Immortal Films

The publisher and the University of California Press Foundation gratefully acknowledge the generous support of the Robert and Meryl Selig Endowment Fund in Film Studies, established in memory of Robert W. Selig.

Immortal Films

CASABLANCA AND THE AFTERLIFE OF A HOLLYWOOD CLASSIC

Barbara Klinger

UNIVERSITY OF CALIFORNIA PRESS

University of California Press
Oakland, California

Library of Congress Cataloging-in-Publication Data

Names: Klinger, Barbara, 1951– author.
Title: Immortal films : Casablanca and the afterlife of a Hollywood classic / Barbara Klinger.
Description: Oakland, California : University of California Press, [2022] | Includes bibliographical references and index.
Identifiers: LCCN 2022008942 (print) | LCCN 2022008943 (ebook) | ISBN 9780520296459 (cloth) | ISBN 9780520296473 (paperback) | ISBN 9780520968950 (ebook)
Subjects: LCSH: Casablanca (Motion picture)—Criticism and interpretation.
Classification: LCC PN1997.C352 K55 2022 (print) | LCC PN1997.C352 (ebook) | DDC 791.43/72—dc23/eng/20220708
LC record available at https://lccn.loc.gov/2022008942
LC ebook record available at https://lccn.loc.gov/2022008943

Manufactured in the United States of America

31 30 29 28 27 26 25 24 23 22
10 9 8 7 6 5 4 3 2 1

In loving memory of Alex Doty

Cultures exhaust themselves; civilizations die. . . . This is nothing we do not already know. There is however a more interesting question: what is it that causes life to perdure?

MICHEL MAFFESOLI,
The Time of the Tribes, 1996

Hey, Bogie . . . Your "Casablanca" opened in 1942 and never really closed. They may respect *Citizen Kane*, but it's *Casablanca* they love. Every day it's playing somewhere, from the Brattle in Cambridge . . . to a television screen at 2 in the morning in a motel in St. Petersburg.

JACK THOMAS,
Boston Globe, 1983

Nothing endures like endurance.

BARBARA HERRNSTEIN SMITH,
Contingencies of Value, 1988

CONTENTS

FIGURES

PREFACE

Casablanca is among the most renowned Hollywood films of all time, regarded as one of the finest movies the studio system ever produced and one of the greatest movies ever made. It has been ranked, since 1977, in the top three in the American Film Institute's influential list of the one hundred best movies in US history and was in the first group of titles added to the National Film Registry in 1989 as most worthy of preserving for the country's heritage. Considered a classic, a cult film, and an all-around entertaining movie, *Casablanca* has also drawn the admiration of myriad kinds of viewers, from cinephiles and cult film fans to more casual audiences.

The film's stature rests on a number of elements and on the legend surrounding its original production. Film critics and viewers laud *Casablanca*'s WWII-era patriotism and sensitivity to wartime refugeeism and its successful fusion of war film and romance. They praise the captivating and chemistry-generating leads of Humphrey Bogart and Ingrid Bergman in their roles as star-crossed lovers, as well as their stellar supporting cast, which included Claude Rains and Peter Lorre. Also highly esteemed are the film's eminently quotable and witty script, cowritten by Julius J. and Philip G. Epstein, Howard Koch, and the uncredited Casey Robinson; the romantic resonance of its theme song, "As Time Goes By"; and its polished studio style, particularly its cinematography and lighting. Admiring critics further examine the contributions of Warner Bros. studio, director Michael Curtiz, composer Max Steiner, and other creative personnel to the finished product. Relatedly, the film's production has received substantial ink, especially as it testifies to old Hollywood's savvy marriage of business, art, and luck that constitutes what André Bazin once called the "genius" of the Hollywood system.

For these and other reasons, *Casablanca* has attained the stature of an iconic film key to understanding classical Hollywood's excellence, cinema as an art form, and the nation's film heritage. Through this lens, *Casablanca* has rewarded repeated viewing over the decades because its richness guarantees an encounter with new layers of meaning. This richness has enabled the film to endure, to stand the test of time for generations of audiences—to become, then, timeless.

While acknowledging *Casablanca*'s iconic status, the pages that follow pursue a different approach to comprehending its meaning, history, and reputation. Rather than embracing *Casablanca*'s timelessness, I want to investigate its "timefulness" by exploring the changing meanings it has had in the course of its rerelease in exhibition venues since its 1942 premiere, from radio adaptations in the early 1940s to streaming today. If the film's iconicity has, in a sense, frozen it in place, I aim to unfreeze it by restoring its historical mobility—and all the complications to its well-known status that may entail—by closely analyzing the impact this mobility has had on its identity and significance over eight decades of circulation.

Focused on circulation, my book engages a mode of film history that generates a set of observations about *Casablanca* that depart from custom, including those that lead us to reconsider certain cherished notions about it. Rather than extolling *Casablanca*'s immortality and endorsing the celebratory ethos that often infuses its interpretations, I will study the industrial, cultural, and historical terms by which it has attained its reputation—as we will see, an altogether different mission. In pursuing this path, I hope to illuminate the conditions under which such high-profile films circulate across large expanses of time and different exhibition platforms and how their temporal persistence reveals not the constancy of their meaning but its volatility and historicity.

ACKNOWLEDGMENTS

This book has been in my life for a long time. One of the best things about its duration has been its reminding me time and again of the generosity of colleagues, archivists, and students in the field. I am immensely grateful to them for their contributions to this research.

My work on this book benefited substantially from themed conferences and symposia where I had the opportunity to present my work-in-progress. The organizers and fellow participants in these meetings helped to shape my thoughts about the project every step of the way. Many thanks to Martin Lefebvre, Charles Acland, Haidee Wasson, and other organizers of the ARTHEMIS International Conference on Moving Image Studies "History, Methods, Disciplines," at the Mel Hoppenheim School of Cinema, Concordia University, Montreal, Canada (2010); Sarah Street and Tim Bergfelder for the Twenty-First Annual International Screen Studies Conference, "Repositioning Screen History," at the University of Glasgow, Glasgow, Scotland (2011); Christian Quendler for the Swiss Association for North American Studies/Austrian American Studies Association "Cultures in Conflict/Conflicted Cultures," at the University of Zurich, Switzerland (2012); Nicola M. Gentili and Meta Mazaj for the First Annual Dick Wolf Penn Cinema Studies Conference, "The End of Cinema and the Future of Cinema Studies," at the University of Pennsylvania, Philadelphia (2013); Paul Young, Lutz Koepnick, and Jennifer Fay for "Ubiquitous Streams: Seeing Moving Images in the Age of Digital Media," at Vanderbilt University, Nashville, Tennessee (2014); Jamie Sexton, Matt Hills, and Kate Egan for "Cult Cinema and Technological Change: An AHRC Global Cult Cinema in the Age of Convergence Network Conference," at Aberystwyth University, Wales (2014); the Chicago Film Seminar, Consortium of the University of

Chicago, Northwestern, Notre Dame, and DePaul Universities, and the respondent to my paper, Neil Verma (2015); and Jan Distelmeyer, Simone Venturini, Hans Michael Bock, and other organizers of the XIX MAGIS International Film and Media Studies Spring School, "Living in the Material World: Transdisciplinary Approaches to Past and Present Media Ecologies," sponsored by the University of Udine and other organizations, Gorizia, Italy (2021). These events fostered a lively intellectual engagement that encouraged me to refine my project in necessary and productive ways.

Special thanks to colleagues who took time out of their hectic schedules, made only more so by the pandemic, to read all or parts of the book: Charles Acland, Caetlin Benson-Allott, Steven Cohan, Claudia Gorbman, Mark Jancovich, Derek Kompare, Mike Levine, Kathleen McHugh, Richard Miller, Ellen Scott, and Matthew Solomon. I cannot imagine the finished manuscript without their insights. I also greatly appreciate the contributions of colleagues who otherwise responded to the project, allowing me to make strategic strikes on issues that required further thought: Peter Balakian, Stephanie DeBoer, Wendy Doniger, Jane Gaines, and Allison McCracken. At the very beginning of my archival work, Eric Hoyt offered to share his research on reissues with me, an act of generosity that helped orient my work on the post-WWII film industry. Kathleen McHugh hosted me on my research trips to Los Angeles, ensuring that fabulous conversation and company were part of the daily equation.

The archives I visited provided assistance and a treasure trove of documents that are at the heart of this book and could easily serve as the foundation of another. My thanks to David Sager and Ryan Chroniger of the Library of Congress; Joshua Larkin Rowley at the David M. Rubenstein Rare Book & Manuscript Library, Duke University Libraries, Durham, NC; Julianna Jenkins and Molly Haigh at the UCLA Library Special Collections/Bob Brooke Lux Video Theatre Collection; Mark Quigley at the UCLA Library Film & Television Archive; Louise Hilton at the Academy of Motion Picture Arts and Sciences Margaret Herrick Library; Brett Service at the Warner Bros. Archives, USC School of Cinematic Arts; and staff at the New York Public Library for the Performing Arts, Dorothy and Lewis B. Cullman Center/Billy Rose Theatre Division. The Internet Archive, particularly its holdings of Old Time Radio programs, has numerous radio episodes useful to understanding the broadcast anthology drama. When the episodes I sought were not available anywhere else, private OTR collectors came to the rescue.

Much gratitude goes to the students who assisted my research: Mark Hain, Lori Hitchcock Morimoto, Lorri Palmer, Justin Rawlins, Will Scheibel, and Sabahat Zeynep Yasar. These students and others that I have had the pleasure of advising on dissertation projects have opened for me a broader window on the field while inspiring my own thinking for this book. Additional thanks in this regard to Michela Ardizzoni, Cory Barker, Mark Best, Shelley Bradfield, Cynthia Erb, Seth Friedman, Daniel Hassoun, Angela Bryant Hofstetter, Bjorn Ingvoldstad, Robert Rehak, Veronica Pravadelli, Margaret Rossman, Brian Ruh, Jeeyoung Shin, Kristin Sorensen, Jason Sperb, Julian Stringer, Jasmine Trice, and Matt Yockey, among others.

Indiana University generously supported my research in the form of a Summer Faculty Fellowship in 2011 from the College of Arts and Sciences, a College of Arts & Humanities Institute Research Fellowship in 2014–15, and an IU College Arts & Humanities Institute Fellowship in 2015. I will always be indebted to my IU colleagues in Film and Media Studies in the Department of Communication and Culture for the collegial and vibrant environment they created for research and teaching—Stephanie DeBoer, Alex Doty, Joan Hawkins, Josh Malitsky, Jim Naremore, Ryan Powell, Susanne Schwibs, and Greg Waller. Alex died suddenly and tragically in 2012; this book is dedicated to his memory.

During the pandemic, when writing on this project proceeded fast and furiously, friends provided a lifeline that made it all doable and bearable through conversation, courtesy of Zoom. Thanks to Fran Bartkowski, Steven Cohan, Patricia Erens, Mark Jancovich, Judith Hiltner, Joanne Hollows, Chris Holmlund, Allison McCracken, Kathleen McHugh, Matthew Miller, Kelsey Mulcahy, Jim Naremore, Carol O'Dea, Darlene Sadlier, Jim Walker, Jeff Wolin, and the "Bisonettes" Judy Allen, Margaret Collins, Sally Kingsbury, and Joanie Stein. Their encouragement and goodwill meant the world to me.

I am especially grateful to my editor Raina Polivka at the University of California Press for giving this project her unflagging support and offering key insights into how to make it a better manuscript along the way. Thanks also to editorial assistant Madison Wetzell for her help and guidance during the production phases, as well as the production team at the press for their consummate professionalism.

Richard Miller and our son, Matt, were an intimate part of this book voyage. My heartfelt appreciation goes to them for their understanding and support, enthusiasm and constructive criticism, shared pilgrimages to see various iterations of *Casablanca,* and the love and care they extend to me every day. No amount of thanks can ever be enough, but this, at least, is a start.

• • •

Portions of the introduction were previously published in "Cinema and Immortality: Hollywood Classics in an Intermediated World," in "Cultures in Conflict/Conflicting Cultures," ed. Christina Ljungberg and Mario Klarer, special issue, *SPELL: Swiss Papers in English Language and Literature* 29 (Fall 2013): 17–29.

Portions of chapter 1 were previously published in "Pre-Cult: *Casablanca,* Radio Adaptation, and Transmedia in the 1940s," in "Cult Cinema and Technological Change," ed. Matt Hills and Jamie Sexton, special theme issue, *New Review of Film and Television Studies* 13, no. 1 (2015): 45–62.

Introduction

THE CULTURAL BIOGRAPHY OF A FILM

THE MUSIC BOX'S SCREENING OF *Casablanca* (1942) in February 2017 was sold out. The five hundred people attending were there to see a special Valentine's Day event, "Sweetheart Sing-Along *Casablanca*," popularly staged for years at this Chicago repertory theater. Unlike other films reissued as sing-along experiences, such as *The Sound of Music* (1965), the interactive dimension did not materialize during the film with audiences performing its musical numbers with its characters. Instead, before *Casablanca* began, attendees crooned vintage love songs like "Let Me Call You Sweetheart," "Moon River," and "As Time Goes By"—the only tune from the film itself—with lyrics posted on the screen and live organ accompaniment by Dennis Scott. After the musical interlude, the host for the evening, Joe Savino, introduced *Casablanca,* identifying it as one of cinema's greatest romances, a perfect fit for this holiday celebration.

At first glance, the Music Box's eventizing of *Casablanca* for Valentine's Day might appear as nothing more than an ephemeral screening featuring a famous old movie with a live-performance twist to lure contemporary audiences. But the event points to a routine aspect of filmic existence that, despite its ubiquity, remains underexplored in film and media studies: numerous films are screened after their theatrical premieres in diverse exhibition forums, potentially achieving an extensive historical life that far surpasses their moments of origin. Typically, film history concentrates on the synchronic moments of a film's existence as they define its original production and exhibition. Its diachronic reappearances, if mentioned in such accounts, tend to be treated as epilogues to the main story of origins or, when its textual longevity is especially pronounced, as evidence of its greatness—that it has stood the test of time because of its stellar features.

In this book, I want to think more precisely and robustly about the factors involved in a film's diachronic journey, particularly how they change our understanding of a film's relationship to history, meaning, aesthetics, and the notion of endurance itself. To do so, I will examine postpremiere modes of film exhibition across media that present rereleased films to the public, thereby grounding and informing their history of circulation. Glossing Igor Kopytoff's work on the cultural biography of things, I will investigate a film's biography, its "career" of dissemination in exhibition venues that mark the periods of its life or lifecycle.[1] Rather than appraising a film's internal elements as responsible for its lasting transit through time, I argue that endurance relies on its construction by social and historical entities that endow it with meaning and continually adjust its aesthetic and cultural standing. By studying the diachronic flow of movies over different exhibition channels, I hope to expose the changing industrial, technological, aesthetic, and cultural forces involved in a film's biography, raising questions about how these forces contribute to its shifting value and how, ultimately, their impact defines cinema itself as an enduring medium.

After a film's premiere, what role do developments in film and media industries, new media, and exhibition play in sustaining its visibility in the public eye decades after its first splash? How do so-called ancillary exhibition markets for films—television, repertory theaters, video—repackage them for new audiences, affecting their presentation, meaning, and value? Addressing different exhibition contexts over time also inspires exploration of film aesthetics and of cinema more generally. How does a film's journey, in which it must mutate to suit the specifications of diverse exhibition venues as a very condition of its endurance, affect our concept of the text? What can an exhibition history that recognizes the essential contributions other media make to a film's circulation tell us about cinema's presumed specificity and autonomy as a medium? How does the phenomenon of longevity illuminate the object we study as film?

To pursue these questions, I turn to *Casablanca,* produced by Warner Bros., directed by Michael Curtiz, and starring Humphrey Bogart and Ingrid Bergman. In a US context, *Casablanca* belongs to a species of classical-era Hollywood films—films produced by studios roughly between 1917 and 1960—that have enjoyed a particularly sustained and visible public presence since their theatrical debuts. I refer to such films as *popular immortals,* known in the trade as "evergreens" or "perennials." Hollywood regularly resurrects these films because they have reliable "extended revenue streams" and continued audience appeal over the course of their histories, a fate that distinguishes them as exceptionally, even excessively, available in comparison to films with more modest distribution.[2] Other vintage popular immortals include *King Kong* (1933), *The Wizard of Oz* (1939), *Gone with the Wind* (1939), *Citizen Kane* (1941), *It's a Wonderful Life* (1946), and, on the classical era's temporal fringes, *The Sound of Music*.[3]

Although there is no single formula for achieving popular immortality, this standing depends not only on patterns of bountiful rerelease but also on extensive recognition across several fronts. These films have earned, among generations of viewers, critical regard as classics, mainstream cult adoration, and otherwise widespread fame as legendary works. Vintage popular immortals thus esteemed have amalgamated identities as classic and cult, a complicated disposition that has given them remarkable commercial viability and cultural staying power. As fixtures of the cinematic lexicon for decades, such texts provide the opportunity to investigate a film's afterlife and the intricacies of textual longevity. These films are also ideally positioned, as long-term survivors in the mediascape, to invite analysis of how meaning, value, and canonical status are generated for texts as they travel across media and historical epochs, lending volatility to what is often presumed to be their inherent value.

While other vintage popular immortals will come into play in this study, my focus on *Casablanca* is inspired by its reputation as a premiere Hollywood cult film and crowd-pleasing, quintessential classic of the studio era, so quintessential, in fact, that it is regarded as an embodiment of cinema itself. With this broader resonance, it offers an exemplary case for investigating both the complex identities a film may accrue through exhibition across time and the phenomenon of endurance as it applies not only to films but also to cinema as a medium. Through my preference for the sobriquet *popular immortals* over other existing labels, I want to emphasize the critical importance of studying what this phenomenon means to individual films and the medium alike. Readers should note that this book is not a celebration of *Casablanca*'s immortality but an exploration of the industrial, cultural, and historical terms by which it has attained this status, a very different undertaking.

Because *Casablanca*'s biography is so extensive, parameters for my study are necessary. I will concentrate on its rerelease in commercial, mass media exhibition venues in the United States, specifically on broadcasting, theatrical, and video platforms.[4] Although outside my project's scope, I mention other facets of its circulation, including an array of spun-off materials that range from ads, production stills, and soundtrack albums to variations produced by live stage performances, remakes, and parodies.[5] Furthermore, since my book centers on *Casablanca*'s national mass-mediatized exhibition, it does not examine the history of its interpretation in academe or its global distribution and reception, both areas deserving of their own studies.[6]

As we will see, *Casablanca*'s trajectory in exhibition has its own specificity, yet it also reveals modes of recycling that have more generally defined classical-era films' travel through time. Numerous films from this era have been, like *Casablanca,* adapted into radio dramas, reissued in theaters, rerun on television, and editioned via different video formats during their exhibition histories. The story of a popular immortal's circulation is, then, a blend of the unique and the general—a special case within normative practices that provides an optic on the exhibition histories of fellow classical-era films that have publicly survived monumental technological, industrial, and cultural changes.[7]

High points that distinguish *Casablanca*'s particular route toward popular immortality include the visibility afforded it by its Academy Award for the Best Picture of 1943, ascension into the cult ranks through Bogart's stardom in and beyond the 1950s, frequent replay in postwar repertory houses and on broadcast TV, rechristening in the video era as both a Valentine's Day cult film and a classic, and its ranking as one of the best films ever made by major industry organs like the American Film Institute (AFI) in the 1990s and 2000s. Throughout the film's life, mass audiences, cinephiles, cultists, scholars, critics, and industry bodies have embraced it, giving it a mix of official and mass-cultural recognition that has allowed it to flourish during its eighty years of existence. As will become clear, Bogart's stardom looms large over much of *Casablanca*'s reception, far outstripping the attention received by accomplished costars like Bergman.

To approach *Casablanca*'s historical circulation, I engage several areas of study in media theory, criticism, and history as particularly central to my research: medium specificity, especially its link to "death" of cinema arguments; exhibition and platform studies; adaptation studies; and the canon, including classic and cult canons. Since I see these areas as interrelated and mutually informing, I am interested in challenging and pushing each beyond its current formulation to uncover the conceptual infrastructure necessary for writing a film's cultural biography. Individual chapters will reveal that investigating this biography as it is shaped by film exhibition across media platforms also involves radio and sound studies, film studies, television studies, video studies, and digital and new media studies—a convergence of fields essential to examining the convergence of media defining film circulation.[8] Throughout, issues of gender and race figure prominently in my understanding of how a film from the 1940s became meaningful within a succession of new social circumstances surrounding its exhibition.

APPROACHES

Medium Specificity

For years, scholarly publications, newspaper articles, and film industry sources have debated the state of cinema in the digital era. For some, the digital revolution, as it altered film production and postproduction from celluloid and analog image and sound to computer-generated codes and files, has thrown cinema's continuing existence into question. Additional concerns, such as the shift in studio productions from adult-oriented quality dramas to the 2000s' CGI-heavy comic book franchises and economically driven "sequelitis," as well as the decentralizing of moviegoing from the dedicated movie theater to multiple smaller screens in the home, have fueled this anxiety. More recently, theater closings due to the pandemic and the success of streaming as an alternative delivery system for movies have elicited numerous meditations on the end of cinema—a concern amplified by WarnerMedia's announcement that it would release its 2021 slate of films simultaneously in theaters and on its streaming service, HBO Max. These and other anxieties about cinema's future as a medium and as an experience have permeated popular culture and informed debates in the field.[9]

I consider these expressions of disquiet as part of cyclical panics about cinema's future, fueled by the threat that changing paradigms of the film business, filmmaking, and moviegoing, elicited by industrial shifts and new technologies and media, represent to prized notions of the cinematic arts. These notions are rooted in a sense of cinematic essentialism based on assumptions about the centrality of celluloid and motion picture theaters to cinema's identity. By contrast, like others questioning this premise, I regard technological and other changes as having always been a part of cinema's basic existential state and history as a medium, seeing arguments about its impending doom as overdrawn. As Caetlin Benson-Allott writes, claims about cinema's "ontological stability [are] historically indefensible" and ignore "the history of cinema's collusion with allegedly competing media."[10] Relatedly, I conceive of cinema's endurance as a medium and a body of films as arising not despite but because of the appearance of new media and the forms of exhibition they represent.[11]

My research historicizes cinema's interrelation with new media to argue that the former has been subject to different kinds of remediation during its history and that such relationships constitute what we understand and experience as cinema—the TV rerun, the video version. Since the exhibition platforms involved in a film's reappearance usually require its conversion into a new format suitable for display, film rereleases embody this process of remediation. Old media are not displaced by new media but are altered in their physicality, function, and status.[12] When placed in historical flow, cinema's accommodation of change, here encapsulated by the rerelease, appears as fundamental to its continuation.

Lisa Gitelman offers a theory of media history that defines media as more flexible and capacious in their definitions and, hence, as less vulnerable to demise in the face of technological, industrial, and cultural developments. She argues that media history charts not only a procession of emergent technologies but also the shifting "structures of communication" and "associated protocols" that surround media enveloped in change. Rooted in "social, economic, and material relationships," these protocols involve clusters of norms and standards that inform the identity, dissemination, and use of specific media over time; as such, protocols are not somehow extraneous to the medium but integral to it and to understanding its history.[13] In fact, mediums continue to flourish precisely because they adapt to profound technological and other shifts that remake the terms of their cultural presence and usage. Enormous differences define cinematic protocols involved in, say, going to a movie theater in 1940 or streaming movies in 2020, but both venues offer feature films and are critical to grasping what constitutes cinema at given moments during its history. The medium of cinema thus encompasses methods of delivery, presentation, and reception.[14]

For more than a century of its history, cinema's complex journey from kinetoscopes to iPhones has involved radical transformations in its materiality as a medium, the film industry, relationships to new media, modes and sites of exhibition, rituals of moviegoing, film cultures, and sociohistorical contexts. Yet cinema, like music and television, remains identifiable as a medium of expression and consumption, while gatekeeping organizations like film festivals, awards organizations, and streaming companies maintain distinctions among mediums as a basic part of their operations. Modifications inevitably govern a medium's continuity through time, making its adaptability to new media climates a prime feature of its historicity.

Rather than conceiving of cinema as a discrete medium defined by films with tidy borders, then, my book regards film as essentially protean and generative—easily "unbound" and remixed by the media involved in circulation. Understanding the specificity of these remixes, I contend, is central to understanding cinema itself as a historically mobile medium. Once cinema is understood as fluid and versatile, new developments, including digital media, appear less as ruptures in its history and more as significant chapters in a lengthy narrative of its associations with media technologies and exhibition platforms. Cinema is thus not "broken" by challenges from other media; rather, it enters into a mutually transformative and sustaining association with them, the exact coordinates of which require study. As we will see, the interventions of other media have not only refashioned films; they have also historically enhanced the medium's vitality and popularity, furnishing increased access to it and expanding its influence.

Ultimately, in a paradox worth exploring, cinematic immortality does not signify immutability; it consists in change through the interventions of other media crucial to sustaining films over considerable expanses of time. Reckoning with enduring films through this lens invites us to examine the notion of the essential cinematic versus remediated cinema, the stability versus the instability of the film text, and the primacy of first-run motion picture theaters versus postpremiere venues. We must also consider the kind of film history and aesthetics best suited to studying cinema's emphatic diachrony—the movement of films through time and space.

Since exhibition reveals cinema as a mobile and variable medium defined by diverse affiliations with other media through time, film's postpremiere circulation in what is often called the aftermarket deserves more scrutiny.

Exhibition and Platform Studies

In the 2000s, the "new cinema history," developed by Richard Maltby et al., defined a movement in scholarship that departs from film history's more traditional focus on films, film production, and authorship to study film "circulation and consumption" in relation to theaters as sites of "social and cultural exchange."[15] Researchers define film distribution and exhibition as influential dimensions of film history, central to understanding, in specific social contexts, the medium's cultural importance and public life, the audience's experience as moviegoers, and the dynamics of reception. Work in this vein also examines the importance of nontheatrical settings like art museums and homes to film exhibition.[16]

In considering film exhibition as critical to film study, my book has a kinship with new cinema histories. I engage areas of inquiry, however, that have thus far been less developed in this approach. Most exhibition histories regard movie theaters as the epicenters of film presentation and a film's original moments of circulation as the focus of research. If histories move beyond theaters to other exhibition sites, these original moments of public exposure still figure prominently in analysis. By contrast, my work conceives of exhibition as not just a synchronic but also a diachronic affair that exceeds the boundaries of theatrical premieres to spill over into numerous other venues responsible for film circulation over time. As Charles Acland phrases it, "film texts *grow old elsewhere*" through exhibition windows that are "major industry sectors in their own right."[17] This aging process necessarily involves the media aftermarket, the "elsewhere" exhibition zone in which films rematerialize postpremiere in forms as diverse as theatrical reissues, TV reruns, and video editions. A film's durability over time owes to its rerelease via a broad network of media industries, platforms, and screens making up the aftermarket. In fact, titles from any medium that travel historically—a movie, song, TV program, or other expressive form—rely on the aftermarket. Postpremiere circulation is the most influential circuit of continued public visibility, representing a mode of textual existence that surpasses the financial motivations behind a rerelease to shape a title's meaning, aesthetics, and place in the canon. As one sign of this impact, the exhibition practices informing the later circulation of media texts eventually sell many of them as "classics," a category freighted with a mixture of nostalgia and canonicity.

Film scholars have examined the aftermarket as an economic, legal, and technological dimension of the film business rather than as a dynamic historical reality rich in implications for theorizing cinema. When aesthetics enters the discussion, especially in the pre-DVD, pre-HDTV eras, major denizens of the aftermarket like televised movie reruns fare badly with critics. Because rerun films are often interrupted by ads and cut to suit programming slots and censorship requirements, critics judge these versions as "mutilations."[18] Such judgments expose the problems inherent in assessing the aftermarket in traditional aesthetic terms. If we uncouple film history from traditional aesthetics, from decisions about savory and unsavory rereleases, scholarship on the aftermarket can approach issues of value through what I call an *aesthetics of circulation* better equipped to explore the film reissue's place in the field. This alternative approach identifies the architectures of transformation that refashion films according to the requirements of new exhibition contexts over time. The changes that occur in these contexts are wide-ranging, affecting the film's materiality, narrative, style, genre, meaning, reception, and canonical status.

An aesthetics of circulation, then, questions traditional judgments that distinguish between "good" and "bad" reissues to analyze, instead, how films are resurrected and modified during the course of their lifecycles. In doing so, this concept obliges cinema's deessentialization. That is, a film's afterlife as it materializes in the aftermarket foregrounds the centrality of cinema's relationships to other media as a defining aspect of its existence and endurance. As Acland asserts, rereleases of popular films "initiate a long intermedia life span" that can be "truly gauged only via cross-media scrutiny."[19]

Studying a film's afterlife provides the opportunity to analyze the nature of cinema's inherent relationship to other media—the different industrial, aesthetic, and cultural forces affecting its translation into new spaces and times—as well as its more expansive implications for theorizing and historicizing cinema. For instance, the radio adaptations of films that proliferated in the 1930s and 1940s, including several of *Casablanca* in 1943 and 1944, presented truncated sound-only versions of their narratives to listeners. If assessed for fidelity, these versions would fall short. Yet radio accounted for the first "viral" spread of movies in another recorded mass medium, its adaptations appearing in homes well before TV reruns of movies began to circulate in this space. Moreover, radio placed Hollywood films firmly within the vibrant sonic landscapes of the time. In trying to ascertain radio's effects on movies outside of the parameters of fidelity, we can address the impact that its sonic renditions of films had on their material broadcast form and how these renditions resonated with the period's sound cultures. Far from destroying the cinematic object, these new iterations extended its territories and influences.

Once we regard the aftermarket as more than an economic zone or place of aesthetic danger for films, a title's iterations—whether they have the patina of a restoration or the disreputable aura of an awkwardly cut print—emerge as essential parts of its history. Denuded of traditional associations with art and authenticity, an aesthetics of circulation focuses on the expansive worlds of cinema's material existence as a disseminated entity, an existence marked by its incorporation into other venues with their own industrial, technological, and medium-specific standards. By directing attention to the principles of film circulation and survival, the concept offers the keys to a more robust understanding of film history that takes stock of cinema's intermedia affiliations as part of its fundamental script. Iteration, in the form of successive rereleases, emerges as a vigorous industrial and cultural force that offers insight into cinema's history as an intermedial enterprise.

The persistence of rereleased films across exhibition forums ultimately raises questions about their protean nature and that of cinema itself. Like other media, film is a shifting prospect in its production, distribution, exhibition, and reception. In this sense, the aftermarket is not really a separate sphere from first-run production and exhibition. It is, rather, part of a continuum that marks cinema as iterable and changeable from the start; postpremiere circulation simply makes this state of affairs strikingly visible.[20] But the aftermarket is distinct from the film's initial moment of exhibition owing to its historical reach and function; it represents a potentially vast and influential network of iterations responsible for the continued dissemination of movies. As cinema's life support system, it is the only dimension of exhibition capable of sustaining or, conversely, marginalizing a film's claim on public attention over time. Aftermarkets provide the conditions necessary for films to become memorable or to be forgotten, to rise or fall in canonical rank, to find or lose audiences, to persist in or disappear from the mediascape.

To consider cinema's historical circulation in diverse modes of exhibition, I adopt the term *platform*. Nick Montfort and Ian Bogost originally used the term to refer to the technological intricacies of computer systems.[21] Industry parlance today regards platforms more generally as digital "pipes" that shape content and media experience, from streaming companies that deliver legacy media like film to social media like Meta (née Facebook). Marc Steinberg contends that this more recent expansive application means that *platform* is becoming "a stand-in term for any media or device after the digital shift"; consequently, platforms are seemingly "everywhere." While maintaining the term's association with digital media ecologies, he notes that some use it retroactively to describe past sites of media distribution, such as brick-and-mortar bookstores.[22]

Although applying contemporary media terms to the past can be problematic, I want to explore *platform*'s productiveness as a retroactive tool for examining film exhibition. Considering film exhibition venues such as movie theaters and streaming both as platforms allows us to recognize connections between different modes of delivering films to viewers that have materialized over time. This more inclusive sense of exhibition windows as platforms recontextualizes the motion picture theater as well. By regarding the movie theater as one platform among others rather than the venue most closely identified with cinema, alternate venues, such as the small-screen experiences of film on post-WWII broadcast television or the iPhone today, emerge less as threats and more as dynamic interfaces for the medium, its films, and its audiences. The movie house thus assumes its place in a series of platforms, while cinema materializes as nimbler and less fragile in the face of inevitable industrial, technological, and cultural change.

Furthermore, as Tarleton Gillespie contends, platforms are not simply delivery mechanisms; they also "afford opportunities to communicate, interact, or sell."[23] Pursuing this observation about the generativity of platforms, I regard those involved in film rereleases like movie theaters, television, and video as industrial nodes of film circulation that, in specific cultural and historical circumstances, deliver and sell films to audiences, negotiate audiences' relationships to films, elicit larger cultural practices and reactions to reissued movies (from film reviews to film cults), and participate in creating or confirming taste formations and canons. Platforms are sites of active discursive confluence with a broad cultural reach.[24]

In *Casablanca*'s case, its aftermarket demonstrates that the proliferation of a title across platforms is not solely a contemporary phenomenon. Additionally, the film's postpremiere circulation shows that it relied absolutely on other media for its continued visibility and that its highly mediated afterlife required textual change and cultural resituating. To fully engage an aesthetics of circulation with respect to these changes, I regard the refashioned films that emerge on media platforms as adaptations.

Adaptation Studies

With its Darwinian drift, the dictionary definition of *adaptation*—"modification of an organism or its parts that makes it more fit for existence under the conditions of its environment"—helps to illuminate the principles governing a film's transit through time.[25] This definition, when reoriented toward texts, suggests that the alterations films undergo in their afterlife to suit new exhibition environments are essential to their survival. Such a general sense of adaptation addresses the historical movement of films by analyzing the mutations they experience over time as key to their continued viability in the mediascape. These mutations, in turn, are central to grasping the aesthetic terms of their circulation.

While neither exhibition nor film reissues—the engine of and forms assumed by these mutations—is customarily seen as related to adaptation, recent developments in the field make their inclusion less surprising. Theorists have recognized media beyond literature as involved in adaptation, the numerous networks of intertextuality generated by a text's reappearance, and the insufficiency of fidelity-driven comparisons of source and adaptation for addressing these more complex situations, resulting in a stronger commitment to postfidelity approaches.[26]

To advance such new directions, Simone Murray proposes a "*materializing* of adaptation theory" in her study of book-to-film adaptations. She envisions the text as a material object produced not only by authors but also by "institutions, agents, and material forces," from book publishers, book fairs, and reviewers to movie producers and screenwriters. All are engaged in a "complex literary economy [that] governs the production and dissemination of books from their earliest phases" while cultivating readers and viewers.[27] By considering the text as a material entity operated on by invested parties, adaptation studies challenge the idea of its discrete boundaries and self-enclosed universe. As Murray writes, "Attention to texts and audiences cannot of itself explain how these adaptations come to be available for popular and critical consumption, nor the intricate production circuits through which they move on their way to audiences, nor the mechanisms of elevation in which the adaptation culture industry—and hence adaptation scholars—is fundamentally complicit."[28] Although she emphasizes the sphere of production, I see exhibition—the site of interface between media industries and audiences—as similarly central to conceiving texts as material objects acted on by a circuit of forces.

Exhibition in a film's afterlife obliges its reissue or rerelease in some form.[29] The new version may appear suspect as a textual form in its own right. When considering the reissue as an alternate version of a film, Thomas Elsaesser contends that we must choose between conceiving of the film as a "mutating strange torso"—a volatile foundation destined to be altered—or a fixed original entity marred by "mutilated changelings" or ruined imposters.[30] The theory of adaptation that informs my book endorses the former perspective, seeing mutations as essential aspects of a film's historicity. Pursuing film history over the long haul foregrounds the inherent changeability of the film body, affirming both the textual validity and historical importance of the aftermarket version as an appropriation with substantial effects on a film's meaning and cultural place. Reissues allow us to grasp the architectures of transformation necessary for textual survival, in which the text becomes fit for existence on television, in repertory movie theaters, and at other locales. Without addressing the filmic shape-shifting that occurs across platforms, a film's history is incomplete, its intimate place in its audience's lives over time difficult to fathom.

Clearly, reissues have a dominant place in the media business and the pleasures of cultural consumption today. But as Eric Hoyt has shown, they have been important to the film business since its origins, making them historically significant forms of film iteration.[31] Over time, classical-era Hollywood reissues have found new homes on radio and broadcast TV, repertory houses and other public screening venues, cable and satellite TV, video formats from VHS to 4K Blu-ray, and streaming sites. While the reissue has not been analyzed as a type of adaptation, it echoes other kinds of texts the field has recently addressed. Reissues assume a place among textual extensions in media culture that include traditional adaptations (i.e., book-to-film), remakes, sequels, reboots, and reimaginings, making them part of a larger catalog of textual "redoings." If, as James Naremore contends, "the study of adaptation needs to be joined with the study of recycling, remaking, and every other form of retelling in the age of mechanical reproduction and electronic communication," placing reissues into this mix brings adaptation studies closer to becoming "a general theory of repetition."[32] Film reissues—the broadcast version, the video version, and so on—represent a type of remaking that joins other modes of textual iteration in illuminating a mass culture dedicated to the serial repetition and viral travel of its artifacts.

As a form of adaptation, the reissue presents a version of the film that assumes the characteristics of its "host environment," including "the media platforms that it traverses."[33] These versions, as they are recycled through time, are adapted on new platforms that remediate the film and enable its continued viability in mass culture. But, as Gillespie's idea of the generativity of platforms suggests, platform adaptation does not simply mean converting a film physically into a different form according to the requirements of the platform itself. A film's resuscitation through the decades also involves it in new industry practices, including changing exhibition practices, and new intertextual networks that affect its meaning, from film releases that accompany its reentrance into the market to reviews and commentaries.

At the same time, classical-era films in reissue interact with the mores of the new cultural, historical, and ideological contexts in which they find themselves. The reissue of these films means the recycling of their cultural beliefs, from segregationist Jim Crow tenets to patriarchal and heteronormative depictions of gender and sexuality. Classical cinema's white heterosexual couples, closeted gay performers, and stereotypical roles for people of color thus bring its racial, gender, and sexual prejudices and prohibitions into new eras. Historically, vintage films' adaptation across platforms has entailed the mediation of these ideologies in later social settings, where the old order might be embraced, renegotiated, critically examined, or rejected. Studying these mediations provides insight into the ongoing impact vintage movies have on the increasingly contemporary contexts that supervise their circulation.

Rather than study *Casablanca* as a self-contained authoritative source in this process of platform adaptation, then, I proceed through a postfidelity lens that deploys a broad sense of platforming as influenced by industry forces, intertextual networks, and social mores that have animated the film's formal features in different ways during its historical rerelease. As I will show, the film's journey across platforms demonstrates how environments involved in its circulation materially excorporated it, remaking the meaning of its textual characteristics for new circumstances of exhibition and reception.

An aesthetics of circulation approach examines such changes without short-circuiting their implications through traditional aesthetic judgments. But circulation deeply involves such judgments as intimate parts of a film's afterlife. The kind of insistent reissue popular immortals have received has kept them in the public eye, providing an opportunity for them to become cultural touchstones and to be otherwise evaluated and remembered. While the tastemaking activities of officially sanctioned institutions like the AFI are important, the more ordinary practices of mainstream exhibition platforms also figure significantly into the formation of value for films. Reflecting on a film's historical platforming means recalibrating notions of the canon beyond sanctioned institutions to include industry discourses and popular modes of reception involved in recycling. *Casablanca*'s platforming over time has been indebted to both elite and mass-cultural tastemakers—taste understood, according to Pierre Bourdieu, as produced by cultural practices rather than by inherent properties of the object itself[34]—that have determined, shifted, and perpetuated the film's value and place in the canon.

The Canon

Casablanca is a clear example of a canonical film. Since its premiere, major institutions have confirmed its peerless virtues through awards and other accolades. At the 1944 Oscars ceremony, it received eight Academy Award nominations from the Academy of Motion Picture Arts and Sciences (AMPAS), winning Best Picture, Best Director, and Best Screenplay for 1943. In 1989, the Library of Congress selected it as one of the first twenty-five entries in the National Film Registry, an honor recognizing titles deemed aesthetically, culturally, or historically important; its firstness here suggests its preeminence among titles deserving of preservation for US heritage. Additionally, the AFI's 1998 list of the "100 greatest American films of all time" ranked *Casablanca* second, after *Citizen Kane*.[35] Along with industry and government stamps of approval, *Casablanca* has received substantial academic and critical attention. Scholars have analyzed it as a model classical Hollywood film and, in the work of Umberto Eco and others, a model of cult cinema.[36] In popular culture as well, *Casablanca* has enjoyed a reputation as a classic and a cult film, while viewers have praised it, along with the Bible and William Shakespeare's works, as among the three most quoted sources in everyday life.[37] These diverse forms of recognition have contributed to *Casablanca*'s reputation as one of the most notable films in US film history.

Casablanca is, then, associated with at least two major variations of the film canon—classic and cult cinemas. Although I will examine theories of cult cinema as they apply to it in the chapters that follow, these theories are generally open to considering postpremiere forces outside the text as creating cult identity.[38] With notable exceptions, those discussing the film as a classic are less amenable to this recognition, seeing its internal features as responsible for its vaunted status.[39] Since *Casablanca*'s place in both cult and classic canons is pervasively underwritten by its classic standing, I want to interrogate this term and its implications for my study here.

The terms *classic* and *classical* originally referred to art created during Greek and Roman antiquity. The classical represents an influential period and style devoted to creating formal unity with a regard for tradition; the classic artwork exemplifies these verities. David Bordwell, Janet Staiger, and Kristin Thompson's *The Classical Hollywood Cinema* bears traces of this terminological ancestry.[40] The authors use this nomenclature to define a coherent filmmaking aesthetic produced by the Hollywood studio system during its growth and decline from 1917 to 1960. The classical embodies the "distinct aesthetic qualities (elegance, unity, rule-governed craftsmanship)" that characterized Hollywood productions during this period. Films like *Casablanca* observed these aesthetic norms, while manifesting their possibilities for ingenuity.[41] *Classic* here, then, exemplifies a text's contribution to thriving in-house traditions, a different inflection from its customary association with enduring value.

This association has inspired debates that tend to split into two lines of thought. The first, tethered to traditional ideas of the canon argued for perhaps most pointedly in the 1980s and 1990s by Allan Bloom and Harold Bloom, invests in the qualities of a text as an explanation of its greatness.[42] Scholars define classics as texts that are formative in the history of the art in question and foundational to fields of study and to cultural literacies. As touchstones in Western and other civilizations, the classic is also a work of genius, a paragon of perfection that contributes to national and international heritages, while communicating a universal truth still relevant to the present.[43] Classics thus represent standards of excellence that authorize their place at the top of textual hierarchies and support their endurance over sometimes vast stretches of time. In this sense, classics establish a common aesthetic ground that offers "continuity . . . and the transmission of tradition,"[44] with the classic's endurance propelled by transcendent textual qualities that give it timeless relevance. Hans-Georg Gadamer writes, for instance, that the classic is responsible for its own successful trajectory through time. It is "self-significant" and "self-interpretive," able to raise itself "above the vicissitudes of changing times and changing tastes" through an immediate accessibility indebted to "something enduring . . . independent of all the circumstances of time."[45] Universal in its appeal and inherently fecund in its possibilities for interpretation over time, "the classic renews itself continuously to pose as a perpetual contemporary: it is a living entity, open to endless intervention in successive acts of reading and interpretation."[46] This kind of aesthetic theory sees the classic's self-determining and self-renewing powers as able to masterfully navigate historical change.

The attribution of *Casablanca*'s status falls within this first, textcentric position. Its reputation is grounded in the period and style of the classical Hollywood studio system. But its standing as a classic exceeds any neutral or normative place in this system because it is prized as one of the most distinguished films the studios ever produced and one of the greatest films of all time. As I outlined in my preface, and will elaborate in more detail in chapter 5, its stature tends to rest on a number of its features, from its wartime love story and stars to its script and deployment of studio style. On this foundation, *Casablanca* emerges as a classic film that testifies to Hollywood's brilliant alchemy of business and art, cinema's capabilities as an expressive form, and American film's rightful place in the nation's history and heritage.

Although canons and the classics they embrace change, the potent virtues of a film like *Casablanca* ensure its perpetuation across time.

In the second line of thought, scholars have mounted counterarguments to the textualist view of the classic's value. In one of the most cogent of these, Barbara Herrnstein Smith holds that the classic's self-determination is an aura produced by the terms of its circulation. That is, its privileged identity arises from an extensive history of having been "thoroughly mediated—evaluated as well as interpreted—*for* us by the very culture and cultural institutions" that have preserved it and shaped our perceptions of it. Hence, an orthodoxy of interpretation and evaluation arising from the cultural reproduction of value penetrates the classic's reception, providing the guise of a stable, enduring canonical identity. In fact, endurance is constituted by "a series of continuous interactions among a variably constituted object, emergent conditions, and mechanisms of cultural selection and transmission." The classic's status as such is indebted, then, to the shifting terms of its continuous circulation, defined by the activities of organizations and people that operate according to certain evaluative standards in historical context.[47] The more the classic continues to circulate, the more its inclusion in the canon seems preordained, justified, as Howard Becker observes, by "common sense and collective experience," by appeals to what "'everyone knows.'"[48] The perpetual presence of a classic in the canon can thus become a self-fulfilling prophecy. As Herrnstein Smith notes, "Nothing endures like endurance."[49]

In this book, I pursue the implications of such counterarguments on the classic canon for theorizing *Casablanca*'s value, departing from conventional wisdom about the film's reputation, in which its outstanding internal elements and circumstances of original production establish the timeless terms of its later regard and enduring appeal. This emphasis has resulted in a fixed identity for the film, diminishing the role its historical journey has played in generating its value. If we can only render texts "timeless by suppressing their temporality," restoring time to a theory of the classic is necessary to fully explore the historicity of texts labeled as such. This means regarding *classic* as a designation that is "historically constituted . . . by identifiable historical forces and within a specific historical context" rather than as a transcendent, universal artifact "independent of all the circumstances of time."[50] My priority with respect to this area of research is to investigate how the institutions and practices involved in *Casablanca*'s movement in and across exhibition platforms created, altered, and sustained its laureled status. Since the film belongs to the traditional film canon, and traditional canons across the arts have been associated with the privileging of white male artists, this priority also means rethinking the identity politics that have shaped the classical Hollywood film's place in film canons.[51]

As a site that registers the converging forces involved in resurrecting films, exhibition is an area of activity worth studying in this regard. Media industries and exhibition platforms that have curated *Casablanca* for the public since the 1940s are invested for financial reasons in establishing value for their products. But this investment resonates far beyond profit motivations into the cultural sphere, requiring attention to the "conditions under which economic objects circulate in different *regimes of value* in space and time."[52] As Erika Balsom contends, the idea that a "strict separation [exists] between the lofty ideals of art and the more earthy concerns of the market is patently false." While these two spheres are not identical, the "financial valorization of art and the cultural and symbolic valorization of art are inextricably tied together."[53] Furthermore, canonization, as Laura Mayne points out, is itself an "ongoing process of negotiation between notions of commercial and cultural value."[54] Exploring aftermarket exhibition illuminates the industrial and cultural factors that treat films as commodities and esteemed objects alike, negotiating their value and meaning across historical periods. Although *Casablanca*'s classic standing either explicitly or implicitly informs its appraisals over time, it was not valued in the same manner in the course of its circulation. We will see that exhibition platforms over time defined its meaning, as well as its classic and cult credentials, differently, revealing its reputation and status as historically changeable entities.

A historical perspective on the classic draws attention to what Janet Staiger refers to as the "politics of canons." Far from being neutral, canons are inflected by the judgments of tastemakers, as well as by ideological agendas that enter into the rituals of selection and its corollary of omission.[55] As Lisa Dombrowski remarks, this selectivity is enormously influential, determining which films "merit recognition, exhibition, and analysis," as well as those "chosen for preservation, and restoration," and a continuing spot in "public consciousness."[56] The dynamic of inclusion/exclusion urges us to consider the canon not as a verity—a list of films judged evermore as cinema's best—but as a mobile construction of status influenced by individuals, institutions, and cultural developments. *Casablanca* has long enjoyed visibility as a member of the orthodox canon as determined by the AFI and numerous other organizations. By examining the agents involved in establishing and perpetuating the film's reputation, I will raise questions about the politics of canons that operate in relation to popular immortals, especially as their inclusion in the canon has excluded other kinds of films from the top ranks, such as those by and for diverse constituencies.

The case of an enduring film from the distant past also invokes a concept that, while further treating the canon as a constructed entity, expressly theorizes the canonizing of older titles: *retrospective cultural consecration*. This term is indebted to Bourdieu's work on cultural consecration, wherein certain objects are given a sacred quality, an "ontological promotion akin to transubstantiation." Bourdieu maintains that aesthetic judgments, in assigning "cultural value to cultural producers and products," consecrate some texts in their original circulation as more "worthy of admiration and respect" than others.[57] Michael Patrick Allen and Anne E. Lincoln identify retrospective cultural consecration, in which films from the past are validated well after their initial play, as a significant variation of the kind of consecration bestowed on films that enjoy immediate success. Older films, given their datedness, potential failure to suit contemporary aesthetic standards and tastes, and need to compete in an ever-expanding field of media choices, are precariously balanced on the knife's edge of being forgotten. With this in mind, Allen and Lincoln propose that when films are retrospectively consecrated, they possess greater legitimacy than newly consecrated texts because these liabilities have been overcome—the oldies have beaten the odds. Since forgetting is such a powerful option, what is selected and remembered attains special value.[58] Moreover, such texts benefit from the claims that surround enduring texts. Their special status relies on the common assumption, in dispute here, that "great art is 'what lasts,'" that "only the most legitimate cultural producers and cultural products survive the 'test of time.'"[59]

Allen and Lincoln examine social processes and agents that confer value on old films, especially institutions like AMPAS and the AFI, "recognized for their authority in granting cultural distinction to films." They identify factors that influence retrospective consecration, from professional and critical recognition through awards and honors to popular registers of approval in box office receipts and audience feedback. Such forces act as "reputational entrepreneurs," invested both in validating a field of cultural production like cinema "by identifying [its] most exemplary achievements" and in securing their own enterprises as authoritative sources of value. Bourdieu calls this reciprocal relationship "consecration through contagion."[60] That is, the activity of creating or endorsing textual value mutually enshrines text, medium, and institution—an activity that we will see at work in the infrastructure defining *Casablanca*'s exhibition.

If films achieve retrospective consecration, they often do so in continuity with their original consecration—*Casablanca*'s Academy Awards in top categories began its veneration in this respect. But they may also be belatedly glorified like *Vertigo* (1958), unappreciated when it was first released and then rapturously received on its rerelease in the 1980s. Longevity can spur less felicitous forms of revisionism, wherein films lose their consecrated status or exist in tension with it, as in the case of D. W. Griffith's *The Birth of a Nation* (1915), a film once sanctified through auteurism and then, because of its overt racism, radically revised in its reputation through Black activism and scholarship. These last two films indicate that retrospective cultural consecration is an ongoing phenomenon as a canonizing force, even for films that, like *Casablanca,* were laureled early in their biographies.[61] Once established, a title's consecration must be further developed and rigorously maintained if it is to endure. This fact separates *Casablanca* from some other Academy Award Best Picture winners; for instance, *The Life of Emile Zola* (1937), another Warner Bros. production, does not enjoy a similar public profile. Maintaining value, even if that value is negotiated differently through time, is one of the reputational entrepreneurs' primary tasks and an essential feature of how classic, cult, and otherwise canonized texts survive. A sense of value is both what sells the film and what makes it meaningful to the public.

Consecration is not strictly an elite enterprise, however, but a heterogeneous cultural activity. Multiple canons coexist at any given time, with multiple agents involved in the process. For cinema, numerous parties, including industry organizations, scholars, archivists, festival programmers, newspapers, and fandoms forge canons.[62] Although I will consider the role of high-profile industry organizations and scholars in value-creation, my book is mainly concerned with lower-profile forces that participate in what I call *banal canonization.* This term does not indicate the insignificance of such forces; to the contrary, it signals their crucial activity in the everyday construction of value. Among other sources, industry trade journals, general circulation newspapers and magazines, TV guides, platform advertising and programming practices, and video special-edition supplements produce discourses that reveal the mass-cultural machinery supporting the routine and prolific dimensions of retrospective consecration.

These four areas—medium specificity, film history and exhibition, adaptation studies, and the film canon—mark the major contours of my inquiry. As I have mentioned and as we will continue to see, *Casablanca*'s biography, as it materializes through exhibition venues over time, cuts across numerous areas in film and media studies, raising other issues relevant to my inquiry.

ORGANIZATION

In each chapter I analyze an individual exhibition platform in the aftermarket, approaching them in rough chronological order, depending on when *Casablanca* initially appeared in that venue (see also appendix 1). The first three chapters concentrate on the film's earliest forms of postpremiere circulation in the WWII and postwar years (the 1940s through the 1970s), starting with radio adaptations in the early 1940s and then moving to the beginning of theatrical reissues in the late 1940s and TV reruns in the 1950s. Although these platforms' inaugural programming of *Casablanca* occurred between 1943 and 1957, theaters and television continued to show the film well after this period, giving it a decades-long presence in the mediascape on two highly influential platforms. The last two chapters and the epilogue concern *Casablanca*'s voluminous history of exhibition on different video formats from VHS to streaming, bringing its biography into the present. The film was released for the first time on home video in 1972 and has since seen dozens of video editions on VHS, laser disc, DVD, and Blu-ray, the latest, as of this writing, in 2018, the year after it also first appeared on subscription-video-on-demand services (SVOD).

Chapter 1, "Listening to *Casablanca:* Radio Adaptations and Sonic Hollywood," examines how the concept of an aesthetics of circulation operates in practice, a necessary theoretical and critical foundation for the chapters that follow. I discuss the film's multiple adaptations by different radio programs between 1943 and 1944, when broadcast radio, a major storyteller in its own right, was the first ancillary platform to recirculate Hollywood's feature films. Like all film-to-radio adaptations, these shows required substantial textual transformations.[63] Radio converted an audiovisual medium into a sound-only medium, while abridging film narratives to fit programming slots. This process condensed *Casablanca*'s story elements, handling what remained through dialogue, sound effects, and music. Radio versions also did not always use performers from the film, making recasting another central component of change. These versions positioned *Casablanca* within a 1940s sound culture that gave its narrative and soundtrack new life, defined the transmedia stardom of its actors, and articulated issues of nationalism, race, and gender in accord with radio's ideological tendencies. By revealing the intricacies of *Casablanca*'s mutation, radio provides a starting point for probing classical Hollywood cinema's reformulation for other media, media markets, and audiences as a constituent part of its social life. Radio did not determine the film's trajectory as a popular immortal but served as the first instance of its influential circulation on and adaptation by an aftermarket platform that kept it in the public eye.

Chapter 2, "Back in Theaters: Postwar Repertory Houses and Cult Cinema," examines the impact of exhibition on reception, with theaters part of a circulatory aesthetic that reshaped films according to where, when, and to whom they were shown. After WWII, conditions in the industry led to the rise of reissues from older catalogs, a development that coincided with the rise of postwar repertory theaters. Repertory movie houses became the center of gravity for the nationwide Bogart cult, a cult formation that deeply affected *Casablanca*'s status. My case study—the Brattle Theatre, in Cambridge, Massachusetts—was one of the earliest and most consequential of these. The theater played a significant role in inaugurating and maintaining this cult, screening *Casablanca* and other Bogart films for Harvard University and Radcliffe College students, as well as for other viewers. Programming Bogart films into annual festivals scheduled during final exam periods, the Brattle created a ritual wherein students interacted with *Casablanca,* engaging in cosplay and quoting dialogue. Between the 1960s and 1970s, students saw the film as the apotheosis of Bogart's persona, the best expression of the actor's "cool" masculinity. This aspect of his persona not only appealed to both men and women but also shaped their navigation of turbulent countercultural times. The Brattle's exhibition of *Casablanca* indicates how transformative reception—informed here by programming, theater and other cultic spaces, and surrounding social environments—was to the film's reputation and cultural stakes.

Chapter 3, "Everyday Films: Broadcast Television, Reruns, and Canonizing Old Hollywood," researches post-WWII television as another prolific early venue of recycling for classical Hollywood. My focus here shifts even more explicitly to the issue of programming as an element of platform adaptation that established and circulated the value of classical Hollywood films and negotiated the terms of their consumption. Despite television's reputation as a low-quality site of film exhibition, multiple forces, from TV stations' rerun programming strategies, including film festivals, to television documentaries extolling old Hollywood, were central to creating canonical status and a sense of American heritage for *Casablanca* and other classical-era titles. My case study here focuses on Chicago's WGN, an independent TV station that, like other independents, was particularly invested in rerunning and asserting the value of older TV series and Hollywood films. In 1957, WGN was one of the first stations to program films from the Warner Bros. library, and for decades, its identity was linked to Bogart's oeuvre. If, along with *The Wizard of Oz, Casablanca* was the "longest-serving and most popular film on American television,"[64] this chapter investigates the granular terms by which one station and a postwar film culture inspired by television contributed to its reputation and aura of immortality.

These three chapters, by examining the changes that films undergo in their physicality, reception, and value across platforms, establish my approach, while addressing older exhibition forums for classical-era films that might not be as publicly familiar today as their video counterparts. Through a more contemporary lens, the last two chapters and epilogue continue to consider the issues these chapters have raised regarding the aesthetic and cultural implications of *Casablanca*'s exhibition. They are, however, more thematically organized to address central identities the film has had between the 1970s and the present as a Valentine's Day cult film and a Hollywood classic. While I discuss other platforms in the book's second half, I concentrate on *Casablanca*'s home video exhibition. Since, after the 1970s, a Hollywood film's rerelease has been driven in the industry by its sales potential on video and since video has been for decades *Casablanca*'s most bountiful sphere of rerelease, focusing on video platforms is necessary to fathom the extensive impact they have had on its more recent exhibition (see appendix 2).

Chapter 4, "Movie Valentines: Holiday Cult and the Romantic Canon in VHS Video Culture," studies *Casablanca*'s second cult identity: as a Valentine's Day film. Movie theaters have ritually screened it on this holiday, while the industry has marketed it on video to consumers searching for ways to celebrate the occasion. Canon-making enterprises that materialize in relation to Valentine's Day, such as newspaper and magazine articles listing the "all-time best" romantic movies on VHS, were intimately involved in its consecration on video. This chapter addresses such value-generating activities in the context of 1980s and 1990s VHS culture and society. It also questions what *Casablanca*'s shifting cult identities, from a masculinized star cult to a feminized holiday cult, signified about its changing meaning with respect to gender; and, more generally, it raises issues about what the film's case suggests about cult cinema itself. *Casablanca*'s circulation as different kinds of cult between the 1950s and 1990s crystallizes questions coursing through this book about the factors that reconfigure a film as it travels historically, giving it divergent identities responsive to shifting industrial and cultural conditions.

Chapter 5, "Happy Anniversaries: Classic Cinema on DVD/Blu-ray in the Conglomerate Age," scrutinizes the old Hollywood film's place in a contemporary media ecosystem dominated by multinational corporations. I will study how a combination of forces—media conglomerates, the video market, and DVD and Blu-ray—contributed to the growth of studio and film anniversaries as rationales for reissue. *Casablanca*'s designation as a classic authorized its gala anniversary rerelease in theaters as an event screening and in anniversary video editions. Anniversary video editions, a subset of special editions, feature supplementary materials particularly important to this release strategy. As is common on these editions, *Casablanca*'s supplements concentrate on its original production—an aspect of its history I have not yet addressed in detail given my focus on postpremiere exhibition. Here, however, that moment is crucial to understanding the film's diachronic journey. *Casablanca* today is surrounded by variations of the same behind-the-scenes stories that, told and retold, accompany it almost everywhere in exhibition, making stories from its past very much a part of its contemporary presentation and reception. By analyzing its 2012 seventieth-anniversary Blu-ray edition, I assess how these stories have created the film's legend, a combination of facts and mystifications that have affected its canonical status and historical importance as a classic. I contend that *Casablanca*'s legendary status has not only obstructed detailed inquiries into its diachronic history but has also fossilized its place in the film canon. Moreover, the persistent presence in canonical hierarchies of enduring classical-era Hollywood films, all of which were produced in Jim Crow America, has cultural ramifications for the film canon's racial politics.

In the epilogue, I discuss the brief history of *Casablanca*'s circulation on its newest video platform beyond physical-format media—SVOD—and reflect on other possibilities for research on aftermarket exhibition. Since streaming has elicited another round of anxiety about the death of cinema, exacerbated most recently by movie theaters closed by the pandemic, I also explore this claim in light of my book's pursuit of the material foundations of immortality.

The chapters' order and overall organization provide a heuristic map of *Casablanca*'s rerelease. I want to emphasize, though, that the film's circulation did not flow in a tidy linear manner wherein one platform successively replaced another. During its history, the film was often simultaneously available across platforms. In the 1950s and 1960s, for example, when fewer exhibition windows for films existed than there are today, *Casablanca*'s repertory house screenings overlapped with its TV reruns. Textual proliferation, a hallmark of the contemporary mediascape, had its own expression in these earlier days. The phenomenon of platform simultaneity characterizing the film's exhibition in these postwar decades became in the 1980s an orchestrated strategy of platform synergy as Hollywood studios and other media companies were increasingly joined under media conglomerate umbrellas. Thus, what appears for clarity's sake in the book's organization to be a linear procession of reissues on different platforms actually rests on the overlapping and cumulative nature of different modes of film exhibition over time. This fact of existence produces a complex, rhizomatic sense of *Casablanca*'s circulation in multiple media in its afterlife, a matter that I will examine.

Today, exhibition platforms for *Casablanca* are numerous—among them, cable TV's TCM, theaters, Blu-ray and DVD release, and streaming on WarnerMedia's HBO Max. But a discernible shift exists from earlier days, when *Casablanca* seemed omnipresent and a vivid part of the cultural conversation, to more recent times, when it appears as an isolated special event or much older title in a sea of new video and streaming releases. To ensure *Casablanca*'s continued circulation in such circumstances, later exhibition forums are even more clearly invested than earlier showcases in maintaining the film's reputation as a classic that belongs in a pantheon of great movies. Once again, such shifts suggest that immortality is not an implacable, constant state of being but a deeply historical phenomenon, subject to the ebbs and flows and promises and threats generated by material historical forces.

As an ensemble, these chapters support my ultimate aims: to explore the range of changing industry practices, exhibition venues, new media, modes of reception, and cultural contexts that define the circulation of classical Hollywood films over the long haul; to understand how such a film's biography is intimately bound to its cross-platform aesthetic reformulation in the aftermarket; and to conceptualize the relationship among history, aesthetics, the canon, and ideology to assess how old Hollywood films have come to have value for successive generations of viewers. Through a single-film study of a popular immortal, I hope to illuminate the materiality and meaning of cinema as distilled in the platformed rerelease of its films, exploring their migration and mutation through time and space as elucidating the terms of its endurance as a medium.

ONE

Listening to Casablanca

RADIO ADAPTATIONS AND SONIC HOLLYWOOD

BETWEEN 1943 AND 1944, five different radio programs adapted *Casablanca,* making it one among scores of Hollywood films to be showcased on this powerful mass medium. Despite early challenges, the association between radio and film industries flourished by the late 1930s and into the 1940s, a period known as radio's "Golden Age."[1] Radio adaptations of Hollywood movies arose from the mutual benefits of this association. Hollywood studios provided radio with stories and stars that had established appeal capable of attracting both advertisers and listeners to its programs, while broadcasters gave studios an influential new venue for promoting their wares.[2] Well before TV reruns, radio repurposed movies for home audiences, allowing Hollywood films to reach expansively into the domestic sphere.

Comedy/variety programs, such as *The Edgar Bergen/Charlie McCarthy Show* (NBC, 1937–48; CBS, 1949–56), were popular in the prime-time slots that film adaptations also often occupied. But anthology dramas—a radio genre that offered a different cast in a different story each week drawn from original material or adapted from literature, theater, and film—were not far behind. *Lux Radio Theatre* and *The Screen Guild Players,* two major anthology dramas featuring film adaptations, found great success with listeners, consistently ranking in the Hooperatings' highest echelon of prime-time broadcasts, the "First Fifteen."[3] As ads on anthology dramas for beauty products like Lux soap suggest, these shows appealed to adult female audiences. Yet while women made up a strong demographic for film adaptations, millions of men and young viewers tuned in as well.[4] Given radio's presence in homes—in 1940, out of thirty-four million US families, nearly 83 percent had radios, a figure rising to 90 percent by 1945—these dramas and their listeners were part of the "greatest national market ... reached by a single medium."[5]

Radio thus assumed a prominent public role as storyteller. Neil Verma contends that from the 1930s to the 1950s, "radio produced content—original and adapted—that made it perhaps the most prolific form of narrative fiction for two decades of the twentieth century."[6] Indeed, anthology dramas alone offered an impressive number of film adaptations. *Lux Radio Theatre* (NBC, 1934–35, 1954–55; CBS, 1935–54) aired roughly six hundred film adaptations during its twenty-year history and could draw an estimated forty million listeners a week. *The Screen Guild Players* (CBS, 1939–48, 1951–52; NBC, 1948–50; ABC, 1950–51) broadcast about four hundred film adaptations to somewhat smaller audiences.[7] Although shows inspired by their success, such as *Theater of Romance* (CBS, 1943–57), aired fewer film episodes, they help to expose how conventional the marriage of film and radio had become industrially, formally, and experientially.

Despite the bountiful presence of radio versions of film, however, with the exception of work by scholars like Michele Hilmes,[8] these versions are not often analyzed for the rich implications they have for our understanding of cinema's life during this era. Reasons for this relative neglect lie in broadcasting's lack of cultural capital as a forum for adaptation in comparison to other arts and the muscular alterations its adaptations exacted on feature films. Radio transformed a medium associated with public film exhibition into a private transmission in the home, while reconstituting an audiovisual text into an audio form in which narration, dialogue, sound effects, and music performed the narrative labor. Radio also abridged feature films' running time to conform to broadcast slots that ranged from thirty to sixty minutes, with host/announcer commentary and commercials further curtailing story time. A film was divided into acts to accommodate such interruptions, thus opening its previously "closed" universe.[9] Moreover, casts often varied between film and radio versions; along with new music and sound effects, new star personas and voices inhabited these productions.

The standard studio contract with anthology drama sponsors further illuminates the conditions informing these alterations. The contract defined fees, performance rights, and allowable changes. For $1,000 (about $16,000 today) studios permitted radio programs to use the film's "script and title on one commercial broadcast and rebroadcast." Shows could also refashion the script through "additions, deletions, and condensations" that they, in their "sole discretion," deemed "advisable."[10] The studio thus regulated performance rights, but levied no restrictions on changes, acknowledging that radio, as a different form of industrial narrative, had to transfigure its sources. Its differences and lack of a visual dimension also ensured that it would provide no real competition to Hollywood films themselves. Yet radio versions had to resemble their sources sufficiently to exploit opportunities for cross-promotion with Hollywood, circumscribing the possibilities of change.

Reviewers in the 1940s, chafed by this sameness in the face of medium differences, complained that radio's film adaptations were nothing more than "telescoped facsimiles" of the originals.[11] More recently, scholars have grappled on different terms with the aesthetics of film's hybrid form on radio, seeing its versions as handicapped by disruption, shallow diegesis, and thin characterizations. At best, with its commercial imperatives and storytelling constraints, radio could only "sketch" its source.[12] With fidelity as the chief criterion of assessment, radio versions thus appear as aesthetically inferior to film originals.

Using *Casablanca* as a case study, this chapter investigates an alternative theory of adaptation designed to explore radio as a momentous forum for film storytelling in the context of 1940s sound culture. Like recent developments in adaptation theory discussed in my introduction, I regard fidelity-based appraisals as unable to grasp the complexities of the textual interplay involved in adaptation. As I have also already mentioned, my postfidelity approach draws from a definition of adaptation infused by Darwinism—"modification of an organism or its parts that makes it more fit for existence under the conditions of its environment."[13] This perspective suggests that a life form's survival is aided by its ability to change when confronted by new milieus and their reacclimatizing processes.

Remobilized for textual analysis, the Darwinian sense of adaptation retains traditional adaptation studies' focus on modification. But rather than using similarities and differences between source and adaptation to establish comparative value, this newer approach draws our attention to what I described in my introduction as an *aesthetics of circulation*—an aesthetics that defines transformation as crucial to a text's durability in diverse media ecosystems. I argue, accordingly, that radio versions of films are generative rather than derivative, productive renditions rather than truncated dead-end copies. Indeed, while allowing us to analyze the nature of "sound-only" versions of films, radio's principles of alteration provide a starting point for exploring how this era's cinema was reformulated for other media, media markets, and audiences as a constituent part of its afterlife. As more than a retelling of a story in a different medium, radio versions of movies signal the institutional and aesthetic practices that repurpose them in new conditions of exhibition. No single platform determines the trajectory of a film's endurance; that is a cumulative activity materializing across platforms and time. Coming early in the history of classical-era films' postpremiere circulation, however, radio begins to demonstrate the importance of other media and media ecologies to a film's continuing public presence.

Casablanca offers a vivid foundation for this investigation, with multiple radio anthology dramas producing versions of it for the airwaves: *The Screen Guild Players, The Philip Morris Playhouse* (CBS, 1939–53; NBC, 1951–52), *Lux Radio Theatre, Crisco's Star Playhouse* (NBC, 1943–45), and *Theater of Romance*. These radio adaptations preceded both the film's theatrical rerelease in 1949 and its reruns on television in the 1950s. Because radio involves the literal adaptation of films, it appears to be a different textual enterprise from theatrical reissues or TV reruns. Granting differences, I regard radio as representing a similar form of aftermarket film exhibition: each platform must modify the films that circulate in its domain to suit its own designs. Moreover, before theater and television rereleases of *Casablanca,* radio was the only exhibition forum available for re-presenting it to the public. Radio's cluster of adaptations constituted the first major means by which the film as a name brand, story, and text went "viral" after its original US theatrical run ended in major cities in mid-1943. As I hope to show, *Casablanca*'s presence and meaning in the 1940s—and, by implication, that of other classical-era Hollywood films as well—cannot be fully grasped without exploring radio's alteration of cinema and its ensuing circulation of films as sonic entities. Perhaps, as I will speculate, radio's platforming of *Casablanca* also represented initial steps toward later identities it would come to have, including that of a cult film.

I begin by studying seemingly contrary but interrelated dynamics defining radio's appropriation of films: contraction and expansion. On one level, radio reduced the scope of film narratives. If we embrace these "sketches" rather than focus on their shortcomings, we can understand how adaptations translated and distilled a film's elements to create a form that could migrate into new broadcast territories. On another level, this migration entailed the aural spread of Hollywood's stories, stars, and sounds, expanding their cultural presence. As a nontheatrical venue bringing Hollywood into millions of listeners' homes, radio enabled film to acquire greater intimacy and familiarity in this new location, while also fortifying cinema's place in the soundscape.

After the "talkies" situated cinema in the sphere of mass-reproduced sound in the late 1920s, radio's conversions of films into an aural language and experience further "audiotized" the medium, amplifying its position in a sonic world that included radio, phonographs, records, sheet music, and live performance. In this sense, radio diversified and rejuvenated film by placing it squarely in aural culture.

Tracking how these adaptations collectively compressed and extended certain features of the film produces a picture of a "sonic" *Casablanca* in the 1940s. That is, by addressing differences among these adaptations, but more fulsomely pursuing their shared features, I can identify facets of the film that had to be present for radio versions to be perceived both as part of its universe and as compatible with radio's conventions of storytelling and sound. I thus examine radio's remodeling of *Casablanca* through two categories: the *story* and *audio cores*. These categories distinguish the elements that transcend individual radio shows to jointly illuminate the most important aspects of the film in broadcast circulation.[14]

For the story core, I discuss radio's distilling of *Casablanca*'s action, settings, and characters. The medium's economy of narrative reveals a significant context for the film less studied than its WWII-era meaning: its colonialist dimensions. Certainly, the film's wartime meaning was earned by its circumstances of release and narrative. Warner Bros. strategized its November 1942 premiere to capitalize on headlines made by the Allies' invasion of then French North Africa (including the Moroccan city of Casablanca), while its general US release in January 1943 corresponded with a major diplomatic event, the Casablanca conference.[15] *Casablanca* itself was infused with wartime concerns. Its action occurs after France's 1940 surrender to Nazi Germany and the ensuing formation of Vichy France, a collaborative puppet government that administered Morocco and other French colonies during the war. Furthermore, the film's narrative arc traces the transformation of isolationist American Rick Blaine (his refrain: "I stick my neck out for nobody") into a WWII freedom fighter, revealing its interventionist, pro-Allied forces stance.[16] Like cinema, radio was heavily defined by the war effort. Yet, as I will argue, *Casablanca*'s radio adaptations, through their intertextual associations with other stories at the time, also call attention to a different meaning: the narrative's subtler relation to 1930s colonialist French cinema set in North Africa. This relation also informs aspects of the audio core.

As we would expect of an audio medium, the audio core characterizing *Casablanca*'s radio adaptations has heterogeneous facets. It is composed, in part, of the adaptations' selection of certain of the film's musical compositions and lines of dialogue that, when subject to radio's powers of dissemination, influenced their place in popular music and language. Performers' voices were similarly amplified on this new media platform, contributing to the construction of their stardom. As an icon of classical Hollywood cinema not typically associated with radio, Humphrey Bogart's performance as Rick Blaine in one of *Casablanca*'s adaptations calls attention to his substantial career on the air and his transmedia stardom. Bogart's voice was, though, only one among others in these radio productions; their overall sonic design relied on a mélange of characters and international accents to articulate the narrative. This mixture, as we will see, evokes the story core's colonialism and 1940s ideologies of gender, race, and nation. Finally, through music and voices, radio played with the film's genre identity, situating it in relation to different genres that created yet other tributaries of meaning for it.

Numerous other films, such as *Dark Victory* (1939) and *It's a Wonderful Life* (1946), enjoyed multiple radio adaptations at this time as well, but few involved the range of programs that produced "Casablanca" episodes. For this reason, before I turn to the story and audio cores, I want to briefly profile these programs. Since performers changed in almost every version, I also consider how recasting demonstrates the importance of stardom across media in the 1940s, a factor that elucidates what might otherwise appear to be inexplicable choices of actors in these adaptations.

ON THE AIR

The radio anthology dramas that adapted *Casablanca* appeared mainly in prime-time evening slots that ran for thirty minutes or an hour; the exception, *Crisco's Star Playhouse,* a daytime serial, ran in fifteen-minute installments for a month.[17] In chronological order, the following lists the shows' titles; air dates and times for its "Casablanca" episode; New York City stations (linked to nationwide broadcast affiliates); cast members (when names are available); advertising sponsors; and hosts, announcers, and narrators. Since these facts often change during a show's history, including its title, they apply here only to this broadcast:

- *The Screen Guild Players,* Monday, April 26, 1943, 10:00–10:30 p.m., WABC (CBS's flagship station in New York). With Humphrey Bogart

(Rick), Ingrid Bergman (Ilsa Lund), and Paul Henreid (Victor Laszlo). Sponsor: Lady Esther Cosmetics. Announcer/Narrator: Truman Bradley.[18]

- *The Philip Morris Playhouse,* Friday, September 3, 1943, 9:00–9:30 p.m., WABC. With Raymond Massey (Rick) and Madeleine Carroll (Ilsa). Sponsor: Philip Morris & Co., Ltd. Announcer: Art Ballinger et al., Host: Charles Martin.[19]
- *Lux Radio Theatre,* Monday, January 24, 1944, 9:00–10:00 p.m., WABC. With Alan Ladd (Rick), Hedy Lamarr (Ilsa), John Loder (Laszlo), Edgar Barrier (Renault), and Ernest Whitman (Sam). Sponsor: Lever Bros.' Lux Soap. Announcer: John Kennedy. Host/Narrator: Cecil B. DeMille.[20]
- *Crisco's Star Playhouse,* Monday–Friday, August 14–September 18, 1944, 11:30–11:45 a.m., WEAF (NBC's flagship station in New York). With Edward Marr (Rick), Peggy Webber (Ilsa), and Ernest Whitman (Sam). Sponsor: Proctor & Gamble's Crisco. Announcer: Marvin Miller. Host and Narrator: Gale Page.[21]
- *Theater of Romance,* Tuesday, December 19, 1944, 8:30–8:55 p.m., WABC. With Victor Jory (Rick), Mercedes McCambridge (Ilsa), Santos Ortega (Renault), and Dooley Wilson (Sam). Sponsor: The Colgate-Palmolive Company. Announcer: Del Sharbutt. Host: Frank Graham.[22]

While we may think of adaptations of the same property as occurring at reasonable intervals to avoid market saturation, here radio exhibits a different economy: an accelerated, concentrated timeline that bespeaks adaptation's importance as cross-promotion for Hollywood and radio, with *The Screen Guild Players'* adaptation airing when the film was still in theaters. Along with revealing the common phenomenon of multiple radio productions of the same film, *Casablanca*'s adaptations also capture the spectrum of programs—famous and obscure, thriving and struggling—that defined film circulation on radio.

Once Lady Esther became its sponsor in the early 1940s, *The Screen Guild Players* (hereafter *Screen Guild*) served to promote the company's wares, but its philanthropic mission otherwise distinguished it from fellow anthologies. Linked to the Hollywood labor union the Screen Actors Guild, the show supported the Motion Picture Relief Fund, founded in 1921 by screen stars Mary Pickford, Douglas Fairbanks, and Charlie Chaplin. They designed the Fund to assist members of Hollywood's community who were impoverished, ill, retired, or "used up" by an industry often unconcerned with its workers' long-term welfare. Studios donated their stars and stories to the show, while performers' compensation went to the fund. Programming it after *Lux Radio Theatre* on Monday evenings gave it a strong position in its time slot as part of a "movie night" double feature, making it "the major show of its kind, the leader in half-hour film fare."[23]

The Philip Morris Playhouse (hereafter *Philip Morris*) had a more modest profile. It produced more than two hundred film adaptations along with other adapted fare, but its lower budget prevented it from regularly featuring A-list Hollywood talent; instead, it often enlisted radio performers for lead roles or relied on character actors from both film and radio. Its tobacco company sponsor Philip Morris & Co. periodically cancelled and resurrected it, making it ultimately into an unsteady enterprise.[24]

Major ad agency J. Walter Thompson backed *Lux Radio Theatre* (hereafter *Lux*), the most influential anthology program of its time. In the 1930s, after initially adapting Broadway plays, the show focused on Hollywood cinema, regarding films as less parochial and better able to attract audiences than stage productions. In its hour spot, *Lux* could mount more elaborate productions and spend more time trumpeting its sponsor's goods than the typical thirty-minute anthology show. During its history, it also offered a prodigious number of adaptations with an impressive lineup of stars, often, like *Screen Guild,* producing multiple versions of the same film. As part of its Hollywood sheen, *Lux* hired Cecil B. DeMille, a film director known for showmanship, as master of ceremonies and narrator. Like other radio drama narrators, DeMille framed the story's beginning and bridged the gap between ads and story acts, smoothing the flow. He also interviewed stars at episode's end to make them more accessible to listeners and to promote their latest films.[25]

Crisco's Star Playhouse (hereafter *Star Playhouse*) aired for less than two years.[26] While films had been profitably adapted into daytime serials, this show proved to be a misfire. *Star Playhouse* episodes were broadcast in fifteen-minute slots common for daytime soaps, but, in an unsuccessful experiment, the show presented them as limited-run serials for a week or month rather than the soap's characteristic span of years. Yet *Star Playhouse* is notable for several reasons. A duo that generated "half of all daytime radio advertising revenue"—radio pioneer Anne Hummert and her husband Edward Hummert—produced it.[27] Moreover, radio and movie actress Gale Page, the only female narrator of programs in my study, hosted for most of the show's history. Finally, the four surviving episodes of *Casablanca*'s serialization extended its story—the action begins in Paris before Rick has even met Ilsa—further distinguishing the show from other adaptations. Although a failure, then, *Star Playhouse* had significant backers and a female host/narrator, while uniquely altering the source's timeline due to serialization's possibilities.

Theater of Romance (hereafter *Romance*) was reportedly a CBS "schedule filler" rather than a marquee show, but it yielded nearly five hundred adaptations of literature, plays, and films.[28] Jean Holloway, another of radio's pioneering women, scripted the program from 1943–46, a period roughly equivalent to *Romance*'s concentration on Hollywood cinema.[29] The show's title suggests that it featured a single genre, but, like other radio anthology dramas, it was generically diverse, airing versions of films that ranged from women's films to westerns.

The casts for "Casablanca" episodes across these programs reflect differences in Hollywood star power, from *Screen Guild*'s Ingrid Bergman to *Star Playhouse*'s lesser-known Peggy Webber as Ilsa. In the process, they reveal the centrality of performers of different statures from film, radio, and other media as leads and supporting players, a combination typical of radio anthology dramas. With exceptions, like the work of Richard Dyer and Gaylyn Studlar, earlier star studies had tended to associate stars solely with their roles in film.[30] More recently, Sarah Thomas, Christine Becker, and Susan Murray have analyzed the interrelationships of film, broadcasting, and other media on star construction.[31] Granting that each medium has its own star system, *Casablanca*'s case indicates how transmediated the careers of leading and secondary players were in the 1940s across stage, film, radio, other sound media, and eventually TV. The multifaceted nature of the careers of those involved in these adaptations also helps to explain the logic of recasting—assigning different performers the same role in different productions of the same text—that defined each of its versions.

With original cast members Bogart, Bergman, and Henreid in *Screen Guild*'s production of *Casablanca,* this version may appear to be the most legitimate. But this aura of legitimacy can obscure the validity of performers associated with the film's other versions and the role their transmedia careers played in their casting. To be sure, several of *Casablanca*'s major stars had such careers. Beyond her film roles, Bergman not only gave patriotic radio talks to US soldiers, as did her peers, but also starred in nearly twenty other radio adaptations of films in which she had originally performed, including *Lux*'s 1948 and *Screen Guild*'s 1949 versions of *Notorious* (1946).[32] Even so, Bergman's costars in *Casablanca*—Bogart, Claude Rains, and Peter Lorre—

had more extensive employment on the air and in other media. Along with credits in film, theater, and TV, Rains was an audio actor on radio programs and spoken-word records, with Lorre sharing a similar profile.[33] Bogart, as we will see, also had an impressive resume across media. But others cast in "Casablanca" radio episodes similarly demonstrated a range of transmedia experience that was a standard feature of entertainment careers at this time.

While numerous factors influenced casting on radio anthology dramas, including budget, star availability, and cross-promotion (whether a star had an upcoming movie to plug), recasting drew on type, radio experience, or both. For example, *Lux*'s Rick, Alan Ladd, began his career as a radio actor in the 1930s working "twenty shows a week."[34] When *Lux*'s version of *Casablanca* aired, he had had his star-making turn as Raven, a psychologically tormented hit man, in the big-screen noir *This Gun for Hire* (1942). Along with other roles, he was featured in additional films of this kind: *The Glass Key* (1942), *Lucky Jordan* (1942), and *The Blue Dahlia* (1946). Rather than simply moving from radio to film, he would star in these film's radio adaptations and his own weekly syndicated radio show, *Box 13* (1947–49), where he played a mystery novelist.[35] Since critics often consider *Casablanca* a film noir and Bogart (fig. 1*a*) the epitome of the noir hero, Ladd's (fig. 1*b*) hard-boiled persona and voice in cinema and radio made him a logical fit for one of the "radio Ricks." Typecasting had racial dimensions as well, influencing not only the choice of white actors like Ladd for lead roles but also, on both *Lux* and *Star Playhouse,* the replacement of the film's original Sam, Dooley Wilson (fig. 2*a*), with actor Ernest Whitman (fig. 2*b*). Even in a nonvisual medium, race factored into audio casting, a topic to which I will return.[36]

The careers of several of the "radio Ilsas" beyond Ingrid Bergman (fig. 3*a*)—Hedy Lamarr (fig. 3*b*), Madeleine Carroll, and Mercedes McCambridge—provide further variation on typing and radio credentials as rationales for recasting. In terms of matching types, Lamarr had starred in *Algiers* (1938), a prototype for *Casablanca* and a remake of the French film *Pépé le Moko* (1937). In *Algiers,* Lamarr plays a beautiful Parisian in this North African city and an unwitting femme fatale in a doomed romance—an influence on the film character of Ilsa, with her romantic links to Paris, arrival in the North African city of Casablanca, and tragic love affair. Critics speculate that Lamarr was Warner Bros.' first choice to play Ilsa; whether or not her role in *Lux*'s version nods to this possibility, she had affinities with this character from her appearance in *Algiers.*

FIGURE 1. Among radio Ricks: *(a)* Humphrey Bogart from *Casablanca* (dir. Michael Curtiz; Warner Bros., 1942); *(b)* Alan Ladd from *This Gun for Hire* (dir. Frank Tuttle; Paramount Pictures, 1942).

FIGURE 2. Radio Sams: *(a)* Arthur "Dooley" Wilson from *Casablanca; (b)* Ernest Whitman from *Jesse James* (dir. Henry King; 20th Century–Fox, 1939).

FIGURE 3. Among radio Ilsas: *(a)* Ingrid Bergman from *Casablanca; (b)* Hedy Lamarr from *Algiers* (dir. John Cromwell; Walter Wanger Productions, 1938).

In terms of radio stardom, Carroll had acted in nearly fifty films in Hollywood and her homeland, England, including Alfred Hitchcock's *The 39 Steps* (1935); she was also a *Philip Morris* regular between 1940 and 1943. She performed, for example, in the show's 1943 adaptations of *The 39 Steps* and *Suspicion* (1941), a film that had starred Joan Fontaine as the heroine. Carroll also worked for *Screen Guild, Lux,* and *Romance,* while having her own radio show, *Madeleine Carroll Reads* (1943).[37] As a mainstay on *Philip Morris,* a radio veteran, and a performer with a European accent—a fixed attribute of Ilsa's film and radio portrayals—Carroll's radio star persona resonated with this role. Similar logic applies to actors who were primarily radio stars. McCambridge, *Romance*'s Ilsa, won an Academy Award in 1949 for her role in *All the King's Men* (1949) and had a series of memorable film parts. But she also performed in scores of original radio dramas, including the popular thriller *I Love a Mystery* (1939–52), and in adaptations on *Screen Guild* and *Romance.*[38] When she performed her version of Ilsa, she was an acclaimed radio actor.

As the logics of typecasting and radio stardom informed recasting, actors might be mainly identified with film or radio and attain various levels of fame in each, but star personas were a transmedia affair, a matter I will pursue in more detail with Bogart. For now, although some performers in *Casablanca* adaptations may be unknown today, their radio voices would not have been alien to 1940s radio listeners. Given its much remarked upon ability to create intimacy, radio could make those appearing frequently on the air familiar to listeners, bringing their voices into domestic space in a compelling manner.

In 1952, *Screen Guild* ended its time on radio as TV became the preferred mode of broadcasting. Some of its fellow anthology dramas, like *Lux,* tried their anthology format on TV, but none lasted beyond the late 1950s.[39] I turn now to exploring how, before this moment, radio anthology dramas transformed film narrative and sound and what the implications of these changes are for grasping the strategies and importance of radio adaptations of films in the 1940s.

THE STORY CORE

Anthology dramas substantially condensed *Casablanca,* with its running time of 102 minutes, to meet program lengths. In this section, I pose two questions about how this affected the film's narrative and shaped its story core, generating patterns of regularity across adaptations: How did radio versions both draw from and transfigure the source, crystallizing its story to circulate on a new media platform? How does the film's extension into this new venue illuminate the larger intertextual narratives to which the story belongs?

The adaptations' differences, evident from the moment their stories open, shed light both on their divergent strategies of reduction and their shared tendencies. The film's introduction to the city offers a series of vignettes depicting wartime refugees and opportunists living under the corrupt, terroristic policies of Vichy France. The vignettes eventually lead to the airport and to Rick's Café Américain, where the major action occurs.[40] On *Lux*, DeMille's narration interweaves soap ads, Hollywood promotions, and WWII context before he launches the action; here his words take the place of and abbreviate the film's vignettes. He remarks that after the "Nazi lash descended upon Europe . . . hordes of refugees" seeking sanctuary flooded Casablanca. German officers were present "when anything unusual happened," like the "murder of two Nazi couriers." This statement leads to the radio program's first scene with major characters—Captain Renault greeting Nazi commander Major Strasser at the airport. As in the film, Renault and Strasser discuss the climates that Germans will have to get used to in their world conquests, the murders of two couriers and the theft of the exit visas they were carrying, the impending arrest of the man responsible for these crimes (who will turn out to be Franz Ugarte), and the centrality of Rick's café to the city. But this same scene in the radio version includes information from subsequent film scenes that it compresses or cuts: Resistance hero Victor Laszlo's arrival in Casablanca, the Nazi's goal of preventing Laszlo from obtaining the exit visas and leaving Casablanca, and the fact that Laszlo is traveling with a "very beautiful young woman." Through narration and dialogue, this radio version economically condenses the events and characters that will define the story, continuing to cut scenes from the film, including those concerning major events like Ugarte's apprehension and killing, which is communicated quickly here through offscreen gunshots.

Aiming for greater economy still, *Screen Guild* centers immediately on Rick. Narrator Truman Bradley begins: "Barely escaping the conquering Germans' entrance into Paris, Rick Blaine fled to Casablanca [where he operated] Rick's American Café." Paving the way for the first scene, Bradley identifies Rick's past and Casablanca as a haven for refugees and a black market in exit visas (also called letters of transit), as well as the locus of Rick's café. Bradley emphasizes Rick's disinterest in the "dangerous business" of selling letters of transit "until the night our story begins," when Renault visits Rick in his office above the café. *Romance,* another thirty-minute program, focuses speedily on Rick, too, but with a difference. After the narrator describes Casablanca's wartime refugee situation, he introduces Rick as the storyteller, making Victor Jory the only actor in these dramas to have a noiresque voice-over. Rick reports that Ugarte gave him the letters of transit before being shot by the Gestapo and that Renault suspects he might have them, a prelude to the opening scene and Rick's visit from Renault. Both *Romance* and *Screen Guild* thus cut the film's prologue, its first scene with Renault and Strasser at the airport, and scenes between Rick and Ugarte, leading the listener instead into Rick's early encounter with Renault.

Given its seriality *Star Playhouse*'s framing narration offers the most dramatic departure from other versions. With roughly half of the fifteen-minute episodes devoted to story (the other time consumed by commercials), and episodes running five days a week for five weeks, *Casablanca*'s story proper ran for two hundred minutes. Part of its expansion offers a prequel to the action as we know it. After commercials, narrator Gale Page sets the stage for the first scene:

> Our story of Casablanca had its beginning in Paris in those last tragic days before . . . Nazi Germany marched in to blacken the glory of that beautiful city. . . . At the window of an apartment overlooking a once gay thoroughfare, Rick Blaine stood looking down at the scurrying life in the street below. Behind him, a sober, middle-aged colored man sat at a small piano idly fingering the keys. Both men were deep in their own thoughts.

This scene between Sam and Rick occurs prior to Rick's first encounter with Ilsa. By launching the action in Paris, a city that appears later and more briefly in the film through a flashback, the version presents Rick, Sam, and Ilsa's origin story, illustrating Rick and Sam's bond before they leave for Casablanca and Rick and Ilsa's first meeting. While altering the story's timeline, this version delves more deeply, as serials do, into characters.[41]

Despite these differences, certain elements of setting, action, and character emerge as key to sketching the film. Like the film, most action across versions occurs in Rick's café; given radio's virtual space, the café becomes an especially centralized and efficient locus for listeners to follow story events. Other settings come consistently to the fore, primarily the airport (in the finale) and Paris as a site of memory. Individual adaptations modestly vary this palette, with *Lux,* for example, featuring a moment with Ferrari, Rick's business competitor, in his Blue Parrot Café. Mainstays of action involve Rick and Renault's wager about Laszlo's escape; Laszlo's arrival with Ilsa and their pursuit of the letters of transit; Strasser's oppressive actions and Renault's complicity; Sam's playing of "As Time Goes By" at Ilsa's request, followed by Rick's anger at hearing the song and surprise encounter with her; Rick and Ilsa's past in Paris and romantic triangle with Laszlo; Ilsa's later appearances at Rick's café, where she at first unsuccessfully and then successfully explains herself to him and declares her love; Rick's plot to get Ilsa and Laszlo on the plane to freedom by tricking Renault; Rick's misleading of Ilsa to think they will remain in Casablanca together; Rick's shooting of Major Strasser; Laszlo and Ilsa's departure by plane; and Rick and Renault's reunion at story's end, where, except in *Romance,* they head off to war.

As these plot points intimate, the scope of radio's downsizing of the film has its clearest impact on characters and subplots, especially given the film's numerous secondary players. In radio versions, Sam, Ilsa, Rick, Renault, Laszlo, and Strasser are the only surefire signature characters. Others are either minimized or cut, with *Lux,* again, the most inclusive. In shorter shows *Screen Guild* and *Romance,* even Ugarte, a vital figure that ignites the film's action around the letters of transit, is mentioned but has no speaking part. Across adaptations, characters like Yvonne, Rick's disappointed ex-lover, and Jan and Annina, a young Bulgarian couple, are excised along with their subplots. The subplots provide evidence, respectively, of Rick's callous disregard for conventional romance, drawn from his lingering bitterness about Ilsa, and of his true compassionate nature as he helps the couple gain passage to freedom. In such cases of omission, radio writers compensated by offering narration and extra dialogue for signature characters that would provide this information about Rick. Although *Star Playhouse*'s length resulted in the creation of new incidental characters and subplots, the show does not appear to shift focus from these major characters.[42]

The story core illuminates radio's productiveness as an adapting platform, particularly its impact on narrative, circulation, and memory. Narratively, radio's condensing of *Casablanca* violates some principles of classical Hollywood cinema, such as cinema's reliance on character ensembles and subplots and its crafting of a closed world—an impossible feat for radio given its commercial interruptions. Yet these adaptations embraced other classical principles, particularly goal-oriented characters with only the traits necessary to drive the story's cause-and-effect chain and linear narratives with clear, unified presentations of action, space, and time.[43] Following such rules and its own strategies of narrative streamlining, radio produced an efficient, communicative brand of dramatic aural storytelling—a highly concentrated or "super-classical" sonic narrative form. Like all adaptations, these stories aimed to be relatively self-sufficient. If they were too elliptical, however, listeners who had seen the films in question could activate their intertextual knowledge of them to fill in the gaps.[44]

Radio's construction of a hybrid broadcast-film form defines one aspect of its narrative generativity. Another lies in its circulation of the story core beyond movie houses. As the adaptations presented a skeletal geopolitical context, cast of characters, and range of story events, they distilled *Casablanca*'s "essence" for dissemination. They created compressed traveling versions of the film's material for listeners, publicly expanding its brand. By repeatedly sketching the film, radio also began to forge an identity for it. After their opening narration about WWII, the programs defined the action, absent the film's large ensemble of secondary characters, as revolving even more explicitly than the film around Rick, accentuating his centrality and that of his café and romance with Ilsa. Additionally, recasting through radio performers allowed the characters a mode of independence as they circulated in a new sphere. That is, substituting Lamarr for Bergman, Ladd for Bogart, or Whitman for Wilson did not destroy the characters but helped to build the legends of Ilsa, Rick, and Sam. Radio's story core thus not only foregrounded certain elements through repetition but also began to influence what became memorable from the film—iteration's mnemonic potential—keeping it alive in the "public ear."

Radio's story core reached into broader spheres as well, affiliated with an intertextual network of other films and radio programs in the 1930s and 1940s. Some of these affiliations explicitly confirmed its standing as a war film. As Colin McArthur argues, *Casablanca* spurred a cottage industry of Bogart-led antifascist WWII movies, such as *Sahara* (1943), that continued its wartime project.[45] The fact that the film's story circulated on radio, a medium that strongly participated in the war effort and enlisted Hollywood stars in the cause, further secures this association. Yet at this time, as Ella Shohat and Robert Stam contend, French-colonized North Africa often served in films as a backdrop for European adventure and romance.[46] This tendency illuminates the colonialist story model that underpins *Casablanca*—a model that radio versions make more explicit: a white European man with a criminal past who, living as a fugitive in North Africa or other Orientalized locale, is exiled from and nostalgic for his place of origin; he dwells among an international populace and becomes involved in perilous situations of romance and intrigue.

This narrative had had its most recent expression in 1930s cinema. In the late 1930s, Julien Duvivier's *Pépé le Moko,* an adaptation of Henri La Barthe's titular 1937 novel, helped to reenergize it. In the film, Jean Gabin plays Pépé, a gangster and jewel thief hiding out in the Casbah section of Algiers in Algeria, an area he cannot leave without being apprehended by the police. A detective in the film's opening explains to visiting Paris police why authorities are unable to arrest Pépé in this part of town:

> The Casbah is like a labyrinth. . . . From the air [it] looks like a teeming anthill . . . a jumble of mazes. . . . Stairways climb steeply like ladders or descend into dark, putrid chasms and slimy porticos, dank, and lice-infested. . . . Many [of its population], descended from the barbarians, are . . . a mystery to us. Kabyles, Chinese, Gypsies, the stateless, Slavs, Maltese, Negroes. . . . And girls of all nations, shapes, and sizes. The tall. The fat. The short. The ageless. The shapeless. Chasms of fat no one would dare approach. [These people] form a city apart, which, from step to step, stretches down to the sea. Colorful, dynamic, multifaceted, boisterous. There is not one Casbah, but hundreds. Thousands. And this teeming maze is what Pépé calls home.

This fever dream of the Casbah indulges in Orientalism by exoticizing the city's peoples and the city itself in charged racial, gendered, Eurocentric, and colonialist language that defines them as alternately dynamic, mysterious, repulsive, dangerous, and utterly Other. Here, Pépé falls for a French tourist named Gaby (Mireille Balin), who reminds him of Paris. Near the end of the film, thinking him dead, Gaby boards a ship headed for home; Pépé races out of the Casbah into town to intercept her. Instead, the police arrest the now vulnerable Pépé on the dock before he reaches Gaby. They allow him to watch the ship sail (fig. 4), an opportunity he uses to commit suicide, knowing he will never see Gaby (or Paris) again.

As Ginette Vincendeau observes, both novel and film drew from 1930s American gangster films, French crime fiction, and fantasies of North Africa in French cinema shaped by colonialist history. Accordingly, Paris and the Casbah became urban icons for this colonialist imagination, with Gabin's Pépé representing authentic French identity and tough masculinity, via an association with the gangster genre, in a colonial milieu both exotically exhilarating and threatening.[47] The film became an influential entry in a body of similar texts. Walter Wanger Productions in Hollywood remade it as *Algiers* (1938), with Charles Boyer and LaMarr as the romantic leads.

FIGURE 4. *Pépé le Moko* (dir. Julien Duvivier; Paris Film, 1937): Pépé's (Jean Gabin) final moments.

While *Algiers* is shot and structured like *Pépé le Moko,* industry censorship sanitized it, toning down some of its Orientalism and other issues.[48] Warner Bros. initially conceived of the unpublished play that became *Casablanca,* "Everybody Comes to Rick's," as its version of *Algiers.*[49] *Algiers* itself was later remade as a musical, *Casbah* (1948), with Tony Martin and Yvonne DeCarlo.

Indebted to French cinema in other ways as well,[50] *Casablanca* reimagines *Pépé le Moko* in a similarly sanitized manner. Tracking parallels, *Casablanca* is set in a North African city that is not only a significant wartime theater but also a French colonial protectorate. Although its opening *March of Time*–like voice-over situates the city in relation to WWII, the vignettes that follow define it as a cosmopolitan crossroads flooded with refugees and defined by intrigue and danger. Characters in this city of international displacement are predominantly Western and, except for Sam and some extras, white, making Casablanca a backdrop to colonialist adventures.[51] Like Pépé, Rick's exile owes to a murky past that prevents him from returning to his homeland. Ilsa, affiliated, as is Gaby, with another man, similarly embodies Paris as the ultimate nostalgic site infused with yearning for a beautiful, ultimately unattainable woman. At film's end, Rick and Ilsa part ways not in a harbor but at another transit site, an airport. Additionally, *Casablanca* embraces the French nationalism of Duvivier's film, particularly in the singing of the French national anthem, "La Marseillaise." While, through Rick's dominance of the narrative, US nationalism reigns in the film, nationalism itself is justified as wartime patriotism, minimizing, if not erasing, colonialism. Nonetheless, Paris and Casablanca are dual urban fantasies characteristic of the colonialist imagination, an imagination that, through Rick, includes America.

These elements of the film inform the story core and, as we will see, the audio core of its radio adaptations, while other related radio shows accentuate the intertextual network at play. The following timeline traces how some iterations of the colonialist narrative drawn from *Pépé le Moko* circulated in both US radio and film in the 1930s and 1940s:

1938	*Algiers,* with Boyer and Lamarr
1938	"Algiers" (NBC, October 23), *The Jack Benny Show,* parody with Benny as le Moko and Andy Devine as Gaby
1939	"Algiers" (CBS, October 8), *The Campbell Playhouse,* with Orson Welles and Paulette Goddard
1941	"Algiers" (July 7), *Lux,* with Boyer and Lamarr
1942	*Casablanca,* with Bogart and Bergman
	"Algiers" (December 14), *Lux,* with Boyer and Loretta Young
1943	"Casablanca" (April 26), *Screen Guild,* with Bogart and Bergman
	"Casablanca" (September 3), *Philip Morris,* with Massey and Carroll
	"Casablanca" (October 17), *The Jack Benny Show,* parody with Benny as "Ricky" Bogart, Minerva Pious as "Ingrid," and Eddie "Rochester" Anderson as Sam
	"Algiers" (October 24), *The Jack Benny Show,* parody with Jack as le Moko
1944	"Casablanca" (January 24), *Lux,* with Ladd and Lamarr
	"Casablanca" (August 14–September 18), *Star Playhouse,* with Marr and Webber
	"Casablanca" (December 19), *Romance,* with Jory and McCambridge

1945–47	*A Man Named Jordan* (CBS West radio series, 1945–47), with Jack Moyles
1946	*A Night in Casablanca,* with the Marx Brothers
1948	*Casbah,* musical with Martin and DeCarlo
1948–50	*Rocky Jordan* (CBS radio continuation of *A Man Named Jordan*), with Moyles
1949	"Casbah" (NBC, June 22), *Screen Director's Playhouse,* with Martin
1952	*Café Istanbul* (ABC radio series), with Marlene Dietrich
1953–54	*A Time for Love* (CBS radio continuation of *Café Istanbul*), with Dietrich

The temporal proximity of these films and radio anthology dramas, comedy/variety programs, and series, along with the iteration of characters and the crossover of stars from film to radio and back again, reinforced affinities among the media and programs involved. Perhaps one of the keenest examples of this arrives when *The Jack Benny Show* (hereafter *Jack Benny*) parodied *Casablanca* and then the following week *Algiers.* The *Algiers* skit continues the *Casablanca* sendup by having "Ingrid" (Ilsa) reappear, further suggesting the films' intertextual links and, because parody presumes audience familiarity with the sources being sent up, their shared resonance with listeners. Later entries in this intertextual network, *A Night in Casablanca* and the musical *Casbah,* obliquely resurrect *Casablanca* by, respectively, invoking the city as a postwar backdrop for a madcap escapade with Nazis and featuring Peter Lorre, the film's Ugarte, as a character.

Casablanca and its aired versions also inspired postwar radio shows *A Man Called Jordan, Café Istanbul,* and their offshoots. These series amplified the film's Orientalism by extending its character types and world into similar "exotic" locales as sites for Western adventures. The shows feature Rick-like characters exiled to North African or Middle Eastern locales, cafés as central spaces, friendly/unfriendly police sidekicks styled after Renault, and international intrigue. In the former series, Jordan, an American, owns the Café Tambourine in Istanbul, before moving his operation to Cairo for *Rocky Jordan.* Collapsing Sam, Ugarte, and figures of African and Middle Eastern origins, Jordan has a "man Friday" named Ali who sounds like Lorre. An early plot involves capturing a Nazi war criminal—its focus on war themes and musical cues that denote Oriental settings echoing *Casablanca*'s blend of war and colonialism. In *Café Istanbul* and *A Time to Love,* Dietrich plays cabaret singer Mlle. Madou. Madou gets involved in police matters in each episode, some of which are located in North Africa.[52] Drawing not only on *Casablanca* but also on Dietrich vehicles like *Morocco* (1930), these radio shows present her as both the desirable Western woman and masculine hero—a surrogate Rick—offering the androgyny for which she had become famous.

These films and radio programs do not erase *Casablanca*'s wartime meaning. Indeed, Benny's parodies of *Casablanca* and *Algiers* followed his return from entertaining troops in North Africa, while Dietrich was heavily involved in the US war effort as spokesperson and entertainer. I propose, instead, that by linking *Casablanca* to films and radio shows with a colonialist pulse, the intertextual network activated reveals a more intricate genealogy for what appears to be solely a wartime fable. In depicting a North African city as an intriguing international crossroads, the national dimensions of a white Western man's masculinity and exilic status, a woman who embodies Europe as the nostalgic epitome of romance, and the subordination of non-Western or Black persons, *Casablanca* and its media relatives show the significance of 1930s French colonialist cinema to US war and postwar variations. Radio, then, not only condenses and disseminates *Casablanca*'s story core; it also calls attention to its more global relation to a supervising system of meaning infusing its narrative.

THE AUDIO CORE

In *Casablanca*'s adaptations, elements of audio—music, songs, dialogue, and voices—were similarly affected by the interaction of compression and extension. Radio crystallized the film's audio elements into what I have termed the audio core, both forging the film's identity in broadcast circulation and linking it to broader worlds of sound and meaning. Given radio's reliance on sound for its expressiveness, the audio core is more multifaceted than that defining the story. Radio versions of *Casablanca* both shaped and were shaped by diverse forces, from developments in popular music, multimedia stardom, and mediatized speech to sonic conventions regarding race, gender, and nation.

My questions here address song, music, dialogue, and voice in relation to these developments. What role did music and song play in the narrative dynamics of audio adaptation? How did the film/media interface situate them in the wider mediascape? What lines in the script did adaptations repeatedly choose, helping to further solidify the film's sonic identity? Using Bogart as a case study, how did the film actor's radio voice and career illuminate transmedia stardom in the 1940s, influencing the reception of *Casablanca*'s film and radio worlds? Finally, how did the vocal ensembles and international accents that characterize the adaptations reflect these mediums' negotiation of cultural identity?

Music and the Popular Song

As Claudia Gorbman observes, *Casablanca*'s earliest shots are "accompanied by a vaguely Middle-Eastern cue"—a clarinet playing a "minor-key melody with much ornamentation to supply the impression of the [city's] exotic streets and markets."[53] Like other film composers, *Casablanca*'s Max Steiner used aural cues to establish time, place, and atmosphere. As an audio storyteller, radio pointedly depended on music to accomplish these feats. Verma remarks that radio used a "set of sonorous marks" to situate listeners spatially and temporally. With just "a few bars," radio music could evoke scenery, signal shifts in action, and span continents and periods. To achieve these effects, it relied on "a network of preexisting associations" that simplified representation "by deploying fertile seeds of information."[54]

Screen Guild uses the minor key clarinet or "Oriental riff" as a sonorous mark to introduce each of its two acts. The riff not only initiates the action but also quickly references a fascination with Otherness. When it reappears in the second act, its already established cues fluidly bridge the transition between ads and the story world. This small aspect of the score resonates with the Orientalist story core I have discussed. The riff was a "fertile seed," a conventional musical shorthand used frequently on radio, including in the *Jordan* radio series and *Benny Show* parodies, harkening back ultimately to music by classical composers enthralled by the East.[55]

Casablanca's song and song-driven tracks provide a fuller sense of the audio core. "As Time Goes By" is the only tune consistently heard in radio versions, with some play for "La Marseillaise," but no presence for other music from the film, such as the "Tango Delle Rose" performed by Corinna Mura. Steiner weaves "La Marseillaise" through the film, culminating in the "battle of songs" in Rick's café between German soldiers singing nationalist anthem "Die Wacht am Rhein" (The Watch on the Rhine) and refugee café patrons singing the French anthem. Despite this scene's significance in the source, adaptations mainly omit it. In *Lux*'s version, for instance, the song duel occurs offstage; to acknowledge its import, characters mention the riot it caused in Rick's café. Under special promotional and patriotic circumstances, *Screen Guild* alone has characters performing the entirety of "La Marseillaise." *Screen Guild* (like *Lux*) was performed in front of a live audience. At the broadcast's end, announcer Bradley tells listeners that two hundred members of the Fighting French (French soldiers combating Axis powers) were in the studio audience, singing the song with performers.[56] Broadcast during WWII and infused with audio values of liveness, this singalong and ensuing applause deliver a rousing anthem that imparts solidarity and patriotism—a morale-boosting affect enjoyed by at-home listeners experiencing the authentic and seemingly spontaneous "hearable audience" as their avatar.[57]

Given radio's customary strategies of abbreviation, no adaptation produced a complete rendition of "As Time Goes By." All versions treat it as a signature song, however, and, as we will see, it had a larger life in 1940s popular music that made including it in these dramas desirable. *Screen Guild*'s version, airing while *Casablanca* was in theaters and featuring its leads, hews closest to the film's soundtrack and maximizes cross-promotion. It also provides a spectrum of possibilities of the song's use in radio drama. In the show's first act, at Ilsa's request, Sam sings the opening bars—

You must remember this
A kiss is still a kiss
A sigh is just a sigh
The fundamental things apply
As time goes by . . .

—before Rick interrupts him. The next scene focuses on Rick's memory of Ilsa in Paris and finds him drunk in his café. Rick orders Sam to "Play it. I've got a date with a memory." As the flashback begins, Sam sings the same bars, but the refrain's last two lines fade out and high-pitched skittering violins fade in to mark the transition to the past as experienced through Rick's subjectivity. During the flashback, more romantic and melodic violin-led strains of the song play. When Ilsa remarks to Rick that they might be forced to part, given the Germans' entry into Paris, her words, "Wherever you are, wherever I'll be" trail off, hinting that the emotion is too strong for words. Instead, "As Time Goes By" swells on the soundtrack. The flashback closes with her saying, "Kiss me as if it were for the last time," as skittering violins lead back to the present and Sam's playing of the same refrain fades in, giving the sequence aural symmetry. The abrupt stop to his singing and his discordant piano chords further denote the flashback's end and announce Ilsa's sudden appearance, along with his exclamation, "Boss, wake up. . . . That lady is here and this ain't no memory from Paris." Further orchestra variations of "As Time Goes By" follow, some to bridge acts. Throughout, the number functions to signify moments overcome with romantic emotion. When Ilsa threatens Rick with a gun in her attempt to get the letters of transit, only to relent and confess her love for him, renditions of the tune punctuate her lines, "Richard, I tried to stay away" and "If you knew . . . how much I loved you, how much I still love you." At episode's end, the orchestra plays a resounding version of the number.

"As Time Goes By" operates in several ways in this adaptation. It provides a transition between acts of the show, creating narrative continuity after commercial interruption. As a device that bridges the story's past and present, it also suggests wide expanses of time and place. Moreover, while foregrounding the story's romantic themes, "As Time Goes By" provides emotion that substitutes for dialogue, suggesting a depth of feeling in the couple's relationship that exceeds words. In this, *Screen Guild* recalls Steiner's use of the song in the film. As Gorbman writes, Steiner was one of the "most melodramatic" of Hollywood composers, emphasizing "narrative actions and moods wherever possible." He thus created a "dramatic universe whose sole transcendental morality might be that of emotion itself"; a Steiner score "wears its heart on its sleeve."[58] *Screen Guild*'s lavish use of "As Time Goes By" functions, too, as a pervasive emotive indicator that emphasizes the story's romantic melodrama.

By contrast, *Lux*'s score relies mainly on in-house melodies unassociated with the film. "As Time Goes By" plays in only three scenes: when Ilsa first asks Sam to sing it, followed by an orchestral flourish at the end of act I; in the background of act 2's first scene, when Rick and Ilsa discuss the past (without a flashback), which concludes with a swelling orchestral version of the song and transition to the next scene; and in act 3, when Ilsa declares her love. While sparsely deployed, the song remains a defining dramatic device for the onetime lovers' surprise meeting, for the emotional texture of their interactions, and for bridging acts.

As usual among adaptations, *Romance* features Sam's performance of the number in Rick's first encounter with Ilsa; unlike others, however, it also ends with the diegetic performance of the tune. Rather than leave Casablanca to fight in the war after Ilsa and Laszlo depart, Rick and Renault return to the café to resume life as usual. Against the backdrop of Sam singing "As Time Goes By," Rick says, "Great tune isn't it? It sort of gets you inside." Then he speaks the drama's last lines: "Sing the song, Sam. Sing the song." Retaining the song as a potent reminder of the past, this closure emphasizes its narrative and thematic import, while hinting at its popularity beyond these adaptations.[59]

The song's pervasive presence in *Casablanca* and iteration in radio versions helped craft its signature status with respect to the story. *Jack Benny* parodies are especially telling in this regard. With the program's typical self-reflexivity, its "Casablanca" episode features Jack as Ricky Bogart, Minerva Pious (as Pansy Nussbaum, her Russian Jewish housewife character) as Ingrid, and Eddie "Rochester" Anderson as Sam. Their skit focuses primarily on one scene—Rick's drunken evening after his first reencounter with Ilsa in the café. Here Ricky repeatedly asks Sam to play "As Time Goes By," which Sam sings in his raspiest voice.[60] Sam exaggerates the number's words ("a SIGHHH is just a SIGHHH") or adds nonsensical new ones ("They still say I love you or cock-a-doodle do!"), effectively deromanticizing it. Ingrid arrives, wailing her own rendition, whereupon everyone onstage joins in to continue to murder the song, eliciting audience laughter. The next week in "Algiers," Ingrid reappears because Benny (now playing le Moko) did not pay her for "Casablanca." Once again assembled performers sing "As Time Goes By" raucously off-key. The show's writers regarded the song as emblematic and sufficiently known to listeners to engineer *Casablanca*'s takedown. A few bars of the tune thus become a prime means of playfully deconstructing the film.

The spread of "As Time Goes By" across a variety of radio programs shaped its early representativeness of the film, its ability to conjure its world. Yet other forces were also at work as radio versions tapped into the tune's mass-cultural popularity. With its ties to Rick and Ilsa's romance, "As Time Goes By" was already a hit as a love song on radio, records, jukeboxes, and sheet music when adaptations aired. By this time, as well, both the music and film business recognized that films often embodied tunes that could be cross-promoted. In fact, *Billboard* routinely published lists of movie songs that could be thus exploited. As films "plugged" songs, they gave them "an impetus" that could result in enthusiasm for both film and song, while generating profits for the involved media industries.[61] Well before "high concept" films in the 1980s made the film/music marriage key to promotion, WWII-era cinema and music helped to sell each other to the public.[62]

Warner Bros. had earlier discovered that even recycled songs could "zoom" to popularity based on their screen appearance.[63] "As Time Goes By" was just such a case. Herman Hupfeld originally composed the song for the 1931 Broadway musical comedy *Everybody's Welcome.* Despite the play's lack of acclaim, in the early 1930s, several musicians recorded the number, including crooner Rudy Vallee and orchestra leader Jacques Renard. It did not become a bona fide hit, though, until Dooley Wilson sang it in *Casablanca* in what was considered a particularly resonant and emotive fashion. As *Billboard* succinctly put it, "Time Goes By and Finally It Clicks via Pic."[64]

Wilson's revival of the song in a popular film finally made it "click," but his record was not among the first to make a splash. The American Federation of Musicians' strike over royalties from record companies (a strike that ran from 1942 to 1943 or 1944, depending on when companies settled with the organization)[65] delayed the release of his rendition. Although they could still perform live, union musicians like Wilson could not participate in recording sessions for major labels. Nonetheless, these labels wanted to capitalize immediately on "As Time Goes By" and the audience's desire to hear it in expected venues. Their general strategy of addressing the shortage of new music during the strike was to reissue "memory tunes" from back catalogs. With oldies, they could continue to release records with low financial outlay, little competition from new recordings, and the potential of increased sales compared to their debuts. In March 1943, RCA Victor rereleased Vallee's version, with Decca Records reissuing Renard's shortly thereafter. Their records sold "over 300,000 copies" by May 1943, as compared to the 40,000 total discs sold in 1931 when the song quickly dropped "from US memory."[66] These recordings jockeyed for months for the number one spot on the charts. "As Time Goes By" also did impressive business on jukeboxes and in sheet music sales.[67] Wilson recorded "As Time Goes By" (with the B side featuring another *Casablanca* tune, "Knock on Wood") in October 1943 for Decca, the first record company to settle with AFM. But the song had reached the apex of its popularity through the earlier recordings and, by December, was off *Billboard*'s charts. Nonetheless, Wilson delivered "As Time Goes By" with great success as the high point of his live performances in nightclubs and other spots.[68] Despite his initial lack of a record and the presence of other renditions, he became definitively associated with *Casablanca* and this tune for the rest of his life and well after.[69]

Along with *Casablanca* adaptations and parodies on radio, the song's airing on this platform included record play and live performances. Both Vallee's and Renard's versions charted in *Radio Daily*'s top ten "Network Song Favorites" until they jointly reached number one in April 1943. That same month *Billboard*'s "Music Popularity Chart" ranked "As Time Goes By" fifth in frequency of play; for the year, it ranked number five among all radio records.[70] Meanwhile, resident singers on radio programs performed it live. In 1943, for instance, *Jack Benny*'s Dennis Day sang the tune sincerely, giving it exposure in straight form on the same program that in the same year had parodied it, a small sign of its popularity.[71] Broadcasts originating in nightclubs featured it as well; in 1944 at the Oran Room of the Algiers Club in Farmingham, Connecticut, for example, the orchestra built "skillfully on the theme from *Casablanca*."[72] With the Algerian city of Oran as the imaginary backdrop for this performance of "As Time Goes By," North Africa materializes once more in relation to *Casablanca* and *Algiers,* suggesting the prevalence of Oriental themes in entertainment businesses more generally at this time.

Thus, as anthology dramas condensed *Casablanca,* "As Time Goes By" performed important aesthetic functions in them and, through its broader distribution in the 1940s music scene, spread recognition of the film. "As Time Goes By" became an aural ambassador for the film that not only further popularized it, but also emphasized its identity as a romance. This identity was supported on film and radio alike by the close association between the song and Rick and Ilsa's relationship in Steiner's emotive score and its translation in adaptations. That "As Time Goes By" was lauded as a love song in its wider circulation and performed by expressive singers like Wilson across platforms further encouraged this affective association, as did ephemera like sheet music covers foregrounding the couple (fig. 5) and the song's play on a daytime radio "soap" adaptation of the film. The radio/film interface begins to illuminate, however tentatively, conditions in *Casablanca*'s early history that shaped its later reputation as a canonical romance (rather than as a war film, for instance)—a status made explicit when it became, as I will discuss in chapter 4, a Valentine's Day cult film decades later.[73]

In the process of its recycling, "As Time Goes By" became a standard in the 1940s and beyond, performed by singers as diverse as Billie Holiday and Barbra Streisand, Barry White and Tiny Tim. In 1998 Warner Bros. began using it as an orchestral flourish during the studio's film and TV credits, making it an emissary for the film, the studio, and, by implication, Hollywood itself. Additionally, the song has become a title meme for novels, plays, TV shows, and academic books and articles.[74] "As Time Goes By" has its own intertextual biography and impact rooted in its cross-platform circulation in

FIGURE 5. Sheet music for "As Time Goes By" (Herman Hupfeld, 1931) as cross-promotion and an extension of the song's life into 1940s musical cultures (Harms Inc. Publishing). Author's collection.

the 1940s, a state of affairs that also characterizes many of *Casablanca*'s other elements, including its dialogue.

Catchphrases and Quotability

Like all films, *Casablanca*'s script furnished ready-made content that radio writers altered for creative reasons and to suit program time slots, while conserving sufficient DNA to produce unmistakable versions of the source. As *Casablanca* adaptations often selected the same or similar lines of dialogue, they privileged certain lines over others, producing a lexical snapshot of the film. Rick's angry response in the film when he hears Sam playing "As Time Goes By"—"Sam! I thought I told you never to play that!"—is among the most frequently repurposed lines across adaptations. Also pervasive is Rick's statement, "I stick my neck out for nobody"; comments about Ilsa, such as, "She's comin' back. I know she's comin' back"; and variations of "Of all the gin joints in all the towns in all the world, she walks into mine." Some of Rick's interactions with Ilsa also make the cut: "I wouldn't bring up Paris if I were you. It's poor salesmanship" and "We'll always have Paris." Except for *Romance,* Rick's "Louis, I think this is the beginning of a beautiful friendship" concludes each version. Other characters' dialogue is iterated as well, including Renault's "I'm only a poor corrupt official"; Ilsa's "Play it, Sam. Play 'As Time Goes By'"; and her poignant invitation to Rick in Paris, "Kiss me, as if it were the last time." In *Lux*'s production, when Renault says, "Round up the usual suspects," the live audience's laughter suggests that they already know this phrase—an example of the film/radio interface's impact on reception, buoyed by the temporal proximity of these adaptations to the film's theatrical release. With radio acting as an amplifying system for film dialogue, hearing "one-liners" like these on the air confirmed their worthiness for replay.

As part of the audio core, repetition of film dialogue also aided the presentation of characters and the narrative. Radio and other audio-only media had to identify characters that were essentially "disembodied" voices. Catchphrases, as Jacob Smith argues, aided this task. The catchphrase—a repeatedly used expression with a distinctive delivery—singled out an individual in aural media, functioning as a kind of "performer ID."[75] Film stars' dialogue (e.g., Mae West's "Come up and see me sometime") had already helped to create and promote celebrity personas in cinema's early sound years. When Hollywood stars became associated with lines of dialogue through iterative screenings or broadcasts, they secured an aural identity that could support their character type or brand across platforms.

The catchphrase, though, not only spread the star's vocal markers and persona, but also functioned as a form of character and narrative ID. In *Casablanca,* Rick's statement, "I stick my neck out for nobody," relays the Bogart persona's cynical toughness, established in his earlier gangster and noir roles, and Rick's corresponding hard-boiled attitude. It also conveys the bitter ramifications of the character's failed romance with Ilsa in Paris, his conflict with other characters who want him to stick his neck out, and a narrative arc tracing the events that change his views. Across radio adaptations, the repetition of "I stick my neck out for nobody" through harsh vocal inflections shared by the actors performing Rick operates as an expressive shorthand similar to that of a catchphrase. In the narratively abbreviated and "disembodied" radio dramatizations of the film, such lines have the ability to function incisively as forms of character and narrative ID, conjuring up character types and narrative developments. Through repeated bits of dialogue in radio versions of *Casablanca,* adaptations both signal their alliance with the film and craft dimensions of its characters and story to create efficient audio worlds.

The audio core around dialogue has additional implications for the circulation and cultural uptake of film lines in larger cultural surrounds. Film and radio were indebted to a history of technological change that had long caused media language to be both memorable and quotable. The catchphrase, as its name suggests, has viral possibilities for everyday language. Prior to film and radio, reproducible sound invited audiences to imitate "recognizable others."[76] In her study of phonography in the late 1800s and Thomas Edison's discovery that tinfoil could record and reproduce sound, Lisa Gitelman writes of the revelation that "oral productions might be textually embodied as aural reproductions." Because of playback, tinfoil provided the basis for a "new, precise sort of quotation . . . or a way of living with the question of quotation as never before." Speakers recording famous phrases on early records inspired individuals to repeat "bits that were already often repeated: a prayer, a lyric, a snippet from a common vocabulary of quotations (like Shakespeare)." Assuming functions of oral culture, early sound technologies showed how "public speech acts made sense as bodily cultural productions."[77]

Hence, what we might call *envoicement*—making mass media phrases one's own through vocal iteration and embodiment—is a long-standing phenomenon in which individuals negotiate mass media by converting them into live performances, a phenomenon perhaps more explicitly associated with songs. As updated forms of tinfoil transmissions and potent linguistic generators in their own right, both radio and film elicit practices of envoicement by their audiences. Through its closely associated audio versions, radio illuminates how *Casablanca*'s dialogue gained traction in the public imagination beyond theatrical exhibition. That these versions generally depended on close miking for rendering voices in story space—a technique that is the sonic equivalent of a film close-up[78]—enhanced listeners' relation to their words. Within the legacy of mass-reproducible sound, radio disseminated catchphrases and other lexical expressions, offering them to audiences for iteration and possibly altering everyday language.

Through radio adaptations, *Casablanca*'s iterated phrases entered broader circulation channels that assisted their public recognizability and, potentially, their survival through time. In the 1940s, dialogue, like the song, began to identify the film—this time not only as a romance but also as the epitome of sophistication and wit. Indeed, many of the lines cited at the beginning of this section are now considered among the film's most memorable. Taking the long view, broadcast iterations helped to initiate the process of popular culture's canonization of film dialogue and, more specifically, *Casablanca*'s reputation for an ingenious and stirring script, a reputation stoked by the Best Screenplay Oscar won by its writers, Julius J. Epstein, Philip G. Epstein, and Howard Koch. We can speculate that the aural dimensions of *Casablanca*'s remediation on radio helped to inform the film's earliest appropriation as cult by postwar university students who practiced envoicement to express their devotion—a subject addressed in the next chapter. At the very least, in repeating film dialogue, 1940s radio served as a public form of audio preservation with mnemonic potential.[79] Some recent viewers regard *Casablanca,* the Bible, and William Shakespeare's oeuvre as the three most quoted sources in everyday life.[80] Among the *Casablanca* voices that enunciated the film's dialogue in both media, perhaps none was more prominent than that of Bogart.

Hard-Boiled Voices

The 1930s and 1940s call attention to the sonic dimensions of Hollywood stardom. As Thomas Elsaesser and Malte Hagener remark, in a time defined by radio, gramophones, and other sound devices, early sound films heightened the presence of audio "in all walks of modern life, from public space to the private sphere." Furthermore, this sonic milieu magnified performers' "marketability and commodification" as they achieved acoustic identities.[81] Radio played no small part in this intensification of the voicescape. Network radio's reach as a mass medium greatly increased public "familiarity with the voices of specific individuals," schooling listeners in the distinctive aural character of certain performing personalities.[82] While music and sound effects are rich components of radio drama, the medium's foregrounding of the voice gave it far-ranging reverberations.

Of Hollywood's relation to radio in this era, Sarah Thomas contends that it was "instrumental in shaping public awareness" of film stars as unique performers.[83] Radio contributed to a requisite feature of celebrity—voice recognition—making it into a prize sensory experience and commodity. In the process, broadcasting at this time helped to constitute transmedia stardom, playing a role in developing stars' traits intertextually across platforms and influencing their reception.[84] As radio offered star voices unvarnished by material visual presence to listeners, it not only spread vocal mannerisms across platforms but also enabled them to "resonate more fully in the listener's sensuous imagination," assisting the penetration of Hollywood stardom into domestic space.[85]

Radio's prominence in this respect suggests that it was much more than a sideline for film performers. Bogart's case allows insight into its historical importance for A-list stars who today may be thoroughly identified with classical Hollywood cinema and not with their work, however bountiful, on other platforms. Besides his stage and TV roles, between 1930 and 1952, Bogart acted in nearly eighty films and more than eighty radio programs.[86] His transmedia stardom reveals how the dynamics of the film/radio interface affected his star persona and created a network of associations surrounding *Casablanca*'s circulation on the air.

In keeping with the early 1950s onus on acting in the new medium of television, Bogart insisted that he was a "motion picture man" rather than a TV performer.[87] But this stigma did not apply in the same way to radio, where film stars had been active in diverse genres since the 1930s and studios considered their stars' ability to translate to radio—a significant promotional venue for their wares—an asset. Accordingly, Bogart had a standard clause in his Warner Bros. contracts regarding permission to appear on radio, permission usually granted if these engagements did not interfere with his film schedule.[88]

On radio, he starred in anthology shows devoted to film and literary adaptations, comedy/variety shows, and original dramas, along with supporting the war effort on such programs as *Command Performance* (Armed Forces Radio Network, 1942–49). Anthologies often featured him in parts he had played in films. Beyond *Screen Guild*'s "Casablanca" episode, he appeared in a dozen of its other productions, including a 1940 reprise of his breakout role as gangster Duke Mantee in *The Petrified Forest* (1936) and 1943 reprise of a role central to his noir mythos, Detective Sam Spade, in *The Maltese Falcon* (1941). *Screen Guild*'s first version of the latter in 1943 featured original costar Mary Astor as femme fatale Bridget O'Shaughnessy; in 1950, its second version costarred Bogart's wife, Lauren Bacall, as Bridget. In between these productions, *Academy Award Theater*'s (CBS, 1946) adaptation again featured Bogart and Astor.[89] On *Romance* in 1945, he starred in the noir *Conflict* (1945), in which he revisited his original role as a murderous husband, and *One Way Passage* (1932), where he assumed William Powell's role as an escaped murderer involved in a shipboard love affair.[90] In 1946 *Lux* cast Bogart in its version of his film *To Have and Have Not* (1944) as a fishing boat skipper enmeshed in wartime intrigue and romance with original costar Bacall as a singer and con woman. *Lux* also adapted his *The Treasure of the Sierra Madre* (1948) in 1949, with him as a greedy gold prospector, and *The African Queen* (1951) in 1952, where he replayed his Academy Award–winning role as a gruff ship mechanic out to destroy a German gunboat during WWI.[91]

In literary adaptations, Bogart performed in significant radio drama series, including *Suspense* (CBS, 1940–62), for which he acted in its 1945 version of James Cain's hard-boiled crime novel, *Love's Lovely Counterfeit* (1942). In 1949 Bogart produced, narrated, and acted in *Humphrey Bogart Presents,* a series devoted to "the great names of the modern short story" like Cain.[92] In original dramas, the early 1950s saw him and Bacall starring in the syndicated radio series *Bold Venture,* set in Havana. Bogart was Slate Shannon, hotel owner and fishing charter boat skipper; Bacall played Sailor Duval, his ward and shipmate; and Jester Hairston was King Moses, Slate's Black sidekick and the hotel's entertainer. Intrigue, adventure, and romance constituted the action, making *Bold Venture* a remix of *Casablanca, To Have and Have Not, Key Largo* (1948), and *The African Queen,* themselves remixes of one another.[93]

Radio and film thus often iterated Bogart's roles in hard-boiled genres, linking the two media and the star's persona through tangled webs of intertextuality. Radio's contribution to his transmedia stardom through this iteration arose from a fluid interplay between voice trademarking and voice typing. Of the former, Gorbman writes that Hollywood stars "with stable and recognizable voices" that conveyed distinctive sonic features, or "trademarks," defined pre-Method film acting.[94] Voice typing indicated an opposing tendency, familiar from casting strategies, wherein an actor's persona and voice become indelibly associated with the same kinds of characters and roles in similar genres. Without a visual register, radio relied both on the singularity of voices to differentiate performers in story space and on typing for the streamlined communication of character, story, and genre information.

In terms of trademarking, what *were* the characteristics of Bogart's voice? Arthur Hopkins, producer of the stage version of *The Petrified Forest* in which Bogart costarred as Duke Mantee, said that he was unimpressed by Bogart at first, "but the voice (dry and tired) persisted and the voice was Mantee's."[95] Bogart's intonations, ranging from "dry and tired" and coolly removed to softly romantic and violently passionate, helped form the sound dimensions of his transmedia stardom. His vocal quirks arose more clearly, though, from his slight lisp, New York/urban accent, nasal timbre, side-of-the-mouth delivery, and cynical inflections. Throughout his roles, his thin baritone had the potential for up-tempo explosive intensity.

Screen Guild's "Casablanca" and the film itself offer a number of these traits, from Bogart's cynical, side-of-the-mouth "I stick my neck out for nobody" to his emotional outburst when he tells Sam to play "As Time Goes By": "If she can take it, I can. Play it!" In the Paris flashback, when Rick and Ilsa are happily together, his lighter and brighter vocal tone, not yet having acquired the sardonic resonance it has in the film's and radio program's present-day Casablanca, marks his different personality. In the film's concluding scene at the airport, after he and Ilsa have renewed their love for one another but must part for the greater good, his voice subtly softens and the tempo slows to reassure Ilsa that "We'll always have Paris," placing him briefly back in romantic mode in an otherwise tense scene. In both film and radio versions, Bergman's gentler, hesitant, and confused response to Rick's decision that she depart with Laszlo not only reveals her vulnerability but also, in contrast to his vocal command, distinguishes between masculine and feminine, a point for more discussion momentarily.

As radio and film reciprocally circulated Bogart's trademark voice in its multiple dimensions, the medium also offered aspects of his vocal persona that his films typically did not. Numerous radio appearances presented listeners with both person and actor. Such an instance occurs in the curtain call after *Lux*'s production of *To Have and Have Not,* when Bogart corrects host William Keighley's reference to Bacall as Lauren, telling him that she goes by

Betty: "Ya only call her Lauren when you're sore with her." That Bogart retained his tough-guy persona, even when he was apparently real, doubled down on his identification with this persona; in promoting his similar "real" and "reel" personalities, radio produced a dual dynamic central to creating celebrities. Because films were abbreviated on radio and, to compensate, radio increased the presence of narration to cover material not otherwise represented, Bogart's persona was also heightened by the isolation of his voice from other elements when he served as narrator. For example, he narrated *Academy Award Theater*'s adaptation of *The Maltese Falcon, Stars in the Air*'s 1952 adaptation of *The House on 92nd Street* (1945), and *Humphrey Bogart Presents.* Of course, male characters often provided voice-overs for detective stories across media in the 1940s. Giving listeners unalloyed access to the grain of his voice, radio's foregrounding of Bogart's solo aural presence in these instances, along with his roles in these and other noiresque programs, defined him as a "voice of noir," suggesting the proximity of voice trademarking and voice typing.

Typing describes a star's repeat performances in certain character molds. Radio dramas consistently confirmed and disseminated Bogart's type by featuring him in roles identical to or reminiscent of those he had originated in film as detectives, gangsters, soldiers, ship captains, adventurers, and romantic heroes, all suffused with tough-guy world-weariness. Bogart's hard-boiled detective and gangster personas composed a particular center of gravity in radio and film, propagating his "city boy" type—an "urban tough guy—small, wiry, savvy, and street-smart."[96] With this physical stature and mentality came a particular voice or range of vocal variations, from the hot-tempered and verbose gangster's slangy, choppy, repetitive, and "impatient and rude" exclamations to the detective's cooler, more measured, and more "civilized" use of voice and language—often resulting in some mix of the two in the detective.[97] Granting variations, voice typing in relation to the tough guy as articulated by these stock urban genre figures consistently expressed a cynical, streetwise, sometimes surly, violent, and exceedingly masculine kind of character.

Typing is also supported both by a pool of fellow performers possessing similar characterological qualities and by genre conventions. In the 1930s and 1940s, Bogart shared the tough-guy designation with numerous others, including James Cagney, George Raft, and Alan Ladd. Recasting often relied on such an intertextuality of personas to manifest type. Other actors besides Bogart—sometimes quite famously—played Dashiell Hammett's Sam Spade and Raymond Chandler's Philip Marlowe across media.[98] Different vocal characteristics defined these actors' performances, but each subscribed to a model of the hard-boiled voice. Radio adaptations' practice of recasting presented this kind of interplay between distinctive and generic voices as they inhabited the same characters. In versions of *Casablanca,* for example, each "radio Rick"—Bogart, Ladd, Massey, Jory, and Marr—lent his unique vocalizations to the role, from Marr's almost whispered, flat existential intonations to Jory's highly enunciated stentorian snarls, but each also strove to produce a clearly legible tough-guy voice. Radio versions illustrate how the character of Rick materialized aurally in different vocal registers in a prolific style of performative masculinity, interlacing actors' trademark voices with demands of voice typing—a process affected by radio genres.

As James Naremore writes, although *film noir* was not a broadly used term until the 1970s, its sensibility was present across the arts well before then. For its part, early radio was crucial to "the history and dissemination of noir taste," with film adaptations and radio shows like *Suspense* helping to popularize crime genres and characters.[99] Bogart's voice on radio and other actors performing Rick indicate that *Casablanca*'s adaptations contributed to the development of a noir sensibility, part of which foregrounded the tough-guy voice as a convention, with Rick fitting comfortably in radio's burgeoning noirverse of types.

Not all performers exhibited such close relations between individual and type in film and radio. For instance, Claude Rains often played villains in both media but also read children's and Bible stories to listeners on radio and LPs.[100] In its consistency, Bogart's vocal career more closely resembles that of Peter Lorre, another *Casablanca* costar. Thomas contends that radio consolidated Lorre's persona in a brand-specific way, culling from his films to feature him repeatedly in radio roles that emphasized his ties to the horror genre.[101] Similarly, radio and film collaborated in developing Bogart as "tough without a gun," as Chandler once described him. With its vococentrism, radio gave Bogart's voice and generic domains further exposure, tendencies especially on display in the many parodies of himself he performed as a tough-guy detective or gangster on its comedy/variety programs.[102]

Animating both individual and collective aspects of Bogart's persona, radio thus advanced his trademarking and typing via repetition in familiar roles, producing a relatively stable star persona that could be branded and sold to the public. In the process, the medium helped to anchor his associations with certain genres that proliferated on film and radio (and literature), placing him and *Casablanca* in a stream of multiplatformed noir and other tough-guy genres. While the dissemination of "As Time Goes By" connected the film to wartime romance, the propagation of Bogart's voice situated it in relation to noir. Radio evoked, then, multiple generic affiliations for the film—affiliations that coexisted in circulation as they promoted its public identities through diverse means.

As we will see in chapter 2, both the distinctiveness and conventionality of Bogart's voice survived this period, not only through the work of legions of impersonators but also through his ascension to cult status in the 1950s. As it had the potential to do with the audio core's other elements, radio, as part of the cross-platform diffusion of his voice and persona, may have laid foundations for enduring stardom that, in turn, kept *Casablanca* publicly visible.

On a larger scale, voice typing persists in *Casablanca*'s adaptations in relation to their ensemble of performers. Along with radio's generative and circulatory activities as a platform for popular film music, dialogue phrases, and the distinctive typed voices of stars, it crafted cultural identities of gender, race, and nation. This returns us to the film's status as an international wartime drama with colonial resonance.

A Choreography of Voices

One of Warner Bros.' press kit articles for *Casablanca,* "All Nationalities Included in Film," promotes the internationalism of the film's personnel:

> They've dubbed Stage 8 at the Warner Bros. Studios, where "Casablanca" was filmed, "The International House." The cast and crew of the production represent so many different nationalities that the set is the most cosmopolitan spot in Southern California. Humphrey Bogart is American, Ingrid Bergman is Swedish, Paul Henreid is Viennese, Claude Rains and Sydney Greenstreet are Englishmen; Conrad Veidt, born in Berlin, is a British subject, Madeleine LeBeau and Marcel Dalio are French and so is Robert Eisner, the technical director. Peter Lorre is Hungarian, as is director Michael Curtiz, Corinna Mura is a South American, Leo Mostovey is Russian, Leonid Kinskey is Polish.
>
> And Dooley Wilson says that he comes from Harlem.[103]

I will return to Wilson's singled-out status here. For now, the film's production, advertised as the meeting place of heterogeneous peoples, extolls a cosmopolitanism that evokes the wartime reality of European refugees fleeing Nazis. As is well known, Hollywood attracted numerous immigrant artists who left Europe during Hitler's rise to power. This ad presents *Casablanca* as a vivid realization of the creative esprit de corps forged from these circumstances; indeed, the film continues to be praised today for casting refugees from different nations.[104]

After the United States entered WWII following the Japanese attack on Pearl Harbor in December 1941, Hollywood became more involved in the war effort, producing government-supervised content to elicit public support and build armed forces' morale.[105] Before this, radio was engaged in uplifting the national spirit regarding freedom and democracy, an uplift that leaned toward interventionism. Given Hitler's racist agenda, both film and radio sought to address racial intolerance and inequity.[106] In the film and radio worlds of *Casablanca,* a "united nations" of characters inhabits the city and, more expressly, the microcosm of Rick's Café Américain, where conflicts between American isolationism and interventionism, the Allies and the Axis, and refugees and Nazi oppressors emerge through a strong pro-Allied forces stance. As Rick and Ilsa are not reunited at the end because each has a different role to play in the war, the story also shows personal sacrifice for the greater good—a fact that inspired government agency, the US Bureau of Motion Pictures, to rave about the film.[107]

Yet, as Hilmes argues of radio, this kind of commitment to a wartime ethos generated a contradiction; the medium that had previously perpetuated aural markers of racial and other social differences now engaged the "urgent task of mobilizing national identity and recruiting excluded groups to the idea of 'Americanness.'" With government pressure, radio broadened its address "to include previously marginalized . . . groups, or at least to mitigate the worst racial and ethnic abuses." This attempt was not entirely successful, however, because of the pervasive hold that segregationist, Jim Crow America had over US institutions, media conventions, and peoples.[108] With its multinational and multiracial voices, *Casablanca* adaptations offer an example of radio's attempts to downplay overt stereotyping during the war that nonetheless retain, as did movies, white male dominance. The arrangement of voices in these shows is central to exploring this issue.

Of cinematic sound, Michel Chion writes, "*There are voices, and then everything else* . . . in every audio mix, the presence of a human voice instantly sets up a hierarchy of perception." Furthermore, he argues, this presence "*structures the sonic space that contains it.*" In his asides about radio, he defines the medium as *acousmatic*—as reliant on voices without visual sources.[109] By this logic, radio is vococentric not only because it lacks a material visual register but also because it privileges the voice over other sonic elements. In my view, the voice's power in radio is attached to the medium's acousmatic status but not exactly because of the lack of a visual corollary. Radio's reliance on sound inspires the listener to imagine the speaker's person from the voice or, in the case of known public personalities, to invoke the face and body that match the voice. The radio voice gains part of its sensorial priority, then, from this active relation in listening between visual absence and inference. This imagining defines all radio sound, but it is especially evocative in relation to the voice as the instrument that heavily defines the medium's expressiveness. As I contend below, affected by radio sound conventions and by the visual absence/inference couplet, the broadcast voice participates in an expansive sound field linked to cultural identity.

Technical, aesthetic, and ideological factors shaped radio's vococentrism. In his work on early radio, Rudolph Arnheim found that, to be legible to listeners, vocalizations had to have peculiarities distinguishing them from one another to avoid a "confusion of vague voices." Moreover, expressiveness did not depend solely on a single voice but on the "interplay of vocal types"; parallels and contrasts among these types were central to conveying meaning.[110] From a similar perspective, Verma observes that radio scenes could bear only so many voices (usually not more than four) without losing coherence, often resulting in the use of "hackneyed accents" to ward off jumble.[111]

Radio's technically circumscribed aesthetic had cultural ramifications linked to vocal types and accents, ramifications enhanced by the medium's ideological imperatives. As Hilmes remarks, without an immediate visual register, radio could have played freely with identities. Instead, the industry saw radio's possibilities in this respect as "slippery," problematic because they could not ensure a "national norm of 'whiteness.'" This norm distinguished between white and Black performers, while fortifying whiteness by minimizing differences among European groups. Hence, early radio "obsessively" performed and circulated identity through "language, dialect, and carefully selected aural context," articulating Blackness, for example, through "minstrel dialect, second-class citizen traits, [and] cultural incompetence."[112]

Casablanca's adaptations demonstrate the impact of such differentiation on vocal choreography in 1940s radio story space. The arrangement of voices in these radio versions conveys similarities and contrasts that aligned them with or distinguished them from one another according to gender, race, and nation, resulting in a set of hierarchies. While Rick's voice is dominant in each adaptation, both he and Sam have distinctive American accents. Other voices conveying wartime internationalism (Renault, Ilsa, Laszlo, Strasser, and supporting players) are pan-European in their inflections of the English language. Performers playing Ilsa, for example, hailed from specific nations—Bergman from Sweden, Carroll from England, Lamarr from Austria, McCambridge and Webber from the United States—but impart, in their in-character foreign voices, no particular nation of origin. Instead, they inhabit the collective vocal space of an indistinct Europeanism. The contrast here, then, exists between American and European accents, with the former, in both its white and Black articulations, differing from the latter, in its construction of a homogeneous internationalism. In their distinctiveness, American voices, particularly Rick's ever-present voice, attain aural priority.

Within this choreographed vocal space, Ilsa's accent associates her with fellow international characters, but she is otherwise set apart as the only woman in the radio versions. With the exception of *Lux*'s Lamarr, who assumes some of Laszlo's and Rick's dialogue from the film and is thus more assertive, the other "radio Ilsas" project what Arnheim would call "delicate helpless" voices.[113] These voices are not only slightly European but also diminutive or emotive (Ilsa, with resignation, to Rick: "I don't know what's right any longer. You have to think for both of us. For all of us."). As it pits Jory's snappish loudness against McCambridge's frail inflections, *Romance* produces gendered aural differences that are especially pronounced.

While Sam may be firmly associated with Rick owing to their shared Americanness, he, even more than Ilsa, is isolated in the film's sound universe. Across adaptations, Sam's Blackness emerges via settings and voice—the café entertainer with the southern-infused elocution of "boss" to address Rick—that clarify his status as a loyal servant. *Star Playhouse*'s first few episodes vary this pattern as each begins with conversations between Sam and Rick that provide a backstory for their friendship. Yet Sam's role as romantic intermediary and Rick's valet, reaffirmed by his subordinate elocutions, indicate significant differences between the two men on the basis of race. Moreover, while these radio dramas minimize substantial vocal differences among European characters, such is not the case here. In his submissive tone and modest drawl, Sam's voice is aurally distinct from other performers, placing him in a racial silo. This recalls the film's press book copy in its similar way of handling racial difference in the midst of international diversity. The copy places Wilson in a sentence and a category of his own, in the "nation" of Harlem rather than of America. Although Harlem as a center of African American creativity was a locus of racial pride, rhetorically presenting it as its own world from which the only Black character in this drama hails defines

Wilson's racial difference as equivalent to national difference, othering him in the process. Radio's conventions of racially based elocutions cement his status in this regard.[114]

Since audiences did not necessarily experience stars in a medium- or sense-segregated way on radio, we can recognize how carefully aligned aural and visual registers were with respect to recasting and race. Although, in theory, radio recasting offered opportunities for change, as I have noted, proximities between actors often underwrote it—Ladd replacing Bogart, for example, based on their shared noir types. Larger considerations also weigh on recasting as radio attempted to ensure that listeners would infer "proper" racial identities. No matter who played the leads or other central performers, almost all were white—something that audiences would know by their conversancy with the stars or by the characters' white American or pan-European accents.[115] Each actor who played Sam in the 1940s, including Whitman in two adaptations and "Rochester" in *Jack Benny*'s parody of *Casablanca,* was African American. In this way, part of the visual inferences or connections radio asked listeners to make between voices and bodies confirmed racial differences and hierarchies.

As radio versions made sonic space legible and meaningful through parallels and contrasts among distinctive voices and by securing inferences about race, they schematized accented characters according to the medium's conventions and concerns. The vocal ensembles captured the wartime internationalism essential to the film, while also conveying a hierarchy of voices in which white US male characters were dominant and affiliated with white Europeans. The European woman, who has access to this brotherhood, is otherwise different because of her delicate aurality and submissiveness, while the African American is isolated and relegated to lower ranks via subservient dialect and social position. In this aural environment, no "confusion of vague voices" could challenge ideologies of gender and race.

It is not that cinema was somehow superior to radio in representing nationalities, accents, or races. Both media often relied on visual and vocal international drag and deployed codes to ensure racial difference, including performances of Blackface or "Blackvoice," in which white film and radio performers played African American characters. Such cases did not depend on inferences to secure matching visual correlates but pushed stereotypical racial differences through vaudeville traditions that favored white performers, often no matter the role.[116] With respect to *Casablanca,* though, radio adaptations' choreography of voices and identities are perhaps more revealing than the film about the stakes involved. By condensing the film's story and sonic elements for broadcast and stripping away the visual aspects of star wattage and lustrous cinematography, radio pointed more clearly to the film's suppositions about cultural identities, invoking its ideological priorities as it marginalized, in different ways, those not white or male.

CONCLUSION

Radio's prolific role as film adapter prompts us to reconsider the standard prioritization in the field of film's relation to literature and stage plays during the 1930s and 1940s. Film adaptation was a multimedia affair that prominently involved radio and its particular kind of sensory makeover. When radio adapted a film numerous times in short order, creating a critical mass of texts bearing the source's name, as it did with *Casablanca,* it also presented challenges for adaptation studies in a different way. How do we analyze such a body of texts and their impact on the source and surrounding sonic cultures? I have pursued this question through a postfidelity approach to adaptation that eschews traditional evaluations, embracing instead an aesthetics of circulation. While this aesthetic does not require a scenario of multiple adaptations of the same source to operate, it is particularly helpful in addressing this phenomenon. It encourages us to track, across versions, the selective foregrounding and transformation of a set of filmic elements that collectively survived the process of translation. In doing so, this approach offers a view both of the source's emblematic features as they emerged on a new media platform and their travel in related and larger mediascapes. This migration, as we have seen, generates a series of paths of meaning that cannot always be reconciled. Radio reduced *Casablanca*'s story and audio elements, only to disperse them into diverse intertextual networks linked to colonial narratives, popular music and language, stardom, and cultural identities.

This untidy picture reveals the forces involved in the push-and-pull of film identity beyond the text itself. With genre, for example, the film's programming as daytime radio fare or the popularity and dissemination of its key song on the air and in other sound media helped to define *Casablanca* in terms of romantic melodrama. Although critics consider *Casablanca* as Bogart's breakthrough as a romantic leading man, the actor's voice and career on the air suggest the prevalence of his strong affiliation with tough-guy genres like noir. Radio also offers a context for the film that strengthens its identity both as a war film and colonialist story. Thus, an aesthetics of circulation, as it engages potentially numerous interrelated spheres of meaning, provides one view of how a text is associated with different generic identities at the same time. Radio alone was not responsible for this state of affairs; rather, it contributed to the fluctuating nature of generic identity in circulation.

Throughout this chapter, I have treated *Casablanca*'s radio adaptation as a case of the source's modification by a sound-only, nontheatrical platform that suggests the importance of pretelevision broadcasting to film rerelease and circulation. Radio adaptations demonstrate the reconfiguration of one influential form of industrial narrative into another, illuminating the intricacies of cross-media conversion while depicting how rapidly and actively versions of the film began to circulate. Clearly the 1940s does not exhibit the corporate conglomeration associated with media convergence, transmedia storytelling, and multiplatform accessibility today. This past is defined, however, by an earlier form of capitalism built on interindustrial affiliations and partnerships that extended story and audio worlds across available platforms, representing a tendency that would later grow exponentially.

Moreover, analyzing story and audio cores not only illuminates the impact of radio adaptation on film narrative and sound in this era but also begins to show how, through this reprocessing, certain film elements gained the potential to become canon. As an initial means of replatforming *Casablanca,* radio became part of a media economy that increased the film's visibility and amplified the presence of its story, stars, characters, music, lingo, and worldview—an uncertain, but potentially important small step on the road toward memorability.[117] Because anthology dramas, like other radio genres, had their own downstream history through radio reruns, commercial rereleases on LP, and radio fan communities, they were present during times when *Casablanca* was reissued on other exhibition forums, thereby continuing to contribute to its visibility.[118]

As we shall see in Chapter 3, *Casablanca*'s broadcast history did not end with radio; television would become enormously influential in shaping the film's fortunes in and after the 1950s. In the next chapter, however, I study another platform of rerelease for the film that began in the later 1940s—theatrical reissues—part of its history critical to understanding its cult status.

TWO

Back in Theaters

POSTWAR REPERTORY HOUSES AND CULT CINEMA

There is evidence that the major studios at last realize the value of their old and, in some cases, forgotten features, and re-issues may become so integral a part of film distribution and exhibition that it will be possible, in a not-too-distant future, to say of movies what is said of books—a good film never dies.

REGGIE HURD JR.,
Films in Review, 1953

Among theologians of the Hollywood cosmogony, Humphrey Bogart ranks as one of the three major deities, the other two being Charlie Chaplin and Greta Garbo. Of the three Bogart alone is dead but only in the transient, off-screen sense of the word. On screen Bogart appears bigger than ever. His films are shown endlessly on TV to never-tiring Bogie buffs who even pay good money at the box office to see the same features repeated in theaters at countless "Bogart Festivals." No other star of the 1930s, a decade loaded with super-stars, matches Bogart's continuing grip on the imagination.

HERM., *Variety*, 1967

DURING THE HEIGHT OF WWII, *Casablanca* premiered in New York City's Hollywood Theater on Thanksgiving Day, November 26, 1942, and opened wide in other US theaters on January 23, 1943. According to industry estimates, the film ran up "smash totals nearly everywhere." *Variety* listed it as Warner Bros.' second most profitable film of the season, bested only by the studio's *This Is the Army* (1943), also directed by Michael Curtiz. In Hollywood, producer Harold "Hal" B. Wallis and Curtiz were "top money getters" for Warner Bros., while *Casablanca* made Humphrey Bogart the "top company star" and Ingrid Bergman the "top femme b.o. (box office) magnet of the year."[1] *New York Times* critic Bosley Crowther bolstered *Casablanca*'s reputation, writing an ecstatic review that ranked it as one of the year's finest films. Indeed, it was nominated for numerous Academy Awards, winning Best Picture, Best Director, and Best Adapted Screenplay of 1943.[2]

Casablanca's initial theatrical exhibition with its wartime relevance, studio and star power, box office and awards success, and favorable reviews had substantial visibility that marked the beginning of its circulation through time, as well as its cultural consecration. In particular, the Oscars it won assigned it superior value in a field of films. As I discussed in the previous chapter, radio adaptations of *Casablanca* in 1943 and 1944 more subtly created value for it. Beyond inaugurating the film's presence in the aftermarket and recirculating its story, characters, and sounds on a new platform to home audiences, radio valorized it by selecting it as worthy of adaptation and acted as a mode of its public preservation.

In this and the next chapter, I examine other platforms involved in *Casablanca*'s early decades of reissue—motion picture theaters and television, respectively—and how they continued to adapt the film to new environments. Like each study in the book, these depict slices of *Casablanca*'s afterlife that reveal how different kinds of exhibition generated different interpretive stakes and values for it in its journey across time. From the late 1940s through the 1970s, theaters and television prolifically screened Warner Bros.' Bogart films, marking the period of *Casablanca*'s most intensive dissemination. This kind of overlap or proximity in platforms indirectly suggested a "consensus around which films should be remembered and which forgotten," particularly as it produced a textual hierarchy of the best Bogart films. That a number of platforms exhibited the same oldies during the same period produced a "cumulative effect" of legitimation,[3] a mutually endorsing proposal about the significance of these films. This interplay began to consolidate facets of *Casablanca*'s reputation as a Hollywood classic, cult film, and Bogart vehicle. Although I examine theaters and television separately, the effects of platform proximity weigh on my consideration of each.

Warner Bros. rereleased *Casablanca* to conventional theaters for the first time in 1949. The studio's reissue of the film occurred in the context of industry developments that fueled a "booming business" in the recirculation of older titles, resulting in new life for many of them. My analysis of theaters commences with a discussion of why the postwar film industry increased its practice of reissue, making films from the past a steadfast part of theatrical programming.[4] I then explore the rise of a particular kind of postwar film theater—the repertory house—that intensively recycled classical Hollywood films for decades, having a significant impact on *Casablanca*'s circulation. Along with older Hollywood titles, repertory houses (also called revival, retrospective, and art houses) screened foreign, documentary and experimental films for audiences in college towns and cities nationwide. In presenting classical-era films outside the customary precincts of first-run theaters and their new movies, repertory houses appeared as alternative venues for audiences whose "routines and practices" deviated from the more sedate moviegoing behaviors of regular theatrical exhibition. Critics thus often regard these theaters' departure from the norm as influencing the development of cult cinema in the United States.[5]

To investigate the repertory house, I turn to the Brattle Theatre in Cambridge, Massachusetts, located near Harvard Square and Harvard University. The Brattle was one of the earliest and most important of postwar repertory houses, as well as the setting most often recognized as contributing to *Casablanca*'s afterlife as a "paradigmatic classical cult film."[6] Critics regard the Brattle as the place where both Bogart and *Casablanca* attained cult status, inspiring the spread of "Bogart-mania" across the nation. While my focus on the Brattle cannot exhaust this phenomenon, the case of a particular movie theater regarded in the postwar years as a center of gravity for the Bogart cult allows me to reflect in detail on the US repertory house's early and continuing role in propagating the intertwined cult standing of actor and film. Here, *Casablanca*'s meaning and status are hitched to Bogart's star, while his stardom, in the eyes of fans, achieves its finest expression in the film. The film became a popular source of access to Bogart's brand of "cool" masculinity and to associated lines of film dialogue, attracting female and male viewers alike to the cult.

In studying the repertory house as an adaptive site for *Casablanca,* we will see that cult responses did not develop solely out of the spontaneous affinities of spectators. Rather, as Mark Jancovich argues, cult developed through the theater's "mechanisms, spaces, and systems of communication" as they produced "a sense of community" and distributed cultural knowledge about cinema to viewers.[7] With this in mind, I examine the Brattle's programming strategies, particularly its organization of Bogart's oeuvre into film festivals, and the relation of these strategies to the rhythms and spaces of student life at Harvard, moviegoers' cultish activities, student newspaper reviews, and the surrounding social environment as they shaped a cult taste formation. Such intensive milieus prepared audiences for a "cultist-like appreciation of cinema."[8]

Historicizing *Casablanca*'s meaning here ultimately obliges a historical lens on cult cinema as well. Rather than regarding cult as determined by inherent textual features, as in Umberto Eco's well-known but ahistorical essay on *Casablanca*,[9] I approach cult as created discursively by institutions, industries, mass-cultural sources, and audience practices in specific social circumstances. A film's textual properties cannot, in my view, define it evermore as cult, nor can they ensure its politics. Social practices mobilize its properties for cult consumption in and through time, subjecting its status and ideological meaning as cult to historical flow and instability.[10] Indeed, as they circulated, Bogart and *Casablanca* had a "double-tiered" status as both mainstream and cult. The film and actor never lost their mainstream credentials, yet through their histories they attained at least two distinctly different cult identities. The Bogart cult was the first but, as we will see in later chapters, not the last of these identities. Furthermore, *Casablanca*'s cult statuses, rather than demonstrating the cult film's purported subversive, counter-to-the-mainstream ideologies, reveal the ambivalences and ambiguities of the historical moments that defined them. No matter what the nuances of cult identity were, however, cult standing provided favorable conditions of recognizability and popularity for certain Hollywood films that offered them a chance at endurance.

THE POSTWAR REISSUE MARKET AND *CASABLANCA*

Today, given video and other outlets, classical-era Hollywood films are rarely reissued in first-run theaters and materialize only periodically in repertory houses. By contrast, in the post-WWII years, theatrical reissues of older pictures were legion. As Eric Hoyt has shown, earlier in film history, these rereleases served as modest additional revenue streams for film companies. After WWII, however, they became "vital profit centers" for the studios until TV reruns assumed this mantle in the later 1950s. So momentous was the postwar industry and audience embrace of reissues that Hoyt hails it as a "turning point in the history of film libraries."[11] This chapter's first epigraph captures this transitional moment, marking the reissue's rise as a financial bedrock for film companies, an incentive to maintain their libraries, and a constituent part of film culture and experience.

Whereas in prewar and wartime America a studio might release one or two of its older pictures annually, the 1949–50 season in which *Casablanca* reappeared "set a record of reissues, with more than 150 oldies" in national circulation. The *Hollywood Reporter* announced another record in 1953–54, with more than two hundred reissues.[12] Since some trade journal tallies did not include independent distributors specializing in reissues such as Astor Pictures and Realart Pictures Inc.—the latter of which, having acquired Universal-International's pre-1948 films, was touted as "the largest reissue company in the world"—the figures are higher.[13] Yet, as Hoyt maintains, not all studios invested in the same way in their back catalogs. In 1949, major studios (studios with production, distribution, and exhibition facilities) reissued small numbers of films—RKO with a high of ten, Paramount with a low of two—an approach that sought both to minimize competition between a studio's old and new films and create a special occasion for films that were reissued. That same year saw smaller studios and film companies adopting a more aggressive stance to exploit reissues' profitability: Columbia Pictures, a major minor (studios without broad theater ownership) rereleased forty-five pictures, followed by Realart with forty-two, and Republic, a minor studio (small studios with few resources) with twenty-two.[14]

These tallies sketch different companies' varying commitments to reissues, while hinting at the variety of films that reappeared. As *Boxoffice*'s Feature Index for 1949 indicates, films ranged from Astor's low-budget *Ghosts on the Loose* (1943), acquired from minor studio Monogram Pictures and starring the East Side Kids, Bela Lugosi, and Ava Gardner, to MGM's *The Wizard of Oz* (1939), with Judy Garland.[15] *Ghosts on the Loose* has since been marginalized or forgotten, whereas other films also reissued in the 1940s—such as *Gone with the Wind* (1939), *The Wizard of Oz,* and *Casablanca*—have become evergreens. Postwar theatrical reissue, then, did not beget popular immortality but represented a mode of rerelease in which films entered a Darwinian textual lottery that might mean eventual accession to this status.

Instabilities in and around the film industry precipitated changing attitudes to reissues in the postwar era. Numerous well-known forces drove industrial precarity after 1946, a banner year at the box office for studios before their fortunes fell. They range from the 1948 Paramount Case, in which the Supreme Court determined that the Big Eight—Hollywood major and major minor studios—constituted a vertical monopoly and had to sell their theaters, to the rise of competition from TV for audiences. Production costs had also increased, resulting in the release of fewer new films.[16] In this climate, theatrical reissues proved to be a financial boon for both studios and exhibitors. They constituted a defense against the postwar industry's difficult conditions by offering, as Hoyt observes, "low-cost, low-risk profit centers."[17] For studios, even when the "'big' pix of yesteryear" like *Gone with the Wind* and *The Best Years of Our Lives* (1946) were given deluxe treatment with new advertising campaigns, they cost far less than new films to release.[18] Profits, in turn, were handsome. In 1955, 20th Century–Fox estimated that it had made $20,000,000 (roughly $200,000,000 today) in reissues since 1946, and RKO, having pocketed millions from several of its 1948 reissues alone, learned that "pictures, like whiskey, improve with age."[19]

For exhibitors, the shortage in new films meant that first-run theaters exhibited them for longer periods. Subsequent-run and neighborhood theaters, which generally changed their bill more frequently, had to wait for the latest fare. In the meantime, they looked for films to fill their schedules—a challenge because, since the 1930s, double features had been the norm in programming. As *Variety* reported, a "flood of reissues" met these "product crises." Since older titles were cheaper to rent and were known quantities to audiences, exhibitors were drawn to them.[20] If an older film had been successful, they promoted it for its winning qualities; if it had been less successful, they emphasized features that new customers might find appealing (e.g., seeing stars in early roles, before they became famous). Exhibitors regarded reissues as a necessary and potentially profitable programming strategy, but they also hoped that, by leasing these films, they could forestall their appearance on TV or at least "grab coin" before the new medium threatened their business.[21] But early postwar theatrical reissue did not keep films from TV play; nor, more surprisingly, did the TV market, as this chapter's second epigraph notes, detract from the appeal of Hollywood oldies in theaters.

Although critics sometimes complained about the reissue boom,[22] movie recycling in regular commercial theaters in the 1940s and 1950s, before repertory houses exploded in popularity, heralded what would become a mainstay of US film programming across platforms.

Casablanca's *First Theatrical Return*

From late 1948 through summer 1949, Warner Bros. released twenty-five new films and six reissues to conventional commercial theaters. Among the latter, *Casablanca* reappeared nationwide in June 1949, paired in a double feature with *G-Men* (1935), starring James Cagney, Bogart's fellow Warner Bros. tough-guy icon.[23] Ads extolled the Bogart/Cagney pairing as "The Big Stars in Their Big Hits! Twice as Thrilling *Together!*" with *Casablanca* in particular promoted as "the most requested picture in years."[24] Reissued films often screened on double bills, with an "A" film at the top and a "B" or lower budget film at the bottom of the bill. A version of this strategy operated in the *Casablanca/G-Men* package in terms of the comparative success of the films, with the less profitable Cagney title occupying second place. This official pairing screened in different settings, from large cities to small rural towns and from first-run to subsequent-run theaters. The "B" film could vary, however; some exhibitors, especially in subsequent-run and Black theaters, changed it to achieve a combination their audiences would find more appealing.[25]

Like all reissues, the Bogart/Cagney program ran in fewer theaters than debut screenings—usually no more than three in a major urban area—but still produced profits. On Memorial Day weekend, *Variety* reported that the *Casablanca/G-Men* program at Chicago's Rialto was a "surprise entry" in the ledgers, doing a robust $16,000 in business (about $190,000 today). In the same market, a new film like Paramount Pictures' *A Connecticut Yankee in King Arthur's Court* (1949) earned $55,000 gross.[26] Although reissues sometimes out-earned new films, even when that was not the case, they made handsome sums; in one theater, the Bogart and Cagney films earned nearly one-third of *A Connecticut Yankee*'s take. Like Warner Bros.' other reissues, *Casablanca* represented a solid source of profit in uncertain times.[27]

The first *Casablanca* theatrical reissue occurred in a broader context of the success that the studio's gangster and noir catalog—two genres in Bogart's métier—experienced in the theatrical aftermarket. In 1947, Warner Bros. rereleased the crime drama *Marked Woman* (1937), a film with Bogart and another popular star in reissue, Bette Davis. A year later, Warner Bros. offered the gangster picture *Angels with Dirty Faces*, starring Cagney, Bogart, and Ann Sheridan in a double feature with the film noir *They Drive by Night*, starring another studio tough guy, George Raft, as well as Bogart, Sheridan, and Ida Lupino.[28] In the early 1950s, Warner Bros. rereleased more films in these genres, including gangster-film double features of Edward G. Robinson's *Little Caesar* (1931) and Cagney's *The Public Enemy* (1931), and Robinson/Cagney's *Smart Money* (1931) and Cagney/Bogart's *The Roaring Twenties* (1939). In 1952, on a double bill that featured Bogart as the undisputed major star, Warner Bros. reissued wartime drama/adventure/romance *To Have and Have Not* (1944) and gangster film *High Sierra* (1941) as a package.[29] At this time, Columbia Pictures also rereleased the Bogart war film *Sahara* (1943).

Between 1947, when these reissues began, and his death in 1957, Bogart made twenty-five new pictures and had, since his breakout role in *Casablanca*, become a bona fide A-list star. But, as this spate of rereleases featuring him begins to demonstrate, his image was defined by the continued circulation of his previous work as well. Along with other Hollywood performers whose work was successfully rereleased at this time, such as Davis, Greta Garbo, Charlie Chaplin, the Marx Brothers, and Mae West, Bogart had become, in Brian Hannan's parlance, a "reissue star."[30] If maintaining stardom as the years passed was a challenge for most actors, rereleased movies magnified their public presence and suggested that they merited the kind of legacy such revivals signified, giving them a chance at longer lasting celebrity. Moreover, although scholars often conceive of a movie actor's persona as confirmed or changed by each new film released, this historical moment indicates that the "persona timeline" is not linear but asynchronous or scrambled, mixing old and new roles and younger and more mature iterations of the star into coexisting portraits.

This aspect of reissue stardom was a crucial feature of the repertory house's Bogart film festivals and the cult taste formations in and beyond the 1950s that they helped to generate. At the same time, repertory houses became the single most important type of theater to screen classical-era titles after the war.

POSTWAR REPERTORY HOUSES AND FILM CULTURES

Warner Bros. continued to reissue its catalog to conventional theaters in the early 1950s, with "single prints seeing quite a bit of use,"[31] creating a public presence for its older films that would gain steam in repertory houses. The studio's films, like many other Hollywood titles, achieved vigorous new life through these houses and TV reruns. Shifting ownership of the studio's library accompanied these developments in exhibition. In 1956, Warner Bros. sold 754 of its pre-1948 titles, including *Casablanca,* to PRM Inc. and Associated Artists Productions (AAP) for a substantial sum. These companies, in turn, sold the library to United Artists (UA) in 1958—not the last time these films would change hands.[32] In 1965 *Variety* reported that UA was taking the "'whimsical phenomenon' of Bogart's theatrical comeback" seriously, emphasizing distribution in college towns since the "Bogart cult" had given his films "unexpected theatrical value" in those and urban locales. For example, that year the 8th Street Playhouse in New York City grossed $10,000 in two weeks (about $90,000 today) from UA's package of Bogart films.[33]

In a US screen culture dominated by Hollywood first-run feature films, post-WWII repertory theaters were not the first to exhibit older Hollywood films, art cinema, and avant-garde movies. In the first half of the twentieth century, museums, specialty cinemas, film societies, and earlier repertory houses programmed such alternative fare. They built a sensibility around movies in niche environments that would influence the cinephilic film culture that flourished from the 1950s through the 1970s.[34] As relatives of these venues, postwar repertory houses offered full-time, highly visible, and broadly available nationwide showcases for this fare that made it into mainstream entertainment. In 1946 Chicago's Clark Theater became one of the earliest repertory houses in the postwar era, with the Brattle Theatre and Berkeley's Cinema-Guild commencing operations in 1953 and 1955, respectively.[35] Repertory houses would soon pervade the country from the New Yorker, Bleecker Street Cinema, and 8th Street Playhouse in New York to the Vagabond, Encore, and Tiffany theaters in Los Angeles.

The repertory house's emergence at this time is due to complex overlapping developments in the film industry and film culture affecting the public presence and impact of old Hollywood films and other alternative theatrical fare.[36] Industrially, repertory houses experienced dramatic growth due to the same changes that affected the conventional theatrical market. The studios' loss of complete control over exhibition and distribution as a result of the Paramount Case, coupled with the fall-off in film production and theater attendance, caused exhibitors to pursue different markets and programming content. The end of the monopolistic relation between studios and theater ownership fueled a surge of independent theater proprietors, new strategies in programming, and different kinds of theaters that formed the backbone of the repertory house phenomenon.

Through a contrast with upscale first-run movie theaters and Hollywood's big commercial machine, repertory houses promoted the sense that they were venues more interested in art and love of cinema than money. Their programming tendencies and institutional features further accentuated this perception. As they screened classical Hollywood movies along with art cinema, documentaries, and avant-garde titles, they created a juxtaposition that allowed older US films to draw from the artistic cachet of fare more clearly produced outside of Hollywood's norms, encouraging an imaginative disassociation of vintage films from the very industry that had produced them.[37] Additionally, repertory house screenings often took place not in well-appointed facilities but in ramshackle buildings or spaces converted to theater use. Platform adaptation in this environment often meant, whether the film was reduced to 16 mm or retained its original 35 mm gauge for projection, the screening of subpar prints that transformed its materiality through scratches, fading, and missing audio or visual segments. Enveloping movies and their patrons in a kind of shabby chic environment, repertory houses redesigned the expected moviegoing experience. They thus materialized as "selective film markets defined by a sense of distinction from 'mainstream, commercial cinema'"—a situation conducive to generating cultish sensibilities and the cultish rediscovery of Hollywood films and stars.[38]

Developments in US postwar film culture further defined repertory houses as unconventional spheres of moviegoing that offered viewers an opportunity to nurture and express distinctive codes of taste. As Greg Taylor contends, film critics, rejecting both what they perceived as the pseudo-sophistication of middlebrow tastes that touted modernism (e.g., abstract expressionism) and lowbrow tastes that lapsed into passive consumerism, embraced movies as a vital, authentic art through which they could exercise their discerning tastes and cultural authority.[39] Postwar film critics eschewed their standard role as "distanced judges," seeing themselves instead as "creative artists" that remade movies through acts of "seized consumerism" that refused "any perceived mainstream of taste while providing a model of resistant, artistic spectatorship." This kind of criticism linked active spectatorship and a countercultural ethos, with movies providing the foundation for self-empowerment.[40] In the moviegoing culture that ensued, newsweeklies and magazines such as the *Village Voice* and *Film Culture* and books such as Arthur Knight's *The Liveliest Art* (1957), Pauline Kael's *I Lost It at the Movies* (1965), and Andrew Sarris's *American Cinema* (1968) bolstered cinema's aesthetic credentials and critics' public profile, while guiding audiences in how to appraise films. This situation amplified the status of films as major topics of popular discussion.

By emphasizing movies as generative forces capable of enfranchising individual tastes as oppositional, this critical attitude fostered a mainstreaming of cult—a "new accessible cultism." Such a sensibility, a form of cinephilia or movie-love, embraced the connoisseurship embodied in the tasteful selection of films. Here, as Jamie Sexton writes, spectators, like critics, could "reclaim mass culture as their own," drawing on a "vast field of valid, potentially useful movies" to build their own aesthetic culture. In so doing, this postwar critical movement helped rescue the term *cult* from its once disparaged status among critics to a more affirmative meaning.[41]

Many of the moviegoers drawn into this film culture were teenagers and young adults. In the postwar era, educated middle-class youth were replacing older, less well-educated viewers from the lower-to-middle class as a dominant demographic in theater attendance.[42] At repertory houses, youth audiences became avid moviegoers in an exhibition venue that fueled the creation of sectarian aesthetic tastes and cult favorites. *Seventeen* magazine reported that "a growing number of young people are gravitating away from plush movie palaces to theaters where the films are vintage, the prices generally lower, and parents or guardians are not required."[43] That repertory houses were often rundown and screened "mutilated" prints with scratches or missing content reinforced a sense of youthful bohemian solidarity that not only testified to a cinephilic commitment to films but also challenged the more respectable parent culture.[44]

As a postwar bastion of American youth, universities were deeply involved in this upswell of interest in movies. The GI Bill funded higher education for many returning veterans, creating the sense that college was a common rite of passage.[45] Students that attended college could encounter film courses offered officially in the classroom, but they also frequented unofficial "film classes" in nearby repertory houses and campus film societies that screened programs of international films, classical-era Hollywood movies, documentaries, and avant-garde cinema. In 1940, fewer than thirty film societies screened films; in the 1960s, their numbers rose to more than four thousand, demonstrating the significant place that alternative fare occupied in this film culture.[46] As a result, "large numbers of college kids for the first time began to center their lives around the movies as an art form . . . [with] something fresh even in old movies."[47]

Showing movies in a college setting not only attracted youth audiences to cinema; it also linked movies and moviegoing to an educational ethos that defined old Hollywood films as an integral part of US history, culture, and heritage. Moreover, campuses in the 1960s and beyond registered important social developments of this era, acting as sites of countercultural political protest and resistance. Against the backdrop of the Cold War and nuclear anxiety, the 1960s alone saw the continuation of the civil rights movement, the rise of the women's and gay liberation movements, and protests against the Vietnam War, developments that inspired youth countercultures and organizations while producing instabilities around culturally established ideologies of race, gender, sexuality, and patriotism. Films could become vehicles for the experience and expression of rebellion against parent cultures as instruments of the "Establishment" that had created the injustices and inequities that fomented this broad range of social causes. Yet moviegoing was not a solemn affair. College youth often made "audible wisecracks" combined with "convulsive laughter." Their "rowdy-ism" caused one reviewer to label them the "sophisticated booboisie."[48] As the Brattle's case will show, cult film behavior—perhaps always tinged with the kind of camp response to older artifacts that can produce this kind of hilarity—was animated by intense vocal participation in the movie experience.

As television reran scores of classical Hollywood films for home audiences, it represented another form of film school. Along with repertory houses, the new medium led to a revived interest in old movies by audiences who might have forgotten or never seen them. As it did, it stoked viewers' desire to experience them "whole," that is, on the big screen and without the editing and commercial interruption they underwent to suit broadcast slots.[49] Through its relentless repetition of old movies that "turned every household into a private film museum," television also had the potential both to school viewers in film conventions, giving them a savvy cinematic literacy, and to inspire cult status for rewatched and beloved artifacts of the past.[50] The impact of TV reruns on film culture in these respects shows that television was not the "enemy" of cinema or film theaters; through platform proximity, it joined with repertory houses to identify classical-era Hollywood movies as central fare for education and entertainment.

Nostalgia, here a yearning for classical Hollywood films and stars and the prewar and wartime eras they represented, was woven through these aspects of film culture. As movies were "becoming aware of themselves as Art," viewers could find immense pleasure in rediscovering "old favorites and famous old faces like Bogart and Clark Gable." Even audiences who enjoyed new Hollywood films like 1967's *The Graduate* and *Bonnie and Clyde* and international films like *Blow-Up* (1966) echoed the often-repeated refrain that movies and stars were better in the "old days."[51] Their superiority issued from what appeared to be their simplicity in comparison to the more explicitly violent and sexual modern films, like those above, produced in the context of the postwar era's seismic social changes. As Fred Davis writes, the "ability to feel nostalgia for events in our past has [to do] with the way they contrast—or, more accurately, the way we *make* them contrast—with the events, moods, and dispositions of our present circumstances."[52] Classical-era films allowed audiences to address the present, often by offsetting and retreating from its tensions—a dynamic, as we will see, important to constituting the cult status of Bogart and *Casablanca*.

The set of developments surrounding repertory houses begins to explain how a film like *Casablanca* could become an object of cult devotion at this time. Major Hollywood movies differed from niche "midnight movies" like *The Rocky Horror Picture Show* (1975) that are typically associated with cult. *Casablanca* fell into a different category—"classical cult"—a category that recognizes films that were produced during Hollywood's Golden Age for mainstream viewers and later rediscovered as especially meaningful to more specialized audiences.[53] Postwar repertory houses and film cultures facilitated the transformation of these films into cultish fare by inspiring youth audiences to remake old titles into signifiers of antimainstream resistance that gave like-minded communities a sense of discerning taste and defiance of prevailing norms.

Buoyed by exhibition practices in regular theaters that had already repackaged Bogart's films for enthusiastic audiences, postwar repertory houses significantly shaped his cult according to their own signature practices.

THE BRATTLE THEATRE AND THE BOGART CULT

In 1953 two Harvard University alumni, Bryant Haliday and Cyrus Harvey Jr., joined forces to renovate Brattle Hall, a building established in the late 1800s for the Cambridge Social Union's meeting spaces and library, to accommodate a movie theater (fig. 6).[54] Harvey had spent time in Paris at the Cinémathèque française, where he immersed himself in its offerings of art cinema and old Hollywood films—an international precedent for their endeavor. Riding the wave of postwar interest in art cinema, Haliday and Harvey wagered that the "intellectual, bohemian population of Cambridge would welcome a chance to view a mixture of the finest . . . American films and . . . most recent avant-garde works of international filmmakers."[55] In 1955 they founded Janus Films primarily to distribute art films nationwide.[56] They expanded their business to include other theaters, but the ownership of the Brattle Theatre and Janus Films would change hands in the ensuing years, the latter becoming affiliated with Voyager and then the Criterion Collection.[57] By the 1970s, Cambridge was a "movie mecca," with an estimated nine commercial movie theaters and repertory houses; besides the Brattle, these included the Orson Welles and Janus Cinema theaters. The university, meanwhile, hosted a dozen film societies.

The Brattle, Harvard Square, and surrounding spaces were defined not only by the tweed often associated with Ivy League schools but also by a

FIGURE 6. The Brattle Theatre: *(a)* early 1950s; *(b)* 2008 (with the Casablanca Club downstairs).

town-and-gown mixture of hippie and radical cultures.[58] Like other Ivy League universities and numerous universities nationwide, Harvard's student body in the early postwar era was largely Christian, male, white, and middle- to upper-class. While the civil rights and women's liberation movements of the 1960s and 1970s helped to change the dynamics of admissions, African Americans continued to account for only a small percentage of Harvard's admissions between the 1950s and early 1970s. Female students from sister school Radcliffe College had been taking classes at Harvard since the 1940s, but women did not constitute a substantial percentage of the university's population until the 1970s.[59] While Bogart had global appeal across genders and races, the demographic constitution of the Harvard University/Radcliffe College matrix in the early postwar decades suggests that the Brattle's Bogart cult had primarily a white male and female following.[60]

Haliday and Harvey facilitated Bogart's US rediscovery, an actor whom they both admired and championed by repeatedly screening his films. After Bogart's death in early 1957, the Brattle programmed *Casablanca* in April of that year, the beginning of a decades-long dedication to the actor and his films.[61] Although it is difficult to pinpoint the exact moment that the cult began, the star's death activated one of the key informing principles of this type of stardom: a poignant contrast between "once vital star personas" and their posthumous screen embalmment as it reanimates their personas for viewers—an interplay we will see more fully in the sections that follow.[62]

Bogart's reanimation at the Brattle was sufficiently powerful to spill beyond the bounds of the theater, creating cult spaces in neighboring areas and affecting other repertory theaters. Harvard Square sported Bogart-themed bars, restaurants, and nightclubs. These included The Blue Parrot, a coffee shop named after Ferrari's (Sydney Greenstreet) business in *Casablanca,* and The Casablanca Club, modeled after Rick's Café Américain with a large mural illustrating many characters from the film (fig. 7). Jukeboxes in such locales repeatedly played "As Time Goes By," with the film's music another locus for the expression and enjoyment of the star/film cult.[63] Meanwhile, the Brattle's screening of Bogart films reached further still in its influences, helping to launch nationwide programming trends in repertory theaters. For example, a reviewer credited the Brattle's Bogart programming as responsible for a 1965 Bogart festival at the New Yorker Theatre, which resulted in "packed houses" for *Casablanca.* These were attended by "collegiate and post-collegiate viewers" that presented "a welter of dungarees, war-surplus coats, and tweed jackets with a scattering of beards, mustaches,

FIGURE 7. The Casablanca Club, 2010. Photograph by David Chin (Prehensile Eye). Mural by David Omar White.

and motorcycle boots." These viewers reveled "in every Bogart mannerism" while "shouting the dialogue" and burying numerous lines in "a wild howl of applause."[64]

The activities of the Brattle and other repertory houses did not, of course, take place in a vacuum. Diverse sources, from national newspapers and magazines and literary and political journals to mass-marketed books, TV documentaries, and Bogart posters, participated in the Bogart-mania sweeping the nation.[65] Woody Allen's hit 1969 Broadway comedy, *Play It Again, Sam,* followed by his 1972 movie adaptation of the same name (both of which may have fueled the rampant misquoting of the film's actual line, "Play it, Sam"), further deified Bogart, capitalizing on and contributing to the fervor surrounding him and his films. Such a concert of forces inspired fans of Bogart's films to develop an "almost worshipful" attitude toward him that made him a "central and engrossing part of [their] lives."[66]

The Brattle's film festivals, as they helped to incite and sustain this Bogart-mania, were, by 1958, programmed during Harvard's reading periods for final exams, quickly becoming a Cambridge institution. At the end of the theater's 1964 Bogart Festival, *Time* magazine estimated that "15,000 viewers had seen 47 showings of 14 Bogey movies." Even "new Bogey fans" had "seen *Casablanca* five times."[67] In the late 1970s, *Variety* reported that, in Cambridge, the cult was "peaking anew with mobs of Harvard studes [students] patronizing the Brattle Theatre for the annual Bogey Festival, an orgy of Bogart films." For undergraduates, the star was "their latest major," with some "fanatic Bogie fans" having seen one of their "fave films [*Casablanca*] 20 times." The festival, the review noted, "brings out audiences who participate in the film" by memorizing and repeating the dialogue.[68] Linked firmly to Bogart, *Casablanca* became a major attraction at the Brattle.[69]

The Brattle's annual ritual of Bogart-themed festivals and other Bogart-centered programming inspired the formation of a cult community, its cinematic tastes, and participatory activities. In this milieu, *Casablanca* was not the only Bogart movie that critics and audiences adored in a cultish fashion,[70] but it had a significant place in his canon as representing his persona's apotheosis: a blend of romantic hero and tough guy of action with "a personal code to pit against corrupt, paradoxical forces."[71] As film critic and avowed film cultist Andrew Sarris wrote in 1977, "*The Maltese Falcon* had made him a star; it remained for *Casablanca* to make him a myth."[72] *Casablanca* entered the cultic zone as a crystallization of Bogart's persona that, in turn, influenced his cult status—the interaction between star and film producing a mutually endorsing "affective contagion."[73]

Within the framework of postwar social developments, I want to examine more closely how the Brattle and its festivals fostered moviegoing communities organized around Bogart, the shape taken by their cinephilic and cultish tastes, and the impact these tastes exercised on *Casablanca*'s meaning.

The Fest Idea and Participatory Culture

Theater exhibitors leased Bogart films from distributors in packages that featured between thirteen and nineteen titles, each mixing well-known and more obscure titles. Repertory houses strategized their programming of these titles as single showings, double features, and festivals. In the 1960s, however, UA wanted to capitalize on the "fest idea" by marketing its packages to exhibitors as suitable for Bogart festivals. In UA's view, the "fest idea" could enhance his oeuvre's appeal because it allowed exhibitors to sell to audiences titles deemed as minor, like his boxing movie *Kid Galahad* (1937) and western *The Oklahoma Kid* (1939), along with more esteemed draws like *The Petrified Forest, Casablanca,* and *The Treasure of the Sierra Madre* (1948)—most of which had already run on TV for free.[74] Exhibitors found the festival as a programming concept additionally compelling because it reaestheticized oldies as a means of reselling them. That is, to ensure older titles' viability for new audiences, film festivals repackaged and recombined them, implicitly promising "improved reception" and a superior aesthetic experience by screening a body of work in a condensed fashion unattainable in ordinary exhibition.[75] This form of programming gave older films added value. If, as Michael Patrick Allen and Anne E. Lincoln remark of the fine arts, the "ultimate form of cultural consecration" lies in a "retrospective exhibition mounted by a major museum," the repertory house film festival featuring a star retrospective routinely operated to define the revived stars and films as worthy of attention and veneration.[76]

In the process of forging a cult film culture based on reissues, the retrospective festival's time and space and the film canons that emerged from programming were significant factors in negotiating the fandom's activities and consecration of oldies. Marijke de Valck writes that international film festivals like Cannes "possess a unique potential to set agendas and intervene in the public sphere [by influencing] our aesthetic tastes, our political beliefs, and our outlook upon life." Furthermore, because of the shared experience that festivals generate, they intimately wed films to the festival's time and space.[77] On this last point, Janet Harbord specifies that festivals are "part of the calendar of local rituals that perform and enact the specific nature and appeal of a location for both inhabitants and visitors." The festival is thus a "model of enclosure" that creates "intense temporal happenings" demanding viewers' presence "within the fold of its moment."[78]

The Brattle film festivals dedicated to reissues were clearly more modest ventures operating at a substantially lower cultural frequency than major international film festivals and their high-profile new films. Yet these observations about festivals' effects on constituting communities of viewers illuminate important contours of the Brattle experience. Besides having a material impact on film prints, platform adaptation obliged, as we will see in this chapter and the next, rewriting films through different programming strategies as well as through different spaces and calendrical times. The Brattle's festivals not only reaestheticized Bogart's films through programming but were also supported by intensive time/space coordinates that offered ideal grounds for cult sensibilities to emerge and flourish. As J. P. Telotte remarks, cults are a "culture in small and thus an island of meaning for [audiences]. . . . Every cult constitutes a community, a group that 'worships' similarly and regularly, and finds strength in that shared experience."[79] Both festivals and cults, then, promote the creation of affective, meaning-making minicultures in temporal and spatial models of enclosure, similarities that allow each to potentially enhance the impact of the other.

The Brattle's relatively rundown and bohemian space, its timing of the festivals during the collegiate pressure-cooker interval of studying for and taking final exams, and the refreshing of oldies through the programming model of the festival created a must-see annual rite of passage for students at exam time. Reviewers for Harvard's student newspaper, the *Harvard Crimson* (hereafter the *Crimson*), wrote that "a Bogart evening at the Brattle during exam period with a packed, unruly, and howling partisan crowd is an experience that no Harvard undergraduate should miss."[80] The *Crimson* saw the Bogart festival as so constitutive of collegiate identity that, when it was canceled in January 1962, the paper called it the "lowest blow of all," especially for "the Class of 1965 [who] will go through their first exams in Cambridge without seeing *Casablanca*."[81]

Although Bogart films and film festivals were programmed at other times, the Brattle's focus on final exam reading periods generated specific kinds of affect and meaning for students. They saw the Brattle and its festivals as an escape from exam stress, a moment of "group therapy."[82] According to *Time* interviews with Harvard and Radcliffe students, they also regarded Bogart and *Casablanca* as providing an attitude and aesthetic that could help them navigate exams and foster a sense of community in the face of this challenge. Hence, students did not run through Harvard Yard emitting a "primal scream in order to relieve exam stress"; instead, they migrated to the Brattle to sing "La Marseillaise" with the characters in Rick's café and each other. In a common refrain, a student remarked that she and her friends found it "the essence of cool" to watch Bogart's films before exams: "There was something just so heroic about going to see something anti-intellectual the night before an exam . . . imitating Bogart's I-don't-give-a-damn attitude." The timing, remarked a Harvard instructor, was "symbolic of the student's identification with him—Bogart's self-reliance like theirs when they had to go into final exams." In chanting Bogart's lines during or beyond screenings, students could "take courage for their ordeal" from the "cynical, hard-boiled, and bitter characters" that he played, like Sam Spade, Rick Blaine, and Philip Marlowe.[83] Screenings also provided the opportunity for boisterous and drink- or drug-inspired behaviors. Perhaps most famously in this respect, Bogart's deep dragging style of smoking cigarettes onscreen transformed his name into a verb—as in "Don't Bogart that joint"—a friendly reminder not to monopolize shared marijuana.

Well before audiences interacted with *The Rocky Horror Picture Show,* the Brattle's Bogart festivals converted screenings into live events via participatory behaviors, many of which practiced what I called envoicement in the last chapter—the adoption of mass media phrases into one's own language through vocal iteration and embodiment. Harvard and Radcliffe undergraduates held parties before the festivals. Imitating Bogart and Bergman, they wore trench coats to *Casablanca* screenings and popped champagne bottles while standing up to sing "La Marseillaise" during the song duel in the film. Their main activity was quoting dialogue aloud—no small feat given that, as one reviewer put it, "every other line is a 'line.'"[84] Cult critic Danny Peary notes that "Bogart addicts" shouted, "Play it again, Tham," mimicking Bogart's lisp. They also quoted his, "I stick my neck out for nobody," "You played it for her, you can play it for me," "We'll always have Paris," "Of all the gin joints in all the towns in all the world, she walks into mine," and "Louis, I think this is the beginning of a beautiful friendship."[85] Their appreciation of the film's dialogue included Renault's (Claude Rains) lines, especially "Round up the usual suspects." This bit's importance was such that, when it was "ruthlessly chopped" from all three showings of *Casablanca* in January 1964 (management had to resplice the film to repair a damaged print, meaning the loss of several seconds of the film), a student wrote about the "tragedy" at the Brattle that prompted "hisses and sobs" from the audience.[86] On another occasion, when the Brattle's projection system lost sound, viewers insisted on continuing the screening and contributed the dialogue track themselves.[87] As these examples show, the repertory house's liabilities could bring heightened affect and participation.

Bogart's fans thus exhibited customary features of cult film behavior in theaters: they attended repeat screenings, engaged in cosplay, quoted dialogue, sang along, loudly interacted with the screen, and experienced solidarity and community in the theater's space at exam time. In another dimension of cult, their attachment to Bogart extended beyond the theater. Since film dialogue is portable into everyday situations, students in Cambridge at restaurants and bars called for "another round of drinks," indulging in the popular misquote, "Play it again, Sam." They also lifted their drinks and proclaimed, "Here's looking at you, kid!" When they were "ready to blow the joint," they asked, "Ya ready, Slim?," borrowing a line from *To Have and Have Not.* When they wanted "to express arrogance or individuality, they spit, 'I don't have to show you no stinking badges,'" from *The Treasure of the Sierra Madre,* writing it into final assignments where professors read "about the 'stinking badges' in papers on the French Revolution."[88]

In the context of this repertory theater and campus, envoicement was a particular mark of social distinction, belonging, and taste. *Time* reported that Bogart's "side-o-mouth repartee had become the canon vernacular of Harvard Yard." If students did not engage in this new linguistic currency, it was the equivalent of digging their "social grave."[89] Popular slang drawn from the actor's movies provided an avenue to what Sarah Thornton calls subcultural capital, a sign of hipness for youth cultures that conferred "status on its owner in the eyes of the relevant beholder . . . in the form of being 'in the know.'"[90] The film's dialogue track not only helped to inspire fans' interactive behavior in and beyond the theater, creating a host of amateur Bogart impersonators, but also delineated a group of film-literate cognoscente for whom an inability to quote lines meant possible ostracism.[91] This dynamic encouraged fans to form communities through exercises of taste that, in enabling them to amass subcultural capital and be positioned favorably in their cohort, crafted the kind of insider/outsider boundaries that give film cults their sense of community.[92]

In this way, the Brattle and its Bogart festivals represented what we can think of, after Pierre Bourdieu's concept of the habitus, as a *cult film habitus*—a terrain of "socialized norms that influence individual behavior and thinking"[93]—here in relation to a mode of film exhibition that resulted in rapt devotion to a star and his work. This habitus may have been initially generated within the theater's four walls, but its live affective dynamics were eminently spreadable to other spaces, constituting a vernacular oral culture arising from the film and grounding a shared culture, as well as a film canon.

The Bogart Film Canon

Distributors' packages and exhibitors' choices mandated diverse selections to represent Bogart's career, with a preponderance of Warner Bros. films, as opposed to films Bogart made with other studios or production companies, drawing most of his fandom's attention.[94] Depending on the screening lineup, viewers could piece together Bogart's trajectory from early bit parts in the 1930s through the classic detective roles of the 1940s to his career's final stage after 1948—a source of star-cult pleasure insofar as it gave them a comprehensive familiarity with and mastery of his career arc and evolution as an actor. At the same time, students did not admire all of Bogart's films equally, and the Brattle often programmed many of the same favored titles. This interplay between exhibition and reception helped to create and maintain a discernible canon in the programming flux.

Bogart connoisseurship meant weighing in on which films best expressed or, conversely, detracted from his persona. In 1963, for example, *Crimson* contributor Charles Whitman wrote that the Brattle's historical survey of Bogart's work through a thirteen-title film festival would be screened in "one-day shots, guaranteed to ruin any carefully planned study schedule." Whitman rated the films, remarking that *The Petrified Forest* was the only notable title among Bogart's pre-1940s films and that *The Maltese Falcon* was a turning point both in establishing the film noir template and "Bogart as the prototype Twentieth Century man"—a point to which I will return. Furthermore, Whitman identified two films as masterpieces, *Casablanca* and *The Big Sleep* (1946), while appreciatively naming "clever near-misses" such as *To Have and Have Not, Key Largo* (1947), and *Dark Passage* (1947). He contended that these latter films "brighten the canon of Bogie films," when compared to "dull patriotic epics" like *Passage to Marseille* (1944). He also saw 1948 as the start of Bogart's serious acting career (when he seemed to escape typecasting) in *The Treasure of the Sierra Madre* and *The African Queen* (1951). Whitman critiques the festival for excluding "splendid" films like *The Roaring Twenties, High Sierra,* and *Beat the Devil* (1954), especially when it screened "mediocre" titles like *Kid Galahad, San Quentin* (1937), and *Passage to Marseille.*[95]

As it educated viewers about a career within its intensive temporal and spatial coordinates, the Brattle festival offered an "erudite salon."[96] Students learned both to periodize Bogart's films and build a hierarchy. They recognized the vintage of his films through his perceived age, signaled by his hairline's position and use of toupees—a vernacular "history by hairpiece." The above review signals a hierarchy of films in the salon as it places *Casablanca* and *The Big Sleep* at the top and allows a significant slot for *The Maltese Falcon,* some gangster films (*The Roaring Twenties* and *High Sierra*), and the actor's post-1948 work. Other movies besides *The Big Sleep* that also starred Bogart's wife, Lauren Bacall (who became part of his mythic status), are esteemed as "clever near misses." Disparaged films are as important to canon formation, with *Passage to Marseille* and other Bogart war films dismissed as "dull patriotic epics."

Each festival, of course, provided the occasion for student critics to vary or consolidate aesthetic priorities. In an earlier review in 1958, a *Crimson* reviewer judged *High Sierra* not as canon-worthy but as a "shuddering loser" with bad lines and performances that would frustrate Bogart fans.[97] In 1964 *Time* commented that Harvard students, showing a proclivity against some of the actor's post-1948 films, "will never forgive John Huston for making

Pauline Kael, the best film critic now at work (in English, anyway), has just published a new collection of essays and short critiques called KISS KISS BANG BANG (Atlantic-Little, Brown, $7.95, available at most bookstores). It's a pleasure to crib most of this program from her new book, hoping that a sample will spur film-lovers to rush out for the whole volume.

Brattle Theatre

TR 6-4226 40 Brattle Street

Performances begin daily at 5:30, 7:30, 9:30
Matinees Saturdays and Sundays at 3:30
Exceptions noted in text

HUMPHREY BOGART Festival

This spring's tribute to Humphrey Bogart is turning into a tribute to John Huston as well: except for the ceremonial showing of Casablanca, the films scheduled are products of that interesting combination of Bogart and Huston -- who is anathema to auteur critics but a pleasure to the dilettanti (fr. prp. of dilettare, to delight).

Sunday-Monday-Tuesday, May 12-13-14

"KEY LARGO"

Based on a rather dreadful play by Maxwell Anderson, Key Largo traps Bogart, Edward G. Robinson, Lauren Bacall, Lionel Barrymore, and Claire Trevor (who won an Oscar for her performance) in a hurricane-swept Florida Keys hotel. A man's gotta do what he's gotta do.

Wednesday through Saturday, May 15-16-17-18
Daily 5:15, 7:30, 9:45
Saturday matinee at 3:00

"TREASURE OF SIERRA MADRE"

"In a brilliant characterization, Humphrey Bogart takes the tough-guy role to its psychological limits: the man who stands alone goes from depravity through paranoia to total disintegration. . . . Bogart's companions are a toothless Walter Huston as a shrewd old prospector, and Tim Holt as a blunt, honest young man. Bogart's character (Fred C. Dobbs) is enough fate for anyone, but it has its outward representative in Alfonso Bedoya as a primitive bandit (if you've never appreciated civilization, the encounter with Bedoya may change your outlook).... One of the strongest of all American movies." - Pauline Kael in KISS KISS BANG BANG

Sunday-Monday-Tuesday, May 19-20-21

THE MALTESE FALCON

"Humphrey Bogart's most exciting role was Sam Spade -- that ambiguous mixture of avarice and honor, sexuality and fear, who gave new dimensions to the detective genre.... It is an almost perfect visual equivalent of the Dashiell Hammett thriller: Huston used [his] plot design and economic dialogue in a hard, precise directorial style that brings out the full viciousness of characters so ruthless and greedy that they become comic. It is -- and this is rare in American films -- a work of entertainment that is yet so skillfully constructed that after many years and many viewings, it has the same brittle explosiveness -- and even some of the same surprise -- that it had in 1941." - Pauline Kael, op. cit.

Wednesday through Saturday, May 22-23-24-25

The AFRICAN QUEEN

"This is a comedy, a love story, and a tale of adventure, and it is one of the most charming and entertaining movies ever made.... Bogart and Hepburn played together with an ease and humor that makes their love affair -- the mating of a forbidding, ironclad spinster and a tough, gin-soaked riverboat captain -- seem not only inevitable, but perfect." - Pauline Kael again. (Bogart won the Academy Award as Best Actor for this one.)

May 26 through June 1 (one week)

CASABLANCA

"Humphrey Bogart as Rick, the most famous saloonkeeper in screen history.... In the role of the cynic redeemed by love, Bogart became the great adventurer-lover of the screen during the war years. There isn't an actor in American films today with anything like his assurance, his magnetism, or his style. In Casablanca he established the figure of the rebellious hero -- the lone wolf who hates and defies officialdom (and in the movies he fulfilled a universal fantasy: he got away with it)." - Pauline Kael

End of Bogarts....

June 2 - 8 (one week) FIRST BOSTON SHOWING!

JEAN RENOIR'S BOUDU SAVED FROM DROWNING
STARRING MICHEL SIMON

"Jean Renoir's Boudu Saved from Drowning was made in France in 1931 when talkies were new and subtitling had not yet become a standard procedure, and so, like many other films of the early sound period, it was not imported. Some of those talkies waited a few years, some a few decades; others are still waiting -- and may go on waiting because of the New York press response to Boudu. . . .

"Boudu is a more leisurely film than we are used to now, not that it is long, or slow, but that the camera isn't in a rush, the action isn't overemphatic, shots linger on the screen for an extra split second -- we have time to look at them, to take them in. . . . Boudu is a simple shaggy-man story told in an open way, and it is the openness to the beauty of landscape and weather and to the varieties of

FIGURE 8. Brattle Festival Program, spring 1968, with film blurbs taken from Pauline Kael's work. Program courtesy of the Academy of Motion Picture Arts and Sciences, Margaret Herrick Library, Los Angeles.

Bogey a boozy simpleton in *The African Queen.* They don't like *The Caine Mutiny* (1954) either—"'Captain Queeg is not good Bogey'"; by contrast, "'*Key Largo* is very good Bogey.'"[98] Students sometimes embraced those titles not typically in favor, including *Dark Victory* (1939), a Bette Davis vehicle in which Bogart plays a secondary role as an Irish stable hand. But in the main, as *Boxoffice* reported of the 1967 Brattle festival, only some of Bogart's movies were consistently "in" for cult fans. These included *The Maltese Falcon, Casablanca, The Big Sleep, The Roaring Twenties, Key Largo,* and *Beat the Devil.*[99] Despite disagreements that otherwise defined aesthetic debate, certain films within this group, particularly the first three, remained largely untouchable consensus members of the star's cult canon. Even Bogart festivals thematized in such a way that would exclude *Casablanca*—a spring 1968 event that focused on the actor's collaboration with Huston, for example—featured the film as a "ceremonial showing" in this lineup, indicating its exemplary, almost obligatory, popular standing in the Bogart cult for this theater and its audiences (fig. 8).[100]

Student and critics' appraisals of worthy versus unworthy Bogart vehicles often hinged on their perceptions of how these films manifested his persona's gendered style. His "boozy simpleton" in *The African Queen,* despite winning him his only Academy Award for Best Actor, and his morally and mentally compromised Captain Queeg in *The Caine Mutiny* did not satisfy those invested in this style. By contrast, the detective characters of Sam Spade in *The Maltese Falcon* and Philip Marlowe in *The Big Sleep* and Rick Blaine's associated noirish tough-guy-with-a-heart in *Casablanca* allowed both male and female students to identify with his "cool" masculinity, outsider status, and antiauthoritarianism, giving them fodder for marshaling their own subcultural capital. *Cool* was an attribution that constituted the most prominent interpretation of Bogart's appeal as it was expressed and understood in the postwar era.

From Icon to Cult Icon: Bogart's Cool Masculinity

The attraction to Bogart's performance of gender was inspired by his physicality, demeanor, voice, and incarnation of principled toughness. Students attending the Brattle screenings located part of his physical allure in his "basset-hound look," which they affectionately called "Basic Bassett." In this look, Bogart appealed to the Brattle's female enthusiasts who were "tired of seeing pretty heroes." Additionally, these fans were drawn to his treatment of female characters, acknowledging that he was "pretty pushy especially with women" but "in a nice, kind of gentle way." For them, "Bogey is everything we wish Harvard men were, in addition to what they already are. Bogey's direct and honest. He gets involved with his women, but he doesn't go through an identity crisis every five minutes. He's the ultimate man. He's so rugged. So absolutely unattainable. The essence of cool." Male students expressed a related desire: Bogart was "a character the average fellow dreams of being but can never hope to be."[101] In these circles, the actor inspired both heterosexual and homosocial fantasies as a paragon of masculinity.[102]

With Bogart as a site of desire, fans chronicled and fetishized his style as an anthology of micromannerisms (fig. 9). As Crowther remarked, Bogart devotees "know his every gesture . . . the cool way he smokes a cigarette, sizes up another person without a flicker of feeling in his face, hikes up his trousers efficiently as he slips a gun under his belt, rolls back the corners of his upper lip." As we saw in chapter 1, Bogart's impact was also rooted in his "dialogue delivery style," his side-of-the-mouth speech.[103] Radcliffe women were report-

FIGURE 9. Bogart's "cool" smoking style in *Casablanca* (dir. Michael Curtiz; Warner Bros., 1942) as one of his attractive micromannerisms.

edly entranced as well by his vocal apparatus more generally, as they "mooned over [his] half lisp and the glistening scintilla of saliva in the corners of his mouth." These fans commented that "it's that special way Bogey grits his teeth, then parts his lips and sort of hisses that makes him so great."[104] Such attention to his nuances shows the impact of repeated screenings on his fandom, while revealing how the smallest details of appearance and performance style contribute to the architecture of cult stardom.

As Mark Jancovich and Shane Brown assert, stars' qualities may serve as the foundation of a cult, but the manner in which audiences appropriate these qualities as alternative to an amorphously defined mainstream is just as crucial to the process. This appropriation fuels their ability to define themselves as similarly oppositional, an identity key to the construction of cult phenomena.[105] The seemingly renegade space of the Brattle, its ritual festival programming of Bogart's films, student desire to rebel against university exam strictures, and the context of postwar countercultures informed and amplified Bogart's contra-mainstream cult identity. The actor served not only as a fantasy gender model and a detailed manual of personal style but also as an antiestablishment figure.

In *Bogart,* a 1967 ABC documentary about the actor's mythification, narrator Charlton Heston discusses Bogart's embrace by youth, stating that while "older fans nostalgically cling to a vibrant memory of the past, whole new generations of fans consider him a significant symbol for NOW." Motivated by Bogart's "nowness," youth audiences lauded his ability to survive by his wits and his underdog values. As one interviewee remarks, "He's always got the jump on everybody. He does good things without being goody-goody.... [He is] the little guy, the guy versus the institution—the man who doesn't knuckle under to police or society or whatever organized force he's up against." Ultimately, "no matter what he does, he is cool."[106]

Critics agreed. Biographer Richard Gehman noted that the actor provided a "clear, if unconscious statement of a kind of revolt expressing a need for something affirmative, something brave, something enduringly cynical, something with a built-in humorous self-perspective." Bogart, with his "I-don't-give-a-damn attitude," was "the ultimate man... the essence of cool."[107] Along with Bogart's hard-boiled independence and "coolness and candor," Crowther commented that Brattle patrons gravitated toward his "disdain for the brass" and "all the manifestations of smugness and hypocrisy that are shown by the Establishment." This aspect of Bogart's persona, especially as distilled in anti-heroes like Spade and Blaine, helped to generate "the mesmerizing myth that is so gratifying to the hip audiences today." Crowther argued that these Bogart characters possessed an enviable personal code of savvy detachment that nonetheless supported fundamental values, doing "what really has to be done... without a lot of clatter." In *The Maltese Falcon*'s conclusion, Spade's decision to surrender his love interest, Brigid O'Shaughnessy (Mary Astor), to the police for murdering his detective partner and, at the end of *Casablanca,* Rick's embrace of the Allied cause, showed them to be men "of strength and essential dignity." The synthesis of cynicism and principle found in Bogart's most representative roles made him, once again, "cool."[108]

Cool is a polyvalent signifier that, unlike other vernacular terms that tend to fade in usage, has served diverse audiences across generations. According to Joel Dinerstein, in the war and postwar eras, cool was "a calm-but-engaged state of mind" that balanced the emotional poles of "hot" (excited, aggressive, intense, hostile) and "cold" (unfeeling, efficient, mechanistic)" by conveying a "relaxed intensity." Cool was gendered, represented by an "implacable male force" using a private code infused with a magnetic brand of dispassionate masculinity to navigate the world. Male figures exhibited control of their emotions through an individual style that exuded heterosexual "sexual charisma accompanied by a cool indifference to women."[109] The figure's appearance of nonchalance in his world, though, was infused by both vulnerability and incipient violence.[110]

Informed variably by French existentialist ideas of alienation, Anglo-American traditions of stoicism, and noir literature and films featuring tough, solitary men, this affective and stylistic gestalt found early expression in the US in the 1940s and 1950s in African American jazz through musicians such as Charlie Parker and Miles Davis. As Dinerstein writes, cool was a response to racial discrimination; to face a hostile world, jazz artists wore "a mask of cool." As cool involved "rituals of self-affirmation" and public composure in the face of "denied individuality," it operated as a "'survival technology' through charismatic self-possession" and an aesthetics of detachment. As white culture appropriated Black cool, it became the "public face of postwar survival" signifying the "rejection of innocence, optimism, and hypocritical morality."[111] In the process, it transformed the specificity of Black oppression into the generalities of white American rebellion. By the mid-1950s, cool came to embody cultural resistance to all authority rather than political resistance to a racist culture. Bogart—whom Heston describes in the ABC documentary as a "man alone, a tough guy with no illusions [who] thinly hid his vulnerability"—performed white cool in an exemplary fashion for his fans.

Audiences found substantial evidence of Bogart's cool persona in *Casablanca*. The film showcases the nuances of performance style parsed in fans' and critics' testimonies, while scene after scene portrays Rick's credentials of cool. For example, Rick refuses Ugarte's (Peter Lorre) pleas to save him, saying, "I stick my neck out for nobody," a signature line that conveys his cynical withdrawal from the world. Rick also dismisses Yvonne (Madeleine LeBeau), a recent lover, who asks him, "Will I see you tonight?" with "I never make plans that far ahead," in a scene that displays both his appeal and indifference to women. Furthermore, when Nazi commandant Major Strasser (Conrad Veidt) shows Rick the dossier compiled on his political past, instead of being nervous in the expected way, Rick looks impassively at the documents and responds with feigned innocence to Strasser, "Are my eyes really brown?" Expressing the anger and sensitivity that also informs cool, Rick calmly handles Ilsa's abrupt reentry into his life in public but privately has a drunken breakdown in which he bitterly recalls their failed Parisian love affair. The film's conclusion finds Rick joining the Allies, saving Ilsa and her freedom fighter husband, Laszlo (Paul Henreid), from the Nazis and breaking off his renewed romance with her to accomplish both aims. The underlying heroic principles that inform his character emerge, verifying that his hard-boiled stance has a moral core.[112]

Dinerstein contends that Bogart's appeal as cool declined when his function as a symbol of the struggles of the Great Depression, wartime America, and immediate postwar adjustment dissipated in the early 1950s and newer brands of cool in the personas of Marlon Brando and James Dean gained greater visibility.[113] As we have seen, however, viewers' readings of Bogart placed him firmly in this category of masculinity and were influential decades after his association with these earlier historical moments had waned.

Reviews provide a sense of how his cool, hard-boiled image both endured and shifted in meaning over time. In 1942 Crowther's review of *Casablanca* mentioned its inspiring and trenchant wartime topicality and deft use of "Bogart's personality . . . to inject a point of tough resistance to evil forces afoot in Europe today."[114] Years later, despite nostalgia for wartime America that some audiences may have felt, Bogart's cult adherents could be inattentive to the war's significance in his movies. Instead, as suggested by the *Crimson* critic who labeled *Passage to Marseille* a "dull patriotic epic" and by another who praised *Casablanca*'s performances for raising "an indifferent story . . . to the level of superlative, escapist entertainment,"[115] his image as a tough wartime hero was losing its historical specificity and being reread according to a new postwar historical script. Like other mainstream US critics, Crowther eventually became immersed in the Bogart cult, writing an extensive article in 1966 on the "Bogart Boom" for *Playboy* magazine, a self-anointed bastion of the contemporary man. Hugh Hefner, founder of the magazine in 1952, reportedly opened his first Playboy Club in 1960 because he identified with Bogart as an antihero and wanted to recreate Rick's café from *Casablanca,* his favorite film.[116] In *True: A Man's Magazine,* Richard Gehman wrote the aptly titled "Bogart: A Cool Cult Welcomes an Old Hero," again confirming the terms of his appeal.[117] This shift from Bogart's and *Casablanca*'s historical specificity to the actor's meaning as the prototypical "Twentieth Century man" suggests that, for cultists, his expression of gender in the form of cool masculinity superseded other interpretive concerns.[118] That is, cultists backgrounded his ties to wartime and other earlier historical moments as they gravitated toward an unimpeded embrace of his mythic masculinity. Bogart's cool quotient and its ability to operate *across* time and historical developments were essential in shaping his cult stardom.

Matt Hills's distinction between icons and cult icons illuminates the relation of cult stars and films to historical flow. Hills argues that an icon is "locked into a given set of social and cultural coordinates," whereas a cult icon transcends these constraints by moving "continuously across social-historical frames, being re-mapped and reworked in this process."[119] Bogart's case depicts how the former can morph into the latter. As Dinerstein suggests, during the 1930s and 1940s, Bogart's roles in gangster, war, and noir films made him an icon of the Great Depression, WWII, and the late 1940s. Audience responses to the actor in the context of repertory houses in the 1950s and beyond remobilized his persona's meaning as representing the epitome of white cool. This shift in emphasis from history-bound icon to transhistorical cult icon was not necessarily a zero-sum game for postwar audiences; historical change rarely proceeds through a simple linear displacement of older for newer identities, meaning his star status as icon and cult icon may have coexisted.[120] Bogart's transhistoricism, however, allowed him to become a floating signifier that viewers could deploy to different ends.

As representing the masculinity of "NOW," Bogart's cool persona modeled self-possessed antiauthoritarianism that responded to different dimensions of student dissatisfaction, social unrest, and political upheaval manifested on college campuses from the 1950s through the 1970s. His characters' stoic personal code and repertoire of physical and vocal mannerisms incarnated a desirable form of masculinity that fans could mine to resist authority across different registers and historical periods. For those involved in the counterculture, as then-Harvard-student Todd Gitlin remarked, *Casablanca*'s antifascist message seemed "specially coded" for his group of "anti-bomb, anti-Cold War" friends.[121] Similar sentiments echoed across campuses. At Stanford University, for example, students remarked that the film instilled a "tremendous sense of patriotism" in them, identifying patriotism as "an emotion we're starved for." Another commented that "in this country . . . most radicals want to be loved. *Casablanca* is the kind of film that makes a radical feel like he is part of the mainstream."[122]

Of this political idealism in relation to *Casablanca,* critic Barry Day considers it "at least part of the film's appeal to successive generations." What, he asks, "is youth if it is not to be radical and what is getting older if it is not a mellowing without admitting to an abandonment of that same radicalism? And what is the essential Bogart persona of the 1940s if not the deification of that premise?" Rick also appealed to countercultural audiences because he made political action seem possible: "he *did* make his mind up, *did* find a solution that was worth a sacrifice, and gave an expression for idealism."[123] As Rick moves from his early position of "I stick my neck out for nobody" to joining the French resistance to fight Nazis, *Casablanca* managed to "energize idealism through vicarious experience by showing audiences how cynicism can be overcome and action taken."[124]

In the postwar countercultural imagination, then, *Casablanca*'s explicit antifascism, expressed in Rick's story arc, as well as in the singing of "La Marseillaise" and other elements, resonated with activists. They updated the film's WWII-based antifascist message to apply to the fascism they saw in current antidemocratic political realities as authorities supported the buildup of nuclear arms, entered a ruinous war in Vietnam, and opposed rights movements. *Casablanca* and Bogart spoke to certain students' patriotic quest for justice, while also demonstrating the persistence of idealism and political commitment in circumstances where cynicism seemed warranted—all in a pleasurable form that mainstreamed radicalism through a cool protagonist. In this respect, Bogart's masculine persona functioned as one of the counterculture's patron saints.

The Harvard and Radcliffe students' reactions to Bogart that we have seen suggest that more localized and transient concerns of youth audiences also informed *Casablanca*'s interpretation via Bogart's cult status. These students mobilized Bogart's cool to express their resistance to exam pressures and university strictures. As Telotte contends, *Casablanca,* and classical Hollywood cult films more generally, allowed "law-abiding, even normally conservative," viewers to momentarily "adapt an outlaw persona [and] transgress the status quo while remaining safely within culture's generally sanctioned patterns of behavior."[125] Bogart's incarnation of the outlaw hero, a traditional US character in movies and other arts that typically eschewed serious political commitments,[126] inspired students to confront the institution of exams through individual and communal cult behaviors that purveyed rebellious attitudes toward the university as the Establishment. Through this lens, Bogart and *Casablanca* operated as a playground for boisterous collegiate behaviors that allowed youth to let off steam around the crucible of final exams—adopting Bogart's persona through behaviors that only appeared to contest the status quo.

Like the *Crimson,* mainstream sources such as *Time* and ABC's *Bogart* documentary bolstered this aspect of his fandom, downplaying politics in their descriptions of why students gravitated to the star. Reports concentrated instead on the fandom's cult rituals as an eccentric display accompanied by a questioning of gender roles and animosities to parent cultures typical of youth. As Dick Hebdige argues, mass media routinely operate to contain the challenges subcultures bring to the status quo, making them legible to their readers by reframing them as innocuous.[127] Here, against the backdrop of postwar social movements, such sources rendered students as young and playful rather than as resistant or potentially violent in their protests—a prevalent identity otherwise for youth cultures during the 1960s and 1970s. Mass and local media reported on students' Bogart-infused rebellion as essentially inconsequential (a means of surviving exam pressures), comical (via cosplay and participatory interaction), and simply youthful (young people negotiating gender roles and social belonging). They thus portrayed Bogart's fans as harmlessly defying authority as they grappled with growing pains, containing the serious issues that many students and other activists raised publicly during this time. In this more conservative dimension of Bogart's reception, he and his films provided a continuum of tradition that students used to negotiate minor crises and that official sources used to explain and tame the category of youth in times of radicalization.

Whether *Casablanca* inspired activist or more transient kinds of rebellion in student populations, though, the transhistoricism of Bogart's cult masculinity has other ramifications for interpreting this aftermarket life. Colin McArthur embraces Bogart's importance as an icon of antifascism in *Casablanca* because it poses "the great political issue [of] whether to go along with or actively resist Fascism." In McArthur's view, the Bogart cult substantially diminished this message as it promoted "masculinity and patriarchy" at the expense of *Casablanca*'s political commitments and Ilsa's political "autonomy and decisiveness."[128] McArthur's position not only suggests a counterargument to the usual association of cult with oppositional fandoms but also offers a view of what I call the *cult repressed,* in which an aspect of a cult phenomenon is overvalued at the expense of the significance of other elements.

The Bogart persona's masculinity inspired gender fantasies of tough forms of white masculinity in the face of social developments that complicated such traditional kinds of identity, developments such as gay liberation, the women's movement, and civil rights. In this sense, this persona often promoted, under the guise of cool, a more familiar past in the face of an uncertain new political climate. The cult's focus on Bogart as a gender exemplar resulted in an undervaluation of femininity, race, and rebellion itself, even when, as we have seen, students transposed, via Bogart's persona, the film's antifascism to address newer forms of oppression.

The critics' and students' glorification of the actor's cool white masculine style depended on conservative notions of femininity and race. One reviewer wrote of Bogart's leading ladies, "Now those were *women*—Lauren Bacall, Ida Lupino, Ava Gardner, Ingrid Bergman.... Still, they had something to play to. Bogart was like that mountain—he was *there*."[129] For like-minded reviewers, in *Casablanca,* Bogart's influential presence and cool relegated Bergman to a warmer, more affective, and ethereal realm. Bogart "crystallizes his persona in *Casablanca* as Rick, the disillusioned, cynical tavern-keeper." Meanwhile, Bergman "was never more beautiful." She is "surpassingly lovely... and natural as the girl and lights the romantic passages with a warm and genuine glow" through a face and voice that "convey great emotion." Critics commented, as well, that no one "can rival Ingrid looking wistful in the fog" or "listening to 'As Time Goes By.'"[130] To return to McArthur's point about Ilsa, interpretations that focus on Bogart tend not to address her attitude or position with respect to the film's major political themes—she, too, has been risking life and limb to fight fascism. As part of the cinematographic fetishizing of her face that defined her early career and reception,[131] Ilsa/Bergman is the to-be-looked-at passive vehicle of beauty, warmth, and emotion, both foil and complement to Rick's hardened yet secretly vulnerable stance (see chap. 1, fig. 3).

At the same time, although fans cherish Sam for his singing of "As Time Goes By," he can otherwise become a footnote to Bogart's performance in cult commentary. In 1942, Crowther wrote glowingly of Wilson as Sam; in his 1966 *Playboy* essay, he simply remarks that Rick has a "close rapport with his Negro pianist (who soothes his melancholy moments by playing 'As Time Goes By'), but he [Rick] is still a remote individual."[132] Through a cult fascination with Bogart's masculinity, Sam, like Ilsa, functions mainly as a means of accessing Rick/Bogart, while Sam/Wilson becomes an anonymous representative of his race. More generally, as viewers defined Bogart as cool, his version of cool became *the* version, making invisible both its whiteness and its indebtedness to African American culture. This construction of Bogart's persona represents a white appropriation of Black culture that supplants the racism and stakes of survival informing the mask of Black jazz cool.[133]

Hence, while the Bogart cult invested in his persona's ability to resist the Establishment, it repressed civil rights–era racial awareness and feminism's progressive conception of women. During the postwar era, viewers' attraction to Bogart/Rick, as he signified "NOW," did not extend to their reconceptualization of other characters through a similarly contemporary lens. While the updating of Bogart's persona via the repertory house helped to create the mix of traditional masculinity and modern cool that defined him at this time, his costars could be interpreted through the singular reactionary register of Hollywood's older gender and racial categories.

As a floating signifier, Bogart's persona thus transformed *Casablanca* into a film that inspired contemporary political commitments, exuberant resistance to university norms, and reflections on youth culture. We have to consider, however, that these responses were informed by a cult that overvalued white masculinity at the expense of other identities in the face of historical developments attempting to rewrite established identity categories. This cult phenomenon, then, drew on and propagated a paradoxical set of values as the center of the moviegoing pleasures it offered to audiences, who were themselves negotiating the struggle between existing and emerging social formations. As part of its paradoxes, it enabled these viewers, through their identification with Bogart's persona, to experiment with their responses to new times while being firmly grounded in older systems of value. Young viewers at the Brattle, situated in the repertory theater's cinematic hothouse in a primarily white and male educational environment, remade the actor and film into the foundation of their fantasies of masculinity and revolt against the mainstream, however sharply or vaguely conceived. As discourses on this cult phenomenon privileged commentary about Bogart, they also repressed attention to femininity and race as possible sites of reinvented thinking about the film and the world during these tumultuous times. Positioned in a network of established and developing cultural and political forces, *Casablanca* thus mobilized the performance of certain reactive white countercultural and gender identities in communities within the *cult film habitus* of the Brattle and its surrounds.

The Decline of Repertory Houses and Cult Exhaustion

In the mid-1980s, repertory houses experienced the so-called repertory theater massacre that saw the extensive failure of this type of venue. Like the rise of these theaters, numerous factors contributed to their decline. Among them was the increasing unavailability of prints owing to the commercial success VHS enjoyed in the decade after its public introduction in the 1970s. With the triumph of home video, studios were inclined to pay even less attention to the costly matters of repairing, storing, and otherwise maintaining their theatrical prints. Furthermore, Casey Scott and Shira Peltzman contend that, as the businesses responsible for distributing film prints began to close, repertory houses experienced more problems with supply, while also juggling rent increases in urban areas. In a reciprocal effect, studios were reluctant to produce new prints for such an unstable market.[134] Repertory houses began to disappear, although they have remained a part of cinema's aftermarket, including the now only occasional screening of classical-era films.

In and after the 1970s, the Brattle's Bogart cult reflects the impact that increasingly ramshackle prints, which could displease audiences rather than engage them in interactive play, and a possible saturation of the market for old Hollywood stars and titles, had on student tastes. A *Crimson* critic wrote of a 1970s Bogart festival that "to avoid the most frustrating kind of rip-off, check out what the print is like from someone before you see the picture. Judging from the Brattle's *Casablanca* last week, your favorite lines are liable to be garbled and flashed out . . . [leaving] huge gaps where . . . favorite lines should be."[135] Critics also experienced what I refer to as *cult exhaustion*. A *Crimson* writer was confounded by the return of "crowdpleaser" *Casablanca*, wondering "why students packed the house and why stock responses like 'Play it, Sam' continued to produce howls of laughter and a sense of togetherness," concluding that the movie "takes the most self-indulgent of campy spirits to be endured." Another complained that "seemingly every joker in the world can imperfectly quote at least three lines from this great movie. After you've seen your fortieth Peter Lorre imitation that's not even close, enthusiasm simply wanes." Some student reviewers thus criticized the very things that had once favorably defined the cult: repetitious screenings, participatory behaviors, and community building. As testimony to *Casablanca*'s perseverance as a ritual, however, the same reviewers might compensate for their negative comments by admitting that it was a "truly great film" and worth seeing repeatedly.[136] Outside of Brattle circles, Sarris also mixed reverence and a concern about saturation, commemorating the twentieth anniversary in 1977 of Bogart's death: "Has he been over-discovered? Is it possible that Bogie has become a cliché?"[137]

In the 1990s and 2000s, the Brattle and Bogart's cachet were challenged by new issues: students' lack of awareness of the theater's location or mission and their eschewing of "Barbara Stanwyck and Jimmy Stewart for Demi Moore and Jim Carrey," with little regard for the "cultural angle" of old movies.[138] Such tendencies indicate how cult stars and films that endure can be subject to rejection by new audiences and to the diminishment of their cult status even as they survive through programming. This is not necessarily a permanent or singular state of affairs. As I. Q. Hunter argues, cult films "dip in and out of cult status," while having "parallel lives [as] classics or 'ordinary' schedule fodder."[139] This variability in and simultaneity of different statuses are hallmark characteristics of *Casablanca*'s circulation here and in its other aftermarket lives.

CONCLUSION

As I have argued, challenges to the postwar film industry shifted its business model toward a greater investment in film reissues in theaters and on television, helping give rise to repertory houses as alternative venues for moviegoing. This shift, along with social developments, forged new film cultures based on reissues and aimed at youth audiences and a film cognoscente. The changing times generated a bonanza in the public visibility and popularity of older movies and stars, orienting part of moviegoing toward nostalgically watching vintage fare in repertory houses. In the process, the repertory house offered viewers a platform and programming model that conveyed a sense of unconventional tastes in comparison to the typical moviegoing experiences represented by Hollywood's new films and first-run theaters. This situation enabled classical-era cinema to gain substantial traction in alternative entertainment environments and to indelibly enter the lives of viewers, sometimes as cult fare.

As an adaptive platform and contributor to the aesthetics of circulation that defined *Casablanca,* the Brattle Theatre and its viewers provide a localized example of the impact that repertory houses and their reissues could have on classical Hollywood films resurrected in the postwar era. The Brattle animated and sustained the dynamics of the Bogart cult, fostering a space that anchored a large local clientele of Bogart and *Casablanca* enthusiasts and that promised intensive immersion in the actor's work through the festival format. In its programming practices, the theater also provided a sense of calendrical time around exams that further molded the communities "in small" that characterized its festivals and film cult. Creating an arena of interpretation, the Brattle and its constituents remade *Casablanca* into a cult film based on its perceived exemplary instantiation of the Bogart persona's cool masculinity, its generativity as a source of quotation, and the opportunities it provided for rowdy behavior, gender exploration, community-building, subcultural capital acquisition, and reaction to challenges that ranged from final examinations to nationwide political developments.

The festival mode of theatrical programming promoted the cultification of film and actor in no uncertain terms. Conventional theaters reissued *Casablanca* in a double feature with Cagney's *G-Men,* creating an intertextual relationship between the two stars and their iconic Warner Bros. roles in gangster and other tough-guy films. Repertory houses programmed single and double features as well, but their "festivalizing" of *Casablanca* placed it firmly in an intertextual network of other Bogart films. This, as we have seen, supplied iterated and condensed doses of the actor's persona that fueled his cult status and facilitated the participatory dynamics that defined reception. While the double-feature of Hollywood oldies had a retrospective dimension that fed Bogart's celebrity, the star-based retrospective festival, with its more extensive historical lens and aura of career completism, made fostering his myth its primary rationale. Repertory house festivals, in expressly amplifying this myth, furnished an awareness of the star's legacy and heritage, canonizing his most highly regarded films in the process.

The kind of popularity and renown that *Casablanca* attained as part of the Bogart cult had an impact on the film's endurance, inspiring its vivid aftermarket presence over decades of film exhibition. The heightened public attention that *Casablanca* drew through a cult formation applied, as well, to other classical-era films that would gain cult audiences and endure in spectacular fashion during the course of their histories, including *King Kong* (1933), *Gone with the Wind, The Wizard of Oz,* and *It's a Wonderful Life* (1946). With its powers of redefinition and ability to inject new life into classical-era films, cult was a key means of recirculation that allowed older films defined under its rubric to compete successfully in a large media marketplace, not despite, but because of, their age. Although, as I have mentioned, a cult designation does not guarantee everlasting life, it inches a film closer to that possibility. Here, in fact, the *Casablanca* cult via Bogart played an immeasurably important early role in its overall arc toward immortality.

If we understand film meaning and value as being constituted in contextual and environmental circumstances, the postwar era's film industry, film cultures, repertory houses, and audiences activated *Casablanca*'s formal features—its major Bogart moments, dialogue, the singing of "La Marseillaise," and so on—as cult. As we will see in chapter 4, under very different conditions when video platforms adapted *Casablanca* in and after the 1970s, the film's most popular identity became that of a cult Valentine's Day film, a standing that found its formal features mobilized to distinctly other ends. The film's constituent elements informed both cults, but the aesthetics of circulation in each—the forces and discourses shaping its reissue, exhibition, and reception—diversely negotiated the meaning, importance, and appeal of these elements.

Casablanca's cult standings begin to show how important discontinuity, rather than notions of continuity or persistence through time, is to grasping a film's historical passage. Since a film's circulation involves multiple forms of exhibition and multiple audiences, its persistence rests on volatile foundations. That is, despite appearances of continuity, a film's survival is indebted to instabilities introduced by material contexts and different interpretations that occur when it is replatformed through time. Even on a single platform, as *Casablanca*'s exhibition in the postwar repertory house attests, it was subject to different tonalities of meaning, from being a youthful playground of star identification and participatory interaction to being a foundation for negotiating, progressively or in a more reactionary manner, contemporary politics. As part of the Bogart cult, the film's postwar meaning also raises the issue of how fascination with the star's projection of cool white masculinity operated to repress similarly vigorous reconsiderations of femininity and race during decades of social upheaval around identity.

Whether in the moment or across historical moments, such shifting affective and interpretive grounds testify to how central the principle of volatility is to a film's history and to comprehending its cultural biography and afterlife. In a point I return to in chapter 4, *Casablanca* is not a timeless film; its endurance rests heavily on the changing terms of its specific historical transit through time.

• • •

For decades after WWII, *Casablanca*'s routine and often simultaneous appearance in theaters and on TV gave classical-era Hollywood fare multiplatform circulation. At the height of its Brattle screenings, *Casablanca* was rerun on TV with reviewers remarking, "Play it again, Sam, and we'll never tire of it."[140] As much as repertory theaters, television was critical to building the fame of actor and film. Moreover, TV fostered its own film culture in which the seventh art became part of home entertainment and life, a process initiated by radio's earlier insinuation of movies into domestic space. *Casablanca* was among countless films circulated on broadcast television, acquiring a reputation as one of the medium's most repeated film reruns.

THREE

Everyday Films

BROADCAST TELEVISION, RERUNS, AND CANONIZING OLD HOLLYWOOD

Nobody except the public likes movies on TV.

RICHARD BLAKESLEY,
Daily Chicago Tribune, 1957

With the extensive sale of old films to television, fireside viewers now have a repertory cinema of their own.

JOHN GILLETT,
Sight and Sound, 1958

If there is one phrase that should be obliterated from the English language . . . it is "old movies." . . . A motion picture is an artistic performance frozen in time. . . . If the *Mona Lisa* is not an "old" painting and *The Count of Monte Cristo* is not an "old" novel . . . then what? . . . Old movies? There is no such thing, and there never has been.

DAN O'BRIEN,
Broadcasting, 1974

ALTHOUGH NOT AS PROLIFICALLY AS RADIO before it, early television produced text-to-text adaptations of *Casablanca* and other Hollywood films. Anthology drama *Lux Video Theatre* (CBS, 1950–54; NBC, 1954–57) aired its "Casablanca" episode in 1955, starring Paul Douglas as Rick, Arlene Dahl as Ilsa, and Hoagy Carmichael as Sam in the character's first white incarnation.[1] Meanwhile, *Warner Bros. Presents* (ABC, 1955–56) used the film as the basis of a short-lived titular prime-time TV series featuring Charles McGraw as Rick and Clarence Muse as Sam (with no Ilsa cast).[2] But postwar television's greatest impact as a platform for films materialized in the phenomenon of reruns. In rerunning feature films, television converted countless movies to broadcast specifications and played a formidable role in creating a film culture in domestic space based on movie iteration. Viewers expected to watch and rewatch older movies at home—to have a "repertory cinema of their own"—a ubiquitous fact of media life today that was relatively new to earlier mass audiences. By the 1970s, along with *The Wizard of Oz*, *Casablanca* was regarded as one of the "longest-serving and most popular films on American television," signaling the entrenched place in moviegoing that reruns had achieved.[3]

As Blakesley's comment above suggests, though, televised films in the postwar era often fared poorly with critics. Many regarded them as debased artifacts, stamped with poor image quality, interrupted with ads, and cut to match program slots or accommodate censors, all for distracted household audiences. Critics deployed graphic language like "movie butchery" and "ax murders" to describe the "violence" done to films by television. This kind of judgment is part of a larger narrative of early television's struggle to attain legitimacy.[4] At the same time, as I have argued in previous chapters, such traditional aesthetic judgments should be understood as a force in the discursive landscape rather than as the last word. They otherwise militate against studying the aesthetic changes media platforms exact on film reissues as vital to their circulation and meaning. Of such intermedial relations, Francesco Casetti observes that "the medium that intervenes does not represent a betrayal, but rather an opportunity: it gives previous media the chance to survive elsewhere."[5] Indeed, because of TV's transfiguration of cinematic texts, viewing classical-era feature films in broadcast form became a pervasively popular new normal.

How do we approach this transfiguration and its crafting of an alternative aesthetics for cinema without savage metaphors? A starting point is recognizing that the sheer importance of media reruns in the circulation and consumption of media content commends them to analysis rather than dismissal for perceived shortcomings. In this spirit, I want to explore broadcast television's sustained impact in the 1950s and beyond on the business and experience of *Casablanca* and other classical-era Hollywood movies, an impact that occurred during the postwar repertory house years and before and as cable TV and VHS were redefining television as a platform for reruns. Of particular interest to me are postwar TV's programming strategies, the "strategies that television companies use to develop and schedule programs with the aim of attracting and sustaining the attention of viewers."[6] Key to understanding film circulation in this medium, programming illuminates television's crucial role, contrary to its reputation as a movie butcher, in producing, mediating, and managing the cultural capital of films like *Casablanca*.[7] These strategies are also responsible for television's retemporalizing of films to suit its scheduling and programming imperatives. Since time—TV's reputed negative impact on a film's running time to conform to these imperatives—has been at the heart of dismissing rerun movies from serious consideration, this facet of platform adaptation similarly invites reappraisal.

As Derek Kompare argues, TV reruns were not only an economic enterprise, a channel's "lifeblood" and the "core" of appeal to advertisers and audiences, but also a semiotic venture as TV stations actively "groomed" reruns for exhibition and consumption.[8] Broadcasters used certain presentational strategies to infuse reruns with an aura of quality that signaled their continued vitality and memorability as American heritage. These strategies were especially important because the rerun's pastness and iteration posed challenges to exhibition. Oldies, while relatively cheap forms of content, were outdated and rigorously repeated on the air and in repertory houses. TV stations managed the rerun's potential liabilities of age and iteration through value-generating tactics. By *value* in this context, I mean the manner in which media industries distributing and exhibiting classical-era Hollywood films in the aftermarket identified them as aesthetically, culturally, and historically worthwhile as a condition of their dissemination as commodities. The construction of value for films in their afterlives is an intimate and pivotal dimension of the aesthetics of circulation at work in their adaptation to new platforms.

Postwar TV's airing of films meant transforming their physicality (through electronic broadcast of prints often reduced to 16 mm from 35 mm), but it also involved remaking them according to the platform's spatiotemporal coordinates. Charles Acland contends that movies and moviegoing more generally should be redefined to accommodate the diverse contexts in which films materialize, given that the spatial and temporal dimensions of exhibition venues deeply affect the film experience.[9] Here, like radio, TV spatially transported a medium associated with public movie theaters to households, expanding the reach and impact of movies and their stars.[10] By bringing movies closer to viewers in their everyday lives, TV provided an increased opportunity for them to become part of the woodwork—a status that enhanced the ordinary intimacy and constancy of their presence.[11] Temporally, a film's running time on TV was usually edited to fit an hour-and-a-half or two-hour time slot and further shortened by commercials; *Casablanca*'s 102-minute length saw modest to significant cuts to accommodate these exigencies. On the one hand, this state of affairs was familiar to viewers, making it a less startling transfiguration than critics might have imagined. As we saw in chapter 1, from the 1930s to the 1950s, listeners to radio adaptations of films were exposed to this kind of abbreviated and interrupted movie presentation. On the other hand, the critical focus on TV's chopping of a film's running time as "murder" obscures the operation of other central aspects of temporal change on this platform. A TV station's brand identity and its desired impact on the public is bound not only to the kinds of shows it airs but also to its programming methods. Examining norms of programming that defined *Casablanca*'s presentation to audiences reveals the temporal practices that regulated its place on broadcast schedules and in viewers' lives, conditions of exhibition necessary to understanding its life in this medium.

Approaching film reruns without savagery, then, means reckoning with television's value generation for and temporal transformations of feature films through programming as one of its most essential and consequential practices. Because the terrain of film reruns on postwar US TV is immense, I will concentrate on the practices that one station—Chicago's WGN—employed to foster the appeal of *Casablanca* and other Humphrey Bogart films. WGN's early investment in feature films was such that it promoted itself as "the nation's first feature film theater" on TV. In the then four-channel commercial TV market in Chicago, WGN emerged as the most prominent film buyer, screening the largest number of feature films (thirty-eight a week).[12] By the 1960s, it had earned the reputation, in its combination of syndicated TV series, feature films, and live local programs, as the "most successful independent in the country."[13] Research on Hollywood films aired on TV at this time tends to focus on networks NBC, CBS, and ABC. But independent TV stations in large urban markets like WGN, licensed to serve customers in their local-regional community as opposed to the networks' national reach, had a long and arguably more robust commitment to Hollywood oldies, often distinguishing their brand by the films they persistently reran.

In 1957, WGN aired its first package of Warner Bros. films from Associated Artists Productions (AAP), a distribution company that had a year earlier obtained the studio's pre-1948 library. Through different distributors, the station continued leasing these films for nearly forty years, prolifically broadcasting Bogart titles in particular. Like the Brattle Theatre, WGN became closely associated with Bogart's Warner Bros. movies, showing *Casablanca* as a highlight of its schedule. Although this chapter examines the terms of *Casablanca*'s more conventional presentation on television, its broadcasts provided another potential place for its enjoyment as part of the Bogart cult discussed in chapter 2.[14] Across repertory houses and TV, the film's popularity in programming was indebted to the actor's stardom.

WGN's case furnishes evidence of how *Casablanca* and other Bogart films materialized in a thriving metropolitan TV market, revealing both the importance of movies as televisual commodities and the intricacies of their exhibition on this platform. To approach these intricacies, I address WGN's programming strategies and other associated programming phenomena as vital to grasping the alternative aesthetics that television brought to classical Hollywood films like *Casablanca* in this part of their afterlife. Rather than gauge WGN's behind-the-scenes activities in this regard, I focus on its public-facing practices—those practices visible to consumers as part of their interface with its feature-film offerings.

The public-facing programming strategies and related phenomena involved in my discussion of time and value—two concerns, as we will see, that are often intertwined—range from seemingly minor materials like movie showcase titles and newspaper TV guides to scheduling models like TV film festivals and the airing of made-for-TV documentaries about Hollywood. Broadcasters often deployed movie showcase titles, as simple as WGN's *Saturday's Best,* to communicate the broadcast time while imbuing the film with an instant stamp of quality. Similarly, just as Chicago-area newspapers announced screening times at local theaters with ads proclaiming the virtues of the movies on offer, newspaper TV-guide sections gave films a temporal anchor in everyday life, informing viewers about when certain programs would air and which films were schedule highlights.[15] While WGN, over its history of broadcasting Warner Bros. films, scheduled *Casablanca* in all available dayparts (or times of day), its use of the film-festival model to program Bogart's oeuvre is especially noteworthy. Festivals made a special event out of oldies the station had already frequently aired and regulated the rhythms of the broadcast week or month. Further establishing the postwar tone for watching older movies, TV documentaries like *Hollywood: The Fabulous Era* (ABC, 1962) chronicled classical Hollywood's history and the careers of its stars, including coverage of Bogart and *Casablanca.* Broadcast initially by the networks and then syndicated—sold as reruns to other channels, including independents like WGN—these shows presented Hollywood as a significant part of American heritage, shaping the audience's conception of historical time in national context.

As I will argue, programming practices, from the modest to the splashier, reveal how granular elements involved in TV's exhibition of movies defined films in relation to broadcast, household, and national rhythms, while creating value for this older fare. These practices thus participate in what I discussed in my introduction as the retrospective cultural consecration of classical-era cinema. By repeatedly rerunning thousands of films for home audiences through programming norms and value-laden strategies, television became a bastion of replay involved in canonizing films, their stars, and old Hollywood cinema itself.

Before investigating how WGN presented *Casablanca* for broadcast circulation, I want to situate my study further by returning in more detail to the station's connection to film exhibition and the Warner Bros. library and by surveying its programming of the film and Bogart's oeuvre more generally.

WGN, CINEMATICS, AND THE WARNER BROS. LIBRARY

WGN (channel nine on the dial) began broadcasting in Chicago in April 1948, initially as a network-affiliate of the DuMont and CBS networks and then, in 1956, as an independent TV station.[16] The *Chicago Tribune* owned the station, its call letters standing for "World's Greatest Newspaper." To serve its audiences and compete against network affiliates, WGN broadcast a mixture of locally-produced original programming, such as children's shows, sports, and news, first-run syndicated series like *The Cisco Kid* (1950–56), and reruns, from syndicated network series like *Perry Mason* (CBS, 1957–66) to Hollywood films.[17] In 1978, WGN became a "superstation," gaining, like WTBS and some other independents, national distribution through satellite uplink and cable TV presence. Despite this change, it maintained its emphasis on local programming and reruns, often airing older and newer Hollywood films in prime-time spots six days a week, along with other times of the schedule.[18] WGN broadcast Warner Bros. and other studio fare until 1995, when it became affiliated with the WB network, partly owned by the Tribune Company and by Warner Bros. Entertainment Division. With its independent status ended, the station started programming original WB shows, and film reruns faded from its schedule.

Like New York's WPIX and other independents, WGN found success in the late 1940s and early 1950s showing movies from foreign companies, independent US companies, and B films from minor studios. Films from the major studios—RKO, Paramount, Warner Bros., MGM, and 20th Century–

Fox—were not immediately available for television owing to studio concerns about releasing their films to an emerging medium they saw as a serious competitor. Realizing, instead, that they could profit substantially from their older assets in this new market, the majors relented during the mid-to-late 1950s, each of them leasing or selling their pre-1948 catalogs to TV.[19]

Reruns had economic advantages for both network and independent TV. In contrast to the expense and risk of producing original programming, reruns represented a cost-effective investment that appealed to a media industry premised on conservative financial management and stability—an advantage especially relevant to independent stations' bottom line, which was less stable than that of the major networks. Reruns also provided content-hungry television with ready-made fare to fill its hours. Because films were recorded rather than live performances, they were repeatable and thus offered flexible scheduling content. Moreover, they had a track record that served as a metric for (though not a guarantee of) performance. If the film happened to be an Academy Award winner like *Casablanca,* all the better; indeed, trade journals advertised the availability of award-winning films for broadcast.[20] Additionally, classical-era feature-film reruns—what *Variety* called *cinematics* to distinguish them from *telefilms* or filmed TV series reruns—did not require the kind of censorship that more contemporary films obliged, especially those produced after 1968, when Hollywood introduced R and X ratings.[21] For independent stations, affiliations with certain studio films, like that between WGN's prominent, but not exclusive, relationship with the Warner Bros. library, helped to establish and sustain their viability as broadcasting enterprises. After major studio films were released to TV, WGN scheduled them into previously underperforming time slots, where ratings could increase fivefold.[22]

Independents reportedly faced "uphill battles" against the networks and network affiliates, forging loyal audiences through original local programming and the "time-tested products" of telefilms and cinematics. A WGN executive remarked that, in addition to local programs that spoke to their constituents, success depended on the "availability of a strong library of product in film and syndicated programming." Along with their other benefits, the Hollywood majors' libraries allowed independents to bring nationally recognized fare to their local-regional brand and to provide counterprogramming to the more powerful networks' lineups.[23] Although independents scheduled cinematics across their schedules, as Kompare writes, their film reruns were competitive in prime time. They were able to secure "the most desirable first-run telefilm and theatrical film packages in their markets" while offering "more prime-time hours" for this fare than networks. Through telefilms and cinematics, independents like WGN forged modes of "distinctive repetition" that informed their "reputation—and survival."[24] WGN programmed more recent Hollywood films after they aired on the networks, but the pre-1948 movie catalogs remained programming staples and station brand identifiers.

According to a trade journalist in 1969, Warner Bros.' films, particularly its Bogart films, were successful among independents: "Whether a café owner in *Casablanca* or a riverboat captain in *African Queen* . . . Bogart is 'pure gold' as a top audience draw for many independents, proving once again that old, but good, movies never die." Bogart's oeuvre became an important part of WGN's signature, so much so that *Variety* considered a September 1964 ratings week as atypical for the station because "no Bogie was screened."[25]

Warner Bros.' library initially came to WGN through AAP.[26] In March 1956, Warner Bros. sold 754 of its pre-1948 feature films, plus short subjects, cartoons, and some silent movies, to AAP, financed by the Canadian investment company PRM Inc. for $21 million (over $200 million today). This deal soon included the studio's 1948–49 productions and, in 1961, its post-1950 films. AAP handled the films' TV distribution in national and international markets and, through its subsidiary Dominant Pictures Corp., their domestic theatrical distribution.[27]

AAP offered TV stations thirteen packages of its feature films, with approximately fifty pictures per package. In September 1957, AAP released fifty-two films that had been kept from TV release for theatrical screenings or remakes, including *Casablanca* and *The Big Sleep* (1946), and films with other big Warner Bros. stars, such as Bette Davis and Errol Flynn. TV station managers were reportedly eager to program these films, regarding them as "the cream of the big Warner backlog." By early 1958, AAP had sold Warner Bros.' films in "fifty markets" with eighteen of those "opting for the entire library," bringing AAP $35 million in TV contracts.[28] United Artists purchased AAP in 1958, creating United Artists Associated Inc. (UAA), a distributor that continued to circulate this library in TV markets. In 1967 Seven Arts purchased Warner Bros. studio, establishing producer/distributor Warner Bros.–Seven Arts, which was sold two years later to Kinney National.[29] The studio and its library would continue to change hands, but this small window of purchases reflects not only the decline of the big studios as they were known during the classical era but also the lucrativeness of TV distribution and the desirability of cinematics in a shifting and competitive industry marketplace.[30]

A 1958 AAP trade journal ad shows Warner Bros.' Bogart, Flynn, and Davis as the winning combination for a slot machine jackpot, exclaiming that the studio's films brought in twice the TV ratings of others.[31] In 1966, when Bogart's cult status was more firmly established, a UAA ad touts the artistic and commercial strengths of his movies (fig. 10). Quoting a *Chicago Daily News* review, the copy reads: "Bogart . . . a stardom that became legendary. *The Treasure of the Sierra Madre, Casablanca,* and *Key Largo* remain . . . the best examples of . . . solid commercial story-telling . . . sophisticated . . . artistic." The distributor promises "45 'Bogies'" or "65 hours 58 minutes of 'Bogie'" programming, describing "the endless demand for Warner features starring Humphrey Bogart [as] the most significant phenomenon of this era in entertainment history." In the ad's emphatic terms, a Bogart film is "*exactly* the kind of movie *most* people like *best.*" Raising gender issues discussed in the last chapter, the ad identifies his works' appeal as resting on "popular tough-guy action . . . bolstered by the unique Bogart approach to the Woman Problem."

To capitalize on available library titles, distributors created packages of mixed quality, meaning TV station managers had to accept "cats and dogs," like low-budget genre fare, to access "product movers," such as blockbusters and star-driven movies. Trade press reports on these packages singled out films and stars that would please advertisers, stations, and audiences alike, with frequent mention of *Casablanca* and Bogart.[32] Accordingly, AAP sprinkled Bogart films in each package as "an attractor" to persuade station managers to buy mixed packages.[33] Indeed, when, in 1961, UAA tallied the top ten Warner Bros. releases during the first four years of their TV circulation, Bogart's *Dark Victory* (1939), *Casablanca, To Have and Have Not* (1944), *Key Largo* (1948), *The Treasure of the Sierra Madre* (1948), and *Chain Lightning* (1950) comprised six of the ten.[34] First-run features—films premiering in a TV market—typically performed better in the ratings than titles already repeated in the same market and were often programmed for Saturday and Sunday late-night (with broadcasts beginning between 10:00 and midnight), two of the most competitive spots in the late 1950s. But repeats broadcast on weekday nights still landed in the top ten movies for the week. In October 1958 in Chicago, for instance, first-run *Lost Horizon* (1937) on WBBM was number one, while a WGN weekday repeat of *Casablanca* earned a respectable number eight ranking.[35]

FIGURE 10. United Artists Associated ad. *Variety*, Sept. 14, 1966, 43.

The industry regarded a "thematic approach" to assembling groups of films as able to "get extra mileage out of cinematics" that would lead to "socko results." Themes blended a batch of movies together so that they could be readily promoted,[36] furnishing a strategy of reselling older films to TV stations and their publics through packaging designed to renew older titles' appeal. Both TV distributors and TV stations engaged in this practice. Using the language of prestige, AAP offered *Casablanca* to stations as part of its "Jupiter" group. But distributor's themes often alluded to genre (e.g., Screen Gems' horror package "Shock!"), popular movie series (e.g., MGM's "Andy Hardy Theatre"), and stars (e.g., National Telefilm Associates Shirley Temple "Pix Binge").[37] In the industry's eyes, WGN, a big spender on cinematics, was also a resourceful programmer, proving "especially adept at lumping well-worn films into thematic packages that have drawn significant ratings."[38] As part of reselling oldies, the station used star themes in its programming of "Humphrey Bogart Weeks."

WGN began broadcasting Warner Bros. films on *The Courtesy Hour,* auto dealer and advertiser Jim Moran's Sunday late-night show, on September 1, 1957, with *Fighter Squadron* (1948).[39] Sunday late-night was the most heated spot for movie competition among Chicago's four commercial stations at this time, WGN, WBBM (CBS affiliate), WNBQ (NBC affiliate), and WBKB (ABC affiliate). This slot was designed for "mature viewers who were presumably less distracted by household responsibilities and therefore willing to invest in longer, more complex and perhaps more serious programs."[40] After weekends spent on other activities, adult audiences looking for some last island of entertainment before the workweek began apparently flocked to TV in Sunday's later hours. On Moran's program, *Fighter Squadron* was followed weekly by other non-Bogart titles like *Captain Blood* (1935), *The Mask of Dimitrios* (1944), and *Edge of Darkness* (1943). *Casablanca,* promoted as an "Academy Award winner with the late Humphrey Bogart and Ingrid Bergman," was broadcast on October 13, 1957. Other Bogart films shown in this same show included *Angels with Dirty Faces* (1938), *High Sierra* (1941), *Key Largo, The Treasure of the Sierra Madre,* and *The Big Sleep.*[41]

The actor's films proved to be a popular weapon in Chicago's Sunday-night "film wars." WNBQ, having purchased United Artists' library package, programmed its Bogart and Katharine Hepburn *The African Queen* (1951) against WGN's "Bogart biggie" *Casablanca.* The former bested the latter in one of its strongest programming hours.[42] Although Moran had once had the most successful show featuring cinematics, he left WGN in 1958 in response to how competitive and expensive the film wars had become. Trade papers reported, in a nod to the association among WGN, Moran, and Warner Bros.' *Casablanca,* that this marked "an end to a beautiful (and once mutually lucrative) friendship."[43] WGN, however, continued to feature Warner Bros. films on Sunday late-night and other movie showcases.

Despite the Sunday late-night hype, WGN scheduled cinematics during all dayparts, allowing it to fill broadcasting hours and pitch old films to potentially new audiences by offering them at different times.[44] In the late 1950s and 1960s, for example, *Casablanca* aired on other days of the week on WGN late-night showcases like *Motion Picture Academy* and *Mages Playhouse.* When WGN began moving to twenty-four-hour programming in the 1960s, *Casablanca* was broadcast during the *All Night: Late Movie* show.[45] Late-afternoon movie showcases *Hollywood Startime* and *Sunday's Best* also screened the film once the station decided to program this daypart for adults rather than children. The film aired as well on *Virginia Gale,* a morning show that had roots in WGN radio as a program designed for adult female audiences at home.[46] The adult orientation of these time slots did not preclude children or teenagers from watching; as we saw in chapter 2, younger demographics constituted a major postwar audience for classical Hollywood films in theaters and, as we will see, on TV as well.

Although the television industry would change dramatically from the late 1940s to the 1990s and WGN would become a superstation competing with cable TV and video, classical-era cinematics remained popular, cost-effective programming on the station. Of WGN's post-1960s feature film showcases, late-night program *WGN Presents* (1975–95) broadcast the greatest number of classical-era and more contemporary Hollywood films. It offered 6,773 episodes predominantly featuring these films but also including TV series, made-for-TV movies, and miniseries. In addition to their prolific presence on the station's other movie showcases, more than forty Bogart films, about half of his oeuvre, aired multiple times on *WGN Presents.* The station screened lesser-known Bogart titles, such as the 1939 gangster films *You Can't Get Away with Murder* and *Invisible Stripes* and the 1941 circus picture *The Wagons Roll at Night.* Bogart's work with other major actors—including James Cagney in *Angels with Dirty Faces, The Roaring Twenties* (1939), and *The Oklahoma Kid* (1939)—were also part of the Warner Bros. packages broadcast on *WGN Presents,* as were his suite of combat films: 1942's *Across the Pacific,* 1943's *Action in the North Atlantic* and *Sahara,* and 1944's *Passage to Marseille.* Films considered to be among his most renowned appeared as well: *The Treasure of the Sierra Madre, The Petrified Forest* (1936), *The Maltese Falcon, High Sierra,* and *Casablanca.* All four of Bogart's films with wife Lauren Bacall, a popular coupling in his oeuvre—*To Have and Have Not, The Big Sleep, Key Largo,* and *Dark Passage* (1947)—were among these reruns, as were other films noir such as *The Two Mrs. Carrolls* (1947) and *They Drive by Night* (1940).

As a movie showcase, *WGN Presents*' title sometimes changed. Under its various titles, including *Those Magnificent Talkies, When Movies Were Movies,* and the *Casablanca*-inspired, *Here's Looking at You Kid Theater, Casablanca* was rerun on November 17, 1975, November 4, 1979, February 28, 1981, and February 27, 1990.[47] As in *Casablanca*'s earlier programming, the film aired on other WGN movie showcases as well, including Sunday afternoon's *WGN Movie Greats* (Jan. 17, 1971) and prime-time's *Thursday Night Movie* (Feb. 27, 1975).[48] This later programming, beyond indicating that classical-era cinematics remained important to late-night television, showed them to be utility players in broadcast scheduling, able to be plugged in almost anywhere. The practices of programming feature films on different days and times and changing a movie showcase's name refreshed these films and gave them the potential to draw new audiences. Such shifts in repackaging oldies for the public offered a central means of managing and selling their iteration—one of the media industry's most important tasks.[49]

Programming practices thus far have defined *Casablanca* as one among many of Bogart's films and other classical-era films in rerun. But television also employed strategies that identified the significance of individual titles. In the next section, I examine the deeper impact of TV programming on *Casablanca,* exploring the temporal and value-laden aspects of its presentation as they shaped the aesthetics of film circulation on this platform.

TELEVISION AND POPULAR FILM LEGACY

WGN's public-facing programming strategies and associated broadcast practices generated value for *Casablanca* through several different avenues: movie showcase titles, newspaper TV guides, TV film festivals, and made-for-TV documentaries about Hollywood. Each of these constituted a means of presenting movies that acted as a promotional interface between classical-era Hollywood films and their audiences. As Arjun Appadurai and Carol A. Breckenridge assert, artifacts of all kinds materialize for their audiences through modes of "exhibition, design, and display" that are not neutral, but offer an agenda-driven vision of the artifacts' aesthetic and historical importance.[50] With respect to TV's presentation of films, the agenda was at once commercial (to resell older films); aesthetic (to show their worthiness as art); affective (to enhance their place in public hearts and minds); and cultural, historical, and ideological (to represent an American past superior to the present). TV's exhibition of cinematics also occurred in the context of broader critical assessments of cinema. By the 1970s, as this chapter's third epigraph suggests, critics argued that vintage films constituted a legacy equivalent to that possessed by older art forms. We can understand TV's activities around feature-film reruns as part of the postwar era's retrospective cultural consecration of classical Hollywood cinema, in which older movies were curated, canonized, and situated within historical legacy and memory.

Curation, canon, and heritage are complex and interrelated terms. For my purposes, curation consists of an "ensemble of activities" that involve "selecting and arranging" objects to add value to them. Value accrues from the way they are "categorized and organized, refined and displayed, and explained and simplified."[51] When intermediaries like museums or media companies curate, they not only define these objects and grant themselves powers of distinction; they also shape consumption as an aesthetic matter.[52] Through value-infused choices, curation negotiates the aesthetic dimensions of viewing, providing potential grounds for establishing heritage-worthy canons.

Resting on curation, canon-building identifies a roster of work deemed as the "very summit of cultural achievement" aesthetically, culturally, and historically.[53] Canon-building is often an elite enterprise, but it is also a heterogeneous activity that fosters the coexistence of multiple canons at any given time. In film and media studies, numerous parties, including film theorists, critics, historians, archivists, museum and festival programmers, newspapers, fandoms, and film and media industries forge, sustain, and alter film canons through time.[54] As Janet Staiger contends, canons, far from being impartial, are inflected by tastemakers and politics.[55] I treat the film canon accordingly, not as a verity—a list of films judged evermore as the best achievements—but as a mobile construction of status influenced by institutional stakes, including those arising from mass culture.

Claims about heritage arise from curatorial and canon-making practices to delineate certain artifacts as so historically significant that they represent not only the best in the art form but also the best of a national culture. As Michael Bommes and Patrick Wright argue, the correlation between art and nation in traditional heritage discourse relies on certain visions of the past and present. In conservative accounts of heritage, the past is posed "against an uncertain present and future that act as a foil to the stability and richness of the past."[56] This kind of heritage discourse has a distinct historiographical signature in which the past is revered above a more complex and threatening present—a signature that entails sanitizing the past of its difficulties.

Together, curation, canon, and heritage discourses negotiate public ideas of what constitutes a memorable artistic history.

In the postwar era, such discourses proliferated on television, mediating the relationship between the public and its consumption of cinematics by producing value for vintage films. Unlike institutions like the American Film Institute (AFI) and the Academy of Motion Picture Arts and Sciences (AMPAS), which bestow major awards on movies, television's contribution to cinema's aesthetic status was not typically recognized or respected. The medium's practices participated in banal canonization, the prolific and insistent daily operations of value creation that fly under the radar because they appear to be lowbrow, nakedly commercial, and relatively meaningless ephemera. Yet the apparatus surrounding TV reruns of films on WGN and other stations, as it rewrote the temporal and aesthetic experience of cinema, helped to create a film culture that embraced older artifacts as the best that Hollywood had to offer.

Movie Showcases

As was the case with other stations, WGN's film program titles could be general (*Feature Film*) but were usually more indicative. Some, such as *Morning Movie, Thursday Night Movie,* and *Saturday Matinee,* were specifically tied to the calendar. Others, such as *Creature Features,* emphasized genre or, like *WGN Presents,* the station's brand. WGN showcase titles also deployed the language of quality in labels such as *Saturday's Best, When Movies Were Movies, Movie Greats,* and *Those Magnificent Talkies.* Each title presumes an activity of curation wherein certain films were chosen for certain showcases. The quality-oriented titles suggest a more privileged status for the station's fare, linking the economic pragmatics of programming reruns to an idea of aesthetically motivated selection.

Airing on all dayparts on WGN, *Casablanca* was programmed in most of its temporally and aesthetically labeled shows. The *Saturday Matinee,* for instance, promoted a leisurely weekend family afternoon as the household rhythm linked to the film's experience. Showcases with titles promising quality films offered additional affective resonances. *Casablanca* aired on the late-night *Saturday's Best* and the afternoon show *Sunday's Best,* titles implying a special standing for films curated for the weekend, and on *Movie Greats,* a late-night program identifying selected films as worthy of that accolade. Another late-night show, *When Movies Were Movies,* offered the mature audiences presumed to tune in during that time nostalgia married to historical legacy. It assumed a value-laden retrospective angle that promoted classical-era films, implicitly opposed to new Hollywood films, as constituting true cinema—a common claim at the time. Like the name *Motion Picture Academy,* such program titles offered movies as a legacy that could educate viewers about the art of cinema by curating films important to its history. Showcases that embedded signifiers of quality in their names sought to elevate both the films broadcast and WGN's brand as a treasure trove of significant movies.

The shifting nomenclature of WGN's showcase titles thus furnished a strategic means of refreshing feature films it repeatedly broadcast, while attempting to instill viewers' experience of them with varying affective and aesthetic values, often in relationship to broadcast times. WGN routinely suggested that it offered a service to audiences through its curatorial activities, selecting, for their leisure, edification, and viewing pleasure, meritorious films from the past. Banal canonization aimed to shape audience expectations and viewing habits around older film commodities, promoting the continued worth of classical-era films in a changing Hollywood and America. TV guides, bound to programming as well, performed their own kind of curation.

Newspaper TV Guides

Chicago's *Television Forecast,* mailed weekly to the area's TV customers, began publication in 1948. That this local publication materialized as the medium was just becoming more established conveys the importance of TV guides to the business, legibility, and audience experience of TV. The nationally published *TV Guide,* commencing operations in 1953 and for decades a commonplace sight in US supermarkets and households, incorporated *Television Forecast* and other local guides as part of its inaugural enterprise.[57] Meanwhile, newspapers like the *Chicago Tribune* (hereafter the *Tribune*) published their versions of guides in daily and weekly TV listings. The *Tribune* often spotlighted cinematics, featuring breakout sections within its listings or separate movie guides that signaled distinction for certain titles.[58] An instrument of curation, the TV guide made programs and their scheduling visible to viewers, allowing them to sort through shows and plan their broadcast day and week. Like WGN's showcase titles, guides managed the iterative programming of cinematics through fledgling canon-building maneuvers.

These maneuvers, my focus here, were manifested in ordinary "elements of exhibition, display, and design" that emphasized certain shows over others. Defined by the economy of space and expression typical of TV listings, these guides suggested the best programs to watch, manufacturing value through movie blurbs in the form of capsule plot summaries, ratings, and graphics/page design. In so doing, TV guides sketched the identity and merit of film reruns at a key everyday interface between mass media and consumers.

Over years of *Casablanca* reruns, blurbs ran the stars' names but otherwise diversely abbreviated its plot—so much so that, were it not for its title and stars, the summaries could almost be construed as describing different movies. For example, *Tribune* writers variously described *Casablanca:* "A woman comes to a café owner in La Medina to seek refuge for herself and her underground leader husband"; "Underground leaders from all parts of Europe hide out in Casablanca during the days of WWII as they try to escape"; "A romantic drama about an underground leader, his wife, and the owner of a small casino. Set in La Medina, the old part of the Moorish city, during World War II."[59] Blurbs in and after the 1960s could also be more evaluative, reflecting awareness of the film's cult reputation in repertory houses: "A man who owns a café in Casablanca finds his life disrupted when an old love walks in with her husband, the leader of an underground movement. Play it again, and again, and again"; "Michael Curtiz directed this World War II drama about a man whose former sweetheart has married the leader of an underground movement. Classic performances plus the beautiful song, 'As Time Goes By.'"[60] As WGN aired *Casablanca* and other Bogart films (and reviewers built the often-misquoted line, "Play it again"—there is no "again" in the film's phrasing—into a perfect phrase for the rerun era), Chicago theaters screened festivals of his work. This amplified Bogart's presence in the mediascape and indicated that the Chicago market could support at least two platforms featuring his oeuvre at the same time.[61] Platform proximities like these operated synergistically to confirm the worthiness of both star and film.

Yet *Tribune* TV guides during these decades could also address the problem of repetition through less affirmative copy (e.g., of *High Sierra:* "Bogart is leading a life of crime again"; or of *The Treasure of the Sierra Madre:* "old, but excellent").[62] By the 1980s, the newspaper's blurbs demonstrated a clear sense of the state of Bogart's canon in relation to how his films had fared comparatively in rampant rerunning. During a 1986 WGN Bogart marathon, for example, the summary for *The Two Mrs. Carrolls* reads, "Bogie plays a painter who kills his wives. Stupid potboiler." Meanwhile those for *The*

Maltese Falcon, The Big Sleep, The African Queen, and *Casablanca* indicate a more secure canonical place. *Casablanca*'s blurb reads, "Venture once again to this most famous of movie saloons—Rick's Café Américain . . . Many people consider it the best movie ever made, and it's hard to argue with them."[63]

These entries function as typical movie blurbs; through bare-bones plot descriptions, they offer general compact statements about lengthier, more complex originals. The plot summary itself is an often-maligned type of film discourse, seen as a low mode of commentary that furnishes superficial guidelines of textual consumption to potential viewers. But reckoning with the capsule's curatorial service as it helped audiences to navigate broadcast schedules and make viewing decisions reveals how it forged microprocesses of ordinary canonization in its evaluative remarks ("Play it again"; "Best movie ever made").

Traces of critical opinion in TV guide plot capsules materialize, as well, in ratings and page design. In the 1950s and 1960s, the *Tribune* periodically employed a ratings system that judged films as "Poor, Fair, Good, Excellent, or Outstanding," often evaluating *Casablanca* as "excellent" or "outstanding."[64] Other means of classifying cinematics emerged in the *Tribune*'s page design. These included terms like the *best,* as in the "Week's Best" (fig. 11*a*) or "Wednesday's Best," and boxed announcements that distinguished certain reruns from others by graphically setting them off on the page (fig. 11*b*). Marrying publicity and aesthetic language, these practices further curated movies for TV audiences.

As I have mentioned, TV's evaluation of films took place in relation to wider critical contexts to which it also contributed. In the 1960s and beyond, the work of Pauline Kael, Andrew Sarris, and numerous others caused film criticism's national stature to grow along with cinema's reputation as entertainment and art.[65] On a local level, Chicago was home to popular film criticism in print and on the air. Mae Tinee, Anna Nangle, and Harriet Choice were among those writing the *Tribune*'s TV and movie guides, and Gene Siskel (of the *Tribune*) and Roger Ebert (of the *Chicago Sun-Times*) wrote higher-profile film reviews for their newspapers. These two critics also hosted the area TV program *Sneak Previews* (1975–82), which became a major entertainment show syndicated nationwide.[66] Film criticism's increasing social presence and popularization, in both its banal and more sanctioned forms, validated movies, including those rerun on TV.

Casablanca and Bogart's other films were among those that WGN and stations around the nation programmed into film festivals. If repeatedly

MOVIE GUIDE

★ Indicates color movie.

SATURDAY

10:00 p. m.—"Bride of the Monster" 7
Bela Lugosi, Tor Johnson, and Loretta King. A mad scientist invents an atomic machine that can turn average people into powerful monsters. [1956]

10:00 p. m.—"Lost Horizon" 2
CHOICE
Ronald Colman and Jane Wyatt. A diplomatic troubleshooter and his brother are kidnaped and brought to a hidden Tibetan community surrounded by treacherous and almost impregnable mountains. [1937]

SUNDAY

9:30 p. m.—"Red River" 5
John Wayne and Montgomery Clift. A man who finds no market for his herd following the end of the Civil war decides to head the first cattle drive over Chisholm trail. [1948]

10:00 p. m.—"Conflict" 9
Humphrey Bogart, Alexis Smith, and Sydney Greenstreet. A detective tries to break the perfect alibi of a man who has killed his wife. [1945]

10:30 p. m.—"Flight Lieutenant" 2
Glenn Ford, Janis Carter, and Barry Sullivan. Young man attending flight school falls in love with the niece of the man who was killed thru the fault of young man's father. [1942]

MONDAY

10:00 p. m.—"The Dynamiters" 9
Wayne Morris, Patrick Holt, and Sandra Dorne. A private investigator tracks down a ruthless gang. [1956]

10:00 p. m.—"Hell's Outpost" 7
Rod Cameron and Joan Leslie. A Korean war veteran uses a trick to get himself a half interest in a million dollar mine but learns that the earned friendship of honest people is worth more. [1955]

10:30 p. m.—"The Dark Past"......... 2
William Holden, Lee J. Cobb, and Nina Foch. An escaped killer imprisons a family and their friends in their summer lodge. [1949]

TUESDAY

10:00 p. m.—"Casablanca" 9
WEEK'S BEST
Ingrid Bregman, Paul Henreid, and Humphrey Bogart. A woman comes to a cafe owner in La Medina to seek refuge for herself and her underground leader husband. [1942]

10:00 p. m.—"Ride the Man Down".... 7
Brian Donlevy, Rod Cameron, and Ella Raines. A young ranch foreman's unselfish loyalty to his cattle king boss wins him the love of his boss' beautiful daughter. [1952]

10:30 p. m.—"East Side of Heaven".... 2
Bing Crosby, Joan Blondell, and Gloria Jean. A singing taxi driver and his roommate inherit a 10 month old baby. [1939]

WEDNESDAY

10:00 p. m.—"The Fighting 69th"...... 9
James Cagney, Pat O'Brien, and Dennis Morgan. Film of the history of the old Irish brigade, the 69th regiment of New York volunteers and later the 165th infantry of the Rainbow division. [1940]

10:05 p. m.—"Secret Venture" 7
Kent Taylor and Jane Hylton. A secret formula for a new type of jet fuel is stolen from a world famous scientist who is kidnaped by a gang of international outlaws. [1955]

10:30 p. m.—"Black Arrow" 2
Louis Hayward and Janet Blair. Sir Richard Shelton is told that his father has been murdered. [1948]

THURSDAY

10:00 p. m.—"Spellbound" 9
CHOICE
Ingrid Bergman and Gregory Peck. Dr. Constance Peterson finds she is falling in love with an amnesia patient who cannot recall whether or not he is guilty of an accused murder. [1945]

10:00 p. m.—"Once upon a Honeymoon" 7
Cary Grant and Ginger Rogers. An American reporter trailing the conquest of Hitler by following the wife of his number one man falls in love with her. [1942]

FIGURE 11. Movie guides and banal canonization: *(a) Casablanca* as "Week's Best"; *(b)* on *Mages Playhouse* as an Academy Award winner. *Chicago Daily Tribune,* Oct. 11, 1958, C6; April 15, 1959, B10.

WEDNESDAY TELEVISION PROGRAMS

CHICAGO TELEVISION CHANNELS
WGN-TV—9 WBKB—7
WNBQ—5 WBBM-TV—2
WTTW—11

• Indicates change in program since your TV Week was distributed.
*Indicates paid listing
★Indicates color broadcast
[Central Standard Time]

Morning

6:15 A. M.
5—TODAY'S MEDITATION
6:20 A. M.
5—★TOWN AND FARM
6:30 A. M.
5—CONTINENTAL CLASSROOM
6:40 A. M.
2—THOUGHT FOR THE DAY
6:45 A. M.
2—FARM DAILY
7:00 A. M.
5—TODAY
2—RAYNER SHINE
7:30 A. M.
7—ROSS AND FACSIMILE
2—PAUL GIBSON
8:00 A. M.
2—MORNIN' MISS LEE
8:05 A. M.
2—WEATHER—P. J. Hoff
8:10 A. M.
2—NEWS—Frank Reynolds
8:15 A. M.
9—TV TEACHERS' COLLEGE
2—CAPT. KANGAROO
8:30 A. M.
7—BOOKS AND BRENT
8:45 A. M.
9—★MORNING EDITION
9:00 A. M.
9—★DING DONG SCHOOL
7—CREATIVE COOKERY
5—DOUGH-RE-MI
2—MORNING PLAYHOUSE
9:30 A. M.
9—★PAUL FOGARTY
7—HERE'S GERALDINE
5—TREASURE HUNT
2—ARTHUR GODFREY
10:00 A. M.
9—FRAN ALLISON
7—JOBBLEWOCKY PLACE
5—PRICE IS RIGHT
2—I LOVE LUCY
10:30 A. M.
7—BEAT THE BUCCS
5—CONCENTRATION
2—TOP DOLLAR
11:00 A. M.
9—★ROMPER ROOM
5—TIC TAC DOUGH
2—LOVE OF LIFE
11:30 A. M.
7—MR. D. A.
5—IT COULD BE YOU
2—SEARCH FOR TOMORROW
11:45 A. M.
2—GUIDING LIGHT
11:55 A. M.
9—★NEWS—Lloyd Pettit

Afternoon

12:00 NOON
9—LUNCH TIME THEATER
7—GEORGE HAMILTON IV
5—PEOPLE'S CHOICE
2—NEWS—Frank Reynolds
12:15 P. M.
2—SHOP WITH MISS LEE
12:30 P. M.
7—PLAY YOUR HUNCH
5—THE LIFE OF RILEY
2—AS THE WORLD TURNS

SPECIAL TV EVENTS

1:55 p.m.—9—Baseball. White Sox vs. Kansas City.

9:00—7—Boxing. Sonny Liston vs. Cleveland Williams in a 10 round heavyweight bout.

1:00 P. M.
9—OUR MISS BROOKS—Connie becomes a June bride by proxy for Mrs. LeBlanche's financee
11—DAVID COPPERFIELD
7—MUSIC BINGO
5—QUEEN FOR A DAY
2—JIMMY DEAN
1:30 P. M.
9—BATTING PRACTICE
11—LAST CONTINENT
7—SUSIE
5—★HAGGIS BAGGIS
2—ART LINKLETTER
1:40 P. M.
9—LEADOFF MAN
1:55 P. M.
9—BASEBALL—White Sox vs. Kansas City
2:00 P. M.

9 WGN-TV
WHITE SOX vs KANSAS CITY ATHLETICS
Tune in pre-game shows at 1:30 P.M.—10th Inning Follows the Game

11—TV COLLEGE—Physical science
7—DAY IN COURT
5—YOUNG DR. MALONE
2—BIG PAYOFF
2:30 P. M.
11—TV COLLEGE—Child psychology
7—GALE STORM—Comedy
5—FROM THESE ROOTS
2—VERDICT IS YOURS
3:00 P. M.
11—TV COLLEGE—Algebra
7—BEAT THE CLOCK
5—★TRUTH OR CONSEQUENCES
2—BRIGHTER DAY
3:15 P. M.
2—SECRET STORM
3:30 P. M.
11—TV COLLEGE—Russian
7—WHO DO YOU TRUST?
5—COUNTY FAIR
2—EDGE OF NIGHT
4:00 P. M.
11—STORY TIME
7—BANDSTAND
5—SHERWOOD FOREST
2—SUSAN'S SHOW
4:15 P. M.
11—COMPASS ROSE
4:30 P. M.
11—TOTEM CLUB
5—JIM BOWIE—Adventure
2—THE EARLY SHOW—"The Marx Brothers of the Circus," with Kenney Baker
4:45 P. M.
9—TENTH INNING
5:00 P. M.
9—★GARFIELD GOOSE
11—FINDER
5—★CHICAGO BANDSTAND
5:30 P. M.
11—MAGIC CARPET
7—MICKEY MOUSE CLUB
5:45 P. M.
9—MAN ON THE STREET
5:50 P. M.
1—TOMORROW
5:55 P. M.
5—★SPORTS ROUNDUP
2—SPORTS

Evening

6:00 P. M.
9—WILD BILL HICKOK—Wild Bill halts the headlong rush into a life of crime by a youngster whose father had been a stagecoach robber
11—TV COLLEGE—Physical science
7—WEATHER BY RADAR
5—★WEATHER
2—NEWS—Julian Bentley
6:05 P. M.
7—NEWS
5—★NEWS—Alex Dreier
6:15 P. M.
7—NEWS—Paul Harvey
5—NEWS
2—NEWS—Douglas Edwards
6:25 P. M.
7—WEATHER BY RADAR
6:30 P. M.
9—★BUGS BUNNY
11—TV COLLEGE—Your Career
7—LAWRENCE WELK
5—WAGON TRAIN—Western. A bird watching school teacher, played by Wally Cox, drives the members of the wagon train to distraction
2—U. S. S.
7:00 P. M.
9—NEWS—Lloyd Pettit
11—LAST CONTINENT
2—KEEP TALKING
7:15 P. M.
9—★WEATHER
7:20 P. M.
9—★SPORTS
7:30 P. M.
9—HUCKLEBERRY HOUND—Huckleberry is an officer in the Northwest Mounties
11—TICKER TAPE
7—OZZIE AND HARRIET—Ricky discovers that being treasurer of his fraternity is a thankless job
5—★THE PRICE IS RIGHT
2—TRACKDOWN—An embittered ex-convict, intent upon revenge, hires a young gunslinger to goad the witness who sent him to prison into a gun duel
8:00 P. M.
9—26 MEN—An escaped convict leads the Arizona Rangers on a trail of re-
11—DAVID COPPERFIELD
7—DONNA REED—Comedy. An immortal all-American fullback is still living off the fame of a 70 yard touchdown
5—BOB HOPE—Comedy. Bob is host to top name entertainment favorites including Jack Benny, Ginger Rogers, Dodie Stevens, Jerry Colonna and his Jazz combo, and Les Brown and his band
2—THE MILLIONAIRE—A bride is so proud of her talented husband that she wants to star him in the movies
8:30 P. M.
9—BOLD VENTURE—A sponge fisherman turns killer. With Dane Clark

8:30 P. M. [continued]
11—PEOPLE AND IDEAS—Guest: Stephen A. Mitchell, former chairman of the Democratic National committee
7—ACCUSED
2—I'VE GOT A SECRET
9:00 P. M.
9—SAN FRANCISCO BEAT—A German refugee who is involved in two crimes—one of cruelty and the other out of loyalty—must learn that his father can never come home
11—JAPANESE TIME
7—BOXING—Sonny Liston vs Cleveland Williams in a 10 round heavyweight bout
5—THIS IS YOUR LIFE
2—DRAMA HOUR—"Trail of Diamonds" is a drama of skill, surprise, and suspense between international crooks and the United States customs in smuggling diamonds
9:30 P. M.
9—NEW YORK CONFIDENTIAL—A taxicab driver thinks his problems are over when he finds the loot from a bank robbery in his cab
11—MEMBER OF THE BOARD
5—MACKENZIE'S RAIDERS—Col. Mackenzie faces mutinous troopers and a cattle thief
9:50 P. M.
7—NEWS—Ulmer Turner
10:00 P. M.

Ingrid Bergman
Humphrey Bogart
Peter Lorre
"CASABLANCA"
Academy Award Winner

11—CALLING ALL DRIVERS
7—WEATHER BY RADAR
5—★NEWS
2—NEWS AND WEATHER
10:05 P. M.
11—TV COLLEGE—Child psychology
7—MOVIETIME U. S. A.—Film. "Canyon Crossroads," with Richard Basehart
10:10 P. M.
5—★WEATHER
10:15 P. M.
5—JACK PAAR—Variety
2—EVENING PERFORMANCE—"Viva Villa," with Wallace Beery
10:35 P. M.
11—TV COLLEGE—Humanities
11:30 P. M.
9—NEWS—Carl Greyson
7—MARTY'S MORGUE
11:45 P. M.
9—ARMCHAIR THEATER—"Polo Joe," with Joe E. Brown
12:00 MIDNIGHT
5—★NEWS—Greg Donovan
2—LATE SHOW—Film. "New Moon," with Jeannette MacDonald
12:05 A. M.
5—MAN BEHIND THE BADGE
12:35 A. M.
5—FEDERAL MEN
1:15 A. M.
2—MEDITATION

broadcasting cinematics acted as a form of their preservation, the star-themed, classical-era Hollywood TV film festival heightened a sense of the rerun's value for the viewer's film education and enjoyment of America's past.

Film Festivals

The film festival, rooted in the term *festival*'s historical association with religious holidays, signifies a cause for textual celebration. This celebratory aura lends distinction to the titles the festival selects and the experiences it offers viewers.[67] Although post-WWII TV film festivals may have lacked the cultural status of equivalent theater-based events, they were equally invested in capitalizing on the concept of the festival to generate value for their wares. Television stations were attracted to the festival concept because it was a particularly promotable means of selling their brand that allowed them, through themed programming, to manage the iteration of classical-era Hollywood films. The stations' festivals combined and recombined titles over time, renovating the appeal of films that had been rerun as singles and as previous festival films.

Stations presented themed film festivals as special events that stood out from television's usual flow, but the festivals, in actuality, operated very much within the medium's programming economy. As Ien Ang argues, regularly scheduled programming on TV was necessary to offset its status as an "uncertain enterprise" in its inability to predict how audiences—the "sine qua non" of its "economic viability and cultural legitimacy"—would respond to shows. Such uncertainty meant that audiences were constantly "seduced, attracted, lured" through practices "aimed at the codification, routinization, and synchronization" of their viewing habits to produce "less capricious and more predictable" results.[68] Festivals airing rerun feature films could accomplish both routinization and lure.

Festivals were broadcast through scheduling norms like once-weekly programs, daily strips (wherein the same program aired each weekday at the same time), or, more rarely, marathons. Their thematic organization over an expanse of time offered TV stations a means of defining and regulating the broadcast day, week, and month and, by implication, viewing habits. Despite presenting what were in fact rerun staples in standard programming slots, festivals constituted a flashy programming strategy. By organizing films into groups through themes such as director, star, period, or genre, they gave individual titles new heft in their connection to such larger categories and promised audiences an enhanced entertainment experience of worthwhile cultural artifacts.[69] They thereby "eventized" reruns, offering viewers focused exposure to a curated assembly of films that emphasized theme as the central presentational logic. In doing so, stations delivered intensified access to a star or other feature of Hollywood cinema as a memorable encounter with vintage movies.

Across decades of changes in the industry and society, WGN branded the actor's festivals as "Bogart Week," "Bogart Festival," or "Humphrey Bogart Theater," broadcasting them on numerous showcases that followed scheduling norms of weekly programming or daily strips. To explore a few of these festivals over the years, weekly programming included the "Humphrey Bogart Theater" on prime-time Saturdays (7:00–9:00 p.m.) that ran from 1966 to 1967 (with periodic breaks). Beginning on September 10, 1966, with *The Maltese Falcon,* the program followed up with seventeen different films, including *High Sierra, Key Largo, Casablanca, Passage to Marseille, The Treasure of the Sierra Madre, The Big Sleep,* and *All through the Night* (1942). Several titles, including *The Maltese Falcon* and *Casablanca,* presumably reliable ratings-grabbers that were identified with Bogart's best work, repeated during the year.[70]

Bogart festivals scheduled in the weekly format continued into the 1980s, with, in 1980–81, WGN's new late-night Saturday show *Here's Looking at You Kid Theater* (hereafter *Here's Looking*) featuring the actor's films. For its title, *Here's Looking* used a well-known line of Rick's dialogue in *Casablanca* that signifies his and Ilsa's (Ingrid Bergman) nostalgia for Paris and their love affair, inviting its audiences to experience their own nostalgia for the star, his films, and a meaningful past. Like repertory houses, WGN saw *Casablanca* as a Bogart urtext, a major attractor for his other films, and part of its own brand identity. WGN's promotion of the festival prominently featured clips from *Casablanca*, while its song "As Time Goes By" played as the soundtrack for the other film clips as well, solidifying *Casablanca*'s signature status.[71] The nineteen broadcasts ran from November to May, mixing, as usual, Bogart star vehicles like *Casablanca* and *The Maltese Falcon* with lesser-known works such as *The Desperate Hours* (1955) and *You Can't Get Away with Murder.* The broadcasts presented films, as was typical of festivals more generally, in achronological order with respect to their original release dates—a point to which I will return.[72]

In a different scheduling model, WGN stripped film reruns in what amounted to de facto festivals. In the mid-1950s, as Kompare explains, stripping represented an inventive scheduling strategy that used telefilms that had been broadcast once weekly and reran them each weekday (e.g., *My Little Margie* then, *Seinfeld* more recently). Stripping created a "horizontal" schedule of the same series shown at the same time, accelerating the series' consumption, while raising "viewer awareness of the local station's schedule" and of the station itself.[73] For film festivals, stripping often meant airing a different film within the themed group at the same time during a particular week. WGN's morning, afternoon, prime-time, and late-night movie showcases stripped feature films of all sorts, Mondays through Fridays, from Bob Hope and Bing Crosby's road movies to Douglas Sirk films starring Rock Hudson.[74]

In relation to Bogart's films, *The Morning Movie* (9:00–11:00 a.m.) began with *The Two Mrs. Carrolls* on Monday, October 6, 1975, followed by, in order of presentation that week, *Dark Passage, Passage to Marseille, They Drive by Night,* and *Dark Victory.*[75] This scheduling continued to demonstrate the versatility of star-themed festivals for different times and associated demographics, suggesting here that Bogart's oeuvre could serve as serialized programming that suited daytime "soap opera" traditions around women's ostensible tastes and household rhythms.[76] No matter the time of day or demographic, though, as a form of scheduling that accelerated consumption and promoted engagement with the station's offerings, stripping also amplified an inherent dynamic of the TV festival's thematic grouping: it gave audiences a predictably scheduled and concentrated dose of Bogart. In all of his festivals, Bogart served not only as the major attraction but also as a principle of programming coherence that bound months, weeks, and days of television offerings together.

Stripping characterized marathon festivals, as well, capitalizing even further on the festival's already intensive features as a programming staple and its promises of immersion in Bogart's persona. For five days in July 1986, WGN broadcast a weekday festival of fourteen Bogart films that were both horizontally and vertically (on the same day) stripped.[77] On each day different films aired at 7:00 p.m., 11:30 p.m., and 3:00 a.m. The prime-time slots featured some of his best-regarded films, *The Maltese Falcon, Casablanca, The Big Sleep, The African Queen,* and *Key Largo.*[78] Later, to counterprogram other holiday TV events on New Year's Day in 1992, WGN promoted Bogart festivals in a vertical strip—the "Day of Bogie"—through a thirteen-hour marathon starting at 1:00 p.m. and ending in the next day's wee hours.[79]

The different means of presenting Bogart festivals to the TV public raise the question of the role played by television's temporal dimensions in adapting *Casablanca* and Bogart's other films to this platform, a conversion that more subtly produces cultural value for them. Film festivals, as vivid examples of programming cinematics, became a steadfast part of TV's temporal ecology, in which the medium routinely fostered an "encounter between scheduling and everyday life." As Jérôme Bourdon remarks, the "repetitive, multiseasonal character of programming (years, months, weeks, days) constantly interacts with the repetitive, multiseasonal character of . . . daily lives." This medium characteristic, in turn, supports television's sense of "ontological security," in which it offers viewers "predictable, well-known contents at regular intervals, contents that are domesticated and appropriated within the safety of the home." In this context, reruns could make films and stars seem like "old family friends."[80] Television converted Bogart and *Casablanca* into comfortable and affective artifacts for household experiences that proceeded according to familiar everyday rhythms interlaced with broadcast schedules.

As we have seen, WGN's programming placed the film in a variety of temporal settings, affiliating it and other Bogart films with the clock and the calendar, while linking them to shifting audiences and colors of daily experience—a fate, as Paddy Scannell has pointed out, that affects all television programming.[81] Watching Bogart's films stripped weekdays on *The Morning Movie* occupied a different constituency, household flow, and cadence than watching them on *Here's Looking at You Kid Theater,* a weekend late-night show aired once weekly over months. The New Year's Day marathon more overtly portrays television's ability to position cinematics in relation to prominent parts of the calendar, especially those tied to the celebratory ethos of national and global holidays.[82] Both within and beyond festival programming, the domestication of *Casablanca* and Bogart on WGN meant their varied, continual alignment with discrete segments and spans of viewers' everyday lives. While TV guides advertised television shows being aired, they also, by publicizing the daily and weekly schedule of programs, made manifest television's intervention into time and, in this study, its ability to reshape the temporal dimensions of film exhibition.

In chapter 2, we saw how Bogart festivals were programmed to coincide with Harvard University's final examination period and, as we will see in chapter 4, *Casablanca* has been unbundled from Bogart's oeuvre in its more recent identity as a Valentine's Day film. Through the TV schedule's intersection with the clock and the calendar, television also muscularly redefined film exhibition through temporality. The connection among festivals, TV, and the viewer's experience of the calendar surface in comments about

WGN's Bogart festivals that suggest they operated as time-bound happenings, as "appointment TV." In one set of comments, a fan remembers looking forward to WGN's "Bogart Weeks." Even when the fan's family was not at home, but on a holiday excursion, they were sure to "catch Bogie movies in the camper all that week."[83] This memory implicitly acknowledges that Bogart festivals were a lure that could draw from the family's station loyalties to routinize viewing habits, while providing meaning to their domestic life. Synced to the clock and the calendar and promoted as special curated broadcasting events, festival films could gain the status of worthwhile experiences with ritual personal significance, marking the sedimentation of affective value into consuming classical-era films on TV.

TV film festivals also trafficked in historical time, influencing the circulation of classical Hollywood films and stars from a different angle. In programming reruns, television acted as a portal to previous historical eras, becoming a prime "technology of memory" with the power to intervene in depictions of the past. Television could produce "prosthetic memories" that invited people to "take on memories of a past through which they did not live."[84] Film festivals, seemingly exceptional programming in television's flow that offered a concentrated view of an oeuvre, had the potential to remain in the viewer's memory—as noted in the fan's comment above—and to provoke awareness of film heritage.[85]

Performers of the classical Hollywood era, aside from gaining new postwar visibility as hosts of and actors on TV shows, operated in these fiestas of oldies as North Stars with which to navigate the films' evocation of the past. Bogart acted tacitly as a principle of legibility across these broadcasts. His celebrity and posthumous "continuing grip on the imagination,"[86] coupled with his service as a unifying factor across films rerun in festival packages, furnished a point of affective identification that underwrote his historical function. If reruns amplified cinema's ability to enter memory, Bogart festivals had the potential to build nostalgic and other affective bridges that could create an emotional bond with viewers. The festival's focused mode of access to the star, coupled with the iterative nature of rerun programming and the "ontological security" of the home, invited viewers to form a "parasocial" kinship with him in which he became a part of their lives. TV marathons provide the clearest instances of this, supplying numerous consecutive hours of Bogart's films to dedicated consumers—earlier versions of what Lisa Glebatis Perks discusses as contemporary media marathons.[87] But because the TV festival is an enterprise that promises intensive and extensive experiences of an aspect of cinema, it invites the cumulative, serial consumption of Bogart as successive characters in vintage movie after vintage movie, immersing audiences not only in his star persona but also in the Hollywood films and worlds of the past.

Moreover, TV festivals, like repertory house festivals, presented Bogart's films in achronological order, mixing helter-skelter his older and younger selves. As we saw with Brattle Theatre viewers in chapter 2, recognizing the changes in his appearance due to age, in conjunction with shifting dialogue styles and mise-en-scènes, became an enjoyable part of watching festivals. Nonlinear presentations could enact a historical sensibility in viewers, engaging them in mental gymnastics aimed at a rough chronological reordering of the films.

This casual, vernacular historicism defined film history as a self-educating sport, a form of play aligned with aesthetic appreciation. In a 1972 *Seventeen* magazine article entitled, "There's No Movie like an Old Movie," teen reporter Ellen Jaffe, acknowledging young people's attraction to vintage films, offered a guide to older Hollywood films packaged in festivals as rich ways to experience stars and genres. Jaffe comments that "one of the best places to view an old movie is your living room . . . a gold mine of vintage pictures." Her guide instructs readers on how to watch, suggesting "several games [that] you can play with old movies." One is "Follow That Star," in which viewers "choose an actor and try to see as many of his [*sic*] pictures" as they can. She remarks that, "it's especially fun to catch someone who is a big star appearing as a juvenile in a twenty-five-year-old film."[88] The value of TV film festivals is located both in the access they provide to classical-era films and in the pleasures of completism and detection they offer. "Follow That Star" asks viewers to watch numerous films in a performer's oeuvre and use their powers of discernment to recognize them in bit parts at the outset of their careers. It thus produces a sense of history, underscored by both the amusement that outdated films could generate and an appreciation of the past anchored by the star and discovered by the viewer's powers of apprehension and connoisseurship.[89]

In a common refrain, Jaffe criticizes contemporary movies as having "no new themes" and as lacking older films' powerful expressions of "peace, love, and unity" that, in a phrase indicating the generational continuum films could evoke, "belong as much to our parents as they do to us." Furthermore, contemporary Hollywood offered few actors that were as funny, versatile, beautiful, or talented as classical-era actors like Groucho Marx, Spencer

Tracy, Greta Garbo, and Katharine Hepburn. As Jaffe concludes, "If you're passing up old films on television, and, possibly, at your local movie house, you're missing some of the greatest entertainment since Clark Gable and Claudette Colbert sent the walls of Jericho tumbling down."[90] This star-defined Hollywood past, delivered by television and repertory theaters, is defined both as true cinema and indispensable heritage.

Hence, the independent station's TV film festivals of classical-era films offered a steady, concentrated exposure to films that rewrote their previous terms of exhibition as transitory fare in first-run motion picture theaters into a domestically and repetitively present and themed ensemble of past productions. The temporal dimensions of TV's adaptation of feature films through the star-themed festival were characterized by programming imperatives that affiliated *Casablanca* and Bogart's other films to everyday broadcast and household rhythms, as well as star-driven panoramas of the past. The redefining of time that occurred in this transit from programming and scheduling to memory and history, fueled by the iterative presentation of star and films, offered an unofficial kind of history that gamified the experience of classical-era films and stars as they aged. This sensibility attained further aesthetic dimensions as their quality was deemed superior to then contemporary cinema and their place in memory, film education, and admiration of America's past embraced.

TV documentaries about Hollywood amplified the kind of nascent claims about classical cinema and US heritage found in these discourses. With the studio system's demise, such shows offered "professional commemorations"[91] that situated Bogart and *Casablanca* in an old Hollywood to be cherished for its contributions to artistic and national heritage. In this form of remembrance, historical chronology was a key currency.

Documentaries

In the 1960s and 1970s, TV producer David L. Wolper was one of the best-known and most prolific independent documentary filmmakers in the medium. He made respected documentaries about twentieth-century US history, such as *The Race for Space* (1959) and *The Making of the President* (1966), in what is considered TV documentary's Golden Age. He also produced dramas with historical content, such as the much-heralded miniseries *Roots* (1977), a story of the US enslavement of African peoples. Wolper's credentials strongly associated him with television, history, and heritage at a time when TV documentaries emerged as "one of the most important vehicles of public education in an age of crisis and uncertainty."[92]

Wolper also made prime-time black-and-white TV specials and series for the networks in the 1960s that saluted Hollywood. Critic Leonard Maltin, on his youthful encounter with these programs, writes, "These were meticulously crafted shows that chronicled film history for the masses, yet didn't talk down to [their] audience in any way."[93] These programs included the sixty-minute TV specials *Hollywood: The Golden Years* (NBC, 1961); *Hollywood: The Fabulous Era*; and *Hollywood: The Great Stars* (ABC, 1963); and the thirty-minute, thirty-one-episode TV series *Hollywood and the Stars* (NBC, 1963–64).[94] Although they aired originally on networks, Wolper sold these shows to local and regional stations, including WGN; enhancing their footprint further, they circulated for years in reruns on both network and independent channels.[95]

Musical star Gene Kelly hosted and narrated *Hollywood: The Golden Years* (premiering on Wednesday, Nov. 29, 1961, 7:30–8:30 p.m.), which traced the early days of silent filmmaking and stardom up to the sound era. Another A-list actor, Henry Fonda, did the honors for the second and third installments, *Hollywood: The Fabulous Era* (Wednesday, Nov. 28, 1962, 7:30–8:30 p.m.) and *Hollywood: The Great Stars* (Wednesday, March 13, 1963, 10:00–11:00 p.m.).[96] Focusing, like *The Golden Years,* on performers and their films, *The Fabulous Era* addressed developments in Hollywood history from the beginning of the talkies in the later 1920s to the studio system's demise in the 1950s and 1960s—the end, then, of the "fabulous era." With some overlapping material, *Great Stars'* chronicle began around 1910, when the fledgling film industry, previously lacking a star system, started to name and promote performers in its films. The program sketched the portraits of major silent and sound-era stars until *The Misfits* (1961), which features Marilyn Monroe and Clark Gable's final performances before their deaths, a conclusion that depicts the star system's apparent demise in elegiac terms. With host Joseph Cotten, *Hollywood and the Stars* premiered with an episode entitled, "The Man Called Bogart" (Monday, Sept. 30, 1963, 9:30–10:00 p.m.), subsequently broadcasting episodes depicting other stars, genres, and periods. Most of these Wolper shows also featured Bogart, along with clips from *Casablanca* and his other films.

This quartet of documentaries operated as influential Hollywood historiographies, generating terms for understanding, remembering, and canonizing the Hollywood past by recounting its major developments, movies, and stars via vintage footage and celebratory narration. They offered Hollywood history through interviews and compilations of archival materials—film clips, photographs, newsreels, press coverage, behind-the-scenes shorts, and home movies—curating signifiers of the past obtained from studios, private collections, film footage companies, museums, and public sources. The archival signature of this producer's work prompted *Variety* to refer to his team as "David Wolper and his pastemakers from the Hollywood vaults" and their formula as creating "sure-fire ratings grabbers."[97]

In doing so, they secured another relationship between TV and cinema at this time and another means of managing classical film iterations through programming. Wolper's shows cut movies into "small pieces and welded them together in a kaleidoscopic view of the filmic evolution," thus repurposing classical films into new products that served both the television and film industries (and fueled the creation of the "film footage retail business") through what became an increasingly common way of memorializing and celebrating old Hollywood.[98] These programs provided television with a different kind of movie-based content and studios and other film library owners with a different means of leasing or selling their footage. Wolper's shows promoted Hollywood's classical-era films and stars in the very medium involved in their renewed cultural display, legitimating both industries as they produced or broadcast this fare. In fact, *Variety* remarked that the programs' "runoff of scenes . . . looked like a string of trailers for the late shows around town." That NBC aired TV series *Hollywood and the Stars* after its Monday night movie further signaled that the shows simultaneously touted TV reruns of feature films and old Hollywood's glories.[99]

More than television's other modes of canonization discussed thus far, these documentaries established silent and classical Hollywood's history, legacy, and memorability. Wolper wanted to counteract the unfavorable public vision of the film industry arising from the Supreme Court's 1948 Paramount Case, which had ended the studios' monopoly over the business. He aimed to tell a "dynamic, upbeat story about Hollywood that [would] help keep the American industry and its traditions alive and important to the entire world."[100] Like his shows, documentaries about classical-era Hollywood that continued to appear—including 1976's *Life Goes to the Movies* (NBC) and *America at the Movies* (PBS), as well as, on the big screen, *That's Entertainment* (1974)—celebrated this past as new films and stars were replacing the old.

Documentaries of this period argued for the relevance of vintage fare in the post–studio system media world and in a changing America. They produced historical commentary and an educational ethos designed to school the public about the industry's earlier history and to portray old Hollywood as a national heritage not to be lost or forgotten. They thus participated in an economy of prestige that sought to elevate the factory system for producing films and stars into a transcendent and indispensable national art.[101] If television as a medium was a "daily teacher" about Americanness and promoted a sense of "national belonging" among viewers—an impact facilitated by the market's concentration around three commercial nationally televised channels and a number of independents—then these programs' mission was enhanced by their very appearance on TV.[102] At the same time, the compilation of movie clips operated as a "stunning advertisement for Hollywood" and an immersive affective experience for viewers as these films embodied a past that provided "a patina composed of . . . private associations and memories . . . as meaningful as a high school album or an old diary rediscovered."[103]

These programs were made in the lavish style of the TV special or spectacular, a postwar currency of prestige for the medium. The broadcasting industry developed the category of the special in the medium's earlier days to designate a program that could be promoted as distinct from the typical procession of TV series and routines of viewing. As Christopher Anderson contends, spectaculars offered broadcasters a means of eventizing TV programs to attract advertisers and audiences on a broad scale. This kind of show transformed "television viewing from a mundane household activity into an irresistible national event."[104] Specials also often preempted regular programming, suggesting further that they were unique, not-to-be-missed events. In the case of Wolper's Hollywood documentaries, this status supplied additional dimensions of glory to the film industry and to the films and stars spotlighted.

Wolper's productions were part of a larger, long-standing trend toward self-reflexivity in media industries. Hollywood films about filmmaking often furnished behind-the-scenes views of production processes and the people involved. As Steven Cohan maintains, while giving audiences an insider's view risks demythologizing the film industry, most self-reflexive Hollywood films, like *Singin' in the Rain* (1952), a musical comedy about the transition to sound in late 1920s motion pictures, tend to minimize unpleasantries. Cohan argues that such films project, instead, "a *fascination with the mystique of commercial filmmaking in Hollywood*." Any criticism they might advance is superseded by a vision of Hollywood as having a "powerful cultural cachet" that offers a "modern-day fulfillment of the American dream"—a place where young talent could achieve success.[105] Self-reflexive films that had played on the big screen became TV reruns, including Bogart's *Thank Your Lucky Stars* (1943),[106] making the self-reflexive mode a familiar presence in the mediascape. TV shows also deployed self-reflexive elements. *Warner Bros. Presents,* for example, ran "Behind the Cameras" segments at the end of its dramas.[107] Alison Trope observes that these segments "enlighten[ed] the audience by making them aware of the production process" but blurred "the lines between knowledge production and complete veneration."[108] As both Cohan and Trope demonstrate, media self-reflexivity is defined by promotional agendas that divulge behind-the-scenes secrets but disguise more troubling elements to sustain a commercially tenable image of Hollywood.

Wolper's documentaries, with their curated recycled footage and special event status, use this self-reflexive sleight of hand to commemorate industry history, promoting Hollywood cinema's place in heritage and memory. The programs' stylistic formula deploys the archival audio-video fragments of compilation films—clips, publicity photos, newsreel footage—and organizes them according to the logic of narration and editing as they forge bonds between images and words. The evidentiary status of resurrected materials, coupled with the explanatory mechanisms of narrative and editing, recontextualize fragments inside an overarching historical narrative about the Hollywood of yore as a precious legacy.[109] In this sense, the programs' producers and broadcasters act as "memory agents" attempting to secure film memories in ways that would not only serve their promotional agendas but also negotiate a collective participation in and remembrance of a particular version of the past.[110] These specials hew closely to traditional heritage aims, avoiding, as their titles suggest, substantial ambivalence about the industry. Like numerous other traditional enterprises that generate memory narratives to establish heritage, their sculpting of history depends on repressing or managing issues that would challenge the celebration of this past, such as the industry's racism, sexism, and exploitation of its labor force. Stars are a major means of engineering Hollywood's allure above other concerns.

The choice of stars for hosts sets the tenor of these programs' homage to Hollywood. Each of the host/narrators' careers is associated with the studio system's heyday, making them appear authoritative in their role as the audience's official history and memory guide. American, white, and male, each host's perceived authority and the intertextual weight of their accomplished personas—their "host effect"—could operate efficiently to help historicize Hollywood as an important site of American achievement and entertainment. Their voices, demeanors, and scripted words are curatorial, mobilizing the archive to convey a cultural heritage that attempts, in turn, to forge a national collective memory. In *The Fabulous Era,* Fonda begins by recognizing Hollywood's power: "Let's go to the movies. For more than half a century these words have meant an invitation to magic—the magic of moving pictures, the spinning of dreams in a darkened theater." Toward the end, he extols the lasting importance of old Hollywood and its stars:

> Times may change, but what will always remain is the public's desire for heroes and heroines and the stories they tell on the screen; Hollywood today is in a state of change, what the future holds in store, no one can tell. However, one thing is certain. [These films] will never lose their power to stir the heart, to fire the imagination, to shape men's *[sic]* dreams. The great stars, the great moments on the screen are cherished and remembered. Over the years, they enrich our experience; they recapture our past.

Fonda inaugurates *The Great Stars* by remarking that stars are

> fantasy heroes and heroines of our time. They are the idolized purveyors of illusion, the vendors of dreams, the public's own creation . . . for more than fifty years glorified and adored. [They have] magical names that conjure up almost a lifetime of wondrous illusions . . . unique personalities . . . in whose images audiences over the years have found some elusive fulfillment. The climate that produced them has changed, but the affections, born out of need for them, remains. This [program] is essentially a love story.

These script segments recognize change and the Hollywood studio era's end, while making emotional, nostalgia-tinged appeals for its incomparable greatness, relevance, and legacy. The narration, authenticated by Fonda's substantial star persona, relies on the language of dreams and illusions, portraying Hollywood and its stars as celestial creations that hold an ineffable and irresistible attraction for audiences.

Topics that are more difficult to square with this romanticization have little place. With the exception of the scene in *Casablanca* when Rick gets drunk and demands that Sam (Dooley Wilson) "Play it," these specials rarely depict African American performers. When controversy is difficult to avoid in relation to race, narrational tools repress it. In *The Golden Years,* for example, Kelly hails D.W. Griffith's *The Birth of a Nation* (1915) as the "first film masterpiece" by "one of the greatest directors the screen has ever known." As clips illustrate Griffith's techniques, we are told that he shaped "the only art form created in the twentieth century." Some clips depict the film's heroically portrayed Ku Klux Klan, leading Kelly to note that its "sympathetic treatment" of the Klan marred Griffith's achievement and caused "furious controversy" and "riots" that left the director "bewildered and shocked." To atone, Griffith subsequently made *Intolerance* (1916), a film "against bigotry across the ages" that "remains the most ambitious movie spectacle of all time." But the end of Griffith's story is not a happy one: "He dies alone and forgotten in a Hollywood hotel room, leaving behind something of himself in every film made since his day . . . but his stars remember him." This last phrase segues to a new subject, Mary Pickford, a recurring performer in Griffith's pictures. Hence, *The Golden Years,* while offering few specifics about the outcry caused by *The Birth of a Nation,* poses Griffith as an unwitting, contrite, open-minded, and ultimately tragic victim who left his mark on filmmaking. Clips and stills from Griffith's other films lend this perspective credence, while the transition to a famous star returns the show to safer ground. The program thus indirectly acknowledges issues, like racism, that run counter to an otherwise celebratory narrative but quickly reframes them to mitigate their threat. This is the sanitizing gesture typical of conservative heritage narratives.

The documentaries also maintain a clear and freighted distinction between genders. In *The Great Stars,* Fonda discusses male actors, from Douglas Fairbanks to Bogart and Marlon Brando, as having created archetypes, while female stars, such as Hedy Lamarr and Rita Hayworth, are depicted through their sexuality, scandals that shaped their careers, and origins in the masses of girls trying to make it in Hollywood. Similarly, in *The Fabulous Era,* Fonda comments that, in the 1940s, Bogart "becomes a screen immortal and Lauren Bacall a sultry near star," while Bergman in *Casablanca* displays a "luminous art." Bacall and Bergman are considered noteworthy because of their physical appeal rather than any enduring and mythic talent that they might embody.

As Fonda's commentary suggests, Bogart's persona figures prominently in these shows and is subject to similar historiographical operations of celebration and sanitization through the by-then-familiar emphasis on his masculinity. Television again participates in the larger mythologizing of his persona occurring across media in the 1960s, this time through an explicitly idealizing documentary mode. Such mythologizing accounts do not feature the real Bogart but a multifaceted construction of his persona that suits the consecrating demands of traditional heritage discourse.

Depicting a lineage of tough masculinity, *The Great Stars'* discussion of Marlon Brando as a rebel segues into a Bogart segment that treats him as a precedent. According to Fonda, *Casablanca* announces Bogart's true stardom and his ruggedly romantic dimensions. One of the most frequently played clips in Bogart's appearances in these documentaries is the aforementioned scene in which Rick tells Sam to "Play it." Here, as a further sign of *Casablanca*'s pivotal and defining position in his career, "As Time Goes By" plays on the soundtrack throughout footage from his other films, while Fonda's narration, until the final clip, substitutes for screen dialogue. The audience is encouraged not only to focus on Bogart's face in different roles but also to continue to associate him with *Casablanca.* In this lengthy sequence, Fonda names the films that further defined Bogart, including *The Petrified Forest* in "the role [Duke Mantee] that made him a star," *They Drive by Night, The Maltese Falcon,* another clip from *Casablanca* (Rick and Ilsa kissing in Paris), *The Treasure of the Sierra Madre, Key Largo, Dark Passage, The African Queen,* "for which he wins an Academy Award," and *The Caine Mutiny* (1954). The montage concludes with a clip featuring dialogue that is also frequently replayed in Bogart's career chronicles: *To Have and Have Not*'s scene in which Bacall kisses and banters with Bogart ("You know how to whistle don't you, Steve?"). The structure of this dedicated Bogart sequence, with "As Time Goes By" as his theme song and *Casablanca* as his signature accomplishment, also privileges *To Have and Have Not,* treating both Bergman and Bacall as his most significant onscreen relationships. Relegated to their affiliations with him, these costars give him status as a leading romantic man.

At the end of *The Great Stars,* Fonda remarks that "the greatest screen heroes are those with whom most people can identify, such as Humphrey Bogart, tough guy, loner, cynical hero of a cynical time. Men like his toughness; women respond to an innate tenderness. And as time goes by through twenty years of his films, they affectionately call him Bogie." These sentiments about Bogart's dual gender appeal are repeated in other Bogart TV documentaries, suggesting the influence and intertextuality of these programs in canon-building.

The first episode of *Hollywood and the Stars,* "The Man Called Bogart," presents a more thoroughgoing history of his career and personal life (fig. 12). Cotten welcomes the audience: "For half a century, movies have stirred our emotions and shaped our dreams. They have become part of us. And so too have the legends of Hollywood's great stars. Compelling personalities whose names conjure up adventure, laughter, and romance." Bogart's story is thus tied to the series' larger project that, consistent with the other documentaries, characterizes Hollywood as an affectively rich dream factory that has

FIGURE 12. Ad for the first episode of *Hollywood and the Stars* (NBC, 1963–64), "The Man Called Bogart." *Variety,* Sept. 25, 1963, 80.

entered into American consciousness and become, through its larger-than-life stars, a US institution.

Although the star system depended on a balance between the performer as type and as unique individual—both forms of recognizability that could distinguish them as part of a studio brand—this episode focuses on the actor's distinctiveness and "compelling personality." The first cue for this lies in the episode's title. By using *the* instead of *a* to modify *man,* it insists that Bogart is not one man among others but a singular entity—"*The* Man Called Bogart." As Cotten comments, both onscreen and off, Bogart had "a style that set him apart from his fellow actors."

The coverage of Bogart begins with a *To Have and Have Not* clip in which Harry Morgan (Bogart) shoots an antagonist. In tough-guy fashion, Harry says to his other antagonists: "Alright, go on, get 'em up. Go ahead and pull your guns. . . . You're going to get it anyway. You've been pushing me around long enough." The clip continues without diegetic sound as Cotten admiringly introduces Bogart to viewers: "Humphrey Bogart brought an unmistakable power and excitement to the screen." Using a script segment from *The Great Stars* to once again define Bogart's dual gender appeal as key to his stardom, Cotten remarks, "Men admired his world-weary toughness; women sensed that underneath lay an innate tenderness." Having established Bogart's broad allure, the episode promises to provide "the story of the man called Bogart, one of the most unforgettable personalities in the history of Hollywood and the stars." Using the archive, Cotten charts Bogart's personal and professional success until his death in 1957, illuminating his biography and a canon of his films, while creating a kind of history that supports the series' overall project.

"The Man Called Bogart" highlights the actor's early, unimpressive roles on Broadway and in Hollywood through stills and film footage, leading to *The Petrified Forest* as the play and film adaptation that gave him his first big break. This break is implicitly aligned with his persona's masculinity; as Alan Squier (Leslie Howard) remarks to Duke Mantee, "You're the last great apostle of rugged individualism." According to Cotten, this first break led Bogart to be cast as a heavy in a succession of Warner Bros. films. The episode curates a flurry of clips from unnamed films in which Bogart's heavies are shot. Yet the narration turns this part of his career into a positive. As Cotten comments, "Bogart takes this kind of fate philosophically. When he begins to die, the audience is his and his alone." Indeed, he "becomes a master at delivering these farewell addresses." Clips featuring his dying words follow ("Do me a favor, will ya? Don't tell them a dame tripped me up."). This part of his career also seeds his battles with Warner Bros. over his roles: "Bogart regards most of his films as mediocre affairs. A proud and sensitive man, he wants to become a serious actor, but he finds himself fighting futilely against roles far beneath his talents." He approaches his goal when he is cast as detective Sam Spade in *The Maltese Falcon,* a part into which he "breathes fire." Cotten says, "This is the turning point in Bogart's career. Through the sheer force of his talent, he has proven that he is not merely an actor; after all of these years, he has become a star."

Two clips from *Casablanca* establish his trajectory from tough guy to tough guy/romantic lead, his rise to "spectacular stardom," and his enduring popularity. The episode shows the first *Casablanca* clip featured in *The Great Stars,* this time with sound: Rick, emotionally distraught after seeing Ilsa earlier in his cafe, proclaims to Sam, "Of all the gin joints in all the towns in all the world, she walks into mine." Sam performs part of "As Time Goes By" before the tune becomes nondiegetic orchestral music supporting Cotten's narration and introduction of John Huston as Bogart's "good friend and great director." The *Casablanca* scene keeps playing, followed by footage from Bogart's career and personal life; as Huston says in voice-over, "I think he is probably a greater star today than he was at any time during his life. That's a unique position." The second *Casablanca* clip cements Bogart's credentials as a romantic leading man, as Ilsa confronts Rick with a gun and then crumbles in emotion as she confesses her undying love for him, a moment followed by their embrace and kiss. As this scene with Rick plays, Cotten remarks that "Bogart's superb performance in *Casablanca* makes him overnight, much to his own surprise, one of the biggest stars in motion pictures." The romantic variation of his tough-guy persona catapults him to superstardom.

Bogart's status as romantic leading man is amplified by another clip that Wolper's "pastemakers" curate from *To Have and Have Not* (also used in *The Great Stars*). Marie "Slim" Browning (Bacall) meets Harry Morgan in his room, sits on his lap, and kisses him, uttering "You know how to whistle, don't you Steve? You just put your lips together and blow" (fig. 13). The episode merges the onscreen chemistry between Bacall and Bogart with their offscreen romance and marriage. Footage from their wedding day follows (fig. 14), along with a recounting of their age difference ("Bogart is forty-five; Bacall is twenty") and an allusion to Bacall as having been a fan of Bogie's tough-guy roles. The connection between *To Have and Have Not* and their

FIGURE 13. *To Have and Have Not* (dir. Howard Hawks; Warner Bros., 1944): romance blossoms between Bacall and Bogart's characters and the actors themselves.

FIGURE 14. "The Man Called Bogart" (NBC, 1963): Bogart and Bacall's real-life wedding day.

personal bond is further sealed when Cotten remarks, "Now she wears a tiny gold whistle that is inscribed, 'If you need anything, just whistle.'"

Cotten remarks that Bogart's late-career films are significant for how they register his artistic growth: "As a dedicated actor over the years Bogart has developed his range and power, and he astonishes even his admirers with a series of brilliant performances." Film clips with sound suggest the range of Bogart's performances in *The Treasure of the Sierra Madre,* in which he captures the "horror of a man twisted by his lust for gold"; *The Caine Mutiny,* where he is "electrifying as he conveys the psychological disintegration of the tyrannical Captain Queeg"; and *The African Queen,* in which he "reveals a surprisingly masterful flair for comedy" and for which he won an Academy Award for "perhaps his finest screen performance."

Bogart's death concludes the episode. Facing his cancer with "characteristic bravado," Cotten explains, he remains "Bogart to the end." Cotten further eulogizes the actor: "His death is felt as an irreplaceable loss. He belongs to a handful of the great stars of his generation who gave the screen a special vigor and excitement and humanity." Excerpts from John Huston's eulogy for Bogart are also included in voice-over: "To begin with, he was endowed with the greatest gift a man can have—talent—and the whole world came to recognize it. . . . He's quite irreplaceable. There'll never be another like him."

Most film clips are from unnamed movies showing the less successful stages of Bogart's career. This makes those named and broadcast with dialogue—*The Maltese Falcon, Casablanca, To Have and Have Not,* and some later films—more potent as signifiers of a career, a persona, and a legacy. The selection and organization of these clips, along with their repetition across documentaries, reveal curation's ties to historical and canonizing tendencies. These fragments act as biographical markers and emblems of achievement for a great man, signaling what details of his personal and professional life should define his remembrance and which films should be canonized. In this way, the logic of narration, the display of archival fragments, and the chronological order of events recontextualize his films through a coherent narrative about old stars and old Hollywood as legacies deserving a place in history and memory.

Yet, to achieve the intimacy with the star that the episode promises, it has to, at least modestly, risk this legacy by addressing more difficult aspects of the Bogart persona's masculinity that had been previously publicized.[111] Cotten notes that in the 1930s, Bogart emerged as "a flamboyant character" offscreen. *Flamboyance* here is a catchall word meant to acknowledge his three divorces, his violent relationship with one of his wives, his alcoholism,

FIGURE 15. "The Man Called Bogart" (NBC, 1963): Bogart aboard the *Santana* with his third wife, Mayo Methot (far right), and friend—surrounded by the "clean world" of the sea.

and his outspoken criticism of Hollywood. Accompanied by footage of him and his third wife, Mayo Methot, Cotten reports, "Friends called them 'The Battling Bogarts' during their turbulent six-year marriage." By Cotten's attributing the nickname's origin to friends, "The Battling Bogarts" seems like an affectionate tag that, rather than treat this turbulence as domestic violence, poses it as the stuff of marital comedy with sparring partners who are equals in the ring. Immediately following this, Cotten characterizes Bogart as "an enemy of sham and hypocrisy," a flattering bridging device that leads from his unsuccessful and violent marriage to his drinking. Against footage of Bogart with friends, including fellow Warner Bros. star Errol Flynn, at a sunny outdoor event, Cotten tells us that "Bogart openly prides himself on his prowess with the bottle. He rates himself with Winston Churchill and Errol Flynn as among the mightiest drinkers of the decade." This scene leads to home movies of Bogart bare-chested and at sea on his sailboat, the *Santana* (fig. 15). Hence, drinking becomes a measure of his authenticity (his antipathy toward hypocrisy) and manliness (his bottle prowess and cohort of distinguished champion imbibers), while the great outdoors emphasizes his vigorous manly health and affinity with nature.

In fact, the episode defines the *Santana* as central to his offscreen life. Cotten discusses Bogart's "passion for the sea" and his sailboat, with numerous clips showing him aboard. The episode reveals that Bogart delighted in "outraging Hollywood" and had antisocial tendencies that prevented people from inviting him to parties for fear he would insult studio bosses. Again, Cotten relays a friend's comments that, on the *Santana,* "Bogie could escape all he detested about Hollywood—the parties, the phonies, the compromises." The sea provided "another world, a clean world." The actor is quoted as saying that unless people really "understand the love of sailing and the feeling of quiet and solitude, [they] don't really belong on a boat. . . . I think Hemingway said the sea was the last free place on earth." The narration thus alleviates Bogart's aggressiveness, translating it into an expression of his rugged individualism, assisted by his philosophical bonding with Hemingway over the sea. By investing in this mode of masculinity, the episode downplays Bogart's real-life labor disputes with Warner Bros. and any alcohol-infused misanthropy to create a picture of a man of uncompromising integrity. The *Santana* becomes a way to offset issues regarding personal dysfunction, explain his relationship to Hollywood, and, ultimately, provide a redemptive arc for his life story.

Just as his sailboat and the sea romanticize him, his relationship with Bacall rescues him from his former life. Cotten follows footage of their wedding with the observation that "they will have two children, and for the rest of his life he will have a strong and almost old-fashioned sense of home and family." The narration certifies his transcendence of his earlier "flamboyance," as his personal story with Bacall as a settled family man matches contentment in his professional life. Against clips of him and Bacall out shopping and then a bespectacled Bogart sitting in a movie theater, Cotten remarks that "Bogart has come a long way from the insecure Broadway juvenile, the trigger man of B pictures, the disillusioned veteran of the divorce court. He has become unmistakably his own man, and, in his face, there is an unstated challenge: 'Take me for what I am or not at all.'" As Bacall and Bogart are seen vacationing in Italy, Cotten comments that Bogart finally learned how to take fame and riches in stride. He quotes him as saying, "Live each moment as well as you can, one moment at a time, and perhaps, when you put all of the moments together, you'll have something worth remembering." Bogart, the rebel, tough guy, and romantic becomes a philosopher, a rhetorical move that interprets his unflinching ways through a meaningful statement about life.

Since part of the enterprise of both canon-formation and traditional heritage discourse is to manage more damning forces potentially disruptive to a celebratory narrative, the episode deploys the *Santana,* the sphere of nature, and Bacall, the sphere of culture, to corral and resolve Bogart's initial bad behavior. The episode's recounting of Bogart's professional path toward accomplishment, philosophical repose, and contentment further bolsters these calmer visions of the actor's persona, while Huston's eulogy and footage from his funeral shift the program to an elegiac tone. Ultimately, the episode's repeated return to Bogart's masculinity effectively mythologizes it. His serious problems are revealed but handled through narration and the selective use and editing of archival materials so that they may support his and his films' enduring legacy. In fact, the airing of these problems enhances the episode's aura of authenticity. One reviewer at the time valued the show's "clear honesty on an outstanding actor" as it offered insight into Bogart's "strikingly individualistic and strong personality."[112]

More contemporary comments also furnish a glimpse of how this series, like the other Wolper documentaries on Hollywood, influenced the taste for and remembrance of Hollywood and its stars, converting some viewers into fans. Maltin wrote that *Hollywood and the Stars* "held great meaning" for him growing up; he "lapped up every episode, then watched them over and over again in reruns." Others remarked that they "love[d] this series" because it taught them in the 1960s to "love classic films at an early age" and introduced them to Bogart, who became "one of their favorite actors."[113] Along with the adults and teens who flocked to Bogart and *Casablanca* in repertory houses and watched older films on TV, children became fans and cinephiles, recruited in this case by the documentaries' highly effective stories about old Hollywood. The cross-generational appeal of classical-era films on TV testifies both to their omnipresence as reruns and their documentary presentations as educational and inspirational.

These programs thus reveal in particularly dramatic terms how television treated Hollywood movies and stars—not as worn-out commodities but as vital and entertaining contributions to US heritage. Defined by Wolper's reputation as a serious documentarian of American history and by heritage-building audiovisual discourses, they identified Bogart as a national icon and Hollywood as a national institution, with *Casablanca* playing a significant supporting role in their accounts. The "history for the masses" represented by these programs depended on an intricate self-reflexive sleight of hand, achieved through a stylistic montage that concealed as much as it revealed.

Distinct from the more trenchant revisionist documentaries about Hollywood that would materialize,[114] this mode of self-reflexivity was central to building public esteem for and knowledge about classical-era Hollywood, its films, and its stars, producing "commercially viable memories" that would ensure a "narrow view" of wider medium and cultural histories."[115] As a result, old Hollywood's equations with whiteness, traditional definitions of gender and sexuality, and the privileged classes represented by its stars became an intimate part of its lesson to audiences. This traditional form of commemoration continues and expands its stakes on later platforms, as we will see in different ways in chapters 4 and 5.

CONCLUSION

The sales of Warner Bros.' pre-1948 library to AAP in 1956 and subsequent distribution of these films to television a year later paved the way for *Casablanca* to find new life on a platform that represented not only the lucrative association of the film and television industries but also an influential system of circulation for classical-era Hollywood films and their stars. In this milieu, Bogart's oeuvre emerged as commercially appealing and popular fare, with *Casablanca* marked as one of his most representative works. As WGN's history of airing the actor's work indicates, broadcasting meant that films were remodeled according to the medium's protocols of programming and additionally refashioned through programming-associated materials like TV guides and documentaries devoted to further defining cinema through television's portal.

Along with editing feature films to fit broadcast slots, the televisual presentation of cinematics involved spatial and temporal reconfigurations, transplanting films into domestic space and aligning them with clock, calendrical, and historical time as experienced in this space. During the course of its WGN broadcasts, *Casablanca* appeared on morning, afternoon, prime-time, late-night, and late-late-night shows on every day of the week, while Bogart festivals could span months. This temporal plasticity demonstrates the relationship of cinematics to broadcasting's structuring of time, as well as the programming utility cinematics afforded television as iterable content. Furthermore, when WGN programmed Bogart films in festivals, it offered an achronological and accelerated experience of the actor and his films, intensifying the star's ability to act as a principle of attraction and coherence across broadcast days and months while providing a quasi-educational sweep of a career. Resituating Hollywood films and stars in a chronological account, Wolper's documentaries were able to make a more pedagogically grounded case for the historical significance and heritage-worthiness of Hollywood cinema, amplifying the pleasures of an informal film education. *Casablanca* was, then, enmeshed in multiple temporal dimensions of broadcasting, from a Saturday matinee slot meant to attract leisured family members to documentaries where it served as an exemplary historical signpost in Bogart's career and Hollywood's evolution. Television's spatial and temporal rewriting of Hollywood movies made films and their stars into everyday experiences, with strategies in place to offset their ordinariness by emphasizing their exceptional status.

Television also presents a vivid instance of how everyday processes of value construction that were visible to home viewers consecrated movies outside of the provinces of institutions, like academe, recognized as more legitimate arbiters of taste. Documentaries on Hollywood officially pronounced the historical significance of classical-era films and stars and Hollywood itself to modern-day audiences, with *Casablanca*'s curation in this context defining it as a memorable part of US film history and legacy. Other banal forms of canonization rooted in aspects of the material culture involved in television programming—movie showcase titles, TV guide plot summaries, ratings systems, page design, and festivals—generated aesthetic, cultural, and affective value for *Casablanca* that continued to demonstrate the multifaceted means by which this platform articulated the film's quality. These means included the standard canonizing language of the "best" deployed by showcases and guides, as well as the festival concept's celebratory elevation of the film from isolated rerun to a themed entry in a special television event. Outside of these more eye-catching practices, *Casablanca*'s broadcast according to TV scheduling norms drew affective value and meaning from the times in which it was slotted, allowing it to enter into different experiential realms in the household. Its domestication meant that it could be personalized and participate in family rituals shaped by the intersection of home life and broadcasting schedule, while acting as a foundation for memories and nostalgia.

Bogart and *Casablanca*'s repeated appearances on television over decades promoted their familiarity and proximity to everyday life. Even when cinematics more generally might have solicited boredom and disinterest, their widespread appearance on broadcast schedules and in homes gave them an omnipresence that remade them into household phenomena that transformed the awareness and appreciation of the place of classical-era movies in US culture.

Postwar repertory houses and television exhibited *Casablanca* in a mix of other Bogart films, where it was lauded for its excellence and singular contribution to the expression of his persona. In aftermarket exhibition, the film would ascend the canonical ladder more clearly as a single title and with more pomp and circumstance after 1980 through the auspices of video, the subject of the chapters to come.

FOUR

Movie Valentines

HOLIDAY CULT AND THE ROMANTIC CANON IN VHS VIDEO CULTURE

> VCRs provide an electronic portal to the world of old movies in their pristine form.
>
> STEPHEN HUNTER,
> *Baltimore Sun*, 1985

> The video-date—boy, girl, and cassette recorder—is the hot *new* way to bring along an affair.
>
> JACK CURRY,
> *Cosmopolitan*, 1985

HOLLYWOOD HAS LONG RELEASED SPECIALLY themed first-run movies in theaters to capitalize on their association with particular holidays, a practice that it has also avidly pursued with its reissues (witness the endless seasonal reappearances of *It's a Wonderful Life* [1946] around Christmas). For decades *Casablanca* has figured centrally in this way of reselling old movies, attaining a familiar presence as popular Valentine's Day fare. Although the precise date that it became indelibly associated with celebrating February 14 in the United States is uncertain, this presence is particularly visible across platforms from the 1970s onward.[1] During this time, independent TV stations, video formats from videocassette to streaming, cable TV channels like TBS (Turner Broadcasting System) and TCM (Turner Classic Movies), and repertory houses, including Cambridge's Brattle Theatre, sold *Casablanca* to viewers as part of Valentine's Day festivities. Today the film remains a standard February presence in many of these venues, while GIFs from it circulate on social media as holiday salutations.

The persistent connection between *Casablanca* and this holiday has led Ernest Mathijs to label it a Valentine Day's cult film, part of a group of seasonal cult films shown "around specific, recurrent periods and dates in the year" and "linked to cultist reception."[2] This chapter examines the film's standing as seasonal cult by focusing on a platform that heavily influenced its broad dissemination as such: home video, specifically analog videocassettes played on VCRs and TVs in US homes from the 1970s to the early 2000s, when DVD became the preferred home technology for watching films.[3] Like other platforms adapting movies to their specifications, video not only transformed *Casablanca*'s material base (here to magnetic tape) but also made it available to new film cultures and kinds of evaluation. The film's association with this holiday emerged as a major means of identifying its appeal to mass-cultural audiences in the video era, bringing film-watching again, as in earlier chapters, into relation to the calendar, a temporal dimension of film reception often overlooked in exhibition studies. *Casablanca*'s standing as a Valentine's Day movie did not, however, supplant other modes of release or interpretation it experienced during these decades. By this time the film had accrued identities that continued to circulate; its seasonal cult status coexisted with and was infused by other modes of consecration linked, for example, to Bogart's stardom and its own repute as a classic. This aspect of *Casablanca*'s afterlife fuels my later remarks on the cult film's amalgamated nature.

Like the Bogart cult in chapter 2, I regard *Casablanca*'s reputation as a movie valentine as one of its cult identities rather than as a singular, eternal designation—a view based on the proposition that cult cinema is a "discursive category" subject to change over time.[4] Indeed, *Casablanca*'s circulation shows that the same film in historically mobile contexts can attain diverse cult (and other) identities as various contexts foreground and frame certain properties to serve different "interests and desirable functions."[5]

To pursue this line of thought for a moment, postwar repertory houses, significant sites for exhibiting classical Hollywood films from the 1950s through the 1970s, spurred *Casablanca*'s early cult formation. As we have seen, one such house, the Brattle Theatre, ritually programmed the film during Harvard University's final exam weeks to showcase Humphrey Bogart and his oeuvre, with the film's cult appropriation tethered to the university calendar, university life, and students. This phenomenon created a star cult that saw *Casablanca* as a perfect vehicle for Bogart's brand of "cool." Repertory house festivals programmed *Casablanca* with dozens of the actor's other films, creating an intertextual cohort that fostered a vernacular genre of "Bogie films" that ignited and supported fans' attraction to the star's imputed cool masculinity.[6] Furthermore, the Bogart cult materialized during countercultural developments, including Vietnam War protests, the civil rights movement, and the gay and women's liberation movements. In this context, the cult could attract youth audiences to traditional values of gender and race, while also offering them, via Bogart's performances, a tool kit of rebellious personal styles they could use to symbolically navigate their social circumstances.

Although *Casablanca*'s consolidation as Valentine's Day cult involves screenings in latter-day repertory theaters as well, its video distribution, particularly in the 1980s and 1990s, gave it a new, lucrative, and pervasive forum for circulation that shaped its ties to this holiday and its audiences. The press identified *Casablanca* as a "must-see" romantic drama for the holiday, also noting the felicitous fit between video and Valentine's Day. A critic remarked that, while the Fourth of July was for "seeing current blockbusters in blissful air-conditioning" and Christmas for "finding a sudden solidarity with classics you find on cable," Valentine's Day was "meant for renting a film [because] February 14 is about going out and finding what fits, no matter what romantic mood you're in."[7] Without erasing Bogart's significance, which continued to be a rationale for rerelease,[8] *Casablanca*'s ties to the holiday altered its previous cult raison d'être and circumstances of consumption. At the most general level, the new platform of video changed the environment for the cult experience from the theater's public space to the home's private space, its ritual timing from winter exam period to Valentine's Day, and its affective function from exam stress relief to romantic celebration.

As we will see, features that made *Casablanca* legible within the Bogart cult—its intertextual cohort, genre, and social context—also shifted dramatically. The video Valentine's Day cult (and its TCM cablecasts) linked *Casablanca* to other reissued classical Hollywood titles deemed great romances, such as *Gone with the Wind* (1939) and *Wuthering Heights* (1939), as well as numerous more contemporary movies that were considered prime Valentine's Day fare in reissue, from *Annie Hall* (1977) and *An Officer and a Gentleman* (1982) to *Sleepless in Seattle* (1993) and *Titanic* (1997).[9] *Casablanca*'s new intertextual cohort thus displaced it from the Bogie genre and brought it firmly into the romance genre fold. Mainstream press around Valentine's Day further secured its place in this latter genre, extolling it as "the most romantic movie ever made" and the "hands-down winner as the greatest romance ever to hit the screen"—tying it seamlessly into the romance and Valentine's Day canons.[10] Here Bogart may have retained his aura as a cult star but became more prominent as half of a Bogart/Ingrid Bergman cult "power couple." Relatedly, whereas the Bogart cult's affective appeal was grounded in his star persona's masculinity during the height of the counterculture, Valentine's Day aroused associations with romance and femininity during a significantly different period. By the 1980s and 1990s, the conservative Ronald Reagan and George H. W. Bush presidencies (1981–89 and 1989–93, respectively) promoted reaction against the counterculture's progressivism, including that of the continuing women's movement. Valentine's Day's explicit ties to romance thus situated *Casablanca* in relation to rituals of love, courtship, and sex in a time of right-wing response to women's changing roles.

Along with these distinctions, the Bogart and Valentine's Day cults experienced different public manifestations on different platforms. Discourse on the former stressed the spontaneity of participatory youth audiences, while commentary on the latter emphasized the seasonal holiday and its commodified trappings.[11] Of course, the screening and consumption of *Casablanca* in each cult involved both attuned audiences and commercial forces; cultural commentary around the film's exhibition simply accentuated different polarities. With this in mind, seasonal cult films, as they reappear annually on holidays tied to consumerism, present an opportunity to explore the commercial apparatus surrounding this form of cult cinema. As I will discuss further, Valentine's Day emerged as a significant event in the US in the 1800s during the industrial revolution—a revolution that inserted marketing into everyday life, including into the personal intimacies of emotions like love. Today, February 14 is among the most consumerist of US holidays,[12] celebrated with greeting cards, candy, flowers, jewelry, and date-night events. As both public and private date-nights might involve dinner and a romantic movie, films have been written into this occasion's rites. My study treats the commercialization of cult cinema not as a sign of its inauthenticity but as an intrinsic fact of its circulation that helps to craft this special status for films.[13]

Postwar repertory houses made cult films and sensibilities more accessible and mainstream while sustaining an aura of niche audiences and subcultural capital. Video, as a "much sought-after commercialized market," moved cult further into the realm of mass media and mass audiences, broadening the number of cult films and types of viewers involved and thus eroding its characteristic "sense of distinction and exclusivity."[14] Yet, as Elena Gorfinkel remarks, video has unique affordances that promote cult consumption: media can be rewound, fast-forwarded, paused, replayed, owned, and collected, bringing the cult experience into "a new sphere of privatization and domestication."[15] David Church observes further that home video fosters recognition of cult cinema not solely as a rare and select breed of films that elicits spectacularly visible fan reactions but also as a product of "situational (though not casual) affective affinities with a range of cinematic texts" in a world of seemingly endless replay, greater textual accessibility, and unrestricted viewership.[16] Video's ability to stimulate the cultification of media and viewing sensibilities calls attention to how the technology's affordances, impact on audiences, and place in the routine domain of domestic space might foster emotional ties to films. Like any aesthetic category, cult is subject to historical change, marking home video as a shift in, rather than a diminishment of, its contours and meaning.

Technological and media industry developments in the 1970s, 1980s, and 1990s underpinned *Casablanca*'s circulation as a cult movie valentine. The industry released *Casablanca* on multiple types of physical-format video, while it produced, disseminated, and evaluated the film as a classic video, giving it the kind of visibility that facilitated its entry into the era's cultural flow.[17] Within this flow, the mainstream press figured prominently in translating the film's reappearance as a classic into seasonal cult status. Whereas film scholars writing at this time often interpreted *Casablanca* as a western or war film,[18] critics from general circulation newspapers and women's magazines like *Cosmopolitan* defined it as a great romance suitable for Valentine's Day celebrations. They invited consumers to participate "in a ritual where the movie is experienced again and again" as an emotionally resonant and memorable event.[19] Even when such discourses did not explicitly label the film as cult, they insistently positioned it as an annual object of viewing indispensable to the holiday experience.

Both industry and press activities around *Casablanca* materialized through an unassuming modus operandi—the list, comprising "best-of" recommendations aimed at steering consumers to top films in video release. These lists, however, were more than consumer guides to videos; they built popular cults and canons and helped to define film culture on video. Here *Casablanca* and other classical-era Hollywood films achieved consistently favorable ratings, becoming holiday staples. Valentine's Day lists had larger outreach still, since their consecrating functions were inseparable from the cultural work they performed in relation to romance. Because this holiday is synonymous in the public imagination with courtship and love, it was a magnet for popular cultural treatises on gender and relationships. Consecrating *Casablanca* as a must-see Valentine's Day film involved it in these discussions, especially as they charted the period's social agitation about women.

Considered one of the most exemplary of all romances, *Casablanca* represented the fantasy memory of what romance and gender roles once were, gaining contemporary cultural relevance in these new circumstances of appropriation.

For my exploration of *Casablanca*'s holiday cult status and meaning, I begin with industrial and technological factors that made it accessible and valuable as a commodity for video platforming by presenting it as a Hollywood classic. As in previous chapters, the industry is a fundamental starting point for studies of historical circulation, since it furnishes the conditions under which films as commercial properties are resurrected and offered to new interpretations and forms of consecration. I then turn to Valentine's Day, briefly discussing its history before examining the connection between this holiday and video culture as they defined *Casablanca*'s place in this new realm. I conclude with thoughts about the film's fate as seasonal cult in the 2000s, where it remains on numerous best-of lists but also often disappears from consideration, particularly on lists focused on racial and sexual diversity. In earlier decades, mainstream press rankings of classical-era Hollywood films on video for Valentine's Day provided an occasion to publicize and affirm white heterosexual romance. More recently, while recycled oldies have continued to receive such affirmation, they have also served as a ground for rejecting traditional identity-oriented conventions of movie romance.

ON VIDEO

Casablanca's presence in the video market was negotiated by, among other factors, the increasing power of corporate conglomerates over Hollywood film studios (discussed in more detail in the next chapter), the consolidation of the video business into a financial and cultural success with Hollywood movies as a major attraction, the selling of old Hollywood films as classics, and advances in home video. Eric Hoyt's observation that libraries became "vital profit centers for the Hollywood studios" after WWII only gained more traction in this later era, with studio film libraries figuring significantly throughout these shifting conditions.[20]

As with radio and broadcast TV, Hollywood was initially ambivalent about video's incursion into the film business, only to embrace it as a major revenue stream and an influential new experience of movies.[21] A convergence of developments in the 1980s and 1990s made movies on video into an immensely profitable enterprise. By the early 1980s, all the major studios had their film libraries on the video market and distribution arrangements in place, increasing the movie supply for video rental and purchase.[22] By the mid-1980s, the infrastructure for delivering video to customers had expanded. Video stores outnumbered movie theaters, while locations renting and selling videos diversified to include common sites like supermarkets, gas stations, and bookstores, making videocassettes seem omnipresent.[23] Additionally, VCR prices fell (from more than $1,000 in the late 1970s to about $200 by the late 1980s),[24] attracting a populace that had also become more comfortable with the technology. This trend helps to further explain the speed with which VCRs penetrated US homes. In the late 1970s and early 1980s, fewer than 5 percent of homes had VCRs. By 1988, the number rose to an estimated 60 percent of homes, increasing another 10 percent a few years later. Except for monochrome TV, VCRs had the fastest penetration rate among home entertainment technologies.[25]

While VCR owners initially used this technology to timeshift (record broadcast programs for later consumption), by 1986–87 video's popularity owed more substantially to Hollywood cinema. Janet Wasko reports that, by then, the main reason consumers bought VCRs was "to view rental movies," with 70 percent choosing prerecorded tapes of Hollywood films to watch. In the early 1990s, films made up 90 percent of rentals and 60 percent of video sales.[26] The sales of films on video in what is called the "sell-through" market was indebted in part to falling prices that encouraged consumers to purchase tapes. Whereas buying a film had once been expensive (around $100), sell-through prices began to be lowered in 1984 to less than $30 per tape with even cheaper bargain prices available. In 1992, consumers spent more than $4 billion buying tapes and more than $7 billion renting tapes, with Hollywood films remaining major attractions.[27] At this time, an industry panel reported that remarketed classics "continued to fuel the sell-through side of the home video business."[28]

Under the category of classics, video gave older films renewed life in the home, contributing vigorously to their continuing viability as modern entertainment. The industry gave variable definitions of what constituted a classic. Although later subject to change, a general definition offered in the 1980s specified high quality, prestigious US or British films produced before 1950 (but including some later titles) that had a track record in reissue that promised their "rentability"—rooting the classic label in both aesthetic and commercial concerns. Although not all classics performed well in retail, with video vendors in certain US rural regions or in convenience stores regarding 1930s and 1940s films as dust collectors on their shelves, some films seemed relatively immune to this fate. A trade journalist reporting on video stores noted, "As we head into the late '80s, certain popular old films are emerging as leaders in the classic video race," with the "five all-time top classics being *Gone with the Wind, The Sound of Music* (1965), *Casablanca, It's a Wonderful Life,* and *White Christmas* (1954).[29] As we will see, *Casablanca* and other classical-era films found their place in the video market primarily in sales.

These developments led to surging video revenues for Hollywood. By 1987–88, studios earned more from video rental and sales than from theaters; by the early 1990s, video provided almost 50 percent of studio income.[30] Meanwhile, video offered consumers more advantageous access to movies. Although analog video has a reputation today as a poor, easily degradable format, media industries promoted it then as superior to both TV and movie theaters. Unlike films broadcast on network or basic cable TV, movies on video were uninterrupted by commercials and generally unedited, improving on the experience of televised films. Home viewing also avoided the hassle and expense of going out to theaters, as well as the rigors of their compulsory silence; in domestic space, viewers could interact freely during screenings.[31]

Moreover, the VCR freed viewers from TV schedules and allowed them to control movies in an unprecedented fashion, pausing, rewinding, fast-forwarding, recording, and renting or purchasing them. Viewers could also rewatch movies and build personal libraries, giving films, as I have mentioned, a potentially intimate place in the home and forming foundations for their cult appropriation. Fostering this sense of intimacy—an affective dimension of video film culture central to the Valentine's Day cult—consumers could program their own screenings in private space, exercising personal choice and curation in selecting what, when, and how to watch. In this sense, physical-format video established central terms by which the "pull" technologies of digital video and streaming today contrast with "push" technologies like traditional television: the latter operate through a set and predetermined schedule, while the former focus on personal interactive control achieved through browsing, selecting, and owning titles matched with the capacity to manipulate the time and space of viewing.[32] Relatedly, as Frederick Wasser writes, the VCR's "combination of product choice and time flexibility was sufficient to make it ideal for a new lifestyle of more work and shifting schedules." When VCRs arrived on the market, more Americans were in the workforce, a situation that generated a sense of less free time and, consequently, the importance of choice in the leisure sphere.[33] If the public was wavering at all in its commitment to Hollywood films at home, video made them into desirable options, placing "film consumption back at the center of people's leisure activities."[34]

Casablanca's video platforming occurred in the context of this consolidation of the video market and video culture. Its circulation was indebted to other forces as well, including reissue on multiple video formats, changing library ownership, and market success.

The Many Video Lives of Casablanca

Casablanca's video release spans the life of physical-format video, reflecting the industry's confidence in its ability both to draw viewers on a succession of video technologies and to compete with films in a congested media climate. *Casablanca* appeared initially on video in 1972 in a short-lived experiment in consumer electronics—Cartridge Television's Cartrivision, the first videocassette format to offer prerecorded content like movies for home viewing. United Artists (UA), a studio that owned the Warner Bros. pre-1950 library from 1958 to 1967 and, after its purchase by Transamerica Corporation in 1967, continued to distribute *Casablanca,* leased it to Cartrivision.[35] Cartrivision was a playback/record precursor to Betamax and VHS that was built into TV sets and priced at $1,600. Before video stores became fixtures of the landscape, Cartridge Rental Network shipped titles to Chicago's Sears, Roebuck, & Company, which rented feature films at its stores for $6 each. Studios were attracted to Cartrivision because it prevented viewers from replaying or copying films, assuaging studio fears about losing control of their product on this new platform—fears that launched the ultimately unsuccessful lawsuits they brought against Sony Corporation of America and its Betamax player.[36] Cartrivision offered color-coded tapes to address this issue: red cassettes for prerecorded content, with one play per tape, and blank black cassettes for recording other content. Because of business problems, viewer dissatisfaction with the red cassette's constraints, and the tapes' lack of quality, however, Cartrivision folded in a year.[37]

Sony's Betamax was released in 1975 and JVC/Matsushita's VHS in 1976, video formats that competed for market dominance for a decade before VHS definitively won the "format wars."[38] *Casablanca* appeared on both from the later 1970s through the mid-1980s and, from 1981 to 1986, on another format that had a shorter shelf-life. With other titles, such as *Citizen Kane* (1941) and *The Wizard of Oz* (1939), *Casablanca* circulated on CED (Capacitance Electronic Disc), a vinyl video disc RCA marketed as SelectaVision.[39] RCA made these disks available to consumers through chain stores like Radio Shack and mail-order companies like CBS Video Club. A modest market force, SelectaVision's operations concluded in 1984, prompted by, among other things, RCA's interest in JVC/Matsushita's technology.[40] Yet, along with Betamax and VHS reissues, *Casablanca* continued to be available on CED into 1986, with the CBS Video Club touting it as one of its top fifty movies in all formats.[41] Between 1985 and 1995, the film also saw multiple reissues on laser disc, another niche technology, before it too faded from view.

During the 1980s and 1990s, *Casablanca* and other earlier Warner Bros. films continued to change hands.[42] MGM bought UA in 1981 and in 1983 formed MGM/UA Entertainment. When, in 1986, the Turner Entertainment Company acquired MGM/UA,[43] Ted Turner used it to stock his cable channels—TBS, TNT (Turner Network Television), and, later, TCM—and to release chosen titles to video. Maintaining the library when he renegotiated his acquisition of the studio with prior owner Kirk Kerkorian, Turner became a central figure in giving classical-era films life on new platforms (and in the colorization controversies that included *Casablanca*).[44] Along with *Casablanca,* Turner's library featured *King Kong* (1933), *Gone with the Wind, The Wizard of Oz,* and *Citizen Kane,* with his cross-platform exploitation of them sustaining their visibility decades after their debuts. In 1996, Turner Entertainment Company became part of Time Warner Inc. (Time having merged with Warner Communications in 1990 in the studio's own history of changing fortunes). As a result, Warner Bros. studio, a Time Warner subsidiary, was reaffiliated with its library for the first time since it was sold in 1956.[45]

During these shifts in technologies and library ownership, *Casablanca* was reissued almost every year after 1980 on physical-format video (see appendix 2). With Betamax phased out of consumer video markets by the late 1980s and laser disc by the mid-1990s, the film continued to appear on VHS through 2001, when DVD replaced it as the reissue format of choice. *Casablanca*'s materialization on video since 1995 also included competing formats HD DVD and Blu-ray (another "format war," this time won by the latter). Each classical-era film has its own home release pattern, but this kind of proliferating reissue is typical of the immortals.

Casablanca's early and consistent presence in multiple video formats indicates media companies' belief that renowned films could draw customers to new technologies and platforms, with the reputation of oldies legitimating and otherwise making uncertain novelties attractive.

The Hit List and Classical Hollywood Cinema

Companies that gambled on *Casablanca*'s success on video had their hopes confirmed. The media industry's metrics, epitomized by *Billboard*'s "Top 40 Videocassettes" charts, indicated the film's significant place in video culture. *Billboard,* a trade publication that had earlier facilitated the crossover into public consciousness of hit charts for popular music,[46] became a major source on hit videos in the 1980s and 1990s. From 1981 to 1983, along with other older titles like *The Adventures of Robin Hood* (1938) and *North by Northwest* (1959), *Casablanca* was one of the few vintage films to land on *Billboard*'s "Top 40 Videocassettes" sales charts.[47] Recent Hollywood feature films, such as *Raging Bull* (1980), dominated both the top rental and sales charts during this time. In August 1981, *Casablanca* entered these charts at number twenty-three. By September, it ranked tenth and stayed in the top twenty titles into the new year, including its return to number ten around Christmas, a major sales occasion for videocassettes. In March 1982, after being on the sales charts for more than thirty weeks, *Casablanca* ranked almost last, only to rise to the top ten in December, again owing to the Christmas spike in video purchases.[48] Although *Casablanca* is not considered a cult Christmas film like *It's a Wonderful Life,* this holiday helped to shape its and many other films' cultural presence. As people shopped for films on video as gifts, video entered into the commercial rhythms and personal rituals that defined publicly meaningful times in the calendar—one of video's many intersections with rhythms and rituals shaped by the holidays.

Because *Casablanca* registered more consistently in the "Top 40" in sales than in rentals, vintage titles appeared to have more success as gifts and collectibles for cinephile, fan, and/or family video libraries than as the kind of transitory fare represented by rentals.[49] The video industry promoted this sense of lasting value for old films. In 1986, one of *Casablanca*'s distributors, CBS-Fox Video, placed ads for its "Cinema Classics Collection" in cinephile periodicals like *American Film,* an American Film Institute (AFI) publication. Illustrated with images from *Casablanca* and *Citizen Kane,* one such ad exclaimed, "own the treasures of the silver screen as you've never seen them before" in "archive-quality videocassettes of the greatest movies ever made." The ad pitted purchased films on VHS against those on TV ("chopped up so

JANE FONDA

Pos. TITLE—Distributor
1 JANE FONDA'S NEW WORKOUT—Karl Lorimar Home Video
2 JANE FONDA'S WORKOUT—Karl Lorimar Home Video
3 PINOCCHIO—Walt Disney Home Video
4 BEVERLY HILLS COP—Paramount Home Video
5 THE SOUND OF MUSIC—CBS-Fox Video
6 JANE FONDA'S PRIME TIME WORKOUT—Karl Lorimar Home Video
7 CASABLANCA—CBS-Fox Video
8 GONE WITH THE WIND—MGM/UA Home Video
9 THE WIZARD OF OZ—MGM/UA Home Video
10 THE BEST OF JOHN BELUSHI—Warner Home Video
11 RETURN OF THE JEDI—CBS-Fox Video
12 MARY POPPINS—Walt Disney Home Video
13 BACK TO THE FUTURE—MCA Dist. Corp.
14 MOTOWN 25: YESTERDAY, TODAY, FOREVER—MGM/UA Home Video
15 ALICE IN WONDERLAND—Walt Disney Home Video

FIGURE 16. Best-sellers overall for 1986. *Billboard,* Dec. 27, 1986, Y36.

brutally you can barely watch") and video rentals, which offered faded, overused copies in short windows for viewing. Oldies for sale, by contrast, were for "true film lovers" to "enjoy again and again" through films that were "complete, unaltered, and . . . meticulously transferred from the finest available master prints to high grade videotape"—presenting, as the first epigraph states, the "world of old movies in their pristine form." Each film was specially packaged in "its own handsome collector's case" with a program guide, reviews, studio photos, and "fascinating behind-the-camera insights." CBS-Fox Video hoped that the promise of quality around film classics would draw customers to its video club (the first classic was priced at $4.95 with subsequent choices offered at $39.95 each),[50] signaling older films' strategic importance as gateway attractions for new subscribers. Observers saw 1986 as a watershed year in video sales, in part because it identified "the strong presence of older catalog titles at lower price points" as an eye-opening trend in the sell-through market, with special praise for CBS-Fox's promotion of *Casablanca* and *The Sound of Music.*[51]

At this time, recent Hollywood films such as *Back to the Future* (1985) still figured prominently in rentals and sales. But original productions and

DEOCASSETTE **SALES**

STBUSTERS—RCA/Columbia Pictures Home Video
DEUS—HBO/Cannon Video
BO: FIRST BLOOD PART II—HBO/Cannon Video
HY SMITH'S ULTIMATE VIDEO WORKOUT—JCI Video
KING AND I—CBS-Fox Video
N—CBS-Fox Video
HY SMITH'S BODY BASICS—JCI Video
BO—Walt Disney Home Video
TE CHRISTMAS—Paramount Home Video
YBOY VIDEO CENTERFOLD #1—Karl Lorimar Home
o
YBOY VIDEO CENTERFOLD #2—Karl Lorimar Home
o
NESS—Paramount Home Video
VIRGIN TOUR-MADONNA LIVE—Warner Music Video
ZI'S HONOR—Vestron
MI VICE—MCA Dist. Corp.
MLINS—Warner Home Video
OMATIC GOLF—Video Reel

33 PATTON—CBS-Fox Video
34 COMMANDO—CBS-Fox Video
35 THE JANE FONDA WORKOUT CHALLENGE—Karl Lorimar Home Video
36 AFRICAN QUEEN—CBS-Fox Video
37 ROCKY IV—CBS-Fox Video
38 WHITE NIGHTS—RCA/Columbia Pictures Home Video
39 COCOON—CBS-Fox Video
40 WHITNEY HOUSTON THE #1 VIDEO HITS—MusicVision
41 WRESTLEMANIA—Coliseum Video
42 WEST SIDE STORY—CBS-Fox Video
43 THE MUSIC MAN—Warner Home Video
44 DO IT DEBBIE'S WAY—Video Associates
45 MASK—MCA Dist. Corp.
46 THE JEWEL OF THE NILE—CBS-Fox Video
47 OUT OF AFRICA—MCA Dist. Corp.
48 ROBIN HOOD—Walt Disney Home Video
49 SILVERADO—RCA/Columbia Pictures Home Video
50 SOUTH PACIFIC—CBS-Fox Video

programming recycled from other media across genres—children's films, fitness instruction tapes (especially those from Jane Fonda's fitness empire), erotica, music performances, comedy specials, and sports events—were increasingly dominant on the charts.[52] Despite this formidable competition, the status of classical Hollywood films and feature-length animation from Walt Disney Productions (like *Pinocchio* [1940]) improved in this period, facilitated by lower prices for tapes and a video market that had grown and stabilized.[53] *Casablanca* thus joined a lasting movement in the media industries toward lower sell-through prices and "giftable" films, fueling its continuation as a video staple.

Best-selling videos for the year 1986 reflect these shifting priorities in content. With Fonda's tapes dominating (fig. 16), *The Sound of Music, Casablanca, Gone with the Wind,* and *The Wizard of Oz* were also part of the top ten, besting an entry in the *Star Wars* saga. With their chart-topping profiles, these older titles proved to the industry that they had enduring market value and popularity, certifying them as "real evergreens."[54] In fact, industry pundits regarded these older films as "responsible for the brisk sales pace" of titles for the year, with "classic movie releases . . . delivering revenues that would never have happened without home video."[55] Indeed, figure 17 identifies a

HIT CLASSIC VIDEO

Following is a recap chart of classic videos which appeared on Billboard's Videocassette Sales chart during the eligibility period of 11/12/83 to 5/9/87.

1. **PINOCCHIO** (Walt Disney Home Video)
2. **GONE WITH THE WIND** (MGM/UA Home Video)
3. **THE SOUND OF MUSIC** (CBS/Fox Video)
4. **SLEEPING BEAUTY** (Walt Disney Home Video)
5. **CASABLANCA** (CBS/Fox Video)
6. **ALICE IN WONDERLAND** (Walt Disney)
7. **MARY POPPINS** (Walt Disney Home Video)
8. **THE WIZARD OF OZ** (MGM/UA Home Video)
9. **WHITE CHRISTMAS** (Paramount Home Video)
10. **DUMBO** (Walt Disney Home Video)
11. **SINGIN' IN THE RAIN** (MGM/UA Home Video)
12. **THE KING AND I** (CBS/Fox Video)
13. **THE MUSIC MAN** (Warner Home Video)
14. **REAR WINDOW** (MCA Home Video)
15. **AFRICAN QUEEN** (CBS/Fox Video)
16. **VERTIGO** (MCA Home Video)
17. **SEVEN BRIDES FOR SEVEN BROTHERS** (MGM/UA Home Video)
18. **MY FAIR LADY** (CBS/Fox Video)
19. **WEST SIDE STORY** (CBS/Fox Video)
20. **SOUTH PACIFIC** (CBS/Fox Video)
21. **NORTH BY NORTHWEST** (MGM/UA Home Video)
22. **THE UNSINKABLE MOLLY BROWN** (MGM/UA)
23. **THE MALTESE FALCON** (CBS/Fox Video)
24. **THE JOLSON STORY** (RCA/Columbia Pictures)
25. **HIGH SOCIETY** (MGM/UA Home Video)
26. **FORBIDDEN PLANET** (MGM/UA Home Video)
27. **AROUND THE WORLD IN 80 DAYS** (Warner)
28. **LOST HORIZON** (RCA/Columbia Pictures)
29. **ON THE WATERFRONT** (RCA/Columbia Pictures)
30. **A STAR IS BORN** (Warner Home Video)
31. **GIGI** (MGM/UA Home Video)
32. **20,000 LEAGUES UNDER THE SEA** (Walt Disney)
33. **MUTINY ON THE BOUNTY** (MGM/UA)
34. **SPARTACUS** (MCA Home Video)
35. **NATIONAL VELVET** (MGM/UA Home Video)

FIGURE 17. Leading classic film sales in the mid-1980s. *Billboard,* May 30, 1987, C-9.

broad selection of classical-era films that had charted favorably in *Billboard* from 1983 to 1987.

Casablanca's fiftieth anniversary, in 1992, prompted another notable moment in its video distribution and another calendar-oriented sales strategy, in this case with a commemorative dimension (a topic that I will explore more fully in the next chapter). A month after its August 1992 video reissue, *Casablanca*'s no-frills fiftieth-anniversary edition was number eight in sales on *Billboard*'s charts, with *Wayne's World* (1992) at number one.[56] This anniversary edition, a single videocassette without extra features, remained in the top ten, climbing to number five during Christmas and remaining in the top five or ten through January and February 1993.[57] Landing in the top one hundred titles in sales for the year, *Casablanca*'s anniversary edition ranked at number thirty-three, between *Wayne's World* and *Playboy's Playmate*

Review '92.[58] Although *Casablanca* rated highest among anniversary editions, others making the top one hundred included *Citizen Kane*, *It's a Wonderful Life*, *King Kong*, and *Singin' in the Rain* (1952).[59]

With their vested interest in the economic stakes involved, industry rankings of and commentary about best sellers on video were not neutral or solely in-house sources of information on these matters. As Liam Cole Young argues in relation to the music industry, beyond their function as financial data, sales charts help to construct the field of popular music. That is, they expeditiously represent dimensions of the business and experience of music, including industry and market tendencies, audience preferences and tastes, and a snapshot of a historical period of media consumption, while acting as a form of communication among producers, critics, and audiences.[60] This set of effects suggests how institutionally sanctioned lists of best-selling films on video, which similarly channeled this information from the industry to the public, revealed industry trends, consumer tastes, and historical instances of film popularity on video, eliciting a sense of film culture in the VCR age.[61]

Furthermore, top-forty and top–one hundred charts and related industry discourses enveloped *Casablanca* in new modes of evaluation, temporality, and intertextual cohorts that also defined the field of popular films on video. Statistics indicated that media industries and consumers valued certain older reissues, especially if they could be defined as high-quality gifts and collector's items. As sales strategies synced films to annual events like Christmas and everyday events like anniversaries, lists demonstrated that *Casablanca* was sold on other occasions besides Valentine's Day, signaling once again the calendar's importance in circulating reissues. These lists additionally situated the film within intertextual cohorts beyond romance films. As Young writes, "any list forges connections between its contents—even if just the basic fact of being placed together—that did not exist prior to the act of listing."[62] Rankings placed *Casablanca* in a new world of video and film releases, from Fonda's workouts to *Playboy* videos and *Wayne's World*. While showing *Casablanca*'s ability to thrive in a changed media ecosystem, such rankings sharpened the sense of its classic status, making it stand out as vintage fare among more contemporary offerings. Since rankings aligned *Casablanca* with films like *The Wizard of Oz* as well, their grouping together as evergreens further consolidated their classic credentials.

Throughout *Casablanca*'s history such cohorts have shifted during circulation, creating networks that recontextualize and redefine its commercial value, terms of consumption, and meaning. Here, it emerged as a classic film commodity, an object of shopping that could facilitate the acceptance of new technologies, enhance the sell-through market, lure customers to video club subscriptions, and function as a holiday gift. In the interweaving of commercialization and best-of-list consecration, *Casablanca* appeared as a classic Hollywood film par excellence, touted as mandatory viewing for video and cultural literacy.[63] With the visibility afforded by its classic status—supported by video stores' classification systems, video guides, and other aspects of video culture[64]—the film was available for mass-cultural appropriation.

As an important part of crafting seasonal cult, newspapers and magazines produced their own video best-of lists, presenting *Casablanca* as a film to be watched annually on Valentine's Day. Well before digital-age algorithms and recommendation engines,[65] a thriving cottage industry of print sources and organizations, operating as aesthetic tastemakers and consumer guides, created rankings that promoted the *crème de la crème* of romantic films. These efforts reflect the post-1960s efflorescence of what James F. English refers to as "institutions of consecration" dedicated to the "maintenance and manipulation . . . of symbolic rank or prestige" for cultural goods.[66] The AFI, a major national organization devoted to film, is recognizably such an institution. But ordinary media were also centrally involved in consecration, producing what I called in chapter 3 *banal* forms of canonization—everyday, ephemeral accounts that routinely construct aesthetic value for texts. As Young reminds us, lists, no matter where they appear or how trivial they may seem, participate in knowledge systems that help to constitute the "infrastructure of culture." They represent some of the "techniques and technologies by which human societies administer, police, and imagine themselves," in the process getting "baked into the circulation of cultural content."[67] Mass-circulation newspapers and magazines, although lacking the prestige of the AFI and other heralded organizations, generated the most insistent and widespread rankings of Valentine's Day films on video, influencing their reception.

While negotiating contemporaneous social developments, press commentary around Valentine's Day videos was more broadly situated in the holiday's historical legacy as a major cultural event.

VALENTINE'S DAY

The origins of Valentine's Day (or St. Valentine's Day) are disputed. Some accounts date it to the third century, when, on February 14, Romans executed two Roman Christians named Valentine. Martyred and then sainted, these figures were not strongly associated with courtship and love until the fourteenth century in England, when poets like Geoffrey Chaucer forged the connection. Centuries passed until the day's celebration as a romantic festivity translated to a US context, where, in the 1840s, it became a "high day" in the nation's calendar.[68]

Leigh Eric Schmidt argues that the industrial revolution, as it gained a broader footprint in American life, fueled this phenomenon, especially as it spurred the intervention of commerce and marketing into everyday life. Valentine's Day was one sign of this, popularized through paper valentines that, whether mass-produced or handmade, drew from the language of love developed by commercial sources. In the process, the noun *valentine* shifted from designating a person to designating merchandise—the Valentine's Day card—as a mode of affectionate exchange between couples, family members, and friends. Marketers promoted these cards as allowing people to escape into the "whimsy, caprice, and romance" of preindustrial folk traditions that could alleviate the burdens of modernity. Romance was thus a nostalgic enterprise tinged with a yearning for the past, a yearning that the old-fashioned paper valentine embodied. Marketers targeted female consumers and children as those most invested in receiving and saving cards as mementos, thereby influencing their consumer choices, as well as, more expansively, their "passage into sentimental and romantic love."[69]

On the one hand, as Schmidt contends, valentines were an enjoyable, relatively risk-free form of communication that offered a "ritualized medium" for navigating the uncertain terrains of the heart in social situations, such as launching a courtship. They thereby asserted individual desires in a codified society. On the other hand, through their "preprinted sentiments and images," the commercially produced valentines that came to dominate this market standardized and commodified not only the holiday but also romance and intimate inner feeling.[70] Valentine's Day and its commercialization thus helped to negotiate cultural values pertaining to consumer culture and gifting; women, children, and sentimentality; romantic affections; and nostalgia for folk traditions as they were being rearticulated through industrialization.

As Schmidt writes, the overarching effect of this dimension of Valentine's Day saw "the impact of expanding markets on holiday traditions." Celebrations were transported from the community public sphere (e.g., streets and taverns) to the private sphere. The private sphere, in turn, was understood as the realm of family and home as it intersected with stores as "primary staging areas for American celebrations"—a development more often associated with Christmas. In the consumer industry that grew in relation to Valentine's Day, cards were joined by other commercial tokens of affection, including candy, flowers, and jewelry, while publications on courtship and etiquette promoted the occasion and surrounding social mores.[71]

The vision of Valentine's Day as a sales event focused on women has spawned objections to its overcommercialization and reliance on stereotypes of women in thrall to romance. The holiday has nonetheless remained popular. In 2009, consumers—mainly couples but also family and friends—spent $14.7 billion on Valentine's Day sundries and date nights, a figure rising to $20.7 billion in 2019.[72] By recommending movies on video as part of the holiday's festivities, late twentieth- and early twenty-first-century magazines and newspapers helped them to become an integral part of this market. The video era, fueled by the rhythms and rituals associated with holidays, created a nexus of video stores and homes as "primary staging areas" for celebration. Capitalizing on films as material commodities available for shopping, this era updated the historical Valentine's Day relationship among commercial sites, the domestic sphere, mass-produced media, and intimate feeling.[73] Against this backdrop and through the intervention of print sources, older titles like *Casablanca* became a standard part of Valentine's Day festivities.

MOVIE VALENTINES ON VIDEO

If, as Thomas Elsaesser argues, a sense of intimacy is "the most powerful bond between the spectator and the film" in theaters, video claimed its own territory in this regard.[74] Home video had deeply social functions, creating and sustaining "different kinds of sociality" that affected families, couples, and friends.[75] Indeed, like the cultural uptake of television, discussions of the VCR often addressed its impact as a new technology and household pastime on interpersonal relationships.[76] Headlines such as "The Human Side: How the VCR Is Changing Us" led to stories on how it influenced parenting, family dynamics, and home life.[77]

In this sense, *Casablanca*'s seasonal cult status arose at an intersection of institutions of consecration and what Lauren Berlant calls "institutions of intimacy." Intimacy promises something shared "within zones of familiarity and comfort: friendship, the couple, and the family, animated by expressive and emancipating kinds of love." Yet it is also haunted by instabilities, ambivalences, and failures. Media institutions of intimacy, like TV talk shows, negotiate the conflicted terrains of intimacy by dispensing therapeutic advice.[78] Commentary about video technology and the Valentine's Day cult canon proceeded in this spirit. By defining the technology and the best romantic films, critics offered tips to readers, irrespective of the stage their relationship happened to be in, on how to achieve the desired emotional resonance for a successful holiday celebration. Along the way, as we will see, they disseminated ideas about romance, dating, love, sex, and marriage inflected by the period's anxieties about women.

In terms of the technology and its affordances, in an earlier version of today's slang linkage of movies and sex, "Netflix and chill," the press assured readers that video's new "high-tech age" would promote the home's intimacies. In 1985, *Cosmopolitan,* a women's magazine known as the "cliff notes of romance" for its emphasis on sex and relationships,[79] published the article, "One VCR—Two Tickets to Romance," which underscored this point. Here writer Jack Curry exclaims that "the video-date—boy, girl, and cassette recorder—is the hot, *new* way to bring along an affair." A couple could get "cozy (or raunchy or tearful) together over a for-snugglers-only double bill!" Better still, VCRs added a "special spice to dating" without altering things that "lovers have always cherished as essential to at-home romance . . . candlelight, cognac, and a fire burning low."[80] Capitalizing on the privacy of the home, video technology supercharged domestic space with romantic and erotic possibilities.

In this milieu, viewers could craft a "*very* personally designed double bill," thus avoiding a "wash-out" date in front of TV and its fixed schedule. Curation meant the ability to choose the type of "thrill" desired: horror films for "cozy[ing] up and shar[ing] scares," X-rated fare like *The Devil in Miss Jones* (1973) or "Hollywood's steamier offerings," like *Body Heat* (1981) for sexual arousal, or "nostalgia nights" that feature people's "most beloved movies" and the opportunity to program, as one possibility, a "Bogie night."[81] Such articles depicted both video's facility at allowing viewers to craft the emotional contours of their romantic encounter and the central place of films in this experience. As one critic noted, while movies "have always been indispensable allies in the pursuit of love," video transformed the old romantic saying, "They're playing our song" into "They're playing our film."[82] Video added "a new element to Valentine's Day . . . rivalling traditional flowers, candy, and cards" by "stirring up the fires of romance [in] a snug room [with] some of the greatest love stories ever put on film."[83] Moreover, couples did not have to fight crowds by going out to movie theaters or restaurants; they could "create [their] own *Casablanca* at home" with "flickering candles, some sensuous food, a bottle of rich, aromatic wine—and their VCR." Whether "in (or out of) their sexiest loungewear," they had "the luxury of celebrating in the warmth and comfort of their own homes without spending a sheik's ransom."[84]

Valentine's Day thus furnished an opportunity to persuade audiences about the connections among video, the home, and romance. Along with the technology's association with privacy and individual choice, the press emphasized how easily films on video could be incorporated into the holiday's expected romantic expressions and surrounding consumer culture, with video rental accompanying candles, food, wine, and wardrobe as means of mixing consumption and eros. Video supplied a financial bonus as well: couples could celebrate without the expense and inconvenience of a night out on the town. Through such discourses, films slipped into the staging of the holiday's intimacies.

As another part of these discourses, the press and other organizations identified films that could successfully function as movie valentines. In a larger media environment with film content also offered by traditional TV, cable and satellite TV, and movie theaters, their best-of lists provided a means of navigating this terrain for video consumers. Lists, finite and value-laden, function as cultural techniques able to make sense of "the vastness of mass culture" by generating distinctions through acts of taste.[85] As Valentine's Day best-of lists were drawn from the writer's own favorites or from polls of fellow reviewers or readers, critics operated as *reputational entrepreneurs;* that is, they shaped the aesthetic and cultural renown of select films by disseminating taste hierarchies and commentaries to their publics.[86] Pieces such as "Eighties-Style Valentines: Old Movies Can Put Romance in Your VCR" or "A Movie Lovers' Guide: Just the Two of You, a Darkened Room . . . and a Classic Romance on the VCR" indicated that classical-era Hollywood films had a place in holiday taste formations.[87]

Best-of Lists and the Cult Canon

Casablanca was christened a movie valentine through different kinds of best-of-list schemata, ranging in style and approach from capsule summary blurbs to detailed analyses. Via capsule summaries, Leonard Maltin, a one-time critic on *Entertainment Tonight* (CBS, 1981–) and author of best-selling TV movie and video guides,[88] published a Valentine's Day list in *Ladies Home Journal* in

1993. Entitled "Leonard Maltin's Ten Most Romantic Movies," this article was dominated by classical-era films. Maltin ranked *Casablanca* first, describing it simply as, "You must remember this triple Oscar–winning romance. Humphrey Bogart, Ingrid Bergman. A café called Rick's."[89] In different articles similarly focused on naming the top ten most romantic films—ten apparently being an ideal number for these lists, given its promise of brevity, readability, and memorability—*Cosmopolitan* called *Casablanca* "the most famous love triangle in cinematic history," while the *Cincinnati Enquirer* praised it as "the movies' greatest doomed romance."[90] Critics attempting to set the romantic scene more broadly also mentioned the film, urging readers to design Valentine's Day around older films by taking out "the dinner jacket or peignoir," setting "the mood with *Casablanca, Gone with the Wind,* or *Wuthering Heights*" and voicing "the classic toast, 'Here's looking at you kid.'"[91] Readers might serve a bottle of Mumm champagne for the occasion—the "champagne Humphrey Bogart poured for Ingrid Bergman in *Casablanca*"—and toast with, "This could be the beginning of a beautiful friendship."[92]

Through similarly telegraphic means, the list's curatorial advice offered readers a comparison of romances according to emotions, explicitness, or themes. Couples could choose "the kind of love story [they] want to see—doomed and overheated *(Body Heat),* comic (*The African Queen* [1951]), classic *(Casablanca),* slavishly traditional *(An Officer and a Gentleman),* violent (*Bonnie and Clyde* [1967]), or simply cornball (*Love Story* [1970]).[93] Critics also urged those interested in star-crossed "tasteful, passionate, and all-consuming" films to select titles by degrees of explicitness, ranging from "sweet ones" like *Casablanca* and *Gone with the Wind* to "hot ones" like *The Devil in Miss Jones.* Others, classifying romances according to their themes, saw *Casablanca*'s worthiness for Valentine's Day as hinging on its central romantic concepts: the "Great Romantic Theme" where Ilsa and Rick pretend to despise each other while "generating enough 'steam' to 'unwrinkle' ties"; the "Noble Parting" in which "sacrifice trumps love"; and "Doomed Lovers," where Bogart and Bergman part in "delicious melancholy."[94]

Assertions about the film's quality circulated throughout these comments. In "The Ten Most Romantic Movies on Video," *Redbook*'s Amy Hufft agreed with the general consensus that *Casablanca* was not only a great romance but also "arguably the best Hollywood film ever made." She remarked that "this Humphrey Bogart–Ingrid Bergman classic is a bona fide three-hankie affair. Set in Casablanca against the backdrop of WWII, Bogie plays the curmudgeonly owner of an expatriate café, seemingly out only for his own good. But when his love for the beautiful Ilsa—and her devotion to war hero Victor Laszlo—is revealed through the brilliant use of flashbacks, his ultimate sacrifice shows *him* to be the real hero."[95] Another wrote, "Does it need any more kudos? No, but what the hell. One-man-island Rick Blaine (Bogart) finds the spark for his buried idealism when eternal flame Ilsa (Bergman) comes into his gin joint . . . The movie is about how we keep coming back, as romantics and as viewers, and how love inspires us to do greater things."[96]

In an epic chronicle in *Redbook,* "You Must Remember Bliss," Judith Viorst chooses the "10 Most Romantic Movies," offering her observations on how *Casablanca,* her number-one selection, became a Valentine's Day favorite:

> It's World War II, and Rick's café, in the teeming city of Casablanca, is a den of intrigue where people desperate to escape the Germans will do anything to get out of town. Humphrey Bogart is Rick, a cool, impassive man who avoids politics and often proclaims, "I stick my neck out for nobody" although he's much more decent than he pretends. Ingrid Bergman is Ilsa, the beautiful wife of a brave Resistance leader who must get to America to continue making the world safe for democracy. Rick and Ilsa once loved each other in Paris, and whenever their eyes meet—with such intensity! With their song, "As Time Goes By," swelling in the background!—it's clear that they love each other still. But Ilsa has broken Rick's heart (for honorable reasons, but he doesn't realize how honorable until much later) and he is bitter. The dilemma: will he help them to escape? I adore this movie—it's the ultimate duty-over-love flick. I know Rick and Ilsa belong together, if anyone on earth ever did, but I fight back tears and accept the fact that Ilsa's husband needs her by his side. In the fogbound airport of Casablanca, in a scene so charged with emotion that I could see it a thousand times and tremble each time, Rick, having arranged their escape, bids Ilsa goodbye. "I'm no good at being noble," etc. "We'll always have Paris," etc. Then, touching her chin in a gallant farewell, he speaks the super-cool words that were always his way of telling her he loved her: "Here's looking at you, kid." Okay, so it's not poetry—but, God, it's romantic![97]

Both the brief and more developed encomiums crystallize the film's romantic components, albeit through different tactics. Lists deploying blurbs variably identified the film's core appeal as a romance, deeming it alternately classic, sweet, steamy, morally virtuous, and satisfyingly tragic. In each case, the film furnished the opportunity to promote specific affective qualities that made it a ranked choice for holiday viewing, based on the columnists' logic that the romantic emotions elicited by the right movie on video would create a premium experience of the holiday. Moreover, in this kind of review, the list, already a form of shorthand, uses the blurb, another form of shorthand, to aesthetic ends: critics presume that audiences are familiar with the film's story and reputation as both classic and romance. This "already-arrived" status materializes further in *Casablanca*'s use as a reference point for staging Valentine's Day celebrations, as readers are advised to create their own *Casablanca* at home through choices of clothing, drink, and toasts featuring film dialogue.

These aspects of holiday discourse define the film as a gold standard of filmmaking and film romance, a standing so well-known that it requires no mention, although, of course, this observation leads to mentioning it again ("Does it need any more kudos? No, but what the hell."). That *Casablanca* features "probably the most famous doomed lovers in screen history and the most effective love theme in history" is something "just about everybody knows."[98] Identifying a film's place in the romantic pantheon as a matter of common sense—something that almost goes without saying—elevates it to the lofty realm of cultural knowledge and competence. This standing is part of the reason critics trade off of *Casablanca*'s elements for article titles (e.g., "You Must Remember Bliss" from "As Time Goes By" lyrics "You must remember this"), borrowing from the film's fame to draw readers and announce their own savvy tastes, while contributing further to the film's renown in their capacity as reputational entrepreneurs. With their swift and succinct communication style, blurbs thus portrayed *Casablanca* as an iconic film and exemplar of romance that, through assumed collective wisdom, merited a strong ranking in the holiday hierarchy.

More developed commentaries provided descriptions of plot, character, and types of romantic affect that resonated with generic formulas of romance that had a foothold in postwar popular culture. This formula, according to John Cawelti, focused on the "development of a love relationship, usually between a man and a woman," confronted by dangers and challenges to the moral order arising from socially or historically charged settings that trouble and then bond the couple. Marriage or the bond's dissolution, sometimes in the form of death, are typical outcomes. In the end, moral order is restored, and the love relationship—no matter whether the couple is together or torn apart—achieves transcendent value that exalts the lovers. This romantic formula, then, fulfills both romantic and moral fantasies, providing emotionally satisfying closure to the love and social/historical plots within an ethos of moral restitution.[99]

Casablanca's cinematic dimensions inform responses to its romance beyond this kind of formula: the charisma of beautifully photographed and dressed stars, Rick and Ilsa's loaded exchange of glances, dramatic moments such as the climax's airport scene, swelling music and "As Time Goes By," and dialogue like "Here's looking at you, kid." Yet, the genre's formula illuminates narrative and thematic elements that course through recommendations. Appraisals of *Casablanca* foreground Rick and Ilsa's romance as the film's nucleus, with WWII serving as the historical conflict that threatens their love and provides the ultimate moral proving ground of their relationship. Victor ostensibly furnishes the romantic conflict, but he is mainly a human embodiment of the war's stakes (as a "war hero" and "brave Resistance leader"). Critics say little about the war, indicating that its main function here lies in the friction it causes in the central relationship and the moral salvation it ultimately offers. When Viorst writes that *Casablanca* is the "ultimate duty-over-love flick," she encapsulates such sentiments concerning the film's emphasis on romantic sacrifice in the name of honor. In the romantic view, *Casablanca* develops from a state of romantic and historical disorder to one that confirms the authentic and lasting nature of Rick and Ilsa's affections ("We'll always have Paris"), while renewing moral order in a weepy and uplifting conclusion: at the airport, Ilsa stays with her husband and escapes to safety; Rick joins the Allied cause. Although the central couple parts at the end, their relationship achieves a transcendent value in this interface of romantic and moral fantasies. Video box art privileges the couple, the setting, and the final airport scene, echoing these readings of the film's narrative (fig. 18).

Casablanca's romantic backbone—the love triangle involving Rick, Ilsa, and Ilsa's husband, Laszlo—has long been recognized as key to its appeal.[100] In the Valentine's Day cult, it becomes *Casablanca*'s dominant feature and organizing principle of appropriation. As in any process of configuring texts to serve specific interpretations, filmic properties falling outside the dominion of the couple are minimized or absent. This includes the film's major plot points of WWII conflicts between the Nazis and Allies, including the singing of "La Marseillaise," that participants in the Bogart cult found so irresistible. Subplots, characters beyond the three romantic protagonists, and quotes from characters popular in other circles, such as the importance that Renault (Claude Rains) and his witty repartee once had to the Bogart cult, fall outside this discussion as well.

These exclusions are an intimate part of how *Casablanca,* adapted to a new media platform and function, achieved cult and canonical identities as a

FIGURE 18. VHS Special Edition (MGM Home Entertainment Inc. and Turner Entertainment Co., 1992). Author's collection.

romance. Moreover, Valentine's Day recommendations articulated 1980s and 1990s social debates that further informed the ramifications of the film's framing as holiday cult. With coverage of movie valentines focused primarily on gender, critics used the optic on the past afforded by classical Hollywood romances to discuss concerns that ranged from cinema's morality to female desire.

Old Romances in New Worlds

Those producing best-of Valentine's Day rankings were at times aware of the classical film's backwardness in social mores, especially because of the impact of second-wave feminism in the 1960s and 1970s. Some regarded old romances as "antifeminist" in their depictions of gender, observing that in "today's light" *Casablanca* has "misogynistic, patronizing moments ('You'll have to think for the both of us, Rick, because I'm just a confused little girl')." But, quoting from the song, this writer nevertheless insisted that "the fundamental things apply, as time goes by." The film "is so well written that it still holds up, still puts a lump in your throat." The fact that "all these decades later . . . a song can evoke such pain and longing keeps *Casablanca* as affecting as ever."[101] Such lists presented *Casablanca* and other older titles as excusably anachronistic, arguing that their emotional strengths offset any retrograde sentiments.

More frequently, commentary accompanying lists simply turned the historical tables by claiming that vintage films were morally superior to newer films. Alterations in Hollywood's censorship codes after WWII allowed more explicit depictions of sex and violence that, along with other phenomena like X-rated films and their video reissues, provided an influential framework for reevaluating oldies produced when earlier versions of these codes forbade graphic content. This perspective was additionally informed by the conservative aura of the Reagan and Bush years and an empowered New Right, a super-conservative amalgam of political actors fueled in part in the 1960s and 1970s by the abortion debates and the women's movement.[102] This convergence sparked clashes between feminist calls for equality and sexual freedom for women and the New Right's opposition to abortion and desire to return to old-fashioned gender roles represented, for them, by TV series like *Father Knows Best* (CBS, 1954–55, 1958–60; NBC, 1955–58).

Unlike *Body Heat* and *Dressed to Kill* (1980), classical-era movies on Valentine's Day lists had no explicit nudity, sex, or violence. In contrast to 1980s and 1990s cinema, in which "anatomy and hydraulics" had become "de rigueur to any film about men and women," older movies defined "romance in a way no other popular medium has achieved. . . . The less you saw, the more you felt."[103] One critic mused, "Wouldn't it be lovely if we could take from romantic old movies some of the things that modern romance has chucked: love's slow unfolding . . . eloquence . . . and sweetness [and] perhaps most important of all [its] redemptive power?"[104] Another cannot understand the female protagonist's decision to let the male protagonist achieve his wish to drink himself to death in *Leaving Las Vegas* (1995), asking incredulously, "Is this supposed to be a loving thing to do?" By comparison, *Casablanca*'s wartime lovers "amounted to more than a hill of beans."[105] Here successful film romance and romantic sentiment itself are only achieved by excluding sexually explicit material and embracing a recognizable and honorable moral code.[106] Such observations posed "sexy movies" and romantic movies as mutually exclusive categories.[107]

Viorst commented more pointedly about the romantic and moral alternatives classic titles presented to contemporary movies and life: "They say romance is dead, but I say it's alive and well—in old movies." Accordingly, her top ten picks are all classical-era films from Hollywood and Great Britain. Of these she writes:

> When real life seems too crazy and complicated, snuggle up, hold hands, and watch one of these four-handkerchief classics, sure to restore your faith in true love, simple values, and happy endings. It may be the most entertaining marriage therapy you'll ever have. Among the many things that I adore about these movies is their focus on courtship rather than consummation. Men and women fall in love before they fall into bed and they rarely fall into bed till they march to the altar, and I (breathing heavy) get to savor the flirting, the touching, the very first kiss—all that foreplay! Now I'm not knocking consummation, but modern movies (and life) get us there too fast. And race us by the romantic yearning and burning of these tantalizing courtships.... But it isn't only love that's getting talked about in these movies. There's ... noble, high-minded stuff as well. Which brings me to the next things I adore about old movies—the willingness to give up love for honor, to forsake individual happiness for duty.... I guess I must also confess that I find romantic old movies romantic because they hark back to a temptingly simpler era when women were women and men were men and, while most of the time I wouldn't want to return to the old arrangements between the sexes, these movies allow me the entertaining fantasy that those old arrangements once worked out just fine.[108]

Classical Hollywood films thus represent simple values versus complex contemporary realities, courtship versus sex, love and moral uplift versus individual satisfaction, and traditional versus changing gender roles. Romantic oldies from roughly eighty years ago do not present outdated concepts of romance or relationships; rather, they incarnate these concepts *because* of their anachronisms, portrayed here as rooted in their nonexplicit intimacies and gender legacies.

Whereas once Rick and Ilsa's adultery was a more contentious issue for film censors and wartime audiences and, a few years later, Bergman's real-life extramarital affair with filmmaker Roberto Rossellini and ensuing pregnancy scandalized the nation and banished her for a time from Hollywood, the video era interpreted their sex scene within different parameters.[109] In Rick's apartment above his café, he and Ilsa verbally renew their love for one another and kiss, but no other onscreen sexual contact is shown. A brief temporal ellipsis stands in for sex (a *Playboy* article in the 1980s raunchily filled in this gap),[110] and Rick's later indirect statement to Laszlo about Ilsa further indicates a liaison. As was customary in censored classical-era films, *Casablanca* expresses eros through implication, placing it on the side of feeling rather than seeing (unlike contemporaneous "sexy" movies) in a sensory register these discussions often privileged. Sublimated under the category of romantic affect, the characters' adulterous liaison is displaced in importance by other concerns about morality. In this same scene, Rick assures a confused Ilsa that he will take command of the situation, with his decision-making resulting in a sacrifice of their relationship for the war effort. Along with elliptical sex, this moment delivers the conventional gender roles and noble morality that columnists saw as key to generating romantic feelings for the holiday.

As lists ranking reissued oldies reacted to the times by responding to perceived problems with then contemporary cinema, they also used movie valentines to negotiate larger issues of sexuality and romance. Press accounts were caught up in debates about feminism, with some writers depicting female sexual liberation as an unwelcome challenge to the nuclear family, particularly to deep-seated ideologies of the family that privileged male authority and normalized female subordination.

Because film recommendations and guides wanted to sell the holiday and videos without alienating readers, commentary on gender politics was subtle. In posing oldies as superior to 1980s and 1990s films—as portals to "a temptingly simpler era when women were women and men were men"—this commentary often indirectly questioned feminism. At the same time, commentary might lean into misogyny, an attitude fueled by the holiday's perceived femininity. Conveyed through a comic writerly tone, this kind of reaction portrayed men as a beleaguered collective in the face of the demands of this occasion or otherwise conveyed the sexual difference that pervaded it. Headlines addressed to men, such as "Valentine's Day Is Monday, and the Pressure Is On. Be Romantic—or Else" furnish a picture of the romantically challenged male.[111] A *San Francisco Chronicle* article by Mick LaSalle and Ruthe Stein, "He Says, She Says," portrayed masculinity and femininity more explicitly as a matter of opposing tastes. The critics developed separate lists of the ten most romantic movies for Valentine's Day "on the theory that men and women may have different opinions on the subject." They also supplied counsel to couples arguing about the best romances to rent, advising men to "Give in. It's the only way to win." In terms of gender and taste, Stein asks of films like *The Clock* (1945), "what woman hasn't dreamed of being wanted that much?" While she selects films that gratify a woman's desire to be desired by men, LaSalle chooses films that invite viewers to be the desirers. He describes *Erotique* (1994), an anthology of films by directors such as Lizzie Borden, as "sometimes idiotic, but sexy enough that you might not make it through the whole thing."[112]

As a holiday devoted to the overt exchange of romantic sentiments, Valentine's Day at this time allowed truisms about men and women to flow, confirming presumptions about sexual difference that coursed through the everyday. As allegedly nonromantic, men had to be nudged into responsibility for the holiday's successful execution, with the vague threat of women making them pay if they failed. Furthermore, classical Hollywood and contemporary films are once again divided into contrasting categories of romantic and sexy, with the female critic preferring older films in which sexuality is sublimated into romantic expression and the male opting for contemporary films that unambiguously generate sexual feelings.

In this sphere of differentiated taste, *Casablanca* emerged as a safe ground for couples. The film was "a celebration of love that both men and women can partake in equally" because "love is played off against responsibility and courage and sacrifice." *Casablanca* was a rare "gold standard in chick flicks that men can go ga-ga for too"[113]—its categorization as a chick flick indicating how close critics perceived its ties to the romance genre and a feminized holiday to be. It is "saved," however, from total feminization by its more serious concerns: a love story infused with the verities of responsibility, courage, and sacrifice. Although, as we have seen, women also gravitated to the "love versus duty" theme, men were assured that the film was not simple romantic fodder with a strictly female appeal, an implicit diminishment of female tastes.

The stirrings of gender wars in Valentine's Day recommendations were part of cultural conversations about movies and romance, especially in women's magazines that featured relationship-oriented articles. Magazines interpreted movie conventions as a way to understand romantic intimacies. A *Ladies Home Journal* piece addressed the convention of "meeting cute" in film romances, in which couples encounter one another for the first time in unusual ways, as a lead-in to interviews with real-life couples about how they met. *Casablanca* serves as an example in Rick and Ilsa's surprise reencounter with each other as Sam plays, "As Time Goes By."[114] More pedagogically,

Cosmopolitan published a short story, "Casablanca Farewell," about a single professional woman who, on the eve of her twenty-ninth birthday, is having "another night alone in New York City." Stopping in a café after work, she has been "soaked by a late spring rain" and is sipping "bitter coffee," recalling a noir scenario, when she is approached by a man who asks her out for a drink. She initially replies, "I have a date to see *Casablanca*" on TV but relents and joins him. Having already had a heartbreaking affair with a married man and remembering her horoscope from earlier that day—"Beware of a new romance"—she figures that he is married and, after substantial indecision, decides to go home. Disappointed, he puts her in a cab. While the cabbie waits, he kisses her and remarks, "This could have been the beginning of a beautiful friendship" (fig. 19). She reminds him that Bogart put Bergman on a plane as the noble thing to do. She leaves, seeking the "safe refuge of a cab" and her TV rendezvous with *Casablanca*.[115]

The film is referenced here not for a feel-good story about meeting cute but for a morality lesson about the romantic plight and general unhappiness of the single working woman—a figure often invoked in the antifeminist imagination for her representation of female success and sexuality outside the traditional nuclear family. While *Cosmopolitan* was famous at this time for selling stories about sex in and outside marriage to female audiences, this particular entry strikes a more conservative note.[116] In a narrative saturated with the heroine's sense of vulnerability and despondency as she approaches thirty, she is lonely, rain-drenched, and drinking bad coffee, left only with married men as potential intimate partners and a televised movie about romance as her sole true companion. The illustration, designed to attract readers to a story of impossible or forbidden love, seems to suggest otherwise. It draws from *Casablanca*'s dramatic airport parting of Ilsa and Rick while summoning the windswept iconography of attractive white heterosexual people verging on passion that was a Harlequin Romance staple at the time. Both references and the noirish setting at the story's outset, though, operate as foils that demonstrate how far the story's working woman is from transcendent love. She parts from her date for sensible reasons, based not so much on ethics as on the desire to spare herself the inevitable pain of insufficient commitment from a married man. But she experiences no rewarding uplift even on these terms: the man is a cad, and she is socially isolated once more, the movie the only salve for her loneliness. "*Casablanca* Farewell" is thus a cautionary tale to single professional women about the treacheries of dating, wherein choosing to work is the same as choosing to be alone. Since women's

FIGURE 19. Illustration from "Casablanca Farewell" by Nora Burns. *Cosmopolitan,* May 1979, 357.

access to professions and to equal pay was and remains a feminist tenet, this scare story about the heroine's misery contributes to a backlash against feminism that, according to Susan Faludi, characterized the 1980s and 1990s under conservative administrations, a point to which I will soon return.

Feminists also deployed classical Hollywood movies as object-lessons for contemporary life. In another *Cosmopolitan* piece, Nancy Friday and several colleagues critique the problematic gender asymmetry produced by the social appropriation of movie fantasies about relationships. They focus on older movies' emphasis on sexual tension—their interplay of "physical attraction and deliberate restraint"—as the fundamental component of screen romance. They revise the idea that such romances were chiefly women's pictures, arguing instead that "truly classic films in American cinema—*Casablanca, Gone with the Wind,* and *Notorious* (1946)—had substantial male audiences." Friday et al. argue that the ideal these films offered of romantic couples that are "handsome, vital, in love, stimulated by each other and everything around them" should be everyone's ideal. But society encourages women to "dream about it," while men "are conditioned to play it down." Consequently, "both sides lose."[117] The films are not at fault for producing fantasies about sex and desire; rather, socially conditioned notions of gender spin the fantasies as appealing to women and not to men, resulting in disparate expectations about relationships.

Valentine's Day lists and this other kind of cultural commentary employ old Hollywood films to express anxieties around women's emerging and established identities, particularly their relationship to men and sex. These films can either fuel traditional ideas about this relationship or, as in Friday et al.'s view, represent an aspirational ideal for both genders. In each case, commentary again distinguishes classical-era films from their contemporary counterparts through the romance/explicit sex dichotomy, a dichotomy further developed in other discourses.

In 1985, Ann Landers (the pen name of Esther Lederer), a well-known media personality who authored a nationally syndicated newspaper advice column read by millions, asked her female readers, "Would you be content to be held close and treated tenderly and forget about 'the act'?" Reportedly, one hundred thousand women replied, almost as many as had responded to a question Landers once posed to them about the possibility of nuclear war. To the sex survey, 72 percent replied in the affirmative; they would indeed rather "be hugged than you-know-what." In preferring to be "cuddled," they "declared themselves willing to forgo intercourse for affection." Reasons varied, from the messiness of sex to the lack of men's lovemaking skills.[118] News outlets quoted Landers as saying, "The importance of sex is overrated. . . . Women want affection. They want to feel valued. Apparently, having sex alone doesn't give them [that] feeling. . . . [Meanwhile many men] are using sex as a physical release and it has no more emotional significance than a sneeze."[119] Although Landers's survey partly faults men for this state of affairs, it suggests that, even under the best circumstances, women are averse to sex and want just to be "cuddled."

Her findings caused a public hubbub. They elicited misogynistic reaction, wherein columnists conducted surveys of married men that found some frustrated by their "cold, unresponsive, and fat wives."[120] More progressively, sex experts chided Landers for embracing 1950s ideologies that viewed women not as sexually desirous and as having a "morally correct" aversion to sex.[121] Furthermore, her work arrived in the wake of more positive surveys on female sexuality inspired by the 1960s and 1970s sexual revolution and the women's movement. In the 1970s, *Redbook* and *Cosmopolitan* queried their female readers via questionnaires about their attitudes toward sex, discovering that numerous respondents actively invested in and experimented with sex. With a title that pointedly contrasts with Landers's later findings, feminists Carole Tavris and Susan Sadd published *The Redbook Report on Female Sexuality: 100,000 Married Women Disclose the Good News about Sex.*[122]

Landers's work signaled the contentiousness and reactionary retrenchment that social developments around female sexuality and women's rights could elicit. As Faludi argues in *Backlash,* the 1980s witnessed a strong adverse reaction to feminism and its calls for equality in professional and personal spheres. During the Reagan and Bush presidencies and the New Right's surge, multiple forces sought to undermine feminism and distort its principles through actions that ranged from legal cases against *Roe v. Wade* to antifeminist myths generated in popular culture. As Faludi contends, such myths blamed feminism (rather than patriarchy) for women's unhappiness, defining it as antifamily and pathologizing professional women. Hollywood produced films in this vein, most infamously *Fatal Attraction* (1987), with its unhinged single professional woman intent on destroying her lover's family, but also in romance films like *An Officer and a Gentleman* that elevated marriage as the ultimate female goal.[123]

Returning to *Casablanca* and classical-era movie valentines in this context: columnists, in opposing explicit films to old Hollywood's sublimated sex and embracing the classics as a fantasy retreat to a time of traditional gender roles, expressed their appreciation of these romances in terms that corresponded to conservative reactions against feminism. Making this connection overt, reporter Stephen Hunter references Landers's survey when he remarks that "love stories in old Hollywood movies" meant the "less you see, the more you feel," especially for the "seventy percent of American women who would rather be cuddled than caressed."[124] Another commented similarly: "The new romance isn't what it used to be and the shift in romantic and sexual attitudes is reflected in books, movies, and videos. Today's woman, however, still craves old-fashioned love."[125] Holiday discourses about romance thereby tended to suppress notions of liberated female sexual desire, offering instead more culturally normative forms of romantic longing and gender roles as what women wanted.

Hence, through Valentine's Day lists and cultural commentary, *Casablanca*'s standing as cult elicited aesthetic and cultural value freighted with romantic emotion and negotiations of gender and sexuality. As this kind of consecration defined the film by emphasizing its nonexplicit doomed-lovers romance and moral rectitude, it became a 1980s and 1990s movie equivalent of a vintage paper valentine. Cultural forces envisaged it as an artifact of a purer time, free of the challenges to human relationships that the modern period witnessed, a fantasy construction based on its representation of an old order around gender. Critics offered classical Hollywood cinema as performing a quasi-therapeutic function for modern audiences, claiming it furnished soothing pictures of the seemingly true nature of romance and chaste female desire in the face of a contemporary culture weighing the impact of second-wave feminism, the sexual revolution, and the promise of liberated women and equitable gender roles.[126] These recommendations thus entered a cultural fray about intimacy in debates about female desire in a conservative climate that pitted a "celebrated past" against a "devalued present."[127]

Mass-media institutions of consecration assumed the function not only of institutions of intimacy but also of institutions of memory. Like other platforms of reissue, home video invited the work of memory institutions because it fostered repeated encounters with the past as a signature element of its cultural impact. Here, the "prosthetic" memories produced by institutions of consecration and intimacy around older reissues encouraged viewers to assimilate a slice of history often beyond their experience as part of their personal repertoire, offering them affective relief from contemporary conflicts through an imagined past.[128] This official mode of memory commodified nostalgia as a desirable emotion as well as an aesthetic lens with which to appreciate the classics.[129] Of course, this mode is one among others affiliated with holiday cult. Holiday films are potentially turbocharged with emotion, generating different modes of memory in their annual pilgrimage through time, including those drawn from personal histories and experiences elicited by the holiday's return.

In their early history, mainstream press Valentine's Day lists, as part of a cultural infrastructure that defined cinema in relation to concepts of romance, charted an aesthetic that was delimited and homogeneous. Because lists are ordered chronicles of culture that are "closed systems," they "set the rules of the game" by defining what does and does not "count."[130] As a sign of this, lists often appeared in magazines, like *Cosmopolitan,* that focused on white women defined as heterosexual for their illustrations and modes of address, while their holiday recommendations emphasized Hollywood films with white heterosexual central characters. If, as Berlant contends, institutions of intimacy build worlds that create spaces for some and usurp those "meant for other kinds of relations,"[131] 1980s and 1990s lists produced visions of love and passion on racial and sexual grounds.

By the later 1990s and early 2000s, however, partly informed by third-wave feminism's commitments to intersectionality, the growing public acceptance of homosexuality, and the continuing activism of civil rights movements, best-of lists targeted diverse audiences for Valentine's Day, championing films with protagonists and story lines representing other races and sexual preferences. In this milieu, *Casablanca* remained on numerous best-of lists but also often disappeared from view, its place as seasonal cult no longer affirmed.

Valentine's Day Cult in the 2000s

In recent years, repertory houses and TCM have continued to program *Casablanca* as a Valentine's Day favorite.[132] Holiday lists have also continued to proliferate in relation to video reissues, now in the form of DVD, Blu-ray, and streaming. While acknowledging the substantial changes in media technologies, the mediascape, and society that characterize the 2000s, this final section considers how elements of *Casablanca*'s seasonal cult identity have both persisted and changed in holiday discourses surrounding digital video rereleases. Notably, the earlier decades' cultural battles regarding gender that spoke through holiday recommendations of classical-era films dissipate in favor of other priorities. *Casablanca*'s more recent circulation as seasonal cult involves its multiple canonical identities, its modernization in relation to new media, and its diminishment or exclusion in favor of titles exhibiting diversity. Given online social networks' imperative to "send small content morsels out . . . to generate clicks, shares, and views," listing itself has become more pervasive.[133]

Certain Valentine's Day rankings perpetuate tradition, drawing from earlier times in terms of the tropes of romantic home viewing, classical-era cinema favorites, and the filmic characteristics they see as significant to the holiday's celebration. Critics advise viewers to avoid the downsides of a public date on Valentine's Day by choosing to watch a movie at home so that they can create the ultimate romantic scene—snuggling up with a significant other, lighting candles, enjoying food and drink, and basking in "the warm glow of the TV set."[134] Titles that had been consecrated as movie valentines, like *Casablanca, Wuthering Heights,* and *Roman Holiday* (1953), are in steady rotation, while sources continue to provide a vernacular typology of films to connect viewers to desired emotions.[135]

In these circles, *Casablanca* has maintained its vaunted place as a cult holiday film, bundled with its identities as a romance and a classic. As a critic remarked in a 2019 Valentine's Day piece, "*Casablanca* is the GOAT [greatest of all time]. Game respects game."[136] Sources salute the film through elements long repeated in Valentine's Day commentary: "Among video rentals, *Casablanca* is the hands-down winner as the greatest romance ever to hit the screen. Start with the beautiful Ingrid Bergman, throw in the hard-boiled but vulnerable Humphrey Bogart, add an exotic locale, play "As Time Goes By," and you have the quintessential love story. The night scene in Rick's when Bogie tells Dooley Wilson to play it again is classic, but still doesn't match the power of the classic goodbye scene at the airfield. 'Here's looking at you, kid.'"[137] The lead performers' appeal, the song, and iconic scenes and lines again provide the ingredients of a canonized romance, while the film also emerges as the greatest film in history. Already having a dual identity as both cult and mainstream, *Casablanca* gains additional layers of value through the mutually reinforcing statuses offered by these other "best-of" categories.

Along with news stories, renowned consecrating institutions boosted the film's standing as a canonized classic and romance. The first selection of films for the newly created National Film Registry in 1989 included *Casablanca,* giving it the official imprimatur of a classic heritage film. In 2002, the AFI conducted a poll among its members asking them to name their top romantic films—an approach that gave the weight of professional recognition and consensus to the selections.[138] The results were published as "AFI's 100 Years . . . 100 Passions," a ranked list of the best one hundred films in this category.[139] In keeping with its national mission, the AFI intended this list to represent "the complex, cinematic tales of the heart that have become an abiding part of American film history," placing romances within US heritage. Movies from each decade made the list, but classical-era films scored the top five positions: *Casablanca* was number one, followed by *Gone with the Wind, West Side Story* (1961), *Roman Holiday,* and *An Affair to Remember* (1957). This poll was part of a family of AFI polls that had become familiar parts of the mediascape. In 1977, ten years after its creation, the organization compiled its first list of the greatest American films: *Gone with the Wind* ranked number one, followed by *Citizen Kane* and *Casablanca.* The AFI's best-of lists reached a crescendo as cinema's centennial approached. In 1998, it designed "AFI's 100 Years . . . 100 Movies" to commemorate cinema's momentous anniversary by once again identifying the greatest Hollywood films ever produced. *Casablanca* ranked second behind *Citizen Kane* and before *The Godfather* (1972), with *Gone with the Wind* falling to fourth place.[140] Meanwhile, in another celebratory list, the AFI's voters declared Bogart the all-time number one male star and Bergman the number four female star.

In these activities, the AFI functioned as a powerful reputational entrepreneur with the authority, visibility, and resources to produce and distribute its consecrating discourses.[141] CBS televised each of these later polls' results in TV specials with star-hosts (Candice Bergen emceed "AFI's 100 Years . . . 100 Passions"). The shows proceeded in countdown fashion, beginning with the one hundredth title and ending with the first. This mode of presentation created suspense about which films or stars would land at the top, infusing their selection with show business glamor and aesthetic gravitas, while positioning the AFI as the gala tastemaker. Within this conspicuous celebration of the industry, *Casablanca*'s status as the best romance and one of the top five greatest films in history and Bogart and Bergman's high standings in the stardom poll enshrined them and one of their signature films as enduring examples of Hollywood's finest achievements.[142] This cross-consolidation of *Casablanca*'s reputation is further accentuated by the listing of "100 Films . . . 100 Passions" on the AFI's website. As the site enumerates the most outstanding romances, a gold star graphically identifies those titles that are also ranked in the AFI's greatest films poll.

Casablanca's canonical standings are thus compounded, with one standing amplifying and justifying another until the best-of ranking in each category attains an unquestionable legitimacy. The film's very definition as seasonal cult rests on an amalgam of canons difficult to separate into isolated identities, suggesting how riven cult titles, especially those with long histories of circulation, may be with polyvalent statuses.

Yet popular immortals are not immune to what Pierre Bourdieu calls "social aging," wherein works are devalued through their overfamiliarity or mismatch with contemporary standards.[143] Unlike the VCR years that embraced *Casablanca*'s age as a distinct merit, its recent uptake in certain Valentine's Day commentary related to DVD/Blu-ray reissue and streaming offers insight into how seasonal cult films can become or verge on becoming relics.

Some lists implicitly registered social aging as an issue. *Casablanca* fell to lower-ranked positions in holiday guides that favored more contemporary fare; for instance, *Ladies Home Journal*'s 2002 "Romance Hall of Fame" readers' poll demoted it in favor of films like *Pretty Woman* (1990). Additionally, in recognition of its vintage, the film served as a historical anchor. Columnists offered historical overviews of romances, explaining that their selections ranged from "the classic *Casablanca* . . . to *Crazy, Rich Asians* (2018)" to highlight the "theme of love [as] one of the most common core themes in film history."[144] The film's inclusion relied on its reputation as a classic and ability, as an aged artifact, to represent the past as part of a temporal record of film romance. *Casablanca*'s pastness also meant, though, that it could generate a quainter self-consciousness about its age and historical value. This kind of evaluation presents *Casablanca,* like an old rock-and-roll song, as "an oldie but goodie," a standard that is a "must-see for any Valentine's movie fan" but is nonetheless dated.[145]

As with the Bogart cult, critics express cult film exhaustion with *Casablanca*'s steadfast Valentine's Day presence. Reporters criticized best-of lists focused on classical Hollywood movies as "old-fashioned" and updated their lists to prioritize more recent fare, like the *Twilight* film series (2008–12). They also suggested that readers forget the always available "classy classics" and opt instead for "quirkier but no less romantic choices," such as *Dead Man Walking* (1995), a film about a nun (Susan Sarandon) and a death row inmate (Sean Penn).[146] *Casablanca* socially ages out of relevance because of perceptions of its over-availability and antiquation, prompting calls for fresher fare to mount a new take on the holiday.

Valentine's Day did occasion attempts to modernize *Casablanca* by bringing it into line with the new streaming protocols.[147] Reporters counseled holiday celebrators to "binge-watch romantic movies until the wee hours of the morning." At almost four hours long, *Gone with the Wind,* an "iconic romance movie that beats all other movies in this genre," constituted its own binge, while *Casablanca,* as one of a number of romances to binge, showed "just how far someone will go for the one they truly love."[148] Conversely, critics argued against binge-watching because it interfered with the desired romantic affect for Valentine's Day. Viewers should instead "cuddle up" with one film like *Casablanca* or *The Princess Bride* (1987).[149]

The most prevalent reason for displacing *Casablanca* from best-of lists, however, arose from the diversification of Valentine's Day recommendations, a tendency energized in earlier lists by the growing number of online critics. *Casablanca* could still find a place on these lists. Indeed, online aggregator of critics' reviews and self-described "recommendation resource" Rotten Tomatoes once named it "the most romantic movie of all time" in its rankings of the "Top 100 Romance Movies," before it was displaced by *It Happened One Night* (1934). Here the film joined the interracial comedy-drama *The Big Sick* (2017), lesbian and gay films like *Carol* (2015) and *Call Me by Your Name* (2017), and *The Shape of Water* (2017), a film featuring a disabled woman, her gay friend, and interspecies love.[150] In this kind of consecration, *Casablanca* was often the only representative of the classical Hollywood era. As such, the intertextual cohort made it look like an odd artifact in the ensemble, implying perhaps the compulsory, reputation-based nature of its inclusion.

Holiday guides might completely eschew classical-era films and their emphasis on white heterosexual couples. The *New York Daily News* included LGBTQ films such as *Blue Is the Warmest Color* (2013), films starring African American performers such as *Carmen Jones* (1954), and Japanese films like *Shall We Dance?* (1996) on its holiday lists.[151] *The Grio,* a website devoted to African American interests, published "10 Black Love Movies to Watch and Chill Valentine's Day Weekend," with *Love Jones* (1997) and *Love and Basketball* (2000) as the number one and number two titles.[152] *Advocate,* an LGBTQ magazine and website, ranked *Brokeback Mountain* (2005) and *Carol* as top choices.[153] Such recommendations show *Casablanca*'s irrelevance for many contemporary viewers, while also demonstrating the important role that shifting dynamics of consecration can play, particularly by the online dissemination of ranked lists in niche and other sources. No amount of canonization guarantees a film's significance for all.

Beyond establishing the continuing prevalence of Valentine's Day film lists in a new media age, these treatments reflect how *Casablanca*'s canonical statuses either gained steam or succumbed to various kinds of social aging. Through the latter lens, critics could keep *Casablanca* in play in relation to present-day technologies and tastes or ignore it. The label "old-fashioned" not only indicated a tired vintage film but also suggested that coverage of the holiday through best-of lists tended to publicize and affirm white heterosexual norms in a way that was out of step with contemporary reality. The 2000s depict a fate for the enduring film that is always possible—that its trajectory of distinction will lead to a "trajectory of extinction," a confrontation between its endurance and "unfavorable conditions" that derail its continued cultural reproduction in certain arenas of consecration.[154]

CONCLUSION

In exploring *Casablanca*'s existence as a cult Valentine's Day film on physical-format video in the 1970s, 1980s, and 1990s, I have examined developments in media industries, video technologies, and markets that informed its successful circulation as an artifact and commodity in these new circumstances. Industry factors enabled and propagated the film's video reissues, while these factors also revealed the popularity and commercial utility of certain older Hollywood films identified as classics on this platform. As we will see more fully in the next chapter, media industries used the classic label as a key means of identifying films from Hollywood's classical era as especially valuable for reissue. This label and the survival in new media markets that it often signified, helped to sustain the visibility of older films, opening them to other kinds of appropriation, including cult appropriation.

Casablanca's identity as cult was forged by mass-media sources that promoted its selection and consumption as a premium Valentine's Day film. Newspaper and magazine reporters defined video's affordances as particularly favorable to celebrating the holiday, specifically as the technology gave consumers the powers of curation so that they could select and watch films to match the nuances of moods appropriate for "snuggling" on Valentine's Day. This technological advantage, coupled with the viewers' ability to enjoy movies in the privacy of their homes, made romantic films playing on VCRs seem like a natural fit for the holiday. The list and associated commentary aimed to shape the intimate dimensions of the technology and experience of movies on home video for Valentine's Day, while also functioning to circulate aesthetic and cultural value for *Casablanca* as a top holiday film. As we have seen, mass media critics mobilized the film's meaning through fantasies of the past elicited in reaction to contemporary social developments. The film became a small soapbox from which to address change around gendered intimacies and femininity, with change presented as a threat rather than a promise. *Casablanca*'s evaluation, then, grew from an intersection among institutions of consecration, intimacy, and memory as they mingled in the banal, everyday form of movie recommendations.

This period of *Casablanca*'s circulation complicated its Valentine's Day cult standing as it flourished in relation to other canons defining the film as a classic and a romance. Although scholars often regard cult identities as singular or exceptional, *Casablanca*'s seasonal cult identity did not simply reside alongside these others but interacted with them as they shared the same space and time of circulation. Together, they created a reciprocal machinery of value-construction, wherein the film's commercial, aesthetic, and cultural worth was confirmed across classic, romance, and cult canons. Although commentary might foreground one identity over others, the film's place in a single system of value drew overtly or implicitly on its compound canonical statuses, on an understanding of its place in a number of aesthetic hierarchies. *Casablanca*'s seasonal cult status, then, involved its continuing fashioning as a classic, a Bogart film, and a romance, with these interpretations and evaluations running parallel to and interfacing with each other. Once a film's temporality is restored, once the terms of its circulation become manifest, it appears as a variable entity that has served multiple and changing interests, potentially accruing numerous canonical identities.

Today the film's seasonal cult standing, understood in this kind of complexity, remains a strong feature of its platforming and circulation. Conversely, this standing also shows wear and tear, whether *Casablanca* is regarded as a historical marker in a lineage of more contemporary choices or disregarded in lists devoted to films with greater diversity and modern pertinence. Films from the past always run the risk of being outdated, meaning that their consecration over long periods, if it occurs, is not a guarantee of life or of appreciation. This facet of the popular immortal's life features most significantly in the displacement of the whiteness and heteronormativity it embodies—an issue I discuss through a different lens in the next chapter.

Aspects of *Casablanca*'s historical existence, however, mitigate against complete exclusion. Although its canonical stature appears timeless in various forms of consecration, its temporality—its vintage and long circulation—are at the heart of its resistance to being forgotten. As Barbara Herrnstein Smith writes, a work's continuous circulation and repeated appearance does not signal its universality but rather an extensive history of having been "thoroughly mediated—evaluated as well as interpreted—*for* us by the very culture and cultural institutions" that have preserved and shaped perceptions of it. Such activities create the appearance of an unassailable orthodoxy around the work.[155] *Casablanca*'s thorough mediation has thus given it a "survival advantage": it has been better preserved than numerous fellow films, extensively reissued, and pervasively referenced. On the one hand, this means that it is more accessible to serve changing social functions and audiences[156] (recall the chapter's opening comparison between Bogart and Valentine's Day cults). On the other hand, this advantage suggests that the diminishment of its seasonal cult status will be partial and that it will resist totalizing trajectories of extinction in this and other canons.

In the chapter that follows, we will see how media industries and critics, particularly from the 1990s to the present, have developed *Casablanca*'s meaning and reputation as a classic in relation to another significant form of reissue: the anniversary celebration. Media industries have coordinated anniversary releases of *Casablanca* across platforms, including special commemorative video editions. These editions involve bonus materials that celebrate the film's birth in 1942 through a compendium of materials chronicling its origins and some of its afterlife. In producing a carefully curated, preferred version of the film's history, these materials raise questions about the nature and influence of institutionally produced histories packaged for entertainment and consumption. By extensively documenting *Casablanca*'s early years, anniversary reissues also bring this book full circle.

FIVE

Happy Anniversaries

CLASSIC CINEMA ON DVD/BLU-RAY IN THE CONGLOMERATE AGE

> Say what you will about Warner's habit of remastering, repackaging, and re-releasing the same films again and again, but it's this practice that grants films like *Casablanca* a fighting chance at immortality.
>
> KENNETH BROWN,
> *Blu-ray.com*, 2012

IN APRIL 1992 TURNER ENTERTAINMENT COMPANY, owner of *Casablanca* (1942), staged a gala "repremiere" of the film at New York's Museum of Modern Art (MoMA), attended by luminaries like company founder Ted Turner; his partner, actor Jane Fonda; Ingrid Bergman's daughters, Pia Lindstrom, Isabella Rossellini, and Ingrid Rossellini; and Julius J. Epstein, one of the film's screenwriters. The occasion was *Casablanca*'s fiftieth anniversary. The museum event launched a limited theatrical run of new 35 mm prints of the film nationwide, a run earning nearly $2 million. It also heralded the film's release on video, where it earned $6 million or three times the theatrical take.[1] In a thriving video market, *Casablanca*'s fiftieth-anniversary edition debuted in the top ten of *Billboard*'s video sales charts, climbing to number five during the Christmas holidays and charting strongly through early 1993. The film ultimately ranked among the top one hundred video sales for 1992 and won the video retailers' award for most popular classic reissue.[2]

Often credited with innovating cross-platform anniversary releases for the classical-era films in his library, Turner saw this reselling strategy as promising in several respects: a classic Hollywood film's birthday furnished a perfect rationale for a high-profile reissue of a heavily recycled movie; theatrical play created a splashy promotion for later video release and its greater profits; and special anniversary packaging encouraged consumers to purchase films, enhancing the growing sales or sell-through market, which was more lucrative for film library owners than rentals.[3] In the early 1990s, *Casablanca* was among a number of classical-era films celebrating elaborate anniversaries and posting impressive video sales. Along with oldies owned by other companies, Turner titles with chart-topping anniversaries included *Citizen Kane* (1941) and *King Kong* (1933) for their fiftieth and sixtieth birthdays, respectively.[4] Turner's earlier cablecasting of these films, along with *The Wizard of Oz* (1939) and *Gone with the Wind* (1939), had already favorably affected their continued visibility.[5] His company found a new way to heighten the profile of classical-era films through a theater/video release strategy that commemorated a film's origins through the anniversary's unique event status. At this time, the market importance of anniversary reissues of lauded old titles was such that one reporter worried that a year without a "major Hollywood classic celebrating a milestone anniversary [to] entice holiday shoppers with pricey collector's editions and flashy cross-promotions" would be a slow sales year for video.[6]

Classical-era anniversary videos were intricate affairs, not only in terms of marketing but also in film presentation. Films were often digitally upgraded and packaged in several editions, including deluxe gift/collectors' sets with supplemental materials. Struck from MoMA's 35 mm fine grain master print, *Casablanca*'s fiftieth-anniversary editions—two on videocassette and two on laser disc—arrived in digitally restored and remastered transfers. Both formats offered consumers lavish and "vanilla" (mainly featuring the film) versions. One VHS edition was a deluxe boxed set ($99.98) with fancy packaging that featured the film on one cassette and supplementary materials on the other. Giving consumers behind-the-scenes insights into the film's production and legacy, the materials ranged from a Turner-produced, Lauren Bacall–narrated documentary short, "You Must Remember This: A Tribute to *Casablanca,*" to hands-on materials like a booklet about the film with commentary by film historian Rudy Behlmer, the shooting script, and a Taster's Choice rebate offer. The other cassette, the one that had charted so well on *Billboard,* was a vanilla version ($24.98) with a few extras. While promising better visual quality than VHS, the laser disc reissues echoed this dual mode of presentation.[7]

Media organizations regularly celebrate milestone anniversaries for films, studios, and cinema itself. With or without theatrical rerelease, film anniversaries have become routine features of the US mediascape, affecting blockbusters like *Titanic* (1997), as well as low-budget horror like *Jack-O* (1995). Any film can potentially gain anniversary recognition, making the criteria for this mode of release somewhat nebulous. Hollywood tends, though, to reserve gala anniversary reissues with extensive publicity for films that have artistic, cultic, historical, or box office prominence. Studios also favor films with proven performance records, print elements amenable to digital renovation, personnel willing to contribute to supplements, and audiences interested in watching them in theaters.[8] In their exacting requirements, anniversary editions resemble special editions, of which they are a subset.

Industry approaches to classical-era film anniversaries differ in certain respects from special and anniversary editions honoring contemporary blockbusters. Blockbusters' spectacular CGI effects, as they endorse the grandeur and quality promised in these reissues, are a major focus of the making-of and other behind-the-scenes documentaries that dominate these discs' content.[9] When classical-era films receive opulent anniversary reissues, their origin stories, although different in nature, are similarly foregrounded. But given their age and laurels accrued over time, editions of these films emphasize the capital that has arisen from their vintage and cultural importance.[10] Their supplements (also known as bonus extras or special features) offer extensive archival materials documenting the past and testimonies from filmmakers and critics on their sterling reputations. These editions, then, are invested in history, remembrance, and the canon for their celebrations.

Film anniversaries flourished during the heyday of the physical video era (1986–2016), when VHS, DVD, and Blu-ray revenues regularly exceeded the theatrical box office before streaming video, rooted in the current "age of intangible media," achieved this financial benchmark.[11] The movie anniversary was popularized in an industry context shaped by media conglomerates that had incorporated film studios and other media concerns into their operations, a video market increasingly aimed at sell-through, and the development of DVD and Blu-ray, with their superior capacity (over VHS) to store information—a technological affordance central to including extensive bonus extras. As the anniversary rerelease was becoming standard practice, the media industry's early treatment of classical-era films influenced the contours of this practice. Moreover, because older films continued to be released through this approach, they registered major developments in home entertainment around special editions The persistence of classical-era film anniversary reissues in the twenty-first century demonstrates both a successful decades-long interaction among conglomerates, video markets, new formats, and films and the possible redefinition or decline of this elaborate release strategy as streaming begins to dominate home entertainment.

Of course, anniversary reissues are not solely financial and technological gambits. Their technoeconomic rationales are inseparable from their production of cultural and historical value for the films being celebrated. Like other exhibition strategies this book has examined, the anniversary reissue is a mode of repackaging old Hollywood films to reestablish both their profitability and reputation. Just as anniversaries in public life more broadly invite evaluation and remembrance of the past, classical-era film anniversaries furnish occasions to canonize and memorialize old Hollywood. Anniversaries supply studios and media companies invested in their film libraries with a prime opportunity to popularize certain historical accounts of films and negotiate how they should be valued and remembered.

If, as John Caldwell argues, "most of what consumers see and know about film/TV behind the scenes was planted or spun as part of formal industrial marketing and publicity initiatives," anniversary video editions and their supplementary materials make the relationship between commerce and consecration especially prominent.[12] Like the Taster's Choice rebate offer, the Bacall-narrated short on *Casablanca*'s fiftieth-anniversary edition is promotional in nature, designed by the industry to sell a vision of itself and the film. Furthermore, unlike newspaper movie ads, bonus extras are packaged with the film as its immediate textual surround, bringing industry promotions and viewers into proximity.[13] Supplemental documentaries meld the industry's desire to hype its products with what I call the anniversary's *celebratory imperative*—the compulsory affirmation of the saluted object—creating a potent union that affects the film's presentation and rendition of its history.

In this chapter, I explore the industrial, historical, aesthetic, and cultural implications of anniversary reissues in *Casablanca*'s domestic circulation in the late 1990s and early 2000s. While I study how anniversary events involve activities across multiple platforms, I eventually focus on movie theaters and physical-format video, treating the latter as the more crucial platform.[14] Here, we will see that *Casablanca*'s contemporary video identity is not just that of a movie valentine (as discussed in chapter 4), but also a classic film.

To start, I situate film anniversaries within the phenomenon of anniversaries more generally, a phenomenon from which they gain their sense of event-status and cultural significance. In everyday life, anniversaries are so commonplace that, as William Johnston remarks, "commemoration industries" have arisen to capitalize on their observances. Counting the film business as among these industries, I address how a combination of forces, from media conglomerates to DVD/Blu-ray, have contributed to the growth of film anniversaries as a standard mode of film reissue. To understand the anniversary's reach and the roles films play in such events, my first case study concerns Warner Bros.' seventy-fifth-anniversary celebration in 1998 of its 1923 origins as a studio. How did such industry events use the conglomerate structure and video for their celebrations? How did individual films like *Casablanca* figure into this occasion?

Turning to the film's exhibition in more recent years, my second case study—*Casablanca*'s seventieth anniversary, in 2012—investigates the evaluative and historical functions of this event, from its museum opening to its video editions. While *Casablanca* saw its seventy-fifth anniversary in 2017, its theatrical reissue was not followed by an explicit anniversary edition. This makes the seventieth anniversary the last to date celebrated through both theatrical rerelease and a new anniversary-branded DVD/Blu-ray gift/collector's set. Although it is too soon to tell, the seventieth may mark a transitional period in the history of anniversary reissues of classical-era films between the earlier video era's gold rush mentality and the later era's more restrained approach due to streaming's penetration of the home and the attendant shifts in the aftermarket it has inspired.

Casablanca's seventieth-anniversary edition is also rich terrain for study because of its place in the film's history of video circulation and the light this later moment sheds on the industry's contemporary historicizing and consecrating aims. By 2012 *Casablanca* had been reissued for forty years in diverse formats on US home video. Its special editioning began in 1989 on a Criterion Collection laser disc, followed by its 1992 laser disc/VHS anniversary editions.[15] Its seventieth-anniversary reissue, then, arrived in the wake of these and numerous other previous editions with supplementary materials. Unsurprisingly, given the industry's repurposing mandates, most of the 2012 edition extras had already appeared elsewhere, making this edition, despite some new touches, into an artifact defined by recycled materials. This boxed set thus offers an interesting historical specimen, a compendium of industry approaches to selling and remembering a legendary Hollywood film. Since classical-era films have also seen decades of canonizing processes, these editions reveal the sedimentation of claims about their enduring value and reputation as well.

Scholars have debated whether audiences actually watch DVD/Blu-ray bonus extras.[16] As I am suggesting, even if they refrain, deluxe anniversary editions play a significant role in film circulation. Often released and critically reviewed prior to vanilla versions, they are glitzy sources of visibility and advance publicity for other editions. Furthermore, many of the materials included, from documentaries to production stills, have not only been released on prior special editions but also have had broader exposure as TV specials and programming on other platforms. Consumers may thus encounter these materials elsewhere in popular culture. Perhaps most important, supplements for the classical-era film anniversary offer heavily recycled propositions about the film and the studio system. In so doing, they consolidate a network of myths that has long accompanied the film, especially regarding the history of its original production. In iterating elements of its origin story, they participate in further building its legend.[17] By *legend,* I do not mean a series of outright falsehoods about the film but a set of both factual and promotional stories about it—a mix of research and hype—that have been repeated so often and in such a celebratory register that they define the popular dimensions of its history and classic standing within a mythic frame.

In this case study I consider the theater/video releases that defined *Casablanca*'s 2012 event, pursuing questions about the historical and canonizing work they performed. How did the chosen museum's gala theatrical "repremiere" at this time contribute to reputation building? What specific materials did media industries produce for the deluxe video edition, and how did this repackaging impact film historiography—the recounting of *Casablanca*'s history? Although scholars do not typically subscribe to a celebratory imperative in their analyses, what role did some historians and critics recruited for this commemoration play in elaborating the film's story? What influence did the film's legend exert on these proceedings, and why does it matter?

In addressing these questions, I ultimately weigh the politics of the canon at work in anniversary editions featuring classical-era Hollywood films to grasp the cultural ramifications of enduring classics' persistence in the canon. Since all canons rest on systems of inclusion and exclusion,[18] the privileged place of old classics in commemorations prompts reflection on the dynamics of these events, including their embrace of films made during the Jim Crow era.[19] Tellingly, anniversary editions of vintage Hollywood films demonstrate the tenacity of industry practices that continued to confirm Jim Crow's segregationist tenets long after the system's legal demise in 1964 through the passage of the Civil Rights Act. With this in mind, how should we reevaluate the cinema classic?

ANNIVERSARIES

Few aspects of life are untouched by anniversaries. Anniversaries annually commemorate the origin of an event, place, or person. Depending on their nature, anniversaries are cause for either somber observance or jubilant celebration globally, nationally, locally, or individually. In the United States, they range from salutes of the nation's independence on July 4 and Martin Luther King Jr.'s birthday on January 15 to fêtes of regular citizen's weddings and birthdays. Anniversaries, numbered by the years since the original moment, are honored on or near the date in question but can also expand to days, weeks, and years of festivities. So-called milestone anniversaries, ending in a five or a zero, generate attention as particularly noteworthy. The further such events are from their origins, the more festive they can grow—a fifth anniversary carries far less weight than a fiftieth "golden" anniversary or a centennial.[20]

The sheer range of anniversaries across the calendar establishes them as recognizable events with possible affective resonance. Their public manifestations have the potential to perform significant cultural functions, creating a shared sense of identity and reverence around the past. In this vein, historian Alfred Andrea writes that there is "something awe-inspiring about looking back across the span of fifty, one hundred, five hundred, or a thousand years to evaluate a distant event that continues to influence our lives and culture. Even the passage of mere decades [situates] a pivotal moment in our collective past into a wider and fuller perspective than was possible at the time it occurred."[21]

Anniversaries have the power to confirm the traditions informing their celebrations of the past, but they are also sites for sometimes contentious revisionism invited by the distance between then and now. For example, historians and activists have disputed the legitimacy of Columbus Day, an annual federal holiday that honors Christopher Columbus's "discovery" of the Americas in October 1492, by questioning this claim's accuracy and the colonialization of Indigenous peoples that his coming wrought. Some states and localities refuse to recognize the anniversary in the traditional way, mounting alternative celebrations of these peoples. Public anniversaries, then, can be occasions for ruptures with the historical record as previously interpreted, provoking discontinuities with tradition and conflicting accounts of the past.

Because anniversaries are designed to enshrine their objects, however, their default mode tends toward continuity with traditions that have established the honoree's significance. In fact, as Johnston writes, a thriving commemoration industry banks on this tendency. Anniversaries are attractive to businesses because they offer dependable calendar points that can accommodate advanced planning. Providing rationales that mobilize organizations and planning personnel, they are thus able to "dictate timing across the whole gamut of cultural production." History meets commercial considerations, as entrepreneurs package and sell the past to consumers, including new generations drawn by the event's visibility, to spark financial rewards for their businesses.[22]

Because commemoration industries stage the past, their choice of features that "deserve to be perpetuated" in cultural memory negotiates how the honoree is remembered.[23] These industries are self-conscious about this dynamic, which is why experts like historians are such conventional icons of anniversary celebration. Owing to the anniversary's default celebratory mode, commemoration industries exert pressure on the proceedings to offer a highly selective kind of memory. While festivities may invest in multiple takes on the saluted object, they tend to avoid conflicts that could undermine its bankable legacy, leaning on its more positive features to maintain its appeal.

Film anniversaries draw cultural capital from the anniversary as a pervasive phenomenon. Through the anniversary sheen, films appear as familiarly intimate yet weighty objects of regard that share the phenomenon's commemorative functions, promotional tendencies, and potential for radical revisionism. Yet the possibility of diverging from traditions of affirmation is rarely realized since media companies have substantial incentives to protect the value of their library assets.[24] Indeed, Hollywood's version of a commemoration industry consists of media conglomerates and their subsidiaries and other cultural and media organizations that stage events, produce materials, and enlist experts to maintain a film's commercial and cultural worth and its ability to function as a studio brand.

After residing in Turner's library for its fiftieth-birthday celebration, *Casablanca*'s subsequent anniversary reissues occurred after Turner Entertainment Company became a Time Warner (1990–2018) subsidiary in 1996, following Warner Bros.' earlier move. Turner's film and television library, comprising MGM, Warner Bros., RKO, and other studio titles, was purportedly the largest in the world, with thirty-eight hundred sound feature films alone. The prospect of exploiting Turner's holdings, especially for home-entertainment platforms, helped to motivate Time Warner's purchase.[25] Shifting ownership of libraries seems to complicate the celebration of a film's birthday: whether or not companies originally produced it, they rerelease it as their own.[26] With possession of media libraries driving mergers and acquisitions, such changes allowed conglomerate subsidiaries to attain a subtle form of public authorship of movies while becoming guardians of their past.

THE COMMEMORATION INDUSTRY, HOLLYWOOD STYLE

Media conglomerates are large multinational corporations that own media and entertainment companies across a spectrum of businesses and platforms, including publishers of newspapers, magazines, video games, and books; radio, television, film, and internet companies; and sports teams and theme parks.[27] Conglomerates often gamble on film blockbusters as high-risk but high-payoff enterprises that, if successful, can realize profitable synergies across their subsidiary companies—the blockbuster franchise that produces movie sequels, TV adaptations and series, video games, and more. As risk-averse as they are risk-taking, conglomerates favor content that they can recycle in this way because it allows them to spread risk and reduce the "uncertain outcomes" represented by new productions.[28] They thus strive to develop content brands that will maximize revenue across media channels. As Simone Murray contends, media conglomerates also focus on "high-profile content" as an effective way to generate consumer loyalty.[29] A film can become an identifiable corporate brand that potentially shapes consumer habits and desires.

Substantial differences in corporate expectations, scope of recycling and synergy, and cultural awareness exist between the way classical Hollywood films and contemporary franchises like *Harry Potter* are treated. But, as the case of Warner Bros.' seventy-fifth anniversary will demonstrate, older titles nonetheless could be subject to Time Warner's synergistic approach. The market reintroduction of a vintage film, a known quantity with its major production costs well in the past, represents an especially conservative, risk-free route toward additional profits. As previous chapters have shown, the oldies' inexpensiveness and proven qualities relative to new productions have long supported their attractiveness to media industries.

In fact, Murray observes that the conglomerate's "optimal commercial goal" is for a "content package to achieve 'classic' status."[30] Whether the classic label is applied to older or newer films, this status allows subsidiaries to reactivate catalog titles with stalled revenue streams in festive, eye-catching fashion, specifically in anniversary reissues that celebrate a film's origins and promise a reborn, revivified artifact. Conglomerates envision films' classic standing and anniversary reissue as attracting consumers to the event itself, as well as to their other offerings, creating an expanded zone of consumer loyalty. As corporate profits relied on video sales, the video business figured prominently in these calculations. In the late 1990s, sales of Warner Bros.' catalog on video constituted more than 50 percent of the studio's revenues.[31] Because of DVD reissues alone, Time Warner's film and television library grew in value by $7 billion between 1997 and 2004.[32] Meanwhile, video vendors regarded anniversaries and the new visibility they brought to films as opportunities to "get titles out in front of consumers" and to identify their stores as destinations for Hollywood's most memorable works.[33]

As we witnessed with *Casablanca*'s fiftieth anniversary, anniversary editions existed on VHS and laser disc before DVD and Blu-ray arrived. The newer technologies, however, with their aura of quality and increased capacity for bonus extras, were ideally positioned to develop this phenomenon into a major means of updating the value of older offerings.[34] Introduced to US consumers in 1997, and into an already successful home video market, DVD added to this market's profitability and reign over the box office. In the early 2000s, North Americans paid $22.5 billion for DVDs and videocassettes, while theaters garnered just over $9 billion.[35] By 2003, with falling prices for home theater equipment and sell-through discs (vanilla editions ran between $10 and $20), and DVD players in nearly 50 percent of US homes, this technology surpassed VHS in profits and popularity.

Consumer familiarity with home video equipment, along with DVD's low pricing, superior image and sound, and apparent durability over time, made the new technology appealing to audiences and compatible with sell-through. With DVDs also making a desirable digital companion to home theater systems, the VHS/VCR market definitively declined by 2006.[36] Blu-ray, arriving in the US market in 2003, successfully won the high-definition format wars with rival HD-DVD but, despite its technological improvements over DVD, did not overtake it in sales.[37] While streaming has recently surged ahead of physical-format video in revenues, during their decades of success, DVD and Blu-ray contributed significantly to the life of reissued films.[38]

The anniversary edition's prestigious connotations, drawing from the event's notable status, as well as that of the special edition, were bolstered further by DVD's digital aura. If studios believed that Red Box's kiosk distribution of DVDs "devalued" movies and studio libraries, the Criterion

Collection, credited with pioneering the special edition, occupied the opposite end of the spectrum.[39] Beginning in 1983 as a high-end laser disc producer for niche collectors before switching completely to DVD in 1998, Criterion developed features for special editions that became industry standards. These include digital remasters; letterboxing; audio commentary by film directors, historians, and critics; and extras like trailers and production stills.[40] Focusing initially on Hollywood classics and international art cinema, Criterion has been associated with superior tastes, a reputation amplified by its early special editions for films like *Citizen Kane.*

These editions seemed to be exceptions to mass culture's undifferentiated media flow, giving them, especially limited editions, a sense of "systematic rarefaction" that promoted their distinctiveness and justified their costliness while downplaying their mass-produced status.[41] Since Criterion's special editions included "exhaustively researched additional materials" and expert testimony with behind-the-scenes information, DVD's storage capacity translated into its archival and educational capacity.[42] Films with the Criterion imprimatur carry the aura of belonging to a select group, giving the company what James Kendrick calls a "legitimizing function" with implications for the canon.[43]

Media companies adopted Criterion's reissue practices in their own claims for the sui generis status of their library titles, with special and anniversary editions generating the desired patina. In the 1990s, classical-era films helped to define the burgeoning film anniversary market. The first films to "make their mark" were the fiftieth-anniversary VHS and laser disc editions of *Gone with the Wind* and *The Wizard of Oz* in 1989.[44] Trade journalists wrote that older classics were "firmly in the spotlight again," attributing their success to several factors. Studios and video vendors regarded classics as having an enduring appeal that enticed consumers to watch them "over and over again, year after year." As known quantities, classics could virtually "sell themselves," at the very least, to nostalgic baby boomers and collectors. Their sales were enhanced by reasonable sell-through prices, their "giftability" for holiday shopping, their deluxe packaging that displayed well in living rooms, and, through supplementary materials, their embodiment of added value for consumers. Indeed, industry pundits saw the remarketing of older classics via anniversary editions as a "phenomenal growth sector" in the sell-through market that would raise revenues over those of video rental. Moreover, classics could "kick up the overall sell-through category," stimulating consumers to purchase films on video more generally.[45]

In these early days, studios deemed "brand-name titles" like *Casablanca,* along with noted children's fare and musicals, as worthy of commemoration. By the late 1990s, however, industry reporters observed that the "floodgates" had opened for anniversary reissues. Studios released new kinds of films in this category—nonfamily-oriented movies like the R-rated *The Exorcist* (1973)—that "no one would have considered classic even five years ago."[46] The successful initial reissue of older titles as classics blazed a trail for different films from different genres and periods to be considered as classics equally worthy of anniversary release.

DVD participated in the anniversary release's growth not only because of expanded capacity but also because this capacity could be exploited to deliver promotional content directly to viewers. As we saw in chapter 3 with 1960s televised documentaries about Hollywood, media industries excel at exposing some of their inner workings to audiences as a means of marketing films and studio brands. Because supplements physically accompany the film, they represented a new frontier in this aspect of the media industry's relation to viewers.[47] Caldwell writes that "one of DVD's chief innovations has been its ability to provide a cultural interface in which critical discourses . . . can be directly discussed and negotiated with audiences . . . without critical/cultural middlemen" like newspaper or TV movie reviewers. In this, DVDs supply a "fundamental connection and means of communication between the industry's producing cultures and the audience's consuming cultures."[48] By opening a direct pipeline, DVD and Blu-ray offer the industry a prime opportunity to negotiate viewers' interpretive, evaluative, and cultural experience of a film. These technologies, then, help to craft a film's "consumable identity" through bonus extras that present to viewers, as a mode of knowledge, the industry's vision of the value of the film and of itself.[49] Offering them command of this knowledge, the industry hopes to make "geeks out of the broader public,"[50] penetrating popular culture along the way with promotions and canon-forming discourses. Home-entertainment media like DVD thus played a role in "legitimating and monumentalizing Hollywood and its history"—one of the industry's most consistent and significant enterprises.[51] Supplemental materials, though diverse, are united by this common function.[52]

Against this backdrop, I want to explore how Time Warner, as part of Hollywood's commemoration industry, approached Warner Bros.' seventy-fifth birthday. This celebration illuminates the manner in which anniversaries inspire conglomerate synergies, performing vital financial and promotional work. Reissues of *Casablanca* and other films in the studio's library were central to this anniversary project.

WARNER BROS.' DIAMOND ANNIVERSARY

In the last chapter, I discussed the AFI's 1998 commemoration of cinema's centennial and related series of best-of lists. That same year, Warner Bros. celebrated its diamond anniversary, another milestone marking cinema's history, by touting its productions. With 1998, then, a banner year for marshaling Hollywood resources of self-celebration, both events acted, through their high-profile salutes to the history of filmmaking, as advertising ventures that could "drive all-important catalog sales" in video.[53]

Although the Warner brothers—Harry, Albert, Sam, and Jack—entered the film business in the early 1900s, the studio's seventy-fifth anniversary was defined by its 1923 incorporation.[54] The occasion sparked stories about the brothers' family background as Jewish immigrants and breakthroughs in the film business, including the invention of talkies. Stories also covered the studio's distinctive socially committed studio philosophy and style and its major successes, genres, and stars.[55] With Warner Bros.' history as content, Time Warner launched the anniversary "at the studio's historic lot," designing the yearlong festivities as an "ultimate test of corporate synergy," a "company-wide" fête encompassing numerous divisions. Activities were spread through the year and across divisions and were intended to build "maximum awareness" of the studio's films. Along with tie-ins with independent companies, promotions offered discounted prices on Time Warner–owned magazines, theme parks, sports paraphernalia, and online access.[56]

The conglomerate's film, cable TV, music, and video divisions were among those with promotions and events. The studio reissued films from its most recent catalog, but in April 1998, under the title "Warner Bros. 75th Anniversary Festival of Film Classics," it released thirty older films in new prints, including *Casablanca*. Theaters showcased the studio's history in a weeklong, decade-each-day program.[57] The success of this event and the studio's Christmas screening of a restored version of *The Wizard of Oz* resulted in the creation of a classic film division with thousands of titles for theatrical distribution.[58] Meanwhile, subsidiary Rhino Records delivered a deluxe four-CD boxed set spanning decades of Warner Bros. film music and songs that included supplements like a booklet on the studio's history and essays by Behlmer.[59] This set featured *Casablanca*'s theme music, composed by Max Steiner, and its theme song, "As Time Goes By," sung by Dooley Wilson.[60] For its part, Turner Entertainment cablecast the studio's films (packaged as "Warner Bros. 75th Anniversary Film Festivals") and, with distinguished TV documentarian David L. Wolper as executive producer, aired *Warner Bros. 75th Anniversary Show,* a four-episode series of original one-hour documentaries on the studio's history.[61] In yet more cable involvement, *Warner Bros. 75th Anniversary: No Guts, No Glory*—a condensed version of these documentaries—aired on Turner stations in November 1998 during the holiday sales period.

The video division reissued more than 350 films—both older and newer titles—on VHS and DVD, shipping millions of units to video vendors. As in other synergistic activities, titles were branded with the Warner Bros. seventy-fifth-anniversary logo, and films with birthdays received special anniversary packaging.[62] Video release patterns indicate that seasonal sales considerations and a desire to maintain hype without oversaturating the market with Warner Bros. titles guided the yearlong celebration. Films thus arrived in different quarterly groupings. Along with *The Life of Emile Zola* (1937) and *Cool Hand Luke* (1967), *Casablanca* was among the first sixty catalog titles reissued on video in February 1998 under the theme of "Awards Winners" to dovetail with the timing of the Academy Awards ceremony. Other, more recent, titles emerged quarterly for Father's Day, then back-to-school sales and year-end holidays. Consumers responded favorably to the studio's anniversary promotions, with major video store chains more than doubling sales of these titles.[63] Video retail seasons were so important to corporate sales strategies that Turner timed the Wolper series' cablecasts to coincide with videos' quarterly release dates.[64] The slow roll-out of Warner Bros. seventy-fifth-anniversary fare in video stores not only provided sustained exposure to the studio's brand and titles but also capitalized on familiar retail periods and their buzz to sell the event's wares.

These subsidiaries constituted an ensemble that produced "maximum awareness" of the studio and its films, while contributing to a "tightly orchestrated display of brand omnipresence." Yet the brand on display was not Time Warner but Warner Bros. Of course, the occasion demanded attention to the studio, but other dynamics were also at play. As Murray contends, media conglomerates are often reluctant to show their substantial footprint—to reveal the "increasingly concentrated ties of ownership between media producers." Accordingly, conglomerates position subsidiary companies, especially those with name recognition, as autonomous brands. In this sense, Time

Warner was a "house of brands" like Warner Bros. and Turner.[65] The conglomerate existed in the background as a savvy steward of companies with their own public identities and creative enterprises. Studio anniversaries, then, helped to further obscure the conglomerates' monopolizing power by celebrating the persistence of studios from early Hollywood, when, it would appear, old-fashioned capitalists and visionaries made movies.

Within this manifestation of Hollywood's commemoration industry, *Casablanca* and Bogart each function as a "brand kernel" of Warner Bros.[66]—a media unit perceived as both its own recognizable brand and an embodiment of the studio. Anniversaries emphasized the film/star/studio identification, enabling each element to cross-promote and confirm the greatness of the other in a process of consecration. Reporters conveyed sentiments in this regard that we will see amplified in the film's own birthday salute. They wrote, "The apogee for both Bogart and Warner came in 1942 with a film called *Casablanca*." Deservedly "showered with Oscars," *Casablanca* was "Warner's finest hour" and Bogart's most consequential role. That Warner Bros. produced a film "so seamlessly perfect, so indescribably 'right' despite a tempestuous production [is] not just a vindication of the Warner house creative process but a justification for the entire studio era." The studio has thus "left behind a filmic legacy that would more than ensure the Warner name would never be forgotten [and would] stay in the artistic and commercial vanguard of movie making down to the present day."[67]

While these comments extol *Casablanca*'s reputation, they also position the film as an ambassador for the studio and the film industry—a media property that is a "component unit in an overarching brand management exercise."[68] In this calculus, the film is an avatar for the success and creativity of Warner Bros. and the old Hollywood studio system that testifies to its legacy in the contemporary mediascape. Through *Casablanca* and other reissued titles, Warner Bros.' events display the studio's own worthiness for commemoration, illuminating its past and present achievements and suggesting its future viability and that of Hollywood itself. In the late 1990s, the anniversary mission would have been additionally energized by the coming millennium and discussions, spurred by the rise of digital technologies, of the "death" of cinema.

As we saw in previous chapters, the industry's financial imperatives rarely define films as mere corporate functionaries; these imperatives elicit value-laden claims that negotiate the meaning of films being honored. My study of *Casablanca*'s seventieth anniversary focuses on this dimension of the anniversary enterprise, examining how the event's theatrical screenings and

DVD/Blu-ray boxed sets generated discourses about the film's aesthetic and historical significance. I am especially interested in how platforms, materials, and people functioning in Hollywood's commemoration industry supported the film's legend—the stories that have long defined it for consumption. Since Hollywood is a memory community invested in negotiating the value and remembrance of its past, with box sets and their supplements forming significant tools in its bid to shape cultural memory, its anniversary efforts are particularly revealing in this regard.[69]

CASABLANCA'S PLATINUM ANNIVERSARY

In February 2012, the Smithsonian's National Museum of American History in Washington, DC, introduced Warner Bros.' $1 million 4K digital restoration of *Casablanca,* minted in honor of its seventieth anniversary. A red carpet, rolled out into the National Mall, led up to the renamed and renovated 261-seat Warner Bros. Theater, with the sold-out screening attended by the glitterati, including, once again, Ted Turner and Jane Fonda. A Moroccan-themed reception preceded the film and, to further set the mood, attendees were encouraged to wear 1940s garb. After the screening, critic and historian Richard Schickel conducted an onstage interview with Stephen Bogart, son of Humphrey Bogart and Lauren Bacall. Anniversary festivities continued on other US exhibition fronts through the year, including a nationwide limited theatrical run and DVD and Blu-ray editions.[70]

This Smithsonian event was not, as we have seen, the first time that museums had shown *Casablanca* to launch an anniversary fête. The museum locus, while not a prolific site of anniversary commemoration like home video, is important strategically to exhibition on such occasions because of its unique ability to merge commercial and consecrating aims. Museums demonstrate what Robert Kapsis describes as the "reciprocity of self-serving relationships" between art institutions and media industries. This reciprocity influences reputation building—the negotiation of public esteem for the parties involved.[71]

The Museum Effect / The Hollywood Effect

The National Museum of American History (NMAH) is part of the Smithsonian Institution museum complex. Founded in 1846 and administered by the government to support the "increase and diffusion of knowledge," the Smithsonian characterizes itself as the "world's largest museum and research complex." NMAH's charter therein is to trace the "American experience from colonial times to the present." Its website describes the part of its mission devoted to cinema as exploring American film's legacy and impact on "how we perceive ourselves as Americans." The new Warner Bros. Theater demonstrates NMAH's pursuit of this cause, while heightening the studio's visibility as an important US institution.[72]

This association bolstered the reputations of Warner Bros. and *Casablanca* through what I call the "museum effect." Like MoMA's celebration of the film's fiftieth anniversary, this setting linked the studio and one of its most celebrated titles with the idea of the museum as a place of sophisticated curation and display of exemplary historical artifacts.[73] Since, as Alison Griffiths argues, museums court "immersion, spectacle, and wonder,"[74] *Casablanca* entered an aesthetic space that not only combined refinement and education but also compounded cinema's affiliation with visual and aural splendor. NMAH, as the Smithsonian's American history museum in the nation's capital, also offered other value. Warner Bros. and *Casablanca* materialized under the auspices of a laureled organization in a setting that defined them as museum-worthy, as meriting artistic recognition in US history and heritage. Furthermore, the Smithsonian's status as a spectacularly appointed tourist destination meant that the studio and film gained additional allure from the institution and DC's appeal to tourist economies. At a major sightseeing crossroads, the studio's offerings were exposed to different audiences and different motivations for attending a movie theater, potentially creating new fans.

NMAH's charged setting thus created a museum effect that consecrated the artistic stature, historical-national importance, and sensational value of Warner Bros. and *Casablanca*. As part of this effect, the museum became a sphere of Hollywood promotion, both during and after the premiere. At the premiere, the postscreening discussion featured personnel key to reputation-building. From 1965 to 2010 Schickel served as a movie critic for *Time* magazine (a Time Warner publication from 1990 to 2014) and had ties to the studio and the Bogart family. In addition to interviewing son Stephen at the opening, he had written two related books with George Perry for sale at this event—*You Must Remember This: The Warner Bros. Story* (2008) and an authorized biography, *Bogie: A Celebration of the Life and Films of Humphrey Bogart* (2006). The first accompanied a five-part documentary series with the same title, written, directed, and produced by Schickel. It aired in 2008 on

PBS's *American Masters* (1986–), a distinguished TV series devoted to nonfiction accounts of significant US artists. Both book and TV series were originally designed to honor Warner Bros.' eighty-fifth anniversary that year and were thus recycled for this newer occasion. Actor and director Clint Eastwood, considered a Warner Bros. auteur because of his long professional association with the studio, wrote the book's foreword and narrated the series. Schickel published his book on Bogart, with a foreword written by Stephen Bogart, to honor the fiftieth anniversary of the actor's death in 1957.

Thus intertwined, Schickel, Eastwood, and Bogart's son have credentials as, respectively, renowned film critic, Academy Award–winning director, and child of a legendary Hollywood super couple. They help to solidify Warner Bros.' brand through multiple kinds of expertise, while cementing the studio's relation to a film and star reputed to be its most representative. The film's enduring reputation depends on the availability of people, especially after the death of its original personnel, who have "a stake in preserving or giving a boost to that reputation."[75] As such reputational entrepreneurs, their presence at this high-profile event maintains and builds the eminence of studio and film, while increasing the luster of their own standings. Laboring within a larger dynamic of reputational entrepreneurship by major players NMAH and Warner Bros., they offer a more subtle guarantee of reliability to the anniversary enterprise. They are the studio's proven friends, tethered to it in various ways, and thus surefire keepers of the flame who will not go rogue with alternative histories that might challenge celebratory narratives.

The museum's promotional impact lasted well beyond the opening. As was industry custom, Warner Bros. saw the opening and *Casablanca*'s later theatrical rerelease as advertising campaigns to stoke consumer desire for the DVD/Blu-ray reissue.[76] But the NMAH theater itself continued to contribute to the Warner Bros. brand. *Casablanca*'s seventieth-anniversary screening inaugurated a weekend tribute there of three other Bogart films—*The Maltese Falcon* (1941), *The Treasure of the Sierra Madre* (1948), and *The Big Sleep* (1946). A series of Warner Bros. film festivals followed through 2014, including a selection of Eastwood's films, a 150th celebration of the Civil War's anniversary with *Gone with the Wind* and *Glory* (1989), and a TCM Classic Film Festival.[77] No matter the film program, though, the Warner Bros. Theater advertised the studio, sustaining the consecrating effects of its museum affiliation.

Because these arrangements have reciprocal benefits for the organizations involved, the museum also profited from this alliance. The gala opening publicized NMAH and the Smithsonian's association with a major Hollywood studio and film.[78] The museums drew from Hollywood's cultural capital, banking on its popular appeal for bringing new audiences to their campus. Moreover, the opening gave NMAH's space an entertainingly immersive dimension through the patrons' introduction to the new theater and novel film presentation, as well as through the Moroccan-themed reception, 1940s cosplay, and live postscreening conversation. But Hollywood ties had longer-term benefits for NMAH as well. The theater, a 2D/3D screening facility with 35 mm and digital capabilities, renovated an old auditorium not at the Smithsonian's expense but through Warner Bros.' $5 million donation.[79] NMAH obtained a new exhibition hall for public programs that involved but also extended beyond the studio's universe to other aspects of the museum's mission. At the same time, this arrangement cemented a relationship with Hollywood in terms of future programming and gifting possibilities.[80] Through Warner Bros., NMAH thus profited from the Hollywood-effect.

As Griffiths observes, like other museums, the Smithsonian had long struggled to balance commercial considerations with its civic mission. Some internal debates on this matter concerned the place of screen media in a museum space committed to three-dimensional exhibits and historical veracity; entertainment media like film could "contaminate" the museum's reputation. But the Smithsonian also wanted to avoid stale, outdated exhibits and the "warehouse atmosphere" that its spaces could unintentionally foster. To this end, it pursued continual modernization and novel forms of engagement for visitors that new media displays seemed uniquely qualified to supply.[81] Corporate sponsors interested in expanding their ventures into the Smithsonian served this drive, as evidenced not only by the Warner Bros. Theater but also by developments like the National Air and Space Museum's Lockheed Martin IMAX theater.

Hence, NMAH's relationship to Warner Bros. enhanced its reputation in the sense of contemporary relevance, making it appear hip to a popular yet artistically and historically worthy American entertainment form. Unlike the IMAX theater's sheer immersive scale, the relatively small Warner Bros. Theater offered an intimate, more traditional filmgoing experience with a Hollywood aura that embraced the past in its 35 mm projection and the present in its digital capacities. The restored digital version of "oldie" *Casablanca* and the Warner Bros. Theater itself, as a new exhibition hall equipped with both legacy and digital technologies, signified the museum's simultaneous commitment to the archive and new display possibilities, attesting to its agility in remaining both a historical and a modern institution.[82] Indeed, as encountered at the Smithsonian, *Casablanca* elicited a "wow" from a critic impressed by the restoration print for its "dark, deep gorgeous shadows" and level of detail previously unavailable in diminished TV and repertory house prints.[83] Fusing old and new in its exhibition, the film encapsulated the museum's mission while showcasing Warner Bros.' devotion to preserving its archive. *Casablanca* and a signature feature of its vintage—its black-and-white cinematography—emerged in freshly consecrated form as an aesthetic, historical, and technological marvel of entertainment with national stature.

Through the museum effect and the Hollywood effect, *Casablanca*'s NMAH anniversary fête was a cross-promoting event with financial and cultural benefits for the studio and museum that endowed each with a trace of the other's reputational cachet. This exhibition platform repackaged *Casablanca* via the museum's distinguished mode of address and setting and Warner Bros. technological makeover. Soon after this screening, video editions found their own way of defining the film's distinctiveness.

Putting the Box in Boxed Set

Warner Bros. and Turner Entertainment Company released *Casablanca*'s seventieth-anniversary videos on March 2012 in a combined DVD/Blu-ray three-disc limited gift/collector's edition set ($64.99) and single-disc vanilla versions on DVD and Blu-ray ($10.20 and $12.97, respectively). Its vanilla versions ranked in the top twenty-five on DVD and Blu-ray sales for a week.[84] Unlike *Casablanca*'s fiftieth-anniversary edition, with its extended run on video sales charts, these editions did not rank highly beyond their debut week, suggesting that the film's place in home video had shifted, perhaps owing to its age and video-market saturation or a home-entertainment business moving away from physical formats.[85] Although *Casablanca*'s chart profile had changed, DVD/Blu-ray aficionados ranked its deluxe version twenty-fifth for 2012, citing the quality of the film, as well as its technological transfer, packaging, and bonus extras, giving it the kind of critical approval that its reissues had long garnered.[86]

Specifically, the deluxe version's elegant boxing and prolific supplemental materials contributed to a sense of its favorable status. Like all product covers, the video cover is an advertisement designed to capture eyeballs in a media milieu full of choices. The physical repackaging of older titles with

FIGURE 20. *Casablanca*'s upscale seventieth-anniversary box-set cover centered on the stars and their characters (Turner Entertainment Co. and Warner Bros. Entertainment Inc., 2012). Author's collection.

flagging sales gains additionally from this mode of visibility.[87] The right package fronted by the right cover, this thinking goes, can jumpstart interest in a title. As one reporter succinctly stated, "Old vids are new again with special packages."[88] Special and anniversary editions also bank on elaborate covers to indicate a movie's unique standing and justify higher prices for fancy versions.[89] In the process, video covers and packaging more generally create a film's consumable identity, emphasizing its most familiar features and their renovation into a fresh product. DVD/Blu-ray packaging distills these features while offering a perceptual and tactile experience that shapes interpretations of films, stars, genres, and studios.[90]

Casablanca's deluxe edition appears in a double-wide white box with a cover photo of Rick/Bogart and Ilsa/Bergman in embrace (fig. 20). The box itself is wrapped in cellophane, featuring the seventieth-anniversary logo and an inset noting the film's Academy Awards (not shown). Embossed lettering in black and red presents the film's title and the three major stars' names. The bottom righthand corner features an airplane (an icon of the film), the anniversary logo, and, on a silver label, the number of the limited collector's edition (out of eighty-one thousand total copies).

The overall design echoes the film's black-and-white cinematography, except for the subtle red of the film's title and characters' first names (to maintain visual branding, the interior box with the discs mimics this design and includes the anniversary logo). The main cover's white background and Bogart and Bergman's white attire blend seamlessly together, setting off their photographically idealized faces as the most dramatic stylistic element. The prominence of these elements indicates what is being sold—the film, its star-studded romantic couple—and how it is being sold. The pristine designscape, constituted by a stylistic minimalism of simple elegance, conveys the sense of an expensive and distinguished presentation of *Casablanca* worthy of its platinum anniversary. The limited edition's number further suggests value by projecting rarity onto what is actually a broadly available film.

This design contrasts with numerous other covers for *Casablanca.* For example, the 2003 two-disc special edition, while also including the Academy Awards inset, features the stars and a group of costars in an action-adventure story with hints of romance and violence in keeping with Bogart's gangster and noir personas (fig. 21). The 2012 and 2003 covers both draw from original 1942 posters and other publicity materials, a convention of packaging for older titles wherein artists recreate the appearance of a classic poster using color and other visual means to modernize it.[91] Yet the differences are clear. The 2003 edition has a crowded frame that suggests action over romance and an ensemble cast; the later edition offers pictorial simplicity that emphasizes the romantic couple and the two stars as the film's most valuable identifiers.

In avoiding intensive detail, the 2012 cover promotes the film's consumable identity in several ways. The white package testifies to *Casablanca*'s milestone platinum anniversary and esteemed standing, as well as to its commodity status as a showable artifact in the home. The black-and-white design intimates that it is a classic film with classic stars and romance. The sparse detail implies further that these elements are iconic and need no further elaboration, fulfilling a fundamental mission of the deluxe boxed set—communicating the legendary status of film and studio, a point to which I will return.

This minimalist design gives way to a profusion of texts in the box. The similarly designed interior case features three discs with 4K Blu-ray and DVD versions of the film and supplements that include behind-the-scenes documentaries, a French *Casablanca* poster, a commemorative book, and beverage coasters bearing the names of the film and its cafés. The film's high-tech transfer, elegant boxing, and keepsakes define it as a collector's item, a

FIGURE 21. The busier 2003 special edition's cover with its multiple ways of defining the film (Turner Entertainment Co. and Warner Bros. Entertainment Inc., 2003). Author's collection.

display-worthy artifact, as do the bonus extras in the form of bountiful documentaries that promise the disclosure of privileged industry information.

The Bonus Overload

Based on its perception that home viewers appreciated directors' commentaries and other value-added materials, Warner Bros. was an enthusiastic proponent of special and anniversary edition bonus extras, embracing a "more the merrier" perspective[92]—a philosophy evident in this platinum edition. Beyond its analog memorabilia, the edition boasts roughly thirteen hours of documentaries, trailers, cartoons, and other audiovisual texts, a tendency toward excess that Caldwell refers to as a "bonus overload" designed to perform industrial functions.[93]

The first disc offers *Casablanca* in Blu-ray with supplementary materials. The second is a supplements-only Blu-ray disc. The third consists of the film and some special features from disc 1 in DVD format.[94] The edition's specific content is as follows:

Disc One: Blu-ray

Casablanca (the film)

Special Features:

"Introduction by Lauren Bacall"

Two Audio Commentaries (by Roger Ebert and Rudy Behlmer)

Warner Night at the Movies:

Now, Voyager Theatrical Trailer

Newsreel

Vaudeville Days

"The Bird Came C.O.D." (1942)

"The Squawkin' Hawk" (1942)

"The Dover Boys at Pimento University" (1942)

Behind the Story:

"Great Performances: Bacall on Bogart"

"Michael Curtiz: The Greatest Director You Never Heard Of"

"*Casablanca:* An Unlikely Classic"

"You Must Remember This: A Tribute to *Casablanca*"

"As Time Goes By: The Children Remember"

Additional Footage:

Deleted Scenes

Outtakes

"Who Holds Tomorrow?" (1955)

"Carrotblanca" (1995)

Audio:

Scoring Stage Sessions

Lady Esther Screen Guild Theater Radio Broadcast (April 26, 1943)

Vox Pop Radio Broadcast (November 19, 1947)

Trailers:

Theatrical Trailer

Re-release Trailer (1992)

Disc Two: Blu-ray

Special Features:

You Must Remember This: The Warner Bros. Story

"The Brothers Warner"

"Jack L. Warner: The Last Mogul"

Disc Three: DVD

Casablanca (the film)

Special Features:

"Introduction by Lauren Bacall"

Commentaries: Rudy Behlmer and Roger Ebert

"Michael Curtiz: The Greatest Director You Never Heard Of"

"*Casablanca:* An Unlikely Classic"

Theatrical Trailer

Re-release Trailer

Beyond the film, disc materials fall into several categories. Most are contemporary documentary shorts, features, TV series, and audio commentaries produced or commissioned by Warner Bros. to recount *Casablanca*'s and the studio's history. The documentaries are in the conventional show-and-tell style, using talking heads and supporting archival clips to emphasize a straightforward delivery of information.[95] Another grouping features Warner Bros.' older productions, such as animated shorts that recreate a

1940s screening program ("Warner Bros. Night at the Movies"), the premiere episode of the studio's 1950s TV series *Casablanca,* "Who Holds Tomorrow," film trailers, and outtakes/deleted scenes. Finally, bonus extras include 1940s artifacts like *Screen Guild Theater*'s radio adaptation of *Casablanca.* Whereas the box-set cover minimizes mention of the studio, here Warner Bros.' logo, its "stamp of proprietorship" in the form of a shield monogrammed with "WB," is pervasive.[96] Disc documentaries on the studio's history and on the Warner brothers themselves further enhance this pervasiveness. As they have been in other settings, *Casablanca* and Warner Bros. are inextricably bound together in this anniversary commemoration.

Rather than analyze each supplement, I want to reflect on their cumulative impact for understanding the historiographical and consecrating strategies of classical-era anniversary reissues. *Casablanca*'s supplements elicit questions about the function of the bonus overload, the sheer plenitude of these materials. They also raise issues about the discs' use of the archive, particularly to support a self-reflexive mode of industry history. By presenting *Casablanca* through a certain kind of historical vision, the supplement's discourses attempt to provide definitive insight into how the film should be interpreted.

Purchasers of the deluxe version are confronted with two major facets of *Casablanca*'s consumable identity: abundance and redundancy. In terms of abundance, the discs generate an aura of plenty designed to "impress consumers with their sheer volume."[97] This aura produces a sense of monumentality for *Casablanca,* suggesting that its enduring reputation requires an immense body of documents to represent its industrial and cultural standing. The extras also convey a sense of informational wealth that lets viewers know they have gotten their money's worth. For their investment, they are gifted a surfeit of features that promises them the most extensive picture of the film available—a desirable commodity for fans and completists.

Along with this general impact, each supplement harbors its own version of plenitude. Documentaries present an array of faces and archival materials. Those testifying include directors like Eastwood, Steven Spielberg, and William Friedkin; other creative personnel such as cinematographers; critics and historians like Molly Haskell and Behlmer; and family members. In fact, many interviewees are essentially family members, understood as immediate kin, as well as creatives who have worked for Warner Bros. and, in some cases, critics/historians with studio ties—Behlmer, like Schickel, had written admiring books about Warner Bros.[98] While mining this expanded sense of family, the procession of faces and voices intimates that the film and studio have consequential legacies able to elicit the enthusiasm of a broad range of experts.

Participants also have effects on the anniversary enterprise specific to them. As Bogart's widow and a Warner Bros. star, Bacall is family in both of the above ways. This special status is conveyed by her multiple stints as a narrator for the bonus extras (in "Introduction," "Great Performances," and "You Must Remember This: A Tribute to *Casablanca*"). As a doubly in-house figure, her ringing endorsements of the studio, *Casablanca,* and Bogart are infused with a personal and professional authenticity that lends credibility to her statements. Other celebrated but more contemporary creatives, such as Eastwood and Spielberg, provide glowing commentary on Hollywood's past affirmed by their authority as renowned filmmakers.[99] Meanwhile, critics and historians tender remarks associated with educated powers of perception and experience as film analysts. The testifiers act as mediators between viewers and the edition,[100] their different areas of expertise securing the integrity of their observations and the superlatives that inform them: *Casablanca* is a "masterpiece" (Ebert), Curtiz is "possibly the greatest filmmaker ever to work in America" (Friedkin, "Michael Curtiz"), and similar sentiments. With few criticisms on offer, these testimonies embrace the superlative as a central form of expression, allowing supplementary materials to function smoothly as industry promotions while they fulfill the anniversary's celebratory imperative.

In another manifestation of abundance, bonus materials furnish an almost unfathomable number of documents assembled from heterogeneous archives, from the Warner Bros. Archives at the University of Southern California to the personal collections of filmmakers like John Huston. These documents include family photos and home movies of studio moguls and stars, past interviews with now-deceased creative personnel, stills and film clips from the history of Warner Bros. productions, newsreels, and public photos representing cinema and US histories. Through the volume and nature of documents, the historical record on display advances another form of authenticity. Encompassing a body of primary documents, the DVD/Blu-ray edition becomes an archive itself, an "archive of archives."[101] This is not, however, a neutral enterprise. As Nathan Carroll observes, DVDs have transformed "old-fashioned archives into commercial markets," shaping both memory and history in an exercise of corporate legitimation.[102] Compiling numerous fragments from different historical records, supplemental materials draw on the evidentiary status of preexisting documents to repurpose them into "new historical narratives and arguments" that supply "particular conceptions of the past and, ultimately, of history itself."[103] On deluxe editions, narrators and those testifying negotiate the relationship between archive and a preferred account of the past, in the process creating a corporate- and consumer-friendly archive that mingles promotion and history.

As I discussed in chapter 3 in relation to Wolper's 1960s Hollywood documentaries, the industry's kind of self-reflexivity informs how old Hollywood is remembered and valued. Industrial self-reflexivity then and now has a revelatory dimension, offering behind-the-scenes stories that give audiences insider knowledge. But this knowledge is fused with a promotional agenda that stokes veneration of the industry. Such documentaries conceal as much as they reveal, managing challenges to Hollywood's mystique, such as racism and sexism, through their scripts.

For instance, in "Jack Warner: The Last Movie Mogul," critic Neil Gabler offers the documentary's last lines: "These moguls left an astonishing legacy . . . a mythology about who we are as Americans, as powerful in shaping lives as any other mythology in this country. . . . There can be no greater legacy than that." Although the documentary delves into Jack's ruthlessness and discloses other flaws, such insights are meant to show the kind of tragic drive and ambition sometimes necessary for Hollywood success at the executive level. The documentary also briefly acknowledges what it calls Warner's womanizing ("He was susceptible to beauty and he liked women. . . . He did a lot of chasing around") but does not mention his well-known assaults of women on his casting couch—a subject addressed in feminist documentaries about Hollywood.[104] This part of his legacy is not easily squared with celebrations of Great Men nor with affirmative accounts of the studio's history.

You Must Remember This: The Warner Bros. Story features numerous *Casablanca* clips with Dooley Wilson, yet the detailed chronicle of the film's production mentions him only briefly in relation to his casting and almost not at all, with the exception of an Ebert comment, in the context of race in the film and in the 1940s. Although race would intersect with the documentary's extolling of Warner Bros.' commitment to social justice issues, materials avoid discussion of it with respect to older and newer films (i.e., narrator Eastwood remarks that Spielberg's *The Color Purple* [1985] features protagonists who had a brutal childhood without mentioning racism as a factor in this abuse).

The anniversary edition thus mythologizes Warner Bros. by using carefully chosen disclosures and omissions to portray difficult aspects of the brotherhood or issues of sex and race without diminishing the otherwise laudatory picture of the studio. Although DVD/Blu-ray's capacity for supplemental materials could support wide-ranging coverage, as Craig Hight contends, discs cannot "disrupt the corporate agenda of the studio that owns the film."[105] The manner in which studios deploy this space "limit[s] interpretation" to protect the film and studio's "commercial viability" through "entrepreneurial modes of selective memory."[106] Those producing *Casablanca*'s anniversary edition consider discussions of sexism and racism as inimical to the film's commercial viability. The problems of selective memory here are compounded by the fact that the gallery of faces in the documentaries is white and often (but not exclusively) male, amplifying Hollywood's lack of diversity in this enterprise, particularly in relation to race.

DVD/Blu-ray's abundancy and its material potential for different kinds of coverage is further hampered by substantial redundancy. Most overtly, both discs 1 and 3 present the film and some of the same bonus extras. But the edition's documentaries have a recycling history that also shows redundancy as a more dominant organizational principle. With the exceptions of "Michael Curtiz: The Greatest Director You Never Heard Of" and "*Casablanca:* An Unlikely Classic," extras have seen previous exposure. For example, before it appeared in 2012, "You Must Remember This: A Tribute to *Casablanca*" surfaced on the film's 1992 deluxe fiftieth-anniversary editions on VHS and laser disc, the 1998 and 2003 DVDs, the 2006 HD DVD, and the 2008 Ultimate Collector's Blu-ray Edition. Similarly, *You Must Remember This: The Warner Bros. Story* premiered at the 2008 Cannes Film Festival to honor the studio's eighty-fifth anniversary and was then, as I have mentioned, broadcast on PBS's *American Masters* series. The 2012 anniversary edition negotiates, then, two conflicting impulses that Pavel Skopal identifies as central to the industry: its desires to differentiate DVD/Blu-ray from other kinds of platforms through their "exclusive materials" and to recycle these materials across media outlets—part of the "endless mutation of content across proprietary host bodies" in the conglomerate era.[107]

Within this industry logic, the anniversary enterprise's reliance on redundancy has canonical and historical implications. *Casablanca*'s discs feature documentaries produced between 1992 and 2012. Those testifying, though, often discuss the same historical facts and offer the same encomiums, with studio memos and other archival materials certifying their statements' authenticity. In the process, they distill a view of *Casablanca*'s legend—the stories that have long accompanied its circulation and forged its status as one of the greatest films ever made. That these stories are repeated over decades exposes how important iterated claims about movies are to reputation and canon building as well as how static traditions of praise can become. Such redundancy also establishes the parameters of acceptable commentary and debate, while articulating a mode of historical writing that circulates influentially in mass culture.

The Legend: Origin Stories

Most of what the anniversary edition repeats about *Casablanca* pertains to its origin story—its production and "making of." Academic analyses of a film's origins are not customarily governed by the kind of prerogatives defining anniversary editions, nor are all such editions the same in the nature of their critical commentary. This edition, however, invokes a common practice of history writing bound to a commercially palatable version of an origin story. For *Casablanca,* the repetition of this story over time has congealed into an influential set of discursive conventions that inform its evaluation and remembrance.

Audio tracks and documentaries reveal core origin story components that range from discussions of the film's adaptation from Murray Burnett and Joan Alison's unproduced play *Everybody Comes to Rick's* (1940) to those about the film's endurance and legacy.[108] The supplements' overarching narrative cites *Casablanca*'s humble beginnings and chaotic production as ultimately offset by the lucky alchemy of the creative collaboration fostered by the studio system, resulting in the unintentional making of a masterpiece. *Casablanca*'s legend extends beyond what follows, but these elements constitute essential aspects of this story:

- *WWII:* The war gave *Casablanca* authenticity, fortuitous timing, and conscience that defined it as a patriotic zeitgeist film. Its 1942 premiere and 1943 general release dovetailed with two major WWII events—the Allies' invasion of North Africa and the Casablanca Conference, respectively—allowing it to speak to wartime audiences. The film gained further realism from this connection, as European refugees who fled Hitler's regime composed part of the cast. This presence gave the film "additional flavor and dimension" in the wartime context (Behlmer, audio commentary). Moreover, for Warner Bros., a studio that made socially aware films about injustice and fascism, *Casablanca* was one of its calls to arms for US involvement in WWII.

- *Studio system:* Despite being a factory system geared toward efficient production, Hollywood and its studio bosses or "titans behind the Golden Era" (Bacall, "Tribute to *Casablanca*") enabled singular directorial visions to emerge, while fostering creative collaborations among the studio's talent. Since critics rarely consider Michael Curtiz an auteur, commentators depict *Casablanca* as produced by the so-called "genius of the system" (Ebert). Yet Warner Bros. did not see *Casablanca* as anything special. In fact, its chaotic production suggested imminent failure: its script was incomplete when filming began and its ending undecided. Because of the factory system's ability to achieve greatness through an alliance of talent, though, *Casablanca* became one of the "best told narratives" of all time (Spielberg, "*Casablanca:* An Unlikely Classic") and remains "one of the greatest examples in Hollywood in which a team produced the movie" (Ebert). Film historian Alan Rode adds the element of accident to this narrative. Citing director John Ford—that "most of the good things that happen in movies are by luck"—Rode characterizes *Casablanca* as just such "an exercise in serendipity" ("*Casablanca:* An Unlikely Classic"). The film's success is thus attributable to collaborative artistry mingled with good fortune during the studio years.
- *Authorship:* When those testifying name the individuals responsible for *Casablanca,* they often give producer Hal B. Wallis credit for being heavily engaged in the production (rather than Jack Warner, who, much to Wallis's consternation, picked up *Casablanca*'s Oscar for Best Film at the Academy Awards). The Curtiz documentary and "*Casablanca:* An Unlikely Classic" cite the director and other studio personnel involved in the film's creation, providing a more detailed picture. Together these accounts continue to confirm the studio system as ultimate auteur.
- *Casting:* This process could also have resulted in disaster. Commentators ask us to imagine how other performers rumored to have been considered for the roles of Rick, Ilsa, and Sam would have dramatically altered and compromised the film's appeal: George Raft or Ronald Reagan as Rick; Ann Sheridan, Hedy Lamarr, or Michele Morgan as Ilsa; and Hazel Scott, Lena Horne, or Clarence Muse as Sam. From the start, however, Wallis wanted Bogart as Rick to begin crafting his image as a romantic hero, a decision that allowed the actor to deliver one of the "most iconic performances in American film" (Friedkin, "*Casablanca:* An Unlikely Classic"). Discussions define the height difference between Bergman and Bogart (he was shorter than she) as an initial problem in casting and relate on-set means of making him taller in certain scenes to successfully craft their romantic pairing. Casting revelations also disclose

that Wilson, a drummer and singer, could not play the piano; another musician, often identified as Elliot Carpenter, appeared as the "piano hands." Commentators address less contested hiring decisions regarding other characters as well, while relating the performers' background stories.

- *Bogart: Casablanca* is recognized as the film that rocketed the actor to A-list stardom. Bogart had performed notable work in *The Petrified Forest* (1936) and *The Maltese Falcon* (1941), but his career prospects had previously been hampered by his continual casting as a heavy or by outright miscasting. *Casablanca,* his lucky break, lent his tough-guy persona a significant romantic dimension. Disc commentary gives Bacall a central place in discourses about Bogart's romantic credentials in reel and real life: how the couple met, their films together, and their marriage and family. Bacall states, "He changed me. He was my teacher, my husband, my friend. . . . He taught me how to live." Bogart incarnated "integrity, truth, and courage." Bacall's testimony in "Great Performances," along with others like John Huston and actor Katharine Hepburn, sustain the legends of film, performer, and man.
- *Bergman:* Bergman's hiring as Ilsa was another stroke of luck. During casting, someone suggested that Wallis hire a European instead of an American actor for Ilsa, leading to negotiations with producer David O. Selznick's company to loan Bergman out to Warner Bros. Other than this backstory and the issue of her height, discussion focuses on two aspects of Bergman's role: her performance and physical appearance. Because the last scene had not been scripted, her confusion about which man she would end up with—Rick or her husband, Laszlo—led her to doubt her performance (Pia Lindstrom, "The Children Remember"). The issue of her appearance elicits comments about her film wardrobe but largely focus on her face. Cinematographer Arthur Edeson used lighting and close-ups to maximize her beauty and the intricacy of her acting, qualities that establish her "luminosity." Among raves about her in *Casablanca,* Friedkin remarks that he has "looked at the Mona Lisa for a long time and could look at Bergman's face a lot longer" ("*Casablanca:* An Unlikely Classic").
- *Adaptation:* An astute script reader for Warner Bros. brought Burnett and Alison's unpublished play, *Everybody Comes to Rick's,* to Wallis's attention, and Wallis purchased the film rights. *Casablanca* drew many of its elements from the play—its wartime café, proprietor, and piano player among them.[109] Otherwise, the change of title and other transformations created great art from a modest, unproven source.

- *Script:* The screenplay is the source of both much of the chaos and the success ascribed to the film. Because the script was not finished by the beginning of production, kept changing during production, and had no ending until the eleventh hour, it was a difficult shoot for performers and the director. Bergman's bewilderment over whether she would ultimately go off with Rick or Laszlo injected uncertainty into her acting (although, citing Aljean Harmetz's study of studio memos, Ebert casts doubt on this story). The participation of different screenwriters—among them Julius J. and Philip G. Epstein, Howard Koch, and the uncredited Casey Robinson—with different writing styles and objectives added to the whirl. The Epsteins contributed wit and sophistication (and many of the film's quotable lines); Koch, politics and social conscience; and Robinson, the love story's development. The synthesis of these disparate contributions resulted in an Academy Award–winning script.
- *Great scenes:* The "song duel" in Rick's café between the French singing "La Marseillaise" and the Germans singing "The Watch on the Rhine," Rick and Ilsa's first reencounter in his café, and Rick's drunken agonizing over Ilsa's return are among scenes commentators mention most as still emotionally powerful. *Casablanca*'s final scene, however, commands the greatest attention in terms of how it was filmed and how the studio's collaborative structure operated. The scene was not shot at Van Nuys airport, like an earlier airport scene, but was photographed on the set, using special effects and fog to make a model airplane look like the real thing on a real runway. More important, individual inspirations, alchemized by the studio's team ethos, created not only a successful ending and "one of the film's great scenes" but also "one of the best closing lines in history" from "one of the best films in history" (Ebert). During the production's final stages, the Epsteins thought of using Renault's standard line, "Round up the usual suspects," to explain his sudden political change of heart and new alliance with Rick and the French underground. Meanwhile, Wallis felt the last moments after Renault's revelation were lacking, but principal photography was complete and the ending could not be reshot since Bergman had already cut her hair for her next film. Wallis conceived of "Louis, I think this is the beginning of a beautiful friendship" as the last line of dialogue, calling Bogart back to the studio to read the line and dubbing it into the film.
- *Music:* Max Steiner composed the score but not most of the songs used, including "As Time Goes By," which had originated in the Broadway play *Everybody's Welcome* (1931). While he disliked "As Time Goes By" and intended to write his own theme song, circumstances intervened

(Bergman's haircut prevented redoing the scene in Rick's café when she hums "As Time Goes By"). Steiner ultimately wove the song, to great emotional effect, throughout the composition. His work resulted in a brilliant score and use of "As Time Goes By," making it "one of the best American songs ever" (Friedkin, "*Casablanca:* An Unlikely Classic"). Spielberg names Steiner as one of his all-time favorite composers, while citing *Casablanca*'s score as one of Steiner's finest and the song as an impressively emotive tune ("*Casablanca:* An Unlikely Classic").

- *Classic status and endurance:* Virtually no aspect of the film escapes superlatives. It is the perfectly timed film with respect to WWII and, through luck and the genius of the system, the perfectly made film in casting, script, style, music, and performances, as well as in its seamless blend of romance, intrigue, wit, and patriotic idealism. One of the greatest films ever produced, *Casablanca* is a cinema classic that has entered the "very fabric of our global consciousness" with dialogue quoted so often it has become part of popular vernacular (Bacall, "Introduction"). The script's wit and quotable lines (e.g., "Round up the usual suspects," "We'll always have Paris," "Here's looking at you, kid") also help to explain the film's enduring appeal. Ultimately, as such an accomplished product of the studio system, *Casablanca* embodies Hollywood's magic and mystique.

Within the origin story, skirmishes are fought over the accuracy of past claims. Did Bergman really know ahead of time which man she would choose? Was Reagan seriously considered for Rick, or was that studio-distributed misinformation to arouse interest in the film? Commentators also correct popular misconceptions about *Casablanca*—for example, they tell us that no one in the film utters, "Play it again, Sam" (the phrase is really "Play it, Sam" or simply "Play it"). Debates like these, rather than being fundamentally challenging, are a staple part of the film's history and legend, part of an iterative origin story that offers viewers knowledge about what happened behind-the-scenes. Since anniversary editions tend to protect and preserve the reputations of film, studio, and media industries, larger battles that could upend the essential terms of official histories have little place in this narrative.

The supplements' pervasive theme regarding the convergence of luck and talent at Warner Bros. speaks to *Casablanca*'s triumph over adversity but also reflects favorably on the old studio system. This system appears capable, against the odds of its factory operations, of successfully fusing business and artistry so that it was able to produce a film that has endured with high public visibility for eighty years—a long stretch given cinema's relatively young age as an art. This idea of the inadvertent classic presents *Casablanca* as a product of an artisanal studio colony that nurtured its success and continues today to create great works grounded in such legacies. The film's legend facilitates nostalgia for old capitalism and the old social order while helping to promote studio identity in the media conglomerate age with its considerably different capitalist configuration. Narratives of luck may indeed be true, but celebratory discourse repurposes them to romanticize films and filmmaking so that other narratives—about the exploitation of labor, for example—would seem discordant and out of place.[110]

My aim here is not to correct the origin story or to examine further its mythification of Hollywood. Rather, I want to interrogate the mode of film history that emerges from its tendencies. Many of the origin story's components draw from studio memos and press books and past interviews with the film's creative personnel. Such primary historical research has been interpreted and published, perhaps most extensively and influentially, by Aljean Harmetz in her *Round Up the Usual Suspects* (1992), reprinted in 2002 as *The Making of "Casablanca,"* in honor of the film's fiftieth and sixtieth anniversaries, respectively.[111] Much of what has since been said about *Casablanca* in commemorations has often been theme and variation of this source's findings.

As Harmetz suggests, the access Warner Bros. has given to its paper archives of memos, ad campaigns, and other documents has provided vital behind-the-scenes insight into its operations in the classical era.[112] On the one hand, this data and its role in constructing *Casablanca*'s origin story are indispensable to research. On the other, its prominence has meant that the film's industrial origins dominate its legend. This attention to origins is on display in anniversary reissues and, because the legend is so generative, in a range of publications from news items to scholarship in the celebratory register.[113] The origin story's iteration over time and across sources has resulted in the repeated endorsement and amplification of similar historical views of *Casablanca*. While the synchronic period of the film's production dominates accounts, commentators also note its diachronic impact and legacy, from the Bogart cult to remakes, sequels, and intertextual references it has spawned in TV series, novels, and other movies.[114] The origin/legacy duo establishes the parameters of what constitutes the film's history and, moreover, what kind of history is suitable to recount. Because anniversaries tend to lionize the industry, studio, and film, they become part of a mass-cultural field of discourse that delimits not only interpretations but also historical analysis. The film history produced by "corporate rationales," as Caetlin Benson-Allott argues, thus has a potentially substantial impact on how classical films are researched, taught, and received, a possibility deserving further scrutiny.[115]

A film's production obviously marks the beginning of its circulation. Yet the authority that origin stories wield as *the* history of a film impedes a fuller engagement, beyond recognition of its intertextual legacies, with its passage across platforms and time as vital moments in its journey. The constraints on historiography extend, as well, to the historian's possible function in these commemorations. Along with the "heightened public interest" that anniversaries bring to an event, the historian's recognized expertise as an interpreter of the past can influentially affect our understanding of yesteryear. Jörg Arnold et al. observe of national anniversaries that they have the "potential to generate or reanimate competing, indeed antagonistic narratives subscribed to by opposing memory communities," as Columbus Day attests. As they note, however, anniversaries put pressure on historians invited to participate to confirm "conventional wisdom" about the object being honored. Contributors are often expected to stoke established narratives, repeating or expanding them in ways that minimize historical antagonisms. Anniversaries thus prompt expert testimonies that "synthesize and popularize existing trends, rather than set genuinely new agendas." This ritualizes memory culture into the same "heroic narratives."[116]

Arnold et al. propose that historians invigorate anniversary events by engaging in "greater historical revisionism or by adding more diversity to the commemorative mix." Although histories going against the grain may be unable to surmount the "grip of historical myths shown on television and other places," or be accepted by those for whom the object has "emotional capital," historians can nonetheless pursue a different agenda. One route is to "historicize memory itself." Here scholars examine involved memory communities, tracing "narratives, symbols, and commemorative practices by which events have been remembered over time." They can thereby "dispel the mistaken notion that memory has no history" by offering "a historical dimension to the competing . . . mnemonic narratives in circulation."[117]

Film anniversaries do not have the gravitas of public anniversary events. Still, Arnold et al.'s points furnish insight into their objectives and into areas of revisionistic historical inquiry. Studio and film anniversary enterprises are populated by "memory agents" such as filmmakers, film historians, and critics that may negotiate collective remembrance of a slice of the past in the context of a promotional ethos.[118] *Casablanca*'s origin story components show how its memory has been historicized and popularized within this ethos—through industry materials and oral practices that have created and fetishized "a commonly accepted vision" of its production.[119] Some revisions to the legend, such as more in-depth examination of these components or the questioning of some claims, can embellish, rather than challenge, its established features. In theory, as I have mentioned, DVD/Blu-ray's expansive storage capacity ought to offer opportunities for other perspectives that diverge more muscularly from ritualized industry-friendly visions.

In terms of such competing mnemonic narratives, if *Casablanca*'s seventieth-anniversary supplements discussed Blackness, Dooley Wilson's iconic performance as Sam would gain a more substantial place therein. As they represent a different memory community, 1940s Black audiences' favorable view of Wilson, his costars, and the film itself could also conceivably participate in this revised story.[120] Such accounts would form part of the public counterformation of anniversary historiography with respect to diversity that Arnold et al. advocate. But these hypothetical additions to the origin story would encounter difficulties in Hollywood's commemoration industry as it materializes on *Casablanca*'s discs. As Delia Malia Konzett has argued, the character of Sam is complicated by *Casablanca*'s Jim Crow racial politics, conveyed in the stereotypical happy subservience of his minstrel role and his narrative marginalization and disposability by the film's conclusion.[121] That anniversary edition testimonies supporting *Casablanca*'s legend barely mention Sam or discuss racial issues confirms tacitly that these topics risk raising awareness of institutional and systemic racism, evidently a third rail in industry commemorative discourses. That there is no commentary from Black filmmakers, historians, or critics as memory agents further legislates Blackness out of the reconstruction of the film's past. Traditional forms of industrial self-reflexivity hitched to the celebratory imperative obstruct the diversification of *Casablanca*'s memory and the production of disc materials to address the film's more complex histories.

In this respect, the 1990s and 2000s anniversary enterprise, although far removed historically from the classical Hollywood era, perpetuates its Jim Crow mentality. As a film produced according to Jim Crow's strictures, *Casablanca* reflects Hollywood's whiteness and the segregationist society of the past. But, more significantly in terms of its historical circulation, after Jim Crow's legal end in 1964, its legacy is alive in the Hollywood that produced the film's commemoration. As Maryann Erigha contends, the "basic structure of Jim Crow remains intact in contemporary US society." As one contemporary US institution, Hollywood continues to articulate "the enduring structure of racialization, or the sorting of groups and individuals along racial lines" through a hierarchical "possessive investment in whiteness" that institutionally fosters racial inequality. Here whiteness is "seen as normal and general ... and Blackness is framed as particular, different, other."[122] *Casablanca*'s 2012 anniversary edition's gallery of faces and archival materials is a microcosm of standard industry practices that maintain the priorities of whiteness into this new century. That this edition echoes the erasure of race that occurred in 1960s documentaries on Hollywood suggests the intractability that institutions of commemoration can exhibit around identity and diversity issues.

These issues are central not only to rethinking the exclusionary modes of film history and memory produced by some classical-era film anniversary editions today but also to their persistent definition of a film's reputation and canonical status. As Konzett writes, while *Casablanca*'s "seriously flawed representation of African American culture does not entirely call into question [its] continuing iconic status and the talents of its [creative personnel], it should give one reason to check cinematic idolatry of Hollywood with a more critical perspective on its collusion with racial segregation in the US."[123] This challenge raises the question of how major industry organs have negotiated their relation to race and racist histories as they canonize classical Hollywood films in and beyond the anniversary context.

A JIM CROW CANON

After George Floyd's murder in 2020 caused a worldwide reckoning with violence against African Americans, the AFI, like numerous other organizations, posted a statement on its website about the necessity of change. This statement pertains particularly to its best-of lists intended to illuminate US film history and reads in part: "Since its inception, American film has marginalized the diversity of voices that make our nation and its stories strong—and these lists reflect that intolerable truth. AFI acknowledges its responsibility in curating these lists that has reinforced this marginality and looks forward to releasing new lists that will embrace our modern day and drive culture forward."[124]

Hollywood and related institutions have long faced concerns about diversity; here, the AFI's new lists, as yet unpublished, promise to address this situation. The 1998 "AFI's 100 Years . . . 100 Movies" list embodies the kind of long-standing limited vision that the organization seeks now to remedy. This chronicle features no films directed by women or persons of color. Its updated 2007 version, celebrating the original list's tenth anniversary, sustains this situation, except for including M. Night Shyamalan's *The Sixth Sense* (1999) at number 89 and Spike Lee's *Do the Right Thing* (1989) at number 96. Few films listed feature lead characters of color.

Like other industry canon-building efforts, the AFI list continues to demonstrate the anniversary's pervasiveness as a mechanism for promoting industry organizations and their cultural functions. As cinema's centennial provided the occasion to celebrate the medium by naming its best films, the AFI positioned itself as an authoritative source of consecration licensed to establish an official film canon. Giving the lists additional credibility, a "blue-ribbon panel of 1,500 film historians, directors, actors, critics, and scholars" selected the final 100 from a preselected list of four hundred films.[125] The panel ranked *Casablanca* as second only to *Citizen Kane* in 1998, and in 2007, with *Kane* retaining top honors, *Casablanca* dropped to number three, after *The Godfather* (1972). Because these lists are presented, publicized, and widely disseminated by a major US film institution, many regard them as definitive accounts of the most noteworthy titles in US cinema.

Like Warner Bros. seventy-fifth-anniversary celebration, AFI's "Top 100" offered a bonanza to media industries. Through the cooperation of the AFI, studios, and video stores, cinema's centennial elicited a multifaceted push to resell older cinematic goods on video.[126] For video vendors, the AFI's celebration of cinema's centennial spotlighted titles, in the digestible form of the list, that the public may have forgotten. Given customers' fondness for lists and titles grouped together—demonstrated in the successful renting and selling of videos thematically through shelving labels like "screen classics"—vendors hoped that the AFI's lists would identify its honored films as "must-have" items. As a mode of advertising suited for sell-through, the lists conveyed a "subliminal message to buy one, then another" in an established consumer trend toward "multiple purchases within a series."[127] The AFI's top one hundred and vendors' use of its lists as a sales strategy, then, offered video stores a means to promote themselves as emporiums of cinema's finest work and for consumers to feel they had purchased titles certified as the best.

In this vein, Jonathan Rosenbaum argues that the AFI's selection of the top one hundred movies championed Academy Award–winning films and films with major stars and directors that served the industry's self-interests rather than representing a record of cinema's best. He blames the AFI's priorities—born of "corporate cultural initiatives bent on selling and reselling what we already know and have, making every alternative appear scarce and esoteric"—for neglecting better Hollywood films and those by independent directors like John Cassavetes.[128] Lists themselves can compound this problem because, as Elena Gorfinkel writes, they tend to "aggregate the already known and consolidate power," reaffirming "hidebound tastes" that coalesce around the familiar.[129]

The vehicle of the list, here in service of an anniversary celebration, not only reveals once again how closely intertwined financial and evaluative considerations are in industry canons but also how the same kinds of titles—proven favorites that perform well in reissue—can endure on such lists over time. Despite their artistic quality and importance to US culture, films seen as more "esoteric" are excluded from these canons for their non-Hollywood status or perceived lack of bankability—the latter a major rationale Hollywood deploys, as Erigha observes, to deny equal opportunity to Black filmmakers.[130] In a vicious circle, because films perceived as outside the usual order have rarely appeared in industry canons, the "commonsense" inclusion of films like *Casablanca* eludes them.[131] These erasures are bolstered by what Jonathan Lupo calls the "stalwart *Kane* canon's" fossilization of the "greatest hits."[132] This stalwartness creates selections so enduring that canons fail to adequately recognize the excellence of directors and films beyond the industry's established white-male domain. The same problems that have plagued the Academy Awards in this respect characterize this enterprise as well—the resistance to changing institutional ideologies that support the priorities of whiteness and patriarchy.

Another prestigious body, Criterion Collection, has an imprimatur with similar symptoms. Avid moviegoers see its holdings as "an authoritative survey" of the most artistic films. Consequently, the near exclusion of Black filmmakers suggests that they have not produced a significant body of work. In a 2020 collection of one thousand movies featuring more than 450 directors from more than forty nations, Criterion's library offered four feature-length films by Black Americans and four by Black directors globally. Todd Boyd contends that this situation owes to selection principles rooted in Criterion's long affinity for classical Hollywood and European art cinemas, producing a taste inheritance defined by a traditionally white catalog. The persistence of this catalog means that "many film ranking systems historically have been forged in echo chambers." The canon that emerges from this process is "so often iterated that it can feel monumental and eternal." Criterion's library thus produced a form of "cinema segregation," representing an example of "how the unexamined racial biases of cultural institutions could have pernicious and long-lasting effects, even without overtly racist intent." As Boyd remarks, this sort of racism stems from "assumptions about what's relevant, what's significant, what's worth seeing."[133]

As I mentioned in the previous chapter, films by and with Black artists often land on alternative pop-culture lists and canons. At the level of major industry institutions, works by Black directors such as Julie Dash and Spike Lee have been reissued in anniversary editions, indicating the greater role that conversations about race and gender might have in this forum and, potentially, the growing place of Black and female filmmakers in the canonizing discourses of commemoration.[134] But these developments cannot fully address how canon formation by the film industry has worked against this kind of recognition because of the countervailing weight of inherited prejudicial traditions. Classical Hollywood studio heads and their films influentially participated in the dissemination of Jim Crow ideologies by rarely including Black performers unless they appeared in stereotypical roles as entertainers or servants and editing them out altogether in films distributed in southern states. Ellen C. Scott has written that, well beyond stereotyping, Jim Crow extended into the industry's policies, including the Production Code Administration's censorship practices as they attempted to repress the "much evidenced truth of America's racial wrongs" through their vetting system.[135] Although contemporary Hollywood films may appear less draconian, the industry involves gatekeepers that "actively create and maintain racial hierarchy in how they discuss, conceptualize, package, produce, and distribute movies and in how they stratify movies, actors, and directors," demonstrating the continuing presence of a Jim Crow racial imagination.[136]

Some classical-era films have been castigated because of their investment in this imagination. Critics have called certain blatantly racist films to account—*The Birth of a Nation* (1915) and *Gone with the Wind,* for example—with variable effects on their canonical place. The former title, listed in the AFI's "100 Films" rankings in 1998, disappears from the 2007 update. The latter fell only two positions (from fourth to sixth) in these rankings, while, in 2019, it enjoyed a deluxe eightieth-anniversary reissue. A year later, however, because of the George Floyd reckoning, streamer HBO Max temporarily pulled *Gone with the Wind* from its lineup until the film's racism could be educationally contextualized.

These films, though, are only overt manifestations of a broader classical Hollywood system that privileged white film artists and stereotyped, diminished, or omitted African Americans. *Casablanca*'s depiction of Sam may seem less egregious than Black characterizations in *The Birth of a Nation* or *Gone with the Wind;* nonetheless, it presents a servant/entertainer figure whose raison d'être is to respond to the needs of the central white couple and to signify their past.[137] Classical Hollywood films of all kinds invite the historical and educational contextualization of race mandated for *Gone with the Wind*'s 2020 streaming reissue, while their place in the canon and the nature of their commemorative discourses are overdue for reconsideration. The point about canon formation, as John Guillory writes, "is not to make judgment disappear but to reform the conditions of its practice."[138]

As I have argued, the repetition of the same classical-era films as the best of cinema has meant the repetition of racial bias, not only because they carry Jim Crow's legacy with them as they continue to circulate but also because high-profile rankings, modes of release, and accompanying commentary have perpetuated this legacy across time. As one form of these evaluations, anniversary celebrations of classical Hollywood fare preserve these films' canon-worthy status, as well as their origin stories, delivered through testimonials, archival materials, and histories that support a vision of a white Hollywood and US culture. *Casablanca*'s origin story has exerted a gravitational pull on critical and historical commentary, drawing it into a well-defined set of coordinates—the components of the film's legend—that confirm a "transmission of tradition" with respect to its reputation. The anniversary edition's unspoken onus on challenging transmitted traditions reveals its continued embrace of embedded cultural standards that have helped both to define the film's status and to recycle segregationist views.[139]

This state of affairs asks us to weigh the impact of oft-repeated origin stories of older films and the commemorative discourses that define them on constraining more inclusive histories. By rethinking priorities that have long governed the industry's canonical selections of films, gatekeepers can approach a more diverse reckoning with artistic talent and commercial success in cinema's history. Such a shift in priorities does not mean dismissing classical-era Hollywood cinema from consideration. In speaking about HBO Max's streaming of *Gone with the Wind,* Jacqueline Stewart remarks that the film should remain in circulation, rather than being completely withdrawn, because its "reposting is an opportunity to think about what classic films can teach us." *Gone with the Wind* is a "prime text for examining expressions of white supremacy in popular culture" and the mythologization of the Civil War and Reconstruction periods for a contemporary culture still defined by racism and historical misrepresentations of this past. As Stewart continues, the film is also "a valuable document of and testimony to Black performance during an era when substantial roles for Black talent were extremely rare in Hollywood films," shedding light on Black actors' ability to "bring humanity to stereotypical roles" through nuanced acting styles.[140]

Each classical-era film has its own interface with Jim Crow prejudices. But Stewart's emphasis on an educational approach and her call to "complicate the pleasures that we get from these works"[141] are instructive for understanding both the particularities of how other films from this period negotiated racism and the discursive activities that have surrounded them throughout their circulation. As we have briefly seen, academic criticism has addressed *Casablanca*'s problematic portrait of Sam. Industry-produced commemorative discourses could enlist filmmakers, historians, and critics to elaborate the film's racial politics, while also considering Dooley Wilson's career in and outside the movies, a standard feature of these discourses in relation to other stars. Furthermore, I have alluded to the fact that *Casablanca* has a Black history in the 1940s. Black audiences and critics admired Wilson's performance in the film, seeing Sam as a sign of progress for Black representation in Hollywood and applauding Wilson's commitment to racial justice in real life.[142] Additionally, many embraced Bogart for his liberalism on race, with Wilson "chewing everybody's ear off around Hollywood about Bogie's man-to-man straight-from-the-shoulder personality, of which he became convinced during the shooting of 'Casablanca.'"[143] The point is not to engage in yet another form of celebration; indeed, Black audiences' praise was inspired by their despair over Hollywood's typical portrayals of African Americans. Rather, we can consider historical perspectives on race that shaped Black stardom in the film, as well as the film's reception by Black audiences during Jim Crow, to provide a different account of its origin story that is responsive to the issue of racial politics.

Coming to terms with *Casablanca* through such perspectives produces competing accounts of its origins that may "complicate the pleasures" it offers to some fans. But this new reckoning restores significant dimensions of the film's life essential to its history and, for Hollywood's commemoration industry, an opportunity to diversify and change customary narratives that continue to shape the film's memory and value. The steadfast presence of transmitted traditions ultimately raises questions about the ethics of memory—about our obligations to the past, to what has been forgotten as well as remembered—that operate in the practices of commercial memory communities like Hollywood, particularly with respect to films that have been longtime studio brands and icons of the system.

Casablanca's endurance—one of its most noted features—results in part from tastemakers' tendencies to draw on familiar stories and traditions of appraisal that repeatedly identify the same worthy titles, in the process resecuring the status quo and insulating influential industry canons from diversity. Like the selections defining the AFI's top–one hundred lists and Criterion Collection's curated library in 2020, the rituals of anniversary celebrations and other industry forms of recognition of classical-era cinema can immobilize the canon, discouraging taste arbiters from recalculating their priorities. As Bill Kramer, the director and president of the Academy Museum of Motion Pictures in Los Angeles remarks, "What we don't want is a celebratory space that doesn't have critical conversations about what we haven't gotten right."[144] Otherwise, endurance is likely to translate into inertia, with regressive cultural ramifications.

CONCLUSION: THE CLASSIC

This chapter has examined the place of anniversary reissues in *Casablanca*'s domestic circulation, the material forces that help to constitute Hollywood's commemoration industry, and the impact these forces have on the production of history and value for the film. Here and earlier in its history, *Casablanca*'s status as a classic has underpinned avowals of its excellence and endurance. Historicizing the idea of its endurance involves destabilizing this idea, which, in turn, injects volatility into its classic standing. As I discussed in my introduction, traditional definitions hold that classics are texts that have stood the test of time owing to the universal appeal of their outstanding features and superb realization of artistry. They attain a stability based on their artistic virtues, a formulation that leaves little room for conceiving of them in more specific historical terms that would introduce variability and contingency into the classic designation.

Casablanca's deluxe seventieth-anniversary edition shapes the film's most recent identity as a classic in several ways. In the term's normative meaning, *Casablanca* is a product of classical-era Hollywood filmmaking that follows the narrative and formal conventions of the studio system and period.

Because of its exceptional animation of these conventions, commentary moves beyond this neutral definition to embrace the label's association with value: *Casablanca* is a touchstone of this period, a diamond in the rough polished to perfection by the genius of the system. Because of its winning textual features and exemplary instantiation of classical style, *Casablanca* appears to be responsible for its own successful trajectory through time.[145] Disc commentary confirms the film's embodiment of standards of achievement that explain its endurance and place at the top of canons. *Casablanca*'s lasting presence communicates its universal appeal, its timelessness and ability to speak to different generations across the world.

In this book, I have argued against such a perspective, examining instead the historicity of interpretation and canonization.[146] In my view, the classic designation is neither textually determined nor forged by the studio system's lucky collaborative brilliance during production.[147] Rather, interested external forces power this designation in specific sociohistorical circumstances of appropriation, with cultural and canonical implications. In *Casablanca*'s case, the 1990s and 2000s saw material conditions governing media conglomerates as making the classic label and anniversary release economically desirable branding tools that could activate productive synergies across subsidiaries and deliver new revenues through video sales. The industry's alliance with museums shaped *Casablanca*'s theatrical reintroduction to the market, with each institution's particular objectives making the film's gala premiere as a restored classic possible. For their part, video businesses promoted "screen classics" in anniversary rerelease as a potential bonanza that could reactivate consumer interest in older titles and spike profits.

Meanwhile, DVD and Blu-ray, with their superior audiovisual quality and suitability for both home theater and special editions, facilitated the joint execution of the industry's promotional and consecrating agendas. On disc, experts testified to the film's classic status, at once enhancing their own reputations and amplifying DVD/Blu-ray's function as an ideal platform for industry-sanctioned celebration. *Casablanca*'s anniversary thus marshaled the activities of different constituencies, platforms, and technologies acting as part of Hollywood's commemoration industry, each contributing to and gaining from the anniversary's event status.

The classic is, then, a constructed entity—not born through its own excellent provenances but made by a consortium of forces "interested in revitalizing old properties within contemporary taste markets."[148] As such, it is a discursive practice mobilized by invested parties that "allocate cultural capital and determine 'greatness'" within specific social and historical contexts.[149] Not timeless, the classic is intricately timebound. *Casablanca*'s endurance as a classic, marked by its seventieth anniversary, stems from its appropriation by industrial, mass-cultural, and individual actors involved in its public reappearances, which often operated within transmitted traditions, to generate its meaning and canonical standing. Understood in this way, *Casablanca*'s reissues more generally have been indispensable to giving it, in Kenneth Brown's words, "a fighting chance at immortality"[150]—a chance based on its successive reappearances and involvement in discursive and material practices over time that adapt it to new platforms and purposes.

The anniversary reissue is a vivid example of how labels like *classic* are deeply rooted in a close relationship between economic initiatives and aesthetic cultures. Recalling Erika Balsom's words, quoted in my introduction, there is no "strict separation between the lofty ideals of art and the more earthy concerns of the market." While not identical spheres, the "financial valorization of art and the cultural and symbolic valorization of art are inextricably tied together."[151] *Casablanca*'s case suggests that classic status for a film is such a doubly determined phenomenon, rooted in the interplay between market imperatives and consecrating institutions in historical context, with Hollywood proving to be particularly agile at producing discourses that conflate commerce and aesthetic value. As we have seen, the interactive commerce/consecration relationship also has deeper cultural implications. Institutions reproduce traditions of meaning and value that police canonizing activities, negotiating cinema's identity and memories of films through practices that sanitize and perpetuate problematic racial and gendered pasts.

• • •

In November 2017, in honor of *Casablanca*'s seventy-fifth anniversary, NCM Fathom Events, a large theatrical content distributor, TCM, and Warner Bros. Entertainment rereleased the film in numerous theaters nationwide as part of TCM's "Big Screen Classics" series—another significant forum by which the film's classic credentials were (re)confirmed, especially considering TCM's already established reputation as a fount of classic film on cable television. TCM host Ben Mankiewicz's introduction accompanied the digital screenings, which used the same 4K restoration the studio had prepared for the film's seventieth birthday. TV shows and magazines ran feature stories on the film, while other press coverage advertised and reviewed it for the occasion.[152] Missing from the usual fanfare was a video release of a special seventy-fifth-anniversary edition. A year later, *Casablanca* was released in a two-disc Blu-ray/DVD set without the anniversary label, a repackaged and less bountiful but otherwise virtual replay of the 2012 anniversary edition. The 2018 version was more a marker, then, of the straightforward recycling logic of AT&T's WarnerMedia (*Casablanca*'s owner at the time—a status that has recently changed) than a bold new film presentation,[153] reflecting streaming's growth as a major force in home entertainment and physical-format video's consequent loss in standing. As this manuscript went to press in early 2022, *Casablanca* had begun to be theatrically reissued for its eightieth anniversary, once again staged by Fathom Events, Warner Bros., and TCM's "Big Screen Classics," with other platforms of celebration yet to materialize.[154]

As we would expect in this evolving mediascape, *Casablanca* has had a streaming life. I turn to this most recent platform of its circulation in my epilogue.

Epilogue

STREAMING *CASABLANCA* AND AFTERTHOUGHTS

SINCE THE 1990S, legacy media like cinema, music, and television have experienced what critics call "digital disruption." While demonstrating some continuity with legacy media practices, this era has seen dramatic changes in, among other things, established businesses and business models, production and postproduction technologies and practices, patterns of release and distribution channels, and modes of media consumption.[1] As in most of its confrontations with major new competitive developments during its history, Hollywood has initially struggled to understand how it could profitably make the transition to this new technological and media entertainment universe, a struggle that has included the disposition of its film libraries.[2]

Hollywood's adjustment is ongoing, but the second decade of the 2000s saw studios, including Warner Bros., commit to digitizing their libraries and to digitally distributing and exhibiting their content in theaters, as well as in homes. Technological advances, the growth of successful business models, and a consumer base with growing access to and familiarity with streaming encouraged Hollywood to pursue more avidly the possibilities of subscription-video-on-demand (SVOD) services. Changes in the video market, a significant financial realm for the studio's bottom line, have also spurred greater interest and investment. Beginning in 2016, streaming video revenues for film and TV content surpassed profits from physical-format video and the theatrical box office. By 2018, revenues from streaming subscriptions and streaming rental and sell-through constituted more than half of US consumers' entertainment spending.[3] The incentive posed by this shift toward the digital delivery of home entertainment, along with the success of Netflix (which, in 2021, had more than two hundred million subscribers worldwide), has led major studios like the Walt Disney Company and Warner

Bros. to launch their own SVOD services, Disney+ in 2019 and HBO Max in 2020.[4]

How have classical-era Hollywood films fared in this emerging environment? In some ways, they are as subject to the dynamics of streaming platforms as other films. All rereleased films as they are adapted to these platforms experience a transformation in their materiality, as well as in the spectator's access to and navigation of their content. They are streamed as digital files in a database rather than in electronic or analog forms. With the exception of one-off streaming events, this fact of existence removes the rerelease from the jurisdiction of the schedule and the realm of special individual presentation. Instead, it is available seemingly at any time in an assembly of titles where almost "every item possess[es] the same significance as any other," and the distinction between reruns and other content can lose relevance.[5] While reissues have always had to compete for attention in a crowded media aftermarket, online platforms incorporate this state of affairs as a signature element of their interface.

With some parallels to physical-format video and cable TV, modes of accessibility to films have also changed. Rereleases on streaming platforms are accessed via SVOD subscriptions, digital sell-through and rental, and acts of streaming or downloading on devices from smart TVs to iPhones. Because numerous devices are mobile and able to maintain continuity of content across their different frontiers, consumers with Wi-Fi access can watch programs whenever they choose at almost any location without serious interruption to the flow of their viewing experience. Modes of navigation have shifted, as well, owing to the specific mechanics of streaming, including online browsing and searching, selecting titles from menus, and other forms of interactivity that, in echoing shopping for titles in a video store, show their roots in protocols of physical-format video. Through methods familiar to consumers of VHS and DVD, customers can rewind, pause, fast-forward, and otherwise manipulate content, watching it according to their own schedules. As these aspects of access and navigation indicate, rituals of streaming spectatorship involve more control, mobility, choice, and interactive engagement, as well as more individuated, solitary forms of consumption, than those commonly associated with movie theaters or physical-format video screenings in the home.[6]

These rituals are additionally affected by what Chuck Tryon and Charles Acland respectively call the "casualization" or "rising informality" in viewing content prompted by the time- and space-shifting affordances of streaming.[7]

The sense of plenty that major streaming platforms exude further emphasizes this mode of transient contact with individual titles. As Derek Kompare observes, while not everything is available, "the new practices have pushed ever more media into circulation; more content now proliferates to more people more widely than ever before."[8] That reissues have to compete with streaming companies' often flashier and more highly promoted original programming—one of their key branding tools—turns this sense of plenty into a highly competitive field for older, previously exposed fare. Casual viewing in a milieu of plentiful choices, coupled with what Caetlin Benson-Allott has identified as a loss of a film or TV show's historical context for viewers on VOD, is counter to the kind of sell-through mentality that characterized analog video. Viewers still curate their content through browsing and selection, but streaming platforms make their contact with any single title more fleeting and less prone to rewatching and collecting and also less exposed to the special edition's version of film history. Such platforms, then, forgo important prior modes of viewer investment, ownership, and cinephilia that defined spectatorial experience with VHS, DVD, and Blu-ray.[9]

As these last considerations begin to indicate, certain dimensions of streaming may operate against a significant place for older classic films in its economy of exhibition and viewing. Indeed, commentators have remarked that "major streaming services have rarely been a friend to classic film fans," citing Netflix's paucity of titles made before the 1970s and the end of FilmStruck, a service that offered vintage classics from both TCM and the Criterion Collection.[10]

On the one hand, even as the classics' age has raised questions about their viability on digital platforms, the films remain visible as ready-made content for those platforms. Numerous classical-era films are currently available on large streaming sites like HBO Max, Amazon, iTunes, and YouTube, as well as on niche streaming channels like Criterion Collection and TCM. *Casablanca*'s own exposure via streaming is instructive for reflecting on the fate of once publicly prominent films in this new media ecology. Beyond Broadcast.com's experimental streaming of it in 1998, its streaming presence has ranged from one-off digital events to more continuous availability on Warner Bros. services and third-party SVODs like Amazon.[11] In terms of one-off events, as part of the multiplatform exposure *Casablanca* received on its seventieth-anniversary celebration in 2012, Warner Digital Distribution sponsored a free screening on Facebook with a live comment

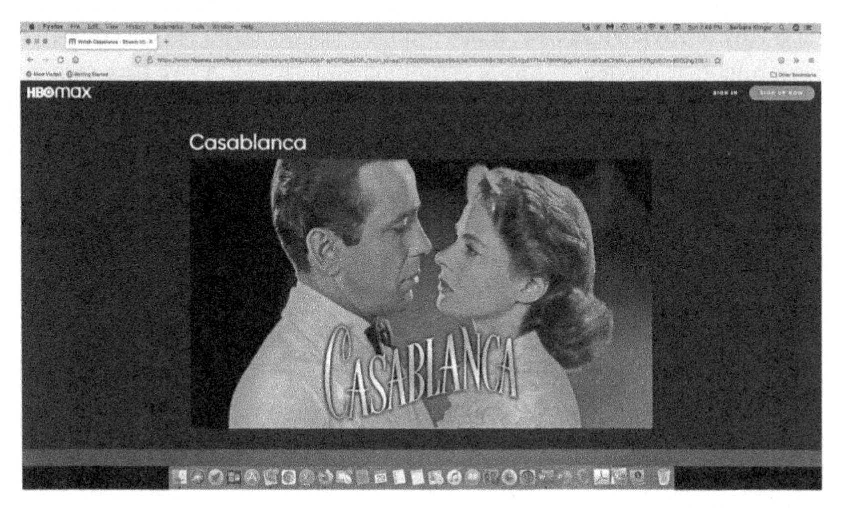

FIGURE 22. *Casablanca* (dir. Michael Curtiz; Warner Bros., 1942) in its newest media ecosystem.

feature, prompting a reviewer to quip, "Here's looking at you on Facebook, kid."[12] The AFI also streamed it in 2020 for its "AFI Movie Club."[13]

Aside from unique streaming events, in the 2000s, Warner Bros. tried leasing parts of its film library to online delivery systems and otherwise engaged with digital and social media.[14] It was not until 2014, however, that the studio began streaming some of its titles, absent *Casablanca,* on its own SVOD, Warner Instant Service, a branch of its DVD/Blu-ray company, Warner Archive Collection (which had launched five years earlier).[15] Warner Bros. halted this streaming service in 2018, when its library became available on the short-lived FilmStruck, developed by Turner Classic Movies (TCM) in partnership with Warner Bros. Digital Networks, both then subsidiaries of Time Warner. Although *Casablanca* streamed earlier in 2017 on third-party SVODs, this marked the studio's initial exhibition of it in one of its dedicated streaming venues.[16] When AT&T purchased Time Warner later in 2018, it phased out FilmStruck. In 2020, WarnerMedia introduced its SVOD, HBO Max, where *Casablanca* streams today, nonexclusively, as part of the streamer's "Classic Movie Collection" (fig. 22).[17] It is available, as well, on TCM's App, "Watch TCM." Before 2020, Warner Bros., which had not initially licensed *Casablanca* to third-party SVODs, leased it to YouTube, iTunes, Google Play, Amazon Prime, and Vudu, where the film also continues to circulate today.

On the other hand, the classic's presence is attenuated in comparison to more recent fare, and it may get "lost" in a competitive streaming environment, especially if this environment is not conducive to the kinds of collecting and cinephilia that previous forms of exhibition had invited. As we have seen in previous chapters, *Casablanca* is no stranger to being released on platforms featuring a glut of Hollywood content—postwar television and repertory houses are cases in point. But one of the most notable differences here is that the film cultures surrounding these platforms were strongly oriented toward classical-era Hollywood fare. The film industry was focused on reselling these titles to new generations, with audiences regarding classics as entertaining exercises in nostalgia, cult appreciation, and cinephilia in relation to a 1940s past that was not too far removed from public memory. From the 1970s to the present, the physical-format video era has marked a gradual shift toward a heavier reliance on reputations and canons for selling oldies to fans, inspired by their increased age, as well as by their diminishing claims on historical memory and popular culture relevance. The rise of contemporary blockbusters and CGI-spectacle films during this period and, more recently, the increased production of films and television programs spurred by streaming companies' investment in new content to attract subscribers, has shifted mainstream film cultures away from Hollywood oldies. In short, oldies are no longer supported by mass-cultural viewing trends as they once were in the early postwar decades. Similarly, where they dominated inquiry in the burgeoning field of film studies in the 1960s, 1970s, and 1980s, they have since been relegated to secondary status in light of diverse developments in the field and its coupling with television and media studies. Classical Hollywood films have become niche fare, not for those dedicated to their enjoyment and study but in terms of larger directions in popular culture and academe.

Today, *Casablanca* demonstrates signs of social aging that characterize it as old-fashioned content within changing priorities in film culture. Eclipsed by contemporary film's appeal to new generations and marginalized by its association with a now too-distant past, the film no longer sustains broad and avid public interest. Even its canonical place signifies a pastness that can deter, rather than attract, contemporary audiences. In this vein, one reviewer assures readers that the film is "much more fun than its stuffy 'Greatest Film Ever Made' tag suggests," highlighting its "literate script, stylish direction, great song, and cinema's most romantic couple in Bogie and Bergman," as features that will overcome spectatorial resistance.[18] Signs of the film's struggle for relevance materialize in other ways, as well. In a review addressed to "young people," an *Entertainment Weekly* writer touts the film's appeal:

> *Casablanca* is the story of a totally badass dude who runs a casino in a city that looks like the Disneyland version of *Raiders of the Lost Ark,* except with more booze and less inhibited sexuality. Said badass dude's love interest is played by a crazy-hot Swedish chick—who is also a badass. The movie also stars Claude Rains, the walking personification of what Colin Firth wishes he saw in the mirror every morning, and Sydney Greenstreet, the greatest Evil Charming Fat Man in movie history. Every line of dialogue is quotable. Everyone smokes. *Casablanca* is *Mad Men* if Don Draper shot Nazis.[19]

Here, the humor and allusions to fare and performers known to younger audiences attempt to translate the film into recognizable terms for a hip taste formation. In the process, the piece signifies not just the film's potential value for viewers but also its otherness as a respected artifact from the deep past.

As we have seen throughout this book, however, *Casablanca*'s temporality—its vintage, long circulation, and reputation—lie at the heart of its resistance to being completely marginalized. The film's mediation by institutions and platforms over the course of its history has given it a "survival advantage."[20] It has been extensively reissued across platforms, pervasively referenced, canonized as classic and cult, and better preserved than many of its fellow films. These activities both preceded and continue in the streaming era and surrounding culture. In the twenty-first century, *Casablanca* remains a cult Valentine's Day film, a classic, one of the best films ever made, a beloved film celebrating its anniversary, and so on. Streaming represents a different media context for oldies, in which their presentation is "de-eventized" in comparison to, say, special screenings in theaters but that demonstrates, nonetheless, the persistence of familiar canonizing verities.

Streaming video guides also help to illuminate how the new market and new film cultures remain in the business of endorsing and amplifying *Casablanca*'s reputation and place in the traditional film canon. For example, Decider.com hailed HBO Max as coming to the rescue of classic films on the strength of its library of Warner Bros. oldies and Criterion Collection films. HBO Max's intervention makes "iconic titles like *Citizen Kane* (1941), *Casablanca,* and *Singin' in the Rain* (1952) *finally* available on a subscription streaming service." With HBO Max alone, viewers can "easily knock off a good chunk of the American Film Institute's 100 best American movies," a timely task since "most of us are still in quarantine [and] now would be a great time to fill in those gaps in your watchlist." Of *Casablanca,* the writer comments, "Like *Citizen Kane,* [its] lasting legacy . . . is almost too significant to put into words. The iconic quotes are endless—'We'll always have

Paris,' 'Here's looking at you, kid,' 'I think this is the beginning of a beautiful friendship'—and the love story between Humphrey Bogart and Ingrid Bergman is one of the most swoon-worthy in history."[21]

As streaming video guides make these older films findable for viewers negotiating a loaded textual environment, they also participate in reputational entrepreneurship, engaging in a value-laden reciprocity between old and new. They promote HBO Max as a purveyor of prestigious movies through its association with the AFI, great films, a great studio, and the Criterion Collection, defining it and streaming itself as significant by linking them to renowned organizations and a renowned past. Meanwhile, vintage films are reintroduced to the public on a new platform, making the past seem less "other" and more intimately compatible with the present.

Casablanca's survival advantage allows it to continue to be accessible through accepted regions of value. At the same time, as it has in previous modes of exhibition, this advantage opens the film to changing cultural functions and meanings. The *Entertainment Weekly* review cited above is both a sign of the film's social aging and a means of viewing it through the lens of popular youth tastes. Decider.com also suggests that in 2020, streaming became linked to stay-at-home pandemic viewing habits in which returning to past films became a significant trend.

The pandemic forced the closing of numerous US theaters and ended, with some exceptions, the theatrical screening of major new releases well into 2021. This paucity of new theatrical content caused the *New York Times* and other newspapers to run columns devoted to remembering and revaluing films from the past. Early in the pandemic, some of these, like *Contagion* (2011), were popular with viewers because they dealt presciently and plausibly with a global virus crisis, holding a mirror up to the viewers' experience with COVID-19.[22] Other films, like *Jurassic Park* (1993), featured disaster on a different imaginative plain as the source of appeal during this time.[23] The audience's attraction to analogous catastrophes in these films seemed to combine pleasurably with their relegation of disaster to the realm of fantasy and the satisfying closure they provided for their respective crises. Thus, their datedness did not detract from their relevance or affective impact, while it also offered viewers a form of escapism to a time before this more contemporary dire period.

Casablanca has been appropriated through COVID-19 inspired readings less interested in onscreen catastrophes than with a different kind of parallelism and escapism. A *Cosmopolitan* reviewer wrote that because the world is a "weird place right now," it was time to revisit beloved oldies and the comfort they offered through nostalgia. This writer cites *Casablanca* as ideal for the occasion, not only because of its reputation as "one of the best films ever made" but also because of the analogies it offers to the pandemic's cultural experience. Like people in 2020, these characters are "trying to survive in a world that suddenly feels way more hostile than it used to." The reviewer continues: "Most people wouldn't think of a movie set in the middle of WWII to be relaxing, but something about this one makes my entire body feel like it's hot chocolate. . . . Whenever Rick says, 'Here's looking at you, kid,' my heart gets a little warmer. Then there are the 'fits. Rick wears a suit the entire movie (and he wears them well). . . . Ilsa's ensembles are so elegant, she might as well be Kate Middleton. Meanwhile, I wear sweatpants literally all day every day." Beyond the "Old Hollywood glamour and big romantic gestures," this commentator extols the movie's theme of personal sacrifice "for the greater good." Citing Rick's speech, "It doesn't take much to see that the problems of three little people don't amount to a hill of beans in this crazy world," the reviewer notes a parallel with the pandemic's world crisis and its indication of the much larger community to which people belong. *Casablanca* becomes a "perfect rewatch because it's one-part escapism and one-part a reminder to look at the big picture."[24]

This description defines *Casablanca* as a therapeutic and instructional film, as part of the quarantine's rituals of "comfort watching" of films from the past that are either "apposite to the pandemic or an antidote to it."[25] In this reading, its WWII setting offers an analogous crisis that makes it relevant to the current time with an ending that resolves that crisis in an uplifting way. Years after *Cosmopolitan* emphasized the film's theme of sacrifice as the height of an expression of love and romance perfect for Valentine's Day viewing, another of its writers now addresses that theme as offering a desirable guide to persevering in the pandemic by recommitting to fellow feeling and humanity. At the same time, the film's costuming and mise-en-scène present a welcome glamorous counterpoint to stay-at-home life during the pandemic with its emphasis on athleisure. Thus, *Casablanca,* like other films from the past interpreted as pandemic films, gains renewed pertinence during an exceptional time in history. Such unexpected readings of the film will continue to arise and shift the grounds of its meanings.

Since films from the past run the risk of being forgotten, their consecration at one or more points in their history does not necessarily guarantee renown over the longer haul. As a popular immortal, *Casablanca*'s survival advantage ensures a more certain prognosis. This status means that it will resist, for the foreseeable future, complete trajectories of extinction in its circulation. It does not mean, however, that its importance in the broader culture has remained or will remain the same; indeed, as I have argued, its life cycle has involved changes to its interpretation, reputation, and public prominence. Most recently, streaming represents both the film's attenuated place in mainstream culture, compared to its earlier life in reissue, and a platform for resuscitating it, opening it to both established and more novel interpretations. No real end to this popular immortal's story materializes, then, as *Casablanca* undergoes ongoing construction by industrial, critical, and cultural forces. As a historical study of the film's meaning and value, this book, too, enters into its biographical flow.

I have tracked and explored the film's career of circulation on exhibition platforms in the aftermarket, offering a diachronic view of the fate of a popular immortal as it has been displayed to audiences over roughly eighty years of its history. Within this history, an array of forces have acted on the film to foreground and define its features for new audiences and new cultural functions. Often, as we have seen, *Casablanca*'s significance has been mobilized for conservative agendas, its age used as a means of denying and otherwise offsetting cultural change and difference. Given the film's large public footprint over many years, though, my study does not exhaust the numerous meanings it has accrued, including those generated in global aftermarkets.

Marc Augé, a French anthropologist, has written resonantly of *Casablanca*'s personal meaning for him after it came out in France in 1947. Among other things, it mapped itself onto his wartime experiences of his family's displacement through its "mythic scenes of departure and arrival" and its evocation of the importance of memory itself.[26] Augé's encounter with the film materialized at a time when French film critics were exposed to classical-era Hollywood titles in great numbers in movie theaters, after the war and the restrictions it had imposed on the distribution of US films in Nazi-occupied European countries had ended. This resulted in a serious reappraisal of classical films in publications like *Cahiers du cinéma,* an appraisal that influenced Andrew Sarris's rendition of the auteur theory and that would go on to affect the programming of these films in US repertory houses like the Brattle Theatre. The situation was quite different in Germany, where *Casablanca* was not exhibited until 1952. To make the film palatable to a postwar, postdefeat nation still recovering from fascism, Warner Bros., in cooperation with the German film board, scrubbed the film of references to

WWII and Nazis (including the excision of the "The Watch on the Rhine" / "La Marseillaise" song duel between Nazi soldiers and refugees). In this edit, Laszlo was not an antifascist freedom fighter but a Norwegian atomic physicist on the run with a precious secret about delta rays. Among other changes, Dooley Wilson was erroneously identified as the musician Louis Armstrong, who had toured Berlin successfully in 1952.[27]

These instances of the immediate postwar exhibition of *Casablanca* in Europe indicate how different experiences of the war affected the film's importance and meaning. But the film has not just circulated abroad in the West or in the distant past. In more contemporary manifestations of its global presence, *Casablanca* has been the subject of stage adaptations in Asia. In 2005, Warner Bros. and the China Arts and Entertainment Group developed a production—*Casablanca: The New Dance Musical*—which debuted at the Third Beijing International Drama Festival at The Great Hall of People. In 2009–10, Japan's Takarazuka Revue, an all-female acting troupe,[28] adapted the film, with the permission of Turner Entertainment, into another epic musical production. In these cases, the film underwent a genre-bending and, in the latter case, a gender-bending transformation that reacclimated it to other performative, artistic, and cultural codes for audiences positioned far beyond the Warner Bros. lot in 1942.

By putting *Casablanca* in historical motion, I have called attention to the significance of domestic forms of exhibition and cultural systems of meaning as they have animated the afterlife of this film. As we can begin to see, the global exhibition of *Casablanca,* beyond moving the conversation about the film's biography and its aftermarket circulation into different geographical terrains, invokes the complexities of transnational media flow, from the relationship among industries involved in the exchange of films to the cultures, cultural codes, and viewers that define reception.

Outside the realm of *Casablanca*'s exhibition, other kinds of circulation that embody the film in some way proliferate, including pastiches, homages, parodies, and remakes. In movies alone, *Casablanca*'s redoings have ranged from Bogart's *To Have and Have Not* (1944) and Woody Allen's *Play It Again, Sam* (1972) to the German art film *Transit* (2018). These and numerous other *Casablanca*-inspired texts—from ads, cartoons (such as *Carrotblanca* [1995]), and cookbooks (*"Casablanca" Cookbook: Wining and Dining at Rick's* [1992]) to theme park rides (Walt Disney World's animatronics display of the film's airport scene in *The Great Movie Ride* [1989–2017])—suggest that a dense intertextual network of related texts accompanies the film's history of exhibition. This network further disperses the film into new territories, lending still other dimensions to the nature of its circulation as an artwork, commodity, and prized Hollywood title.

As a striking example of an immortal film, the terms of *Casablanca*'s endurance do not map directly onto other classical-era films' fates or, more broadly, cinema's persistence as a medium. But its case is suggestive for both. All films that survive diachronically have life cycles that materialize through a succession of exhibition platforms over time that transfigure them in every respect. Their biographies are similarly punctuated by the activity of reputational entrepreneurs engaged in retrospective cultural consecration and by the resulting classifications and canons that negotiate the historical terms of their interpretation and value. Moreover, this discursive surround helps to illuminate cinema's persistence as a medium insofar as multiple media keep individual films and cinema not only afloat but thriving.

Cinema itself has a complicated life support system, constituted by technological, industrial, and cultural factors that have ensured its survival for more than a century. If the current moment is any indication, cinema will continue to exist despite challenges from new media that appear to augur its death as a medium but actually promise it new life in a new form and context. Furthermore, cinema's history as a medium provides a practical view of this endurance. Cinema has a past that will continue to invite research and teaching that equips students with literacy in the field, a past that helps to preserve its identity as a medium. While it has been deeply affected by digital technologies, cinema also has a present in which it exists as a category of production, distribution, and exhibition with audiovisual conventions of storytelling that remain recognizable to mainstream industries and audiences. Additionally, platforms from motion picture theaters to streaming are still in the business of featuring films, while distinctions between media like film and television are maintained by involved organizations and parties, from the film and media industries to film critics and reviewers. Gatekeeping structures such as these undoubtedly help to perpetuate cinema's identity as a vital commercial and aesthetic sphere with a substantial consumer base. Finally, cinema has a future that is already under way, given its place in a congested entertainment landscape definitively characterized by fraternization among industries, technologies, and media—a place that will continue to shape and disseminate its artistic products for new and old publics alike.

APPENDIX ONE

Casablanca's *First Appearances on US Platforms/Formats*

November 26, 1942	Thanksgiving Day Premiere, New York City's Hollywood Theater
January 23, 1943	Wide release in theaters
April 26, 1943	*Screen Guild Players* adaptation (widely available, including on YouTube)
September 3, 1943	*Philip Morris Playhouse* adaptation (missing)
January 24, 1944	*Lux Radio Theatre* adaptation (widely available, including on YouTube)
August 14–September 18, 1944	*Crisco's Star Playhouse* (Library of Congress—four episodes)
December 19, 1944	*Theater of Romance* (Internet Archive)
1949	Nationwide theatrical reissue
1954–57	The Brattle Theatre
1957	WGN television
1972	Cartrivision video release
1979–80	VHS and Betamax (See appendix 2 for more detail on video releases)
1981	SelectaVision videodisc
1984	Early cable television (TBS) showing
1985	Laser disc
1997–98	DVD
1998	Streaming (Broadcast.com experiment)
2005	CD-ROM, "*Casablanca:* A Digital Critical Edition"
2006	HD DVD
2008	Blu-ray

2017	Streaming: Vudu, Amazon Prime, Google Play, iTunes
2018	Streaming: FilmStruck
2020	Streaming: HBO Max
2021	Streaming: HBO Max, Apple TV, Amazon Prime, YouTube, Vudu

APPENDIX TWO

Casablanca's *Physical-Format Video Rereleases*

Vanilla editions unless otherwise noted.

1972	Cartrivision
1979–80	VHS; Betamax
1981	SelectaVision videodisc; VHS; Betamax
1983	VHS; Betamax
1984	VHS; Betamax
1985	Laser disc
1988	VHS
1989	VHS and laser disc—Criterion Collection special editions; VHS—colorized version
1990	VHS
1991	VHS and laser disc—Criterion Collection special editions
1992	VHS and laser disc—Fiftieth-Anniversary editions
1994	VHS
1995	VHS; laser disc
1997–98	VHS; DVD; VHS—The Humphrey Bogart Collection *(The Big Sleep, The Maltese Falcon, Casablanca, Key Largo)*
1999	VHS and DVD—special edition
2000	VHS; DVD—snap case; DVD—Limited Edition Collector's Set; DVD—The Humphrey Bogart Collection *(The Big Sleep, The Maltese Falcon, Casablanca, Key Largo)*
2001	VHS and DVD—special editions
2003	DVD—special edition; DVD—The Bogart Collection *(Casablanca, The Big Sleep, The Maltese Falcon, To Have and Have Not,* and *The Treasure of the Sierra Madre)*

2005	DVD
2006	HD DVD; DVD—Humphrey Bogart: The Signature Collection *(Casablanca, The Treasure of the Sierra Madre, They Drive by Night,* and *High Sierra)*
2007	DVD—Essential Classics: Romances *(Gone with the Wind, Casablanca, Doctor Zhivago)*
2008	DVD and Blu-ray—Ultimate Collector's Edition
2009	DVD—TCM Greatest Classic Films Collection / Best Picture Winners *(Casablanca, Gigi, An American in Paris,* and *Mrs. Miniver);* DVD—special edition
2010	DVD; Blu-ray; Blu-ray—Academy Awards sleeve
2012	DVD and Blu-ray—Seventieth-Anniversary editions; Ingrid Bergman Collection *(Autumn Sonata, Anastasia, Gaslight, Casablanca, For Whom the Bell Tolls, Arch of Triumph)*
2013	DVD and Blu-ray—Best of Warner Bros. Fifty-Film Collection; Academy Awards Sleeve/seventieth-anniversary edition; *Casablanca* and *The African Queen* twin pack
2014	DVD and Blu-ray—The Best of Bogart Collection *(The Maltese Falcon, Casablanca, The Treasure of the Sierra Madre,* and *The African Queen)*
2016	Blu-ray
2018	DVD; Blu-ray
2017	DVD—Silver Screen Icons: Best Pictures *(Casablanca, Mrs. Miniver, An American in Paris, Gigi)*
2018	DVD; Blu-ray

NOTES

INTRODUCTION

1. Igor Kopytoff, "The Cultural Biography of Things: Commoditization as Process," in *The Social Life of Things: Commodities in Cultural Perspective,* ed. Arjun Appadurai (Cambridge: Cambridge University Press, 1986), 66, 68.

2. Patrick Healy, "Like the Movie, Only Different," *New York Times,* August 4, 2013, AR1. Circulation is not a free-flowing phenomenon equally applicable to all films. It is adjudicated by numerous considerations, from industry assessments of a film's ability to generate revenue to forces that hinder or prevent film distribution. On the complex dynamics of circulation, see Brian Larkin, *Signal and Noise: Media, Infrastructure, and Urban Culture in Nigeria* (Durham, NC: Duke University Press, 2008); and Jeff D. Himpele, *Circuits of Culture: Media, Politics, and Indigenous Identity in the Andes* (Minneapolis: University of Minnesota Press, 2008). On the unavailability of certain films, see Caetlin Benson-Allott, *The Stuff of Spectatorship: Material Cultures of Film and Television* (Oakland, CA: University of California Press, 2021), 59–93.

3. This kind of status also extends into the postclassical era with such films as *Star Wars IV: A New Hope* (1977).

4. Although I do not devote a case study to cable television, I discuss cable's importance to *Casablanca*'s circulation periodically in the book. For more on cable TV and Hollywood classics, see my *Beyond the Multiplex: Cinema, New Technologies, and the Home* (Berkeley: University of California Press, 2006), 91–134; Alison Trope, *Stardust Monuments: The Saving and Selling of Hollywood* (Hanover, NH: Dartmouth College Press, 2011), 134–47; and Benson-Allott, *The Stuff of Spectatorship,* 94–132.

5. Colin McArthur refers to *Casablanca* as "possibly the richest generator of other texts of the past fifty years." Colin McArthur, *The "Casablanca" File* (London: Half Brick Images, 1992), 5. Others treating the film's dissemination beyond the sphere of exhibition include Kathy Merlock Johnson, "Playing It Again and Again: *Casablanca*'s Impact on American Mass Culture," *Journal of Popular Film and*

Television 27, no. 4 (2000): 33–41; Aljean Harmetz, *The Making of "Casablanca": Bogart, Bergman, and World War II* (New York: Hyperion, 1992/2002), 338–54; and Noah Isenberg, *We'll Always Have "Casablanca": The Life, Legend, and Afterlife of Hollywood's Most Beloved Movie* (New York: Norton, 2017), 201–75.

6. Jack Nachbar lists sources on the film in "'Nobody Ever Loved Me That Much': A *Casablanca* Bibliography," *Journal of Popular Film and Television* 27, no. 4 (2000): 42–45. The spread of "Rick's Cafés" around the world hints at the film's global reach; see "'Play It Again, Issam': In Casablanca, a Cafe is Still a Cafe," *New York Times,* July 1, 2018, www.nytimes.com/2018/07/01/world/africa /casablanca-morocco-ricks-cafe.html.

7. For my earlier work on longitudinal studies of film phenomena, see my *Melodrama and Meaning: History, Culture, and the Films of Douglas Sirk* (Bloomington: Indiana University Press, 1994). For another treatment of a single film through the lens of exhibition, see Cynthia Erb, *Tracking "King Kong": A Hollywood Icon in World Culture,* 2nd ed. (Detroit: Wayne State University Press, 2009). For a work tracking a film's dissemination more generally, see Jon Solomon, *"Ben-Hur": The Original Blockbuster* (Edinburgh: Edinburgh University Press, 2016).

8. Charlotte Brunsdon, cited in James Bennett and Tom Brown, "Introduction: Past the Boundaries of 'New' and 'Old' Media," in *Film and Television after DVD,* ed. James Bennett and Tom Brown (London: Routledge, 2008), 10.

9. On both sides of the debate, see in the popular press, Manohla Dargis and A. O. Scott, "Film Is Dead? Long Live Movies," *New York Times,* Sept. 9, 2012, 1, 50; Matthew Jacobs, "Not to Be Melodramatic, but Movies as We Know Them Are Dead," *Huffington Post,* June 9, 2016, www.huffpost.com/entry/hollywood-sequels-will-they-ever-end_n_575813f8e4b00f97fba6b1e3; A. O. Scott, "Cinema Is Dead? Telluride Says Not Yet," *New York Times,* Sept. 5, 2016, www.nytimes.com/2016/09/06/movies /telluride-film-festival.html; Martin Scorsese, "The Dying Art of Filmmaking," *New York Times,* Nov. 5, 2019, A25; A. O. Scott, "The Flickering Future of Movie Theaters," *New York Times,* Oct. 17, 2020, C1, C2; Brooks Barnes, "Hollywood's Obituary, the Sequel: Now Streaming," *New York Times,* Nov. 28, 2020, www.nytimes.com /2020/11/28/business/media/hollywood-coronavirus-streaming.html; Brooks Barnes and Nicole Sperling, "Warner Bros. Will Stream Movies," *New York Times,* Dec. 4, 2020, B1, B4. In the scholarship, see Paolo Cherchi Usai, *The Death of Cinema: History, Cultural Memory, and the Digital Dark Age* (London: BFI, 2001); Lev Manovich, *The Language of New Media* (Cambridge, MA: MIT Press, 2001); Philip Rosen, *Change Mummified: Cinema, Historicity, Theory* (Minneapolis: University of Minnesota Press, 2001); D.N. Rodowick, *The Virtual Life of Film* (Cambridge, MA: Harvard University Press, 2007); Dudley Andrew, *What Cinema Is!* (West Sussex, UK: Wiley-Blackwell, 2010); Francesco Casetti, *The Lumière Galaxy: Seven Key Words for the Cinema to Come* (New York: Columbia University Press, 2015); André Gaudreault and Philippe Marion, *The End of Cinema? A Medium in Crisis in the Digital Age,* trans. Timothy Barnard (New York: Columbia University Press, 2015).

10. Caetlin Benson-Allott, *Killer Tapes and Shattered Screens: Video Spectatorship from VHS to File Sharing* (Berkeley: University of California Press, 2013), 8.

11. For my earlier arguments about the importance of new media and technologies to cinema's nontheatrical exhibition and reception, specifically in the context of late twentieth- and early twenty-first-century developments, see my *Beyond the Multiplex.*

12. Jay David Bolter and Richard Gruisin, *Remediation: Understanding New Media* (Cambridge, MA: MIT Press, 1999).

13. Lisa Gitelman, *Always Already New: Media, History, and the Data of Culture* (Cambridge, MA: MIT Press, 2008), 6–8.

14. Defining the forces responsible for change is especially important because theorists often treat change as something the medium itself engineers—as if media are "self-acting agents of their own history . . . purposefully [able to] refashion each other." Bolter and Gruisin and Casetti are among those discussing media without "mention of human agents" (Gitelman, *Always Already New,* 9).

15. Richard Maltby, "New Cinema Histories," in *Explorations in New Cinema History: Approaches and Case Studies,* ed. Richard Maltby, Daniel Biltereyst, and Philippe Meers (West Sussex, UK: Blackwell, 2011), 3–4.

16. See, for example, Haidee Wasson, *Museum Movies: The Museum of Modern Art and the Birth of Art Cinema* (Berkeley: University of California Press, 2005); and, on home cinema, Klinger, *Beyond the Multiplex.*

17. Charles Acland, *Screen Traffic: Movies, Multiplexes, and Global Culture* (Durham, NC: Duke University Press, 2003), 65–66.

18. See, for example, Kerry Segrave, *Movies at Home: How Hollywood Came to Television* (Jefferson, NC: McFarland, 2009).

19. Acland, *Screen Traffic,* 22–23, 65–66.

20. During initial theatrical runs, films often appear in different versions. See Thomas Elsaesser, *Metropolis* (London: BFI, 2000).

21. Nick Montfort and Ian Bogost, *Racing the Beam: The Atari Video Computer System* (Cambridge, MA: MIT Press, 2009); see also Ian Condry, *The Soul of Anime: Collaborative Creativity and Japan's Media Success Story* (Durham, NC: Duke University Press, 2013).

22. Marc Steinberg, *The Platform Economy: How Japan Transformed the Consumer Internet* (Minneapolis: University of Minnesota Press, 2019), 1–2.

23. Tarleton Gillespie, "The Politics of Platforms," *New Media and Society* 12, no. 3 (2010): 351.

24. See also Benson-Allott, *The Stuff of Spectatorship,* on the difference that platforms make to media meaning.

25. *Merriam Webster's Collegiate Dictionary,* 11th ed. (2003), s.v. "adaptation"; Linda Hutcheon, *A Theory of Adaptation* (New York: Routledge, 2006), is among adaptation scholars who deploy Darwin's sense of adaptation.

26. James Naremore, introduction to *Film Adaptation,* ed. James Naremore (New Brunswick, NJ: Rutgers University Press, 2000), 15.

27. Simone Murray, *The Adaptation Industry: The Cultural Economy of Contemporary Literary Adaptation* (London: Routledge, 2012), 12–13 (Murray's emphasis).

28. Murray, 12.

29. Historians often differentiate between *reissues* and *rereleases,* associating the former term with theaters. With my use of the more neutral term *platform* to define exhibition across media, I employ the terms interchangeably.

30. Elsaesser, *Metropolis,* 37.

31. Eric Hoyt, *Hollywood Vault: Film Libraries before Home Video* (Berkeley: University of California Press, 2014).

32. Naremore, introduction, 15.

33. Karin Littau, "Media, Mythology, and Morphogenesis: *Aliens,*" *Convergence: The International Journal of Research into New Media Technologies* 17, no. 1 (2011): 22, 26.

34. Pierre Bourdieu, *Distinction: A Social Critique of the Judgement of Taste,* trans. Richard Nice (Cambridge, MA: Harvard University Press, 1984).

35. "National Film Preservation Board: Film Registry," Library of Congress, www.loc.gov/programs/national-film-preservation-board/film-registry; "AFI's 100 Years . . . 100 Movies," American Film Institute, www.afi.com/afis-100-years-100-movies.

36. See, for example, Robert B. Ray, *A Certain Tendency in Hollywood Cinema, 1930–1980* (Princeton, NJ: Princeton University Press, 1985); and Umberto Eco, "*Casablanca:* Cult Movies and Intertextual Collage," in *Travels in Hyperreality,* trans. William Weaver (New York: Harcourt Brace, 1983), 197–211.

37. David Lipson, letter to the editor, "We'll Always Have *Casablanca,*" *New York Times,* July 8, 2018, A20.

38. I. Q. Hunter writes that "cult films are not defined by their textual qualities so much as by wider criteria. . . . The cult film is a discursive formation . . . a term of art constructed by rough agreement by audiences, distributors, critics, and so on as it circulates through culture." I. Q. Hunter, *Cult Film as a Guide to Life: Fandom, Adaptation, and Identity* (London: Bloomsbury, 2016), 3.

39. Exceptions to this insular way of approaching classics include Ross P. Garner, "'The Series That Changed Television'? *Twin Peaks,* 'Classic' Status, and Temporal Capital," *Cinema Journal* 55, no. 3 (Spring 2016): 137–38.

40. Prior to Bordwell, Staiger, and Thompson's work, André Bazin recognized cinema as having achieved a "well-balanced stage of maturity" by 1938–39 that he identified as "classical art" and "classical perfection" in *What Is Cinema?,* trans. Hugh Gray (Berkeley: University of California Press, 1967), 29, 30.

41. David Bordwell, Janet Staiger, and Kristin Thompson, *The Classical Hollywood Cinema: Film Style & Mode of Production to 1960* (New York: Columbia University Press, 1985), xiv, 3–4.

42. Allan Bloom, *The Closing of the American Mind* (New York: Simon & Schuster, 1987); Harold Bloom, *The Western Canon: The Books and School of the Ages* (New York: Riverhead, 1995).

43. For example, in his 1940s lecture, "What Is a Classic?," T. S. Eliot defined Virgil's epic poem *The Aeneid* (ca. 19–29 BCE) as the "classic of all Europe." T. S. Eliot, *On Poetry and Poets* (New York: Farrar, Straus and Cudahy, 1957), 52–74.

44. Ankhi Mukherjee, "'What Is a Classic?': International Literary Criticism and the Classic Question," *PMLA* 125, no. 4 (2010): 1030.

45. Hans-Georg Gadamer, *Truth and Method,* trans. Joel Weinsheimer and Donald G. Marshall (New York: Crossroad, 1991), 288–89.

46. Sainte Beuve, quoted in Mukherjee, "'What Is a Classic?,'" 1030.

47. Barbara Herrnstein Smith, *Contingencies of Value: Alternative Perspectives for Critical Theory* (Cambridge, MA: Harvard University Press, 1988), 47, 50-52 (Herrnstein Smith's emphasis).

48. Howard Becker, *Art Worlds* (Berkeley: University of California Press, 1982), 365.

49. Herrnstein Smith, *Contingencies of Value,* 50.

50. Herrnstein Smith, 50–52; J.M. Coetzee, "What Is a Classic?," *Stranger Shores: Literary Essays, 1986–1999* (London: Vintage, 1992), 12.

51. In their respective books, Allan Bloom and Harold Bloom represented a conservative reaction to feminism, critical race theory, postcolonial theory, and other approaches critiquing the hegemony of works by white Western male artists in the canon.

52. Arjun Appadurai, "Introduction: Commodities and the Politics of Value," in *The Social Life of Things: Commodities in Cultural Perspective,* ed. Arjun Appadurai (Cambridge: Cambridge University Press, 1986), 4 (Appadurai's emphasis).

53. Erika Balsom, paraphrasing Isabelle Graw, "Original Copies: How Film and Video Became Art Objects," *Cinema Journal* 53, no. 1 (Fall 2013): 100.

54. Laura Mayne, "Assessing Cultural Impact: Film4, Canon Formation, and Forgotten Films," *Journal of British Cinema and Television* 11, no. 4 (2014): 462.

55. Janet Staiger, "The Politics of Film Canons," *Cinema Journal* 24, no. 3 (Spring 1985): 4–23.

56. Lisa Dombrowski, "Canon and Canonicity," Encyclopedia.com, www.encyclopedia.com/arts/encyclopedias-almanacs-transcripts-and-maps/canon-and-canonicity.

57. Bourdieu, *Distinction,* 6.

58. Michael Patrick Allen and Anne E. Lincoln, "Critical Discourse and the Cultural Consecration of American Films," *Social Forces* 82, no. 3 (March 2004): 873–75.

59. Allen and Lincoln, "Critical Discourse," 873; Becker, *Art Worlds,* 365–66. For work on retrospective cultural consecration in a British context, see Joseph Lampel and Shivasharan S. Nadavulakere, "Classics Foretold? Contemporaneous and Retrospective Consecration in the UK Film Industry," *Cultural Trends* 18, no. 3 (Sept. 2009): 239–48.

60. Allen and Lincoln, 874–75; Pierre Bourdieu, *Homo Academicus,* trans. Peter Collier (Stanford, CA: Stanford University Press, 1988), 259.

61. Insofar as both canonization and retrospective cultural consecration can "confer legitimacy on a symbolic product long after its initial release," they are equivalent terms (Mayne, "Assessing Cultural Impact," 464). But canonization—the distillation of what is considered the best art—is a subset of this form of consecration, which can extol older texts without placing them into a canon.

62. Dombrowski, "Canon and Canonicity."

63. Although they may seem more like remakes than reissues, I consider radio adaptations of films as the latter. From the 1930s to the early 1950s, studios used radio as a primary nontheatrical means of recirculating their goods. These adaptations represented an early full-scale cooperation of film studios and radio broadcasters in iterating and disseminating movies beyond theaters, presaging TV's later broadcast of films.

64. Brian Hannan, *Coming Back to a Theater Near You: A History of Hollywood Reissues, 1914–2014* (Jefferson, NC: McFarland, 2016), 300.

CHAPTER 1. LISTENING TO *CASABLANCA*

1. On early challenges to the radio-film alliance, see Michele Hilmes, *Hollywood and Broadcasting: From Radio to Cable* (Chicago: University of Illinois Press, 1990), 49–77.

2. Hilmes, 93–96.

3. "Radio: The Hooperatings for '43," *Billboard,* Jan. 15, 1944, 8. *Lux* ranked fifth and *Screen Guild* eleventh. C. E. Hooper Company's audience measurement system, an industry standard from 1934 until 1950 (when Hooper sold his business to A. C. Nielsen, Inc.), based its ratings on phone interviews with radio listeners.

4. "Airers Rated by Circulation: The Billboard-Hooper Urban Circulation Index," *Billboard,* Dec. 16, 1944, 5, 8. These findings gave broadcasters and advertisers demographic figures on listeners' gender and age in thirty cities. For the week ending November 30, *Lux* ranked no. 2 (after *The Pepsodent Show Starring Bob Hope* [NBC, 1938–48]) with ten million listeners—five million women, three million men, and two million "juveniles." *Screen Guild* drew more than seven million listeners—four million women, two million men, and one million juveniles.

5. William C. Ackerman, "The Dimensions of American Broadcasting," *Public Opinion Quarterly* 9, no. 1 (Spring 1945): 3; M. H. Shapiro, "The Market for Radio in 1945," ed. Jack Alicoate, *Radio Daily: The 1945 Radio Annual* (New York: Barnes Printing, 1945), 57.

6. Neil Verma, *Theater of the Mind* (Chicago: University of Chicago Press, 2012), 2.

7. Connie Billips and Arthur Pierce, *Lux Presents Hollywood: A Show-by-Show History of the "Lux Radio Theatre" and the "Lux Video Theatre," 1934–1957* (Jefferson, NC: McFarland, 1995); "Jerry Haendiges Vintage Radio Logs: *The Screen Guild Theater,*" Old Time Radio, http://otrsite.com/logs/logs1010.htm; John Dunning, *On the Air: The Encyclopedia of Old-Time Radio* (New York: Oxford University Press, 1998), 416.

8. Hilmes, *Hollywood and Broadcasting;* Matthew Solomon, "Adapting 'Radio's Perfect Script': 'Sorry Wrong Number' and *Sorry, Wrong Number,*" *Quarterly Review of Film and Video* 16, no. 1 (1997): 23.

9. Hilmes, *Hollywood and Broadcasting,* 108–9.

10. A letter cosigned by Warner Bros. and the Biow Company—the ad agency for the Philip Morris account behind *The Philip Morris Playhouse*—represents the

standard agreement; see folder 12732A, Warner Bros. Archives, University of Southern California School of Cinematic Arts, Los Angeles.

11. Shirley Frohlich, "Program Reviews: *Screen Guild Playhouse,*" *Billboard,* Oct. 31, 1942, 7.

12. Hilmes, *Hollywood and Broadcasting,* 108–9.

13. *Merriam Webster's Collegiate Dictionary,* 11th ed. (2003), s.v. "adaptation."

14. Although I use the concept of core elements differently, it has similarities to what Seymour Chatman calls "kernels"—central narrative features defining a plot's backbone. Chatman opposes kernels to "satellite" elements that provide character depth and other story lines but are not strictly necessary for narrative comprehension. See Seymour Chatman, *Story and Discourse: Narrative Structure in Fiction and Film* (Ithaca, NY: Cornell University Press, 1978), 53–56.

15. The Casablanca Conference was attended by US president Franklin Roosevelt, British prime minister Winston Churchill, Free French Forces leader General Charles de Gaulle, and other top Allied leaders. They agreed that only the Axis powers' unconditional surrender would end WWII. As for Morocco, it is no longer a French protectorate; in 1956, it became an autonomous nation and is now considered part of the Middle East and North Africa (MENA).

16. For analysis of *Casablanca*'s conversion narrative, see Robert B. Ray, *A Certain Tendency of the Hollywood Cinema, 1930–1980* (Princeton, NJ: Princeton University Press, 1985), 89–112.

17. On December 17, 1946, Warner Bros. produced a version of *Casablanca* on its LA radio station KFWB as the first episode of its show *Star Makers' Radio Theater.* Director Michael Curtiz narrated and the studio's young talent performed to hone their radio acting. The episode is lost, but the sparse details that remain suggest how important radio was to training movie actors. "Radio: Warners Push Own Talent on KFWB," *Billboard,* Dec. 14, 1946, 5.

18. "The Week's Radio Programs," *New York Times,* April 25, 1943, 10; Dunning, *On the Air,* 600.

19. "Radio Today," *New York Times,* Sept. 3, 1943, 33; *The Philip Morris Playhouse* files, New York Public Library for the Performing Arts, Lincoln Center, New York.

20. "Radio Programs of the Week," *New York Times,* Jan. 23, 1944, 8; Billips and Pierce, *Lux Presents Hollywood,* 305–6.

21. "Hollywood Theater of the Air," *Billboard,* July 24, 1943, 13; Ron Lackmann, *The Encyclopedia of American Radio* (New York: Facts on File, 2000), 89; Dunning, *On the Air,* 211.

22. "Radio Today," *New York Times,* Dec. 19, 1944, 37; Old Time Radio Downloads, *Theater of Romance,* "Casablanca," www.oldtimeradiodownloads.com/drama/theater-of-romance/casablanca-1944-12-19 ; Dunning, *On the Air,* 583–84. The KNX collection at the Thousand Oaks Library in LA has a script collection from this show and from *The Crisco's (also known as Dreft) Star Playhouse.*

23. "'Screen Guild' Renewed on Full CBS Network," *Radio Daily,* Jan. 15, 1943, 1, 2; Dunning, *On the Air,* 601. Given the electronic transcription of numerous

episodes, *Lux* and *Screen Guild* are the most widely available shows in my study. Outlets include DVD bonus features (e.g., *Screen Guild*'s version on *Casablanca* DVD releases), online collectors like Jerry Haendiges and his Old Time Radio site (otrsite.com), and other internet sites, podcast apps, and satellite radio. The Margaret Herrick Library in Los Angeles has *Lux* scripts, and Special Collections at the University of California, Santa Barbara, houses *Screen Guild* scripts from 1942 to 1948.

24. This *Casablanca* episode appears to be lost, although fragmentary descriptions of it exist.

25. See Hilmes, *Hollywood and Broadcasting*, 62–63, 96–110; and Michele Hilmes, *Radio Voices: American Broadcasting, 1922–1952* (Minneapolis: University of Minnesota Press, 1997), 214.

26. The Sound Online Inventory and Catalog (or SONIC database) in the Motion Picture, Broadcasting, and Recorded Sound Division of the Recorded Sound Reference Center at the Library of Congress has the most episodes of *Crisco's Star Playhouse* (categorizing it as *Star Playhouse*). These include four episodes of its "Casablanca" (1, 2, 3, and the penultimate episode). My thanks to NBCUniversal, the sole owner of all copyrights and exclusive rights to this material, for permission for phonoduplication from the LOC for research purposes. Thanks also to David Sager, reference assistant in the LOC's Recorded Sound Reference Center, for locating these episodes and to Ryan Chroninger, public service assistant for the LOC, for duplicating and delivering these episodes to me.

27. "She Made It: Women Creating Television and Radio—Anne Hummert, Radio Producer, Writer, Executive," Paley Center for Media, www.shemadeit.org/meet/biography.aspx?m=124; "Radio—Hummert's Mill," *Time*, Jan. 23, 1939, 38; Jim Cox, *Frank and Anne Hummert's Radio Factory* (Jefferson, NC: McFarland, 2003).

28. Dunning, *On the Air*, 583. *Theater of Romance*'s "Casablanca" (and episodes featuring other films) can be streamed or downloaded on My Old Radio, www.myoldradio.com/old-radio-episodes/theater-of-romance-casablanca; and the Internet Archive, https://archive.org/details/Romance_339/Romance44-12-19083Casablanca.mp3).

29. "Radio Is My Beat," *Radio Daily*, Feb. 4, 1943, 4; Burt A. Folkart, "Radio, Television Writer Jean Holloway Tobin Dies," *Los Angeles Times*, Nov. 16, 1989, www.latimes.com/archives/la-xpm-1989-11-16-mn-1884-story.html.

30. Richard Dyer, *Heavenly Bodies: Film Stars and Society* (New York: Routledge, 1986); Gaylyn Studlar, *This Mad Masquerade: Stardom and Masculinity in the Jazz Age* (New York: Columbia University Press, 1996).

31. Sarah Thomas, *Peter Lorre: Face Maker: Constructing Stardom and Performance in Hollywood and Europe* (New York: Berghahn, 2012); Christine Becker, *It's the Pictures That Got Small: Hollywood Film Stars on 1950s Television* (Middleton, CT: Wesleyan University Press, 2008); and Susan Murray, *Hitch Your Antenna to the Stars: Early Television and Broadcast Stardom* (New York: Routledge, 2005).

32. "Notorious," *Lux* (Jan. 26, 1948) and *Screen Guild* (Jan. 6, 1949). Among other roles, Bergman performed in *Lux*'s version of *Gaslight* (1944) (April 29, 1946)

with original costar Charles Boyer and assumed new roles like the title character in *Jane Eyre* (1944) on *Lux* (June 14, 1948). For a broader view of her work, see David Smit, *Ingrid Bergman: The Life, Career, and Public Image* (Jefferson, NC: McFarland, 2012).

33. For more on Rains's career, see Ronald L. Smith, *Horror Stars on Radio: The Broadcast Histories of 29 Chilling Hollywood Voices* (Jefferson, NC: McFarland, 2010), esp. 171–81. For more on Lorre, see Thomas, *Peter Lorre.*

34. Dunning, *On the Air,* 111.

35. On *Screen Guild* Ladd starred in "This Gun for Hire" (April 2, 1945), "The Glass Key" (July 22, 1946), and "The Blue Dahlia" (April 21, 1949).

36. Both Whitman and Wilson had careers that crossed media, though they were constrained by Jim Crow. For more on Whitman's transmedia career, see, on vaudeville, "Ernie Whitman's Vaude Act," *Billboard,* April 16, 1932, 8; and on radio, Hilmes, *Radio Voices,* 80, 263. Whitman also had numerous movie credits in supporting roles, including *Jesse James* (1939) and *Cabin in the Sky* (1943), and a starring role in 1952 on TV sitcom *The Beulah Show* (ABC, 1950–53). Wilson performed live in vaudeville, nightclubs, and theater and also appeared on radio, film, and television. He sang on radio's *The Chamber Music Society of Lower Basin Street* (Blue Network, 1940–44), for example, and acted, beyond his role in *Casablanca,* in such films as *Cairo* (1942) and *Stormy Weather* (1943). On TV, he also starred in *The Beulah Show.* See "Dooley Wilson Signs Long-Term Contract," *Pittsburgh Courier,* June 26, 1943, 20; "Dooley & Dodo," *Time,* May 10, 1943, 68.

37. Beyond *Philip Morris*'s "The 39 Steps" (May 21, 1943) and "Suspicion" (Oct. 15, 1943), Carroll also starred in its adaptations of *The Shop around the Corner* (1940) (April 16, 1943), *Now, Voyager* (1942) (Oct. 30, 1943), and other titles. *Philip Morris Playhouse* file, New York Public Library for the Performing Arts, Lincoln Center, New York.

38. McCambridge's film roles included *Johnny Guitar* (1954) and *Touch of Evil* (1958). Beyond her work in original radio dramas, she played in *Screen Guild* versions of *The Informer* (1935) (Oct. 19, 1950) and *The Guilt of Janet Ames* (1947) (March 1, 1951).

39. On television's foray into anthology dramas, see Becker, *It's the Pictures,* 189–220.

40. *Casablanca*'s script is in the Warner Bros. Archives, University of Southern California School of Cinematic Arts, Los Angeles; it is available online at ScreenplayExplorer.com.

41. In *Serial Television: Big Drama on the Small Screen* (London: BFI, 2004), 107–8, Glen Creeber discusses the serial's ability to offer greater character development than more finite forms.

42. *Star Playhouse* introduces, for example, a spy who threatens Ilsa in Paris. But the first few installments are divided into two parts that demonstrate the priority of signature characters: they begin with Sam and Rick and then move to Rick and Ilsa. The penultimate episode occurs at the airport with story core elements in place (e.g., Rick's trickery of Renault, his noble deception of Ilsa). That said, the story's longer

running time likely included new characters and subplots that, for now, remain unknown.

43. See David Bordwell, "Classical Hollywood Cinema: Narrational Principles and Procedures," in *Narrative, Apparatus, Ideology: A Film Theory Reader,* ed. Philip Rosen (New York: Columbia University Press, 1986), 17–34.

44. Janet Staiger, *Interpreting Films: Studies in the Historical Reception of American Cinema* (Princeton, NJ: Princeton University Press, 1992), 101–23.

45. Colin McArthur, *The "Casablanca" File* (London: Half Brick Images, 1992).

46. Ella Shohat and Robert Stam, *Unthinking Eurocentrism: Multiculturalism and the Media* (London: Routledge, 1994).

47. Ginette Vincendeau, *Pépé le Moko* (London: BFI Classics, 1998).

48. In *Algiers,* the detective's description of the Casbah cuts some offensive passages from Duvivier's film, as well as its sex and suicide.

49. Jerry Wald to Irene Lee, "*Everybody Comes to Rick's,*" Warner Bros. interoffice memo, Dec. 23, 1941, box 4B, file 1881A F005191, Warner Bros. Archives, University of Southern California School of Cinematic Arts, Los Angeles.

50. *Casablanca*'s "battle of the songs"—between German soldiers singing "Die Wacht am Rhein" and refugees singing "La Marseillaise"—borrows from Jean Renoir's *La Grande Illusion* (1937), where a battle of the same songs occurs in a German prisoner-of-war camp. *Casablanca*'s platonic ending may have been inspired by the revised ending of Julien Duvivier's *La belle équipe* (1936), where Jeannot (Jean Gabin) does not kill his friend Charlot (Charles Vanel) over the woman they love—Gina (Viviane Romance)—but dismisses her, investing instead in male friendship.

51. Extras include some Asian actors, shown briefly in the opening scenes of Rick's café. Excepting the uncredited Abdullah Abbas, very few Arabs are cast in the film, making the predominance of whiteness in the fictional Casablanca additionally pronounced.

52. See Amy Lawrence, "The Voice as Mask," in *Dietrich Icon,* ed. Gerd Gemünden and Mary R. Desjardins (Chapel Hill, NC: Duke University Press, 2007), 79–99.

53. Claudia Gorbman, *Unheard Melodies: Narrative Film Music* (Bloomington: Indiana University Press, 1987), 82–83.

54. Verma, *Theater of the Mind,* 33.

55. Derek B. Scott, "Orientalism and Musical Style," *Musical Quarterly* 82, no. 2 (Summer 1998): 309–35.

56. Richard Raskin argues in "*Casablanca* and United States Foreign Policy," *Film History* 4, no. 2 (1990): 161, that the US did not recognize the Free French diplomatically until 1944. Furthermore, US support of the North African Vichy France leadership saw the arrest of "men like Victor Laszlo." Despite the "anti-Free French orientation" of the US and "support of Vichy leaders in North Africa," the film and radio shows projected solidarity with the Free French for patriotic and promotional purposes.

57. Jacob Smith, *Vocal Tracks: Performance and Sound Media* (Berkeley: University of California, 2008), 34–35. As Smith observes, magnetic tape and multitrack-

ing technologies that radio networks used to manipulate the studio audience track did not come into broad commercial usage until 1947. Prior to this, though, liveness was not a simple signifier of authenticity; networks used its spontaneity as a commodity to sell shows. On another note, the presence of the Fighting French at the radio studio recalls a promotion featuring Allied French forces that Warner Bros. used at *Casablanca*'s New York premiere. See Richard Maltby, "'A Brief Romantic Interlude': Dick and Jane Go to 3½ Seconds of the Classical Hollywood Cinema," in *Post-Theory: Reconstructing Film Studies,* ed. David Bordwell and Noel Carroll (Madison: University of Wisconsin Press, 1996), 458.

58. Gorbman, *Unheard Melodies,* 7. See also Birger Langkjær, "*Casablanca* and Popular Music as Film Music," *P.O.V.* 14 (Dec. 2002): http://pov.imv.au.dk /Issue_14/section_1/artc7A.html.

59. On the song's romantic and nostalgic value in the film, see Caryl Flinn, *Strains of Utopia: Gender, Nostalgia, and Hollywood Film Music* (Princeton, NJ: Princeton University Press, 1992), 108.

60. Smith, *Vocal Tracks,* 134–38. He identifies the rasp as a central Black performative elocution at this time.

61. "Picture Tie-Ups for Music Machine Operators," *Billboard,* June 26, 1943, 72; "Pubs Plug More Oldies as Wax and Pix Hypo Pay-Off," *Billboard,* July 8, 1944, 16.

62. Justin Wyatt, *High Concept: Movies and Marketing in Hollywood* (Austin: University of Texas Press, 1994).

63. Philip Scheuer, "This Town Called Hollywood," *Chicago Sunday Tribune,* Oct. 3, 1943, 7, discusses how Warner Bros.' *The Great Lie* (1941) catapulted Tchaikovsky's 1888 "Piano Concerto No. 1 in B Flat Minor, Op. 23" to hit status.

64. "Time Goes By and Finally It Clicks via Pic," *Billboard,* August 28, 1954, 36. *Casablanca*'s version of the song deleted the first stanza (with lyrics like "This day and age we're living in / Gives cause for apprehension"), focusing more explicitly on its romantic tenor.

65. "Petrillo to Face Courts for Record Ban," *Broadcasting, Broadcast Advertising,* July 27, 1942, 7–8, 52. The strike was over royalty payments—a dispute the union would win.

66. "Public Demand Forecast by Kids," *Billboard,* June 10, 1944, 13, 19; "Time Is Now for 'As Time Goes By,'" *Billboard,* March 6, 1943, 23; "Dooley & Dodo," *Time,* May 10, 1943, 68.

67. "National and Regional Best-Selling Retail Records" and "National and Regional Sheet Music Best Sellers," *Billboard,* May 1, 1943, 22; "Recordings: Most Popular Juke Box Records," *Billboard,* Sept. 25, 1943, 122.

68. "Dooley & Dodo," 68.

69. As an example of this lasting association, Wilson's hometown of Tyler, Texas, erected a commemorative plaque that reads, "Cast as pianist, Sam, in *Casablanca* performing 'As Time Goes By.'" See Faith Harper, "Dooley Wilson, Actor Known as Sam in *Casablanca,* Honored with Downtown Marker," *Tyler Morning Telegraph,* Jan. 10, 2017, https://tylerpaper.com/news/local/dooley-wilson-actor-

known-as-sam-in-casablanca-honored-with-downtown-marker/article_376d6783-8216-5bb8-a0b4-c7c466f83fff.html.

70. "Network Song Favorites," *Radio Daily,* March 29, 1943, 6 and April 12, 1943, 6; "*Billboard* Music Popularity Chart," *Billboard,* May 1, 1943, 22; "ACI Hits for 1943," *Radio Daily,* Jan. 10, 1944, 6.

71. Day sings "As Time Goes By" on two episodes of *Jack Benny:* "From Quantico, Virginia," Jan. 31, 1943 (where Benny was entertaining troops) and "Little Red Riding Hood" (hosted by Orson Welles), April 4, 1943.

72. "Radio Reviews: 'As Time Goes By,'" *Variety,* Dec. 20, 1944, 37.

73. Ernest Mathijs, "Time Wasted," *Flow* (March 2010), www.flowjournal.org/2010/03/time-wasted-ernest-mathijs-the-university-of-british-columbia.

74. Thomas Sebeok's *A Sign Is Just a Sign* (Bloomington: Indiana University Press, 1991) is one of the academic works that references the song in its title. It also lists other works that refer to the song and film in their titles (4–6).

75. Jacob Smith, *Spoken Word: Postwar American Phonograph Cultures* (Berkeley: University of California Press, 2011), 188. Smith discusses catchphrases in relation to comedy, but they have broader application in sound media owing to their efficient expression of performer and character.

76. Smith, 188–92, 124.

77. Lisa Gitelman, *Always Already New: Media, History, and the Data of Culture* (Cambridge, MA: MIT Press, 2006), 40, 35–36.

78. Smith, *Vocal Tracks,* 103.

79. Seán Street, *The Memory of Sound: Preserving the Sonic Past* (London: Routledge, 2015).

80. David Lipson, "We'll Always Have *Casablanca,*" letter to the editor, *New York Times,* July 8, 2018, A20.

81. Thomas Elsaesser and Malte Hagener, *Film Theory: An Introduction through the Senses* (London: Routledge, 2010), 129.

82. Smith, *Spoken Word,* 10, 124.

83. Thomas, *Peter Lorre,* 167.

84. Susan Murray, "I Know What You Did Last Summer: Sarah Michelle Gellar and Crossover Teen Stardom," in *Undead TV: Essays on "Buffy the Vampire Slayer,"* ed. Elana Levine and Lisa Parks (Durham, NC: Duke University Press, 2007), 43–44, 53.

85. Jesse Schlotterbeck, "Radio Noir in the USA," in *A Companion to Film Noir,* ed. Helen Hanson and André Spicer (New York: Wiley-Blackwell, 2013), 435.

86. Gerald Duchovnay, *Humphrey Bogart: A Bio-Bibliography* (Westport, CT: Greenwood Press, 1999), 315–18. Not all of the author's list of radio appearances are correct or complete. I have sought to verify and cross-check Bogart's appearances through studio files, radio program logs, and newspapers. "The Humphrey Bogart Collection," a selection of his radio performances (available through Otrcat.com and iTunes) was also helpful.

87. "Bogart's on Television—But Not for Long," *New York News,* May 30, 1955, 7.

88. For each invitation to perform, the studio produced "letters of clearance"—standard agreements authorizing Bogart to appear on radio and specifying which films of his to plug. For the radio clause in such contracts, see negotiations between Bogart's agent, Sam Jaffe, and Warner executives Steve Trilling, Jack Warner, and Hal Wallis, Dec. 27, 1941, file 28248 and F000635 in the Warner Bros. Archives, University of Southern California School of Cinematic Arts, Los Angeles.

89. *Screen Guild* aired "The Petrified Forest" on January 7, 1940, and "The Maltese Falcon" on September 20, 1943, and May 18, 1950. This show's other adaptations with Bogart included *The Amazing Dr. Clitterhouse* (1938) (Nov. 2, 1941); *High Sierra* (1941) (Jan. 4, 1942, and April 17, 1944); *If You Could Only Cook* (1935) (Jan. 26, 1941, and Nov. 23, 1941); *Across the Pacific* (1942) (Jan. 25, 1943); and *13 Rue Madeleine* (1947) (Nov. 25, 1948).

90. "Conflict" and "One Way Passage" aired, respectively, Sept. 11, 1945, and Dec. 18, 1945.

91. *Lux*'s "To Have and Have Not" aired on Oct. 13, 1946, "The Treasure of the Sierra Madre" on April 18, 1949, and "The African Queen" on Dec. 15, 1952. Other productions featuring Bogart on *Lux* were *Bullets or Ballots* (1936) (April 17, 1939) and *Moontide* (1942) (April 30, 1945).

92. "Love's Lonely Counterfeit" aired on *Suspense* (March 8, 1945); "Dead Man" on *Humphrey Bogart Presents* (Sept. 17, 1949). Whether this radio program continued beyond this pilot episode is unknown.

93. As just one example of this, *To Have and Have Not* invokes aspects of *Casablanca.* It is set in 1940 in the French colony of Martinique, which was part of Vichy France. Bogart plays a cynical fishing boat owner who initially refuses to help two Resistance fighters to escape. Marcel Dalio plays a French character known as "Frenchy" and Hoagy Carmichael plays Cricket, a piano player in the local café. Bogart and Bacall have a romance and, at the end, Bogart obtains harbor letters necessary for him and his friends and the Resistance fighters to escape Martinique.

94. Claudia Gorbman, "The Master's Voice," *Film Quarterly* 68, no. 2 (Winter 2014): 9. I am indebted to Claudia for her helpful comments here.

95. Arthur Hopkins, quoted in Jeffrey Meyers, *Bogart: A Life in Hollywood* (London: Deutsch, 1997), 49.

96. Robert Sklar, *City Boys: Cagney, Bogart, Garfield* (Princeton, NJ: Princeton University Press, 1992), 12.

97. Sarah Kozloff, *Overhearing Film Dialogue* (Berkeley: University of California Press, 2000), 202, 205–6.

98. Before Bogart played Philip Marlowe in *The Big Sleep* in 1946, Dick Powell had the role in 1944's *Murder, My Sweet.* Both Robert Montgomery in *Lady in the Lake* (1947) and George Montgomery in *The Brasher Doubloon* (1947) followed. On radio, first Van Heflin and then Gerald Mohr starred as the title character in *The Adventures of Philip Marlowe* (1947–51). Among others, Howard Duff played Spade on radio in *The Adventures of Sam Spade* (1946–50).

99. Naremore, *More Than Night* (2008 ed.), 10, 259-260; Schlotterbeck, "Radio Noir," 423–39.

100. Smith, *Horror Stars on Radio,* 171–81.

101. Thomas, *Peter Lorre,* 167–68.

102. See, for example, *The Eddie Cantor Show* (NBC, March 5, 1941) (available from "My Old Time Radio," www.myoldradio.com/old-radio-episodes/eddie-cantor-humphrey-bogart); and "The Frightwig Murder Case," *Jack Benny* (Jan. 25 and Feb. 1, 1942) (available on YouTube, www.youtube.com/watch?v=DOvc4dURldk).

103. "All Nationalities Included in Film," part of the Warner Bros. press book for *Casablanca* in the Warner Bros. Archives, University of Southern California School of Cinematic Arts, Los Angeles.

104. See Noah Isenberg, *We'll Always Have "Casablanca": The Life, Legend, and Afterlife of Hollywood's Most Beloved Movie* (New York: Norton, 2017), 123–62.

105. See, for example, Clayton R. Koppes and Gregory D. Black, *Hollywood Goes to War: How Politics, Profits, and Propaganda Shaped World War II* (Berkeley: University of California Press, 1990).

106. Hilmes, *Radio Voices,* 230–70; Thomas Cripps, *Making Movies Black: The Hollywood Message Movie from WWII to the Civil Rights Era* (New York: Oxford University Press, 1993).

107. Lillian Bergquist, "*Casablanca:* Feature Review," Office of War Information, Bureau of Motion Pictures Hollywood Office, Oct. 26, 1942, from the National Archives, https://soar.kennesaw.edu/bitstream/handle/11360/3570/Casablanca-review.pdf?sequence=1&isAllowed=y.

108. Hilmes, *Radio Voices,* xxi, 235.

109. Michel Chion, *The Voice in Cinema,* ed. and trans. Claudia Gorbman (New York: Columbia University Press, 1999), 5, 21 (Chion's emphases).

110. Rudolph Arnheim, *Radio: An Art of Sound,* trans. Margaret Ludwig and Herbert Read (New York: Da Capo, 1972), 39–40.

111. Verma, *Theater of the Mind,* 36.

112. Hilmes, *Radio Voices,* xix, 21, 76, 93, 235–36. Hilmes details how US awareness of Hitler's racist agenda inspired radio to join other efforts to address the problem at home.

113. Arnheim, *Radio,* 47.

114. Later revisionist work on *Casablanca,* such as Michael Walsh's novel *As Time Goes By* (1998), addresses issues of gender and race. In providing both a prequel and sequel to the film, Walsh makes Ilsa an action heroine and Sam more integral to the story.

115. The exception was Latino actor Santos Ortega, who played Renault in *Romance.*

116. *The Amos 'n' Andy Show* (NBC, CBS 1928–55) is a famous case of white men playing the Black title characters. Adding gender switching to this formula, the Black maid, the title character of *The Beulah Show,* was played by white men before Hattie McDaniel assumed the role in 1947.

117. For more on this, see my "Pre-Cult: *Casablanca,* Radio Adaptation, and Transmedia in the 1940s," *New Review of Film and Television Studies* 13, no. 1 (2015): 45–62.

118. See Eleanor Patterson, "Capturing the Flow: The Growth of the Old-Time-Radio Collecting Culture in the United States during the 1970s," *Journal of Cinema and Media Studies* 59, no. 3 (Spring 2020): 46–68. Today the internet is a rich resource for "Old Time Radio" film adaptations, while theater troupes also perform radio adaptations of films on stages across the United States, providing a live analog dimension to these revivals.

CHAPTER 2. BACK IN THEATERS

1. "Top Grossers of the Season," *Variety,* Jan. 5, 1944, 54; "14 Warner Bros. Films Headed for $36,000,000," *Variety,* Jan. 5, 1944, 55. *Casablanca* earned $3,700,000 (around $64,400,000 today, adjusted for inflation) and *This Is the Army* $4,800,000 ($83,500,000).

2. Bosley Crowther, "Casablanca," *New York Times,* Nov. 27, 1942, www.nytimes.com/1942/11/27/archives/casablanca-with-humphrey-bogart-and-ingrid-bergman-at-hollywood.html. Oscar nominations without a win were Best Actor, Humphrey Bogart; Best Supporting Actor, Claude Rains; Best Music Score, Max Steiner; Best Film Editing, Owen Marks; and Best Cinematography-Black and White, Arthur Edeson.

3. Julian Stringer, "Raiding the Archive: Film Festivals and the Revival of Classic Hollywood," in *Memory and Popular Film,* ed. Paul Grainge (Manchester, UK: Manchester University Press, 2003), 81.

4. Gorham Kindem, "The Postwar Motion Picture Industry," in *Boom and Bust: American Cinema in the 1940s,* ed. Thomas Schatz (Berkeley: University of California Press, 1997), 293; Brian Hannan, *Coming Back to a Theater Near You: A History of Hollywood Reissues, 1914–2014* (Jefferson, NC: McFarland, 2016).

5. Mark Jancovich and Shane Brown, "'The Screen's Number One and Number Two Bogeymen': The Critical Reception of Boris Karloff and Bela Lugosi in the 1930s and 1940s," in *Cult Film Stardom: Offbeat Attractions and Processes of Cultification,* ed. Kate Egan and Sarah Thomas (Basingstoke, UK: Palgrave Macmillan, 2013), 243. While arguing that cultish reading strategies were already evident in Hollywood's earlier years, the authors cite the impact of postwar retrospective houses on forming movie cults.

6. J. P. Telotte, "The Classical Cult Film," in *The Cult Film Experience: Beyond All Reason,* ed. J. P. Telotte (Austin: University of Texas Press, 1991), 40.

7. Mark Jancovich, "Cult Fictions: Cult Movies, Subcultural Capital and the Production of Cultural Distinctions," *Cultural Studies* 16, no. 2 (2002): 308.

8. Ernest Mathijs and Jamie Sexton, *Cult Cinema* (West Sussex, UK: Wiley-Blackwell, 2011), 32, 39.

9. Umberto Eco, *Travels in Hyperreality* (1973; New York: Harcourt, Brace, 1983), 198. Eco writes that beyond being loved, the cult film "must provide a completely furnished world so that its fans can quote characters and episodes as if they were aspects of the fan's private sectarian world. . . . [It] must be already ramshackle, rickety, unhinged in itself."

10. On the discursive constitution of cult, see I. Q. Hunter, *Cult Film as a Guide to Life: Fandom, Adaptation, and Identity* (London: Bloomsbury, 2016), 3; and Jamie Sexton, "From Bad to Good and Back to Bad Again: Cult Cinema and Its Unstable Trajectory," in *B Is for Bad Cinema: Aesthetics, Politics, and Cultural Value,* ed. Claire Perkins and Constantine Verevis (Albany: State University of New York Press, 2014), 142.

11. Eric Hoyt, *Hollywood Vault: Film Libraries before Home Video* (Berkeley: University of California Press, 2014), 4, 109.

12. Hoyt, 112–13; "Record Reissues," *Hollywood Reporter,* Sept. 18, 1950, 1; "Re-Issue Record Set in 1953–54: More Than 200 Re-releases Save the Day in Product Shortage," *Hollywood Reporter,* July 22, 1954, 1, 9.

13. "Reissues Playing in 8,000 Theatres, Budd Rogers of Realart Reports," *Boxoffice,* Oct. 22, 1949, 21; "Feature Film Index: A Complete Production Record for the Year," *Boxoffice,* Dec. 3, 1949, C107–48.

14. "Feature Film Index," *Boxoffice,* Dec. 3, 1949.

15. "Feature Film Index."

16. Kindem, "Postwar Motion Picture Industry," 285–328; James M. Jerauld, "Features Down to 368 as Film Drop Continues," *Boxoffice,* June 20, 1953, 9. See also Hoyt, *Hollywood Vault,* 106–41.

17. Hoyt, *Hollywood Vault,* 139.

18. "Bring-'Em-Back-with-Live-New-Bally for 100 Reissues Now Booked," *Variety,* July 7, 1954, 11.

19. "$20,000,000 from 20th Reissues in Past Nine Years," *Hollywood Reporter,* Oct. 27, 1955, 1, 4; "Pictures: 'Pompeii,' 'She' to Add 500G for RKO," *Variety,* Dec. 1, 1948, 5. As Hannan notes, not all theatrical reissues (including *Casablanca*'s rerelease in regular theaters in 1957) found consistent success (*Coming Back,* 90).

20. "Bring-'Em-Back-with-Live-New-Bally" (see note 18 above).

21. "Over 160 Re-releases in Circulation to Fill Gaps, Grab Coin before TV Sale," *Hollywood Reporter,* July 19, 1956, 1, 4; "Stations Offered 13 Pkgs. of Warner Films by AAP," *Billboard,* April 21, 1956, 12. When AAP bought the Warner Bros. library primarily for TV distribution in 1956, it agreed to offer theater owners "TV protection" until September 1, 1957. Television stations had to delay showing the films until then, while theater owners were given a short respite from broadcast competition. This agreement responded to theater owners' initial objections, but AAP subsequently granted them little further protection.

22. Complaints about reissues often targeted their radical alteration. Some silent and sound films were rescored and retitled to update them or feign their newness, or they were edited to suit exhibitor slots for double features and 1950s-era censorship. Critics saw these practices as tampering with a film's authenticity or making it incomprehensible and open to audience derision. See Edward Connor, "Ruining Re-issues," *Films in Review* 5, no. 5 (May 1954): 221–23, 235; and Richard Kraft, "Audience Stupidity: The Pleasure of Old Films Can be Spoiled by the Laughter of Empty Minds," *Films in Review,* no. 3 (March 1954): 113–14.

23. Besides the *Casablanca/G-Men* double feature, other Warner Bros. reissues at this time were *Angels with Dirty Faces* (1938) / *They Drive by Night* (1940), and *Castle on the Hudson* (1940) / *Sergeant York* (1941).

24. See, for example, the *Washington Post,* May 24, 1949, 14; and May 25, 1949, 12. *Casablanca* Publicity: folder F002562, Warner Bros. Archives, University of Southern California School of Cinematic Arts, Los Angeles.

25. In February 1950, for example, the Royal Theatre, located in a Black neighborhood in Atlanta, debuted *Casablanca*'s reissue with a presumably crowd-pleasing installment of *Bruce Gentry: Daredevil of the Skies* (1949), a Columbia Pictures serial in the science fiction / action genre (advertisement, *Atlanta Daily World,* Feb. 7, 1950, 3). See also Douglas Gomery, *Shared Pleasures: A History of Movie Presentation in the United States* (Madison: University of Wisconsin Press, 1992), 77–79.

26. "Chi Soars to Strongest Biz in Weeks," *Variety Picture Grosses,* June 1, 1949, 9.

27. Interoffice Communication, Warner Bros. Pictures Distributing Corporation, Home Office / Benjamin Kalmenson, Vice-President in charge of distribution, April 29, 1949, folder F008496-15502A, "49–52 Incomplete Designations," Warner Bros. Archives, University of Southern California School of Cinematic Arts, Los Angeles. Rental terms are specified in this boilerplate memo sent to theaters. The standard arrangement between Warner Bros. and theaters fell into either "percentage situations" (35 percent for the program) or "flat rental situations" (50 percent over the top flat rental for the program). If pictures played in a single bill, the studio contracted for 25 percent of the theater's ticket income.

28. "Feature Chart," *Boxoffice,* Feb. 28, 1948, B4-B9. *Marked Woman* appeared on a double bill with *Dust Be My Destiny* (1939), starring John Garfield; "Feature Index," *Boxoffice,* Dec. 3, 1949, 140–42.

29. Interoffice Communication, Warner Bros. Pictures Distributing Corporation, Home Office / Benjamin Kalmenson, Vice-President in charge of distribution, a boilerplate memo for theaters, May 14, 1952, folder F008494, "Warner Circuit—1952," Warner Bros. Archives, University of Southern California School of Cinematic Arts, Los Angeles.

30. Hannan, *Coming Back,* 5.

31. A. E. Piggins, Warner Bros. Picture Distributing Corporation in Toronto, to Home Office, Feb. 4, 1954, on 16 mm billings, folder 12678, box 3, Warner Bros. Archives, University of Southern California School of Cinematic Arts, Los Angeles.

32. "Warners Sells 750 Features to PRM, Inc.," *Motion Picture Daily,* March 2, 1956, 1, 6. Warner Bros. sold its pre-1948 library for $20 million (over $200,000,000 today). For other terms of this sale, see P. D. Knecht to Robert W. Perkins, Esq. Warner Pictures, Inc., memo, June 14, 1956, "Casablanca Picture File," folder F002953-2870, and Warner Bros. Pictures to Vivienne Nearing, Esq., memo, Dec. 11, 1959, folder F000750-001, box 2, 1956, both in the Warner Bros. Archives, University of Southern California School of Cinematic Arts, Los Angeles. For more on the early shifting ownership of Warner Bros.' titles, see Hoyt, *Hollywood Vault,* 167–94.

33. "'Whimsical Phenomenon' of Bogart's Theatrical Comeback after TV Play-off," *Variety,* June 16, 1965, 4. UA was attracted to this "comeback" because it meant that these oldies could be "taken out of the flat rental field into the percentage class," offering them potentially better profits from ticket sales.

34. In their respective books, Haidee Wasson and Dana Polan have shown that postwar retrospective houses were not the start of institutional or cultural interests in exhibiting alternative movies in unconventional surroundings. Rather, the decades that preceded this era witnessed the growth of museum film libraries, academic curricula, specialized "little cinemas," film societies (including those at Harvard University), and public critics that raised the profile of the art, history, politics, and educational potential of cinema. See Haidee Wasson, *Museum Movies: The Museum of Modern Art and the Birth of Art Cinema* (Berkeley: University of California Press, 2005); and Dana Polan, *Scenes of Instruction: The Beginnings of the U.S. Study of Film* (Berkeley: University of California Press, 2007).

35. Ben Davis, *Repertory Movie Theaters of New York City: Havens for Revivals, Indies, and the Avant-Garde, 1960–1994* (Jefferson, NC: McFarland, 2017), 18. See also Jim Lane, "Critical and Cultural Reception of the European Art Film in 1950s America: A Case Study of the Brattle Theatre (Cambridge, Massachusetts)," *Film History* 24, nos. 3–4 (1994): 51–64.

36. Davis, in *Repertory Movie Theaters,* provides a more comprehensive view of the postwar rise of repertory houses.

37. Mathijs and Sexton, *Cult Cinema,* 32–33. The authors discuss the closeness of art cinema and cult cinema exhibition, as both venues rely "heavily on a loyal audience that is heavily invested in film taste," but with the latter defined by "a more lively, visceral attitude."

38. Jancovich, "Cult Fictions," 317.

39. Greg Taylor, *Artists in the Audience: Cults, Camp, and American Film Criticism* (Princeton, NJ: Princeton University Press, 1999), 15.

40. Taylor, 75, 96, 98. On an earlier generation of influential film critics, see David Bordwell, *The Rhapsodes: How 1940s Critics Changed American Film Culture* (Chicago: University of Chicago Press, 2016).

41. Sexton, "From Bad to Good," 136.

42. Davis, *Repertory Movie Theaters,* 18–22.

43. Ellen Jaffe, "There's No Movie like an Old Movie," *Seventeen,* Jan. 1972, 135.

44. Such prints arose from cost cutting by companies, rights holders, or regional distributors unwilling to strike new prints for theaters that would not quickly recoup the investment, leading to shortages and overuse of prints in circulation. For testimonials from repertory theater attendees on how their cinephilia intersected with the dilapidated condition of these theaters, see Davis, *Repertory Movie Theaters,* 20–22.

45. Hoyt, *Hollywood Vault,* 109, 118–19; Kathryn J. Frydl, *The G.I. Bill* (New York: Cambridge University Press, 2009).

46. Taylor, *Artists in the Audience,* 75.

47. Richard Shepro, "The Movies in Cambridge: Some Thoughts, Some History," *Harvard Crimson,* April 29, 1974, www.thecrimson.com/article/1974/4/29/the-movies-in-cambridge-some-thoughts.

48. Kraft, "Audience Stupidity," 113–14. Wasson also details MoMA's problems with rowdy audience members (*Museum Movies,* 176–82).

49. Davis, *Repertory Movie Theaters,* 20. See also Bosley Crowther's series of articles about reissues, including "Remember This One? Public Interest in Old Films Is Gauged," *New York Times,* March 14, 1954, 11; "Revivals Return: New Business Found in Good Old Films," *New York Times,* March 4, 1960, 81; and "Boom in Revivals: More New York Houses Showing Old Films," *New York Times,* Jan. 21, 1962, 93.

50. J. Hoberman and Jonathan Rosenbaum, *Midnight Movies* (New York: Da Capo, 1983), 30–31; Robert B. Ray, *A Certain Tendency of the Hollywood Cinema, 1930–1980* (Princeton, NJ: Princeton University Press, 1985), 264.

51. Robert Joseph, "Cinema," *Arts and Architecture,* Oct. 1950: 42–43; J.Z., "That Old Time Revival," *Cue,* Sept. 2, 1950, 12–13.

52. Fred Davis, *Yearning for Yesterday: A Sociology of Nostalgia* (New York: Free Press, 1979), 11–12.

53. Telotte, "The Classical Cult Film," 40.

54. John Engstrom, "As Time Goes By: 100 Years of the Brattle," www.brattlefilm.org/brattlefilm/first100.html; "Timeline of Brattle History," www.brattlefilm.org/brattlefilm/history.html; Gavin W. Kleespies and Katie MacDonald, "The Brattle Theatre," www.harvardsquare.com/History/Glimpses/The-Brattle.aspx; George H. Watson, "Anniversary of a Theatre," *Harvard Crimson,* Feb. 16, 1957. Polan has shown that, since the early 1900s, Harvard University has explored ways of incorporating film into study and the campus's intellectual life, including creating the Harvard Film Society in 1936 (*Scenes of Instruction,* 113–74).

55. Shawn Levy, "Miracle on Brattle Street," *Boxoffice,* April 1, 1990, 38–39.

56. Levy, 38–39. A Janus Catalog (undated) shows that the films of Michelangelo Antonioni, Ingmar Bergman, Federico Fellini, and Akira Kurosawa, along with *Citizen Kane* (1940), *King Kong,* and a few other US films, were staples for the company. See also Peter Cowie, "Janus and the Art House Legacy," in *Essential Art House Cinema: 50 Years of Janus Films,* ed. Elizabeth Helfgott (New York: Janus Films, 2006), 10–31.

57. Engstrom, "As Time Goes By." The Brattle's economic situation varied during the years, with video the greatest intrusion on the retrospective house business in the 1980s. On the Brattle's rise and decline, see Mo Lotman, *Harvard Square: An Illustrated History Since 1950* (New York: Stewart, Tabori & Chang, 2009), 30–31.

58. For broader chronicles of the postwar era and the counterculture, see John Morton Blum, *Years of Discord: American Politics and Society, 1961–1974* (New York: Norton, 1991); and David Steigerwald, *The Sixties and the End of Modern America* (New York: St. Martin's, 1995).

59. Jerome Karabel, *The Chosen: The Hidden History of Admission and Exclusion at Harvard, Yale, and Princeton* (New York: Houghton Mifflin, 2005), 400–405,

439–46. By 1955, Harvard accepted approximately six African American students a year out of starting classes of about one thousand; in 1970, an only marginally better 8 percent of its students were Black. Still, because it admitted some Black students, it earned the reputation as the most progressive of the Ivy League schools. In terms of female students, by the late 1970s, the number of women had grown to 35 percent of incoming classes. Karabel writes broadly about the discrimination and antidiscrimination admissions policies at Ivy League schools affecting Jews, African Americans, and women.

60. Although little evidence exists of a Black audience for Bogart at the Brattle, in the United States more generally the appeal of his stardom crossed racial boundaries. For example, African American audiences in the 1940s selected Bogart as their number one male star, while luminaries such as Malcolm X and James Baldwin later professed their admiration for the star. See "Bette, Bogart 1 and 2 in Negro Houses," *Variety,* March 31, 1943, 1, 44; Alex Haley and Malcolm X, *The Autobiography of Malcolm X* (New York: Ballantine, 2015), 102; James Baldwin, *The Devil Finds Work* (New York: Vintage International, 1976), 30.

61. Aljean Harmetz, *The Making of Casablanca: Bogart, Bergman, and World War II* (New York: Hyperion, 1992/2002), 344.

62. Mathijs and Sexton, *Cult Cinema,* 79. The timeline concerning the origin of Bogart Festivals at the Brattle is not exact, however. A 1964 article marking the festivals' tenth anniversary ("Old Faces: Bogey Worship," *Time,* Feb. 7, 1964, 82) places its origins in 1954, three years before the actor's death, though other sources disagree.

63. "Old Faces," 82. For the fate of these businesses and a historical account of Harvard Square more generally, see Nell Porter Brown, "25 Years in Harvard Square," *Harvard Magazine,* Sept.-Oct. 2011, https://harvardmagazine.com/2011/09/25-year-retrospective-on-harvard-square.

64. "Old Bogart Films Packing Them In: 'Cult of Personality' Attracts Diverse 'Hip' Crowds," *New York Times,* Jan. 28, 1965, New York Public Library for the Performing Arts, "Bogart File: 1960–69," MFL fnc 2270.

65. In 1965 alone, five books were published about Bogart: Richard Gehman's *Bogart: An Intimate Biography* (New York: Fawcett Gold Medal); Ezra Goodman's *Bogey: The Good-Bad Guy* (New York: Lyle Stuart); Paul Michael's *Humphrey Bogart: The Man and His Films* (New York: Bonanza); Clifford McCarty's *Bogey: The Films of Humphrey Bogart* (New York: Cadillac); and Jonah Ruddy and Jonathan Hill's *Bogey: The Man, the Actor, the Legend* (New York: Tower). Joe Hyam's, *Bogie: The Biography of Humphrey Bogart* (New York: Signet) came out in 1966. For more on this phenomenon, see Jack Nachbar, "'Nobody Ever Loved Me That Much': A *Casablanca* Bibliography," *Journal of Popular Film and Video* 27, no. 4 (2000): 42–45. As we see throughout the chapter, Bogart's nickname could be spelled Bogey or Bogie.

66. Telotte, "Beyond All Reason" and Wade Jennings, "The Star as Cult Icon: Judy Garland," both in *The Cult Film Experience: Beyond All Reason,* ed. J. P. Telotte (Austin: University of Texas, 1991), 8–9, 91, respectively.

67. Lotman, *Harvard Square,* 30–31; "Old Faces," 82.

68. "Harvard's Affair with H. Bogart," *Variety,* April 27, 1977, 6. On the 1960s collegiate reception of Bogart, see also Noah Isenberg, *We'll Always Have "Casablanca": The Life, Legend, and Afterlife of Hollywood's Most Beloved Movie* (New York: Norton, 2017), 209–16.

69. Levy, "Miracle on Brattle Street," 38–39.

70. Other Bogart films had cult followings, although without *Casablanca*'s longevity. See T. J. Ross, "*Beat the Devil* or Goodbye, *Casablanca*," in *The Cult Film Experience: Beyond All Reason,* ed. J. P. Telotte (Austin: University of Texas Press, 1991), 79–89; and, on *The Big Sleep,* Anne Jerslev, "Semiotics by Instinct: 'Cult Film' as a Signifying Practice between Film and Audience," in *Media Cultures: Reappraising Transnational Media,* ed. Michael Skovmand and Kim Schroder (London: Routledge, 1992), 181–98.

71. Joe Goldberg, "The Death of Sam Spade," *Evergreen Review* 7, no. 28 (Jan.-Feb. 1963): 107–16; TV movie, *Bogart* (ABC, aired April 23, 1967).

72. Andrew Sarris, "Here's Looking at You, Bogie," *Village Voice,* Feb. 14, 1977, New York Public Library for the Performing Arts, MPL fn c2270. See also Richard J. Anobile, ed., *Michael Curtiz's "Casablanca"* (London: Pan, 1974) for another manifestation, in book form, of the cinephilic and cultish attachment to Bogart and *Casablanca* at this time. Part of the press's Film Classics Library series, Anobile's book reconstructs the film through more than a thousand photos taken from its negative and reproduces its dialogue.

73. Levy, "Miracle on Brattle Street," 38–39; Matt Hills, "Cult Movies with and without Cult Stars: Differentiating Discourses of Stardom," in *Cult Film Stardom: Offbeat Attractions and Processes of Cultification,* ed. Kate Egan and Sarah Thomas (Basingstoke, UK: Palgrave Macmillan, 2013), 21.

74. "'Whimsical Phenomenon,'" 4.

75. Derek Kompare, *Rerun Nation: How Repeats Invented American Television* (New York: Routledge, 2005), 171. What Kompare identifies as cable TV's distinctive forms of repetition as it repackaged old TV shows applies more generally to the repackaged iteration of films I discuss in this and other chapters of this book.

76. Michael Patrick Allen and Anne E. Lincoln, "Critical Discourse and the Cultural Consecration of American Films," *Social Forces* 82, no. 3 (March 2004): 873.

77. Marijke de Valck, introduction to *Film Festivals: History, Theory, Method, Practice,* ed. Marijke de Valck, Brendan Kredell, and Skadi Loist (New York: Routledge, 2016), 9.

78. Janet Harbord, "Contingency, Time, and Event," in *Film Festivals: History, Theory, Method, Practice,* ed. Marijke de Valck, Brendan Kredell and Skadi Loist, (New York: Routledge, 2016), 70, 80.

79. Telotte, "Beyond All Reason," 13.

80. [Charles S. Whitman], "Humphrey Bogart Festival: At Brattle for Two Weeks," *Harvard Crimson,* May 27, 1963, www.thecrimson.com/article/1963/5/27/humphrey-bogart-festival-pit-has-become.

81. Raymond A. Soxolov Jr., "*The Bicycle Thief* and *Ivan, Part I,*" *Harvard Crimson,* Jan. 8, 1962, www.thecrimson.com/article/1962/1/8/the-bicycle-thief-and-

ivan-part. Bogart films screened at the Brattle at times other than examination periods when they operated as "traditional tension-busters." That they were sometimes not as successful during these alternative occasions suggests the close relationship of the cult to exam timing. See Maxine S. Paisner, "Legend Loses Lengthy Lines," *Harvard Crimson,* August 23, 1965, www.thecrimson.com/article/1965/8/23/legend-loses-lengthy-lines-pwhen-the.

82. Harvard alumnus and actor John Lithgow, quoted in Lotman, *Harvard Square,* 31.

83. "Old Faces," 82; Robert Sklar, *City Boys: Cagney, Bogart, Garfield* (Princeton, NJ: Princeton University Press, 1992), 251.

84. "6th Bogart Festival at Brattle Theatre," *Boxoffice,* Jan. 16, 1967, NE-2; and Peggy Nelson, "Brattle Film Theatre Notes," *Brattle Blog,* Nov. 23, 2009, http://brattleblog.brattlefilm.org/2009/11/23/casablanca-664/#.UsW8QvosoYU.

85. Danny Peary, *Cult Movies: Over 100 Films from the Silent Era to the Present* (New York: Gramercy, 1981), 47.

86. "Suspects Unrounded Up in Tragedy at Brattle," *Harvard Crimson,* Jan. 22, 1964, www.thecrimson.com/article/1964/1/22/suspects-unrounded-up-in-tragedy-at.

87. Rebecca Mazur, "Past Tense: The Brattle Theatre," *Harvard Crimson,* Feb. 14, 2013, www.thecrimson.com/article/2013/2/14/brattle-theater-past-tense.

88. These lines, respectively, occur in a conversation between Bogart and Bacall's characters in *To Have and Have Not* and between a Mexican character (who utters the fabled line) and Bogart's character in *The Treasure of the Sierra Madre;* "Old Faces," 82.

89. "Old Faces," 82.

90. Sarah Thornton, *Club Cultures: Music, Media, and Subcultural Capital* (Middletown, CT: Wesleyan University Press, 1996), 11–12.

91. *Casablanca* continued to be associated with its dialogue's performativity. In the 2005 American Film Institute's list of the one hundred best movie quotes of all time, *Casablanca* has the most entries. In the Internet Movie Database's "quotables" section for the film, familiar one-liners run beside long exchanges between characters deemed worthy in this respect.

92. Thornton, *Club Cultures,* 11.

93. Marijke de Valck, "Fostering Art, Adding Value, Cultivating Taste," in *Film Festivals: History, Theory, Method, Practice,* ed. Marijke de Valck, Brendan Kredell, and Skadi Loist (New York: Routledge, 2016), 109.

94. The dominance of Warner Bros. Bogart films in the Brattle's Bogart festivals reflects, of course, the actor's long association with the studio and the popularity of distribution packages of the studio's films. Bogart made movies for other production companies, including *Knock on Any Door* (1949) and *In a Lonely Place* (1950), produced by his own Santana Pictures in league with Columbia Pictures as distributor. Because they were not a part of Warner Bros. distribution packages, these movies tended not to be included in the Brattle's Bogart festivals. But their lack of status in the lineup might have other roots. Some Bogart titles could undermine his myth as it appealed to cult fans—particularly *In a Lonely Place* and its depiction of Bogart's

character as unattractively unhinged in his brutality. We can speculate that such films might not have found favor with those viewers embracing the Bogart myth of cool. For more on why Harvard students ignored the more troublesome aspects of Bogart's films, see "Nobody Is: Who Is Nicer Than Bogey?," *Harvard Crimson,* May 23, 1961, www.thecrimson.com/article/1961/5/23/nobody-is-pthere-is-a-convention. For a scholarly study of how aspects of Bogart's performance style disrupted his mythos, see Steven Cohan, *Masked Men: Masculinity and the Movies in the Fifties* (Bloomington: Indiana University Press, 1997), 9–121.

95. [Whitman], "Humphrey Bogart Festival" (see note 80 above).

96. Cindy Hing-Yuk Wong, "Publics and Counterpublics: Rethinking Film Festivals as Public Spheres," in *Film Festivals: History, Theory, Method, Practice,* ed. Marijke de Valck, Brendan Kredell, and Skadi Loist (New York: Routledge, 2016), 86.

97. Daniel Field, "*High Sierra,*" *Harvard Crimson,* Oct. 6, 1958, www.thecrimson.com/article/1958/10/6/high-sierra-pthe-brattle-management-has.

98. "Old Faces," 82. This take on *The African Queen* did not foresee the public embrace of the film in the mid-to-late 1960s. See Hannan, *Coming Back,* 205–6.

99. "6th Bogart Festival" (see note 84 above). Similar taste formations operated elsewhere. In New York, for example, the New Yorker Theatre programmed four Bogart films in 1963 to commemorate its second anniversary as a retrospective house. Besides "the obligatory 'Falcon,'" the theater screened *Casablanca, The Big Sleep,* and *The Treasure of the Sierra Madre.* In November 1970, Chicago's Clark Theater programmed a "Humphrey Bogart reissue quartet" of *The Maltese Falcon, Casablanca, Key Largo,* and *The Treasure of the Sierra Madre* ("Chi Soars," *Variety,* Nov. 25, 1970, 8). Assessments, of course, were tethered to prints in distribution and the fact that "against-the-grain" Bogie cultists might gravitate to films not typically in the 1960s and 1970s canon (e.g., *Dark Victory* and *The African Queen*).

100. Demonstrating the influence of popular film critics on postwar film cultures, film notes for each title in this spring festival program were "cribbed" from Pauline Kael's latest book, *Kiss Kiss Bang Bang* (New York: Little, Brown, 1968); see "John Huston" file, Margaret Herrick Library, Academy of Motion Picture Arts and Sciences, Los Angeles.

101. *Bogart* (ABC, April 23, 1967), UCLA Film and Television Archive, UCLA, Los Angeles; "Old Faces," 80; Bosley Crowther, "The Bogart Boom," *Playboy,* June 1966, 158.

102. *Casablanca* has been overtly queered, whether in interpretations that stress the bond between Renault and Rick (Peter Kunze, "Beautiful Friendship: Masculinity and Nationalism in *Casablanca,*" *Studies in Popular Culture* 37, no. 1 [Fall 2014]: 19–37), the bond between Rick and Victor (Eco, *Travels in Hyperreality,* 207–8), or the 2018 lesbian staging of *Casablanca,* "Casablanca Live Read," with an all-female cast, including then Ellen Page (now Elliot Page) as Rick and Kiersey Clemons as Ilsa.

103. Rick Altman, *Sound Theory, Sound Practice* (London: Routledge, 1992), 13.

104. "Old Faces," 80.

105. Jancovich and Brown, "'The Screen's Number One,'" 244.

106. Richard Gehman, "Bogey's New Boom: Hollywood's Famed He-Man of Yesterday Is Top Hero with Today's Young Crowd," *This Week Magazine,* August 8, 1965, New York Public Library for the Performing Arts, "Bogart File: 1960–69," MFL fnc 2270; and interviews from *Bogart.*

107. Gehman, "Bogey's New Boom."

108. Crowther, "The Bogart Boom," 112, 158.

109. Joel Dinerstein, *The Origins of Cool in Postwar America* (Chicago: University of Chicago Press, 2017), 87. For another history of cool, see Peter N. Stearns, *American Cool: Constructing a Twentieth-Century Emotional Style* (New York: New York University Press, 1994).

110. Dinerstein, *Origins of Cool,* 9–10, 22, 87.

111. Dinerstein, 12, 24, 37, 39.

112. In an otherwise critical take on *Casablanca* that saw few prospects for its future, Pauline Kael wrote that, in the "role of the cynic redeemed by love, Bogart became the great adventurer-lover of the screen during the war years. There isn't an actor in American films today with anything like his assurance, his magnetism, or his style. . . . He established the figure of the rebellious hero—the lone wolf who hates and defies officialdom." Kael, *Kiss Kiss Bang Bang,* 303.

113. Dinerstein, *Origins of Cool,* 232–37.

114. Crowther, "Casablanca" (see note 2 above).

115. Walter E. Wilson, "Casablanca: At the Brattle," *Harvard Crimson,* April 23, 1957, www.thecrimson.com/article/1957/4/23/casablanca-pthe-brattle-has-timed-icasablancasi.

116. Crowther, "The Bogart Boom." This issue of *Playboy* also included Kenneth Tynan's article on Bogart, "The Man and His Myth," and a Bogart quiz, filmography, and bibliography for Bogart cult completists; Susan King, "Hugh Hefner Helps Present a Humphrey Bogart Retrospective," *Los Angeles Times,* March 3, 2010, www.latimes.com/entertainment/la-xpm-2010-mar-03-la-et-classic-hollywood3-2010mar03-story.html.

117. Richard Gehman, "Bogart: A Cool Cult Welcomes an Old Hero," *True: A Man's Magazine,* Sept. 1965, 50–54, 107–21.

118. Postwar French sentiments did not tend to separate Bogart and *Casablanca* from wartime urgency. French film critic André Bazin's Bogart tribute characterized him as the "actor/myth of the war and post-war period," and Marc Augé extols *Casablanca*'s ability to "shimmer with history." See André Bazin, "The Death of Humphrey Bogart," in *Cahiers du cinéma: The 1950s: Neo-Realism, Hollywood, and the New Wave,* ed. and trans. Jim Hillier (Cambridge, MA: Harvard University Press, 1985), 98 (originally published as "Mort d'Humphrey Bogart," *Cahiers du cinéma,* Feb. 1957); and Marc Augé, *Casablanca: Movies and Memory,* trans. Tom Conley (Minneapolis: University of Minnesota Press, 2007), 55. Bazin also indicates, though, that the emotions aroused by Bogart's death are motivated by a sense of loss of his brand of virility, suggesting its inescapable centrality, along with his postwar credibility, to his affective impact. As Bazin writes, "The popularity of Bogart is virile. Women may miss him, but I know of men who would weep

for him were not the unseemliness of emotion written all over this tough guy's tomb" (98).

119. Matt Hills, *Fan Cultures* (London: Routledge, 2002), 140.

120. In *Masked Men,* Cohan counters the idea that the Bogart cult was transhistorical—that his tough-guy persona could outrun its complex symptomatic postwar meaning as it performed and disturbed notions of masculinity during this era (79–121). Critical opinion during the height of the Bogart cult could also sustain his wartime meaning. See Sarris, "Here's Looking at You, Bogie."

121. Harmetz, *The Making of Casablanca,* 344.

122. Barry Day, "The Cult Movies: *Casablanca,*" *Films and Filming* 20 (August 1974): 21.

123. Day, 21.

124. Sexton, "From Bad to Good" (summarizing one of Day's points), 138.

125. Telotte, "The Classical Cult Film," 40; J. P. Telotte, "*Casablanca* and the Larcenous Cult Film," in *The Cult Film Experience: Beyond All Reason,* ed. J. P. Telotte (Austin: University of Texas Press, 1991), 52.

126. See Ray, *A Certain Tendency,* 89–112, on how the outlaw hero in *Casablanca* is used to navigate and reduce ideological tensions.

127. Dick Hebdige, *Subculture: The Meaning of Style* (London: Methuen, 1979), 96–97.

128. Colin McArthur, *The Casablanca File* (London: Half Brick Images, 1992), 7–8.

129. Eugene Archer, "Man and Superman," *New York Times,* Jan. 3, 1965, X9, New York Public Library for the Performing Arts, "Bogart File: 1960–69," MFL fnc 2270.

130. Wilson, "Casablanca at the Brattle"; Margaret A. Armstrong, "*Casablanca:* At the Brattle Monday," *Harvard Crimson,* Jan. 25, 1960, www.thecrimson.com/article/1960/1/25/casablanca-pthe-usual-shoot-em-up-effects; "Kubrick Gets His Kicks; Hawks Hyperventilates," *Harvard Crimson,* April 27, 1978, www.thecrimson.com/article/1978/4/27/kubrick-gets-his-kicks-hawks-hyperventilates.

131. Ora Gelley, "Ingrid Bergman's Star Persona and the Alien Space of *Stromboli,*" *Cinema Journal* 47, no. 2 (Winter 2008): 26–51.

132. Crowther, "The Bogart Boom," 161. These comments do not fully represent Crowther's position with respect to the depiction of race in Hollywood films but rather the way the cult could contribute to its discursive erasure. Against other backdrops, Crowther wrote about cinema's ability to address the injustice of "anti-Negro prejudice," especially during the period of postwar conscience liberalism. See his "'Home of the Brave', at the Victoria," *New York Times,* May 13, 1949, 29.

133. This migration of Black cool to white masculinities through Bogart was potent enough that, decades later, when the Black historical newspaper the *Los Angeles Sentinel* reviewed a reissued collection of Miles Davis's romantic ballads, the reporter referred to the "smoky eloquent lyricism" Davis performed on his trumpet as possessing "the terseness associated with the Bogart of *Casablanca* . . . alone in a bar at closing time and trying to forget" ("This Valentine's Day, Miles Does It like

No Other," *Los Angeles Sentinel,* Feb. 11, 1999, B7). This review may have also promoted Davis's romantic ballads in relation to Bogart and *Casablanca* since the actor and film were a Valentine's Day cult phenomenon.

134. Shira Peltzman and Casey Scott, "This Is DCP: Digital Projection in Repertory Theatres," Tisch Preservation Program, www.miap.hosting.nyu.edu/program/student_work/2012spring/12s_3049_Peltzman_Scott_a2.docx (download only).

135. One of the lines left out in this screening was Renault's, "Well, Rick is the kind of man that . . . well, if I were a woman, and I were not around, I should be in love with Rick." Richard Turner, "The Screen," *Harvard Crimson,* Dec. 5, 1974, www.thecrimson.com/article/1974/12/5/the-screen-pbthe-orson-wellesb-it. See also, on this subject, Richard Shepro, "The Movies in Cambridge: Some Thoughts, Some History," *Harvard Crimson,* April 29, 1974, http://www.thecrimson.com/article/1974/4/29/the-movies-in-cambridge-some-thoughts/.

136. "The Screen," *Harvard Crimson,* August 7, 1973, www.thecrimson.com/article/1973/8/7/the-screen-pbthe-harder-they-comeb; "Kubrick Gets His Kicks" (see note 131 above).

137. Sarris, "Here's Looking at You, Bogie."

138. Sarah J. Schaffer, "Discover the Brattle," *Harvard Crimson,* Nov. 3, 1995, www.thecrimson.com/article/1995/11/3/discover-the-brattle-pforty-years-ago.

139. Hunter, *Cult Film as a Guide,* 8.

140. Lester F. Greenspoon, "Television," *Harvard Crimson,* Nov. 7, 1974, www.thecrimson.com/article/1974/11/7/television-pbtodayb-pbcourse-of-our-times-historyb.

CHAPTER 3. EVERYDAY FILMS

1. *Lux Video Theater* was broadcast from 10:00 to 11:00 p.m., with actor James Mason hosting for part of its run. Its version of "Casablanca" (season 5, episode 28) aired on March 3, 1955. *Lux*'s episode of *Casablanca* appears to be missing, but the broadcast's full script is in Bob Brooke's papers in the "*Lux Video Theatre* Collection," folder "*Casablanca,* 1955, March 3: Scope and Content Revised Script—Entire Spoken Dialogue of the Broadcast," Box.001, TN: 58874, Special Collections, Charles E. Young Research Library, UCLA.

2. *Warner Bros. Presents* comprised three rotating shows—*Cheyenne,* an original TV western, and versions of *Casablanca* and another feature-length film, *King's Row* (1942). Warner Bros. canceled both film adaptations within a year and ultimately the show itself; *Cheyenne* became a hit and went on to a long run. The UCLA Film and Television Archive is one of the few to house the program's "Casablanca" episodes. For more on *Warner Bros. Presents* and the early TV/Hollywood relationship, see Christopher Anderson, *Hollywood TV: The Studio System in the Fifties* (Austin: University of Texas Press, 1994). For a study of the complexity of media stakeholders involved in this relationship, see Jennifer Porst, *Broadcasting Hollywood: The Struggle over Feature Films on Early TV* (New Brunswick, NJ: Rutgers

University Press, 2021). Another TV series named after *Casablanca* (NBC, 1983), starring David Soul as Rick and Scatman Crothers as Sam, was also unsuccessful.

3. Brian Hannan, *Coming Back to a Theater Near You: A History of Hollywood Reissues, 1914–2014* (Jefferson, NC: McFarland, 2016), 300. See also Gerald Duchovnay, *Humphrey Bogart: A Bio-Bibliography* (Westport, CT: Greenwood Press, 1999), 47–48.

4. Gary Deeb, "Tempo: TV and Radio," *Chicago Tribune,* Nov. 19, 1979, A7. For more on the postwar film industry's objections to films on TV, see Eric Hoyt, *Hollywood Vault: Film Libraries before Home Video* (Berkeley: University of California Press, 2014), 186–90; on the medium's historical difficulties with status, see Michael Z. Newman and Elana Levine, *Legitimating Television* (New York: Routledge, 2012).

5. Francesco Casetti, *The Lumière Galaxy: Seven Key Words for the Cinema to Come* (New York: Columbia University Press, 2015), 27.

6. Michael Curtin and Jane Shattuc, *The American Television Industry* (London: Palgrave Macmillan, 2009), 58.

7. James F. English, *The Economy of Prestige: Prizes, Awards, and the Circulation of Cultural Value* (Cambridge, MA: Harvard University Press, 2005), 75, 79.

8. Derek Kompare, *Rerun Nation: How Repeats Invented American Television* (New York: Routledge, 2005), xi, 171–72.

9. Charles Acland, *Screen Traffic: Movies, Multiplexes, and Global Culture* (Durham, NC: Duke University Press, 2003), 59–71.

10. Broadcast TV's association with Hollywood stars exceeds this chapter's parameters. Stars were featured in programming that included TV series, documentaries, interviews, made-for-TV movies, and other kinds of shows. See Christine Becker, *It's the Pictures That Got Small: Hollywood Film Stars on 1950s Television* (Middletown, CT: Wesleyan University Press, 2008); Mary R. Desjardins, *Recycled Stars: Female Film Stardom in the Age of Television and Video* (Durham, NC: Duke University Press, 2015). Bogart drew substantial attention on television: there were interviews with him and Bacall, such as on Edward R. Murrow's *Person to Person* (CBS, 1954), documentaries like *Bogart* (ABC, 1967), made-for-TV movies such as *Bogie* (CBS, 1980), and of course adaptations starring him, like *The Petrified Forest* (NBC, 1955).

11. TV's relationship to domestic space and time have long been matters of critical concern. See, for example, Tania Modleski, *Loving with a Vengeance: Mass-Produced Fantasies for Women* (New York: Methuen, 1982), 85–109; Lynn Spigel, *Make Room for TV: Television and the Family Ideal in Postwar America* (Chicago: University of Chicago Press, 1992); David Morley, *Television, Audiences, and Cultural Studies* (London: Routledge, 1992); Roger Silverstone, *Television and Everyday Life* (London: Routledge, 1994); and David Gauntlett and Annette Hill, *TV Living: Television, Culture, and Everyday Life* (London: Routledge, 1999).

12. *Billboard*'s survey of early nationwide patterns of movie programming on TV found that the average station in four-and-more-channel markets like Chicago broadcast over 30 percent more feature films weekly than one-and-two-channel markets (which aired a high of nineteen films weekly). "Spotlight on Feature Film Programming: Movie Patterns-1," *Billboard,* August 11, 1956, 15.

13. "Moran Pays Big for WGN Film Package," *Billboard*, August 19, 1957, 7; "Hit 'Em Where They Ain't Is WGN-TV's Formula to Lick Web O&Os in Chicago," *Variety*, August 17, 1966, 26, 36.

14. Television could turn "living rooms into private revival houses for a gamut of old Hollywood features" (Greg Taylor, *Artists in the Audience: Cults, Camp, and American Film Criticism* [Princeton, NJ: Princeton University Press, 1999], 75). It thereby provided "seedbeds for the kind of ritualized viewings associated with cult cinema" (J. Hoberman and Jonathan Rosenbaum, *Midnight Movies* [New York: Da Capo Press, 1983], 30–31).

15. On TV guides as part of material culture, see Caetlin Benson-Allott, *The Stuff of Spectatorship: Material Cultures of Film and Television* (Oakland: University of California Press, 2021), 2–7.

16. WGN left CBS in 1953 and DuMont in 1956 after it ceased operation.

17. For a snapshot of WGN's mid-1960s programming, see Marion Purcelli, "On Channel 9 This Fall!," *Chicago Tribune*, Sept. 10, 1966, C18.

18. Kompare reports that, by the early 1970s, owing to microwave retransmission, WGN and other independents were already large-market regional independents on cable TV. With satellite transmission in the late 1970s, WGN became a "reluctant superstation," one that could not risk losing its local/regional market through a national form of address. It thus kept its local programming strategies, "with old films, off-network reruns, cartoons, and sports filling [its] schedule" (*Rerun Nation*, 175–76). As evidence of this, Robert Feder wrote in 1987, "While ABC, CBS, and NBC roll out their new and returning weekly series, three of Chicago's four major independent stations (WGN, WFLD, and WGBO) will continue to rely on movies as key to their prime-time programming strategy this fall." In fall 1987, WGN would air "as usual" movies during prime-time Mondays through Saturdays. Top titles included *Amadeus* (1984), *The Breakfast Club* (1985), *The African Queen*, and *Casablanca*. "Independents—Stations Show Movies at the Flick of a Switch," *Chicago Sun-Times*, Sept. 13, 1987, 15.

19. The history of the relationship of Hollywood feature films and TV is amply discussed in the scholarship. Besides Anderson *(Hollywood TV)*, Hoyt *(Hollywood Vault)*, Kompare *(Rerun Nation)*, and Porst (*Broadcasting Hollywood*), see, for example, Tino Balio, ed., *Hollywood in the Age of Television* (Boston: Unwin Hyman, 1990); Michele Hilmes, *Hollywood and Broadcasting: From Radio to Cable* (Chicago: University of Illinois Press, 1990); William Boddy, *Fifties Television: The Industry and Its Critics* (Urbana: University of Illinois Press, 1990); and Kerry Segrave, *Movies at Home: How Hollywood Came to Television* (Jefferson, NC: McFarland, 1999).

20. "Guides for Tricky Business of Purchasing Feature Pictures," *Billboard*, August 11, 1956, 29, 30. TV executives identified "five key check points" for "establishing a feature film's quality for TV": the film's theatrical sales formula, theatrical track record, running time (below ninety minutes indicated a low-budget film), vintage (before 1933 indicated bad sound quality; before 1939, unless the film was a classic, outdatedness), and stars. Additionally, trade journals showcased Academy

Award-winning films for broadcast. See "TV Oscar Winners," *Billboard,* August 11, 1956, 16.

21. In 1968, the Motion Picture Association of America (MPAA) introduced its voluntary ratings system for films, superseding the old Production Code and creating the G, M, R, and X categories.

22. Richard Blakesley, "Good Old Movies View Like New!," *Chicago Daily Tribune,* Sept. 14, 1957, C7. Trade journals also reported the ratings success of feature films on independent stations like New York's WPIX and Los Angeles's KTTV. See "NTA's Statistical Joy on Network's Combined Ratings," *Variety,* May 1, 1957, 29, 50.

23. Jack Jacobson, "Independent Ideas, or Programming Can Be Fun," *Back Stage,* Feb. 20, 1976, 24, 36; Robert A. Malone, "The New Tricks of Counterprogramming," *Broadcasting,* Nov. 10, 1969, 36–37. Other articles on WGN's counterprogramming strategies include "Hit 'Em Where They Ain't"; and Clay Gowran, "On TV 9: It's Going to Be a Great Year," *Chicago Tribune,* August 11, 1966, 66.

24. Kompare, *Rerun Nation,* 49, 78.

25. Malone, "New Tricks," 36–37; "Variety ARB Feature Film Chart," Sept. 9, 1964, 4.

26. Trade journalists considered AAP's formation a decade earlier, when it acquired TV rights to 199 Monogram movies, as the "earliest milestone" in the history of film distribution on TV. See Gene Plotnik, "History of Feature Films: Movies Get Better Than Ever," *Billboard,* August 11, 1956, 1, 6.

27. "Warner Control Passes to Investors," *Broadcasting, Telecasting,* May 14, 1956, 40; "Post-1950 WB Pix in 39 Markets," *Variety,* Feb. 8, 1961, 77; "Warners Sells 750 Features to PRM, Inc.," *Motion Picture Daily,* March 2, 1956, 1, 6. For more on this sale and the shifting ownership of Warner Bros. titles over the years, see Hoyt, *Hollywood Vault,* 167–94. For other terms of this sale, see P. D. Knecht to Robert W. Perkins, Esq., Warner Pictures, Inc., memo, June 14, 1956, "Casablanca Picture File," folder F002953-2870; and Warner Bros. Pictures to Vivienne Nearing, Esq., memo, Dec. 11, 1959, folder F000750-001, box 2, 1956, both in the Warner Bros. Archives, University of Southern California School of Cinematic Arts, Los Angeles.

28. "Big Packages Sell at a Steady Pace," *Billboard,* August 11, 1956, 16; "Storer Stations Buy WB Bundle," *Variety,* April 23, 1958, 23; "Breakdown on TV Cinematics," *Variety,* May 1, 1957, 50; "Stations Offered 13 Pkgs. of Warner Films by AAP," *Billboard,* April 21, 1956, 12. Conceding to theater exhibitors, AAP provided "TV protection" for them by having TV stations delay broadcasts of their films until after September 1, 1957. This allowed for unopposed theatrical exhibition—AAP's Dominant Pictures reissued more than one hundred Warner Bros. films to theaters before this deadline, including *Casablanca, King's Row, Mildred Pierce* (1945), and *Rope* (1948). AAP would not commit again to TV protection; in fact, it spent the summer of 1957 promoting its packages to both TV executives and theater exhibitors.

29. "Warner Bros.-Seven Arts Ltd," *Wall Street Journal,* June 26, 1968, 22; "Warner Completes Sale of Stock to Seven Arts," *Boxoffice,* Dec. 5, 1966, 5.

30. On profits of TV distribution in the early years of post-studio releases, see "Breakdown on TV Cinematics," *Variety,* May 1, 1957, 50; for comparative statistics

on theatrical versus TV revenue in these early years for the Warner library, see Hoyt, *Hollywood Vault,* 174.

31. AAP ad, *Variety,* Dec. 10, 1958, 53.

32. "How Top Five Users Program Features," *Billboard,* August 11, 1956, 31; "Multi-Million Warner Deal," *TV & Video Screen International,* July 10, 1982, 15.

33. Hoyt, *Hollywood Vault,* 173.

34. "WB's Top 10 Pre-'48 Releases," *Variety,* Feb. 8, 1961, 77.

35. "*Variety*-Pulse Feature Chart," *Variety,* Nov. 26, 1958, 42. Survey dates ran from October 10–17, 1958, and measured 1,815,000 Chicago TV homes. *Lost Horizon*'s ratings high was 29.7, and audience share was 58, while *Casablanca*'s repeat earned a ratings high of 13.0 and audience share of 29. The TV industry had several other ratings systems besides Pulse, including Nielsen and ARB (American Research Bureau). Such measurements are not an exact science but provide a glimpse of how cinematics fared in their broadcasts.

36. "Extra Mileage on Cinematics," *Variety,* April 23, 1958, 23.

37. "AAP Now Springs Its 'Jupiter' Group," *Variety,* April 23, 1958, 23.

38. Malone, "New Tricks," 36–37; "Extra Mileage on Cinematics," 23.

39. "Jim Moran Goes the Limit (500G) in New Bid as Chi Feature King," *Variety,* April 21, 1957, 42.

40. Curtin and Shattuc, *The American Television Industry,* 61, 65.

41. "Courtesy Film Series Begins Ninth Year: Pioneer Show Keeps High Rating," *Chicago Tribune,* Sept. 1, 1957, SW4.

42. Les Brown, "Sun. Nite Brawl Top Headliner," *Variety,* Oct. 16, 1957, 27, 57; and "Chi WNBQ Hot for Aft. Features," *Variety,* April 2, 1958, 28.

43. "How Top Five Users Program Features," 31 (see note 32 above). See also "Auto Dealer Jim Moran, Caught in Chi Feature Wars, Makes a Detour," *Variety,* May 14, 1958, 20; "Jim Moran Deplores High Cost of TV Cinematics in Chi Pullout," *Variety,* April 27, 1958, 24.

44. "Movie Patterns," *Billboard,* August 11, 1956, 16.

45. From the *Chicago Tribune*'s "TV Movie" guides (citations are in parentheses): early showcases on WGN airing *Casablanca* included the *Motion Picture Academy,* Tuesday, Oct. 14, 1958, 10:00 p.m. (Oct. 11, 1958, C14); *Mages Playhouse,* Wednesday, April 15, 1959, 10:00 p.m. (April 15, 1959, B10); *Saturday's Best,* June 30, 1962 and August 15, 1964, 10:15 p.m. (June 30, 1962, B27; August 15, 1964, C18); and "All Night—Late Movie Channel 9," Friday, August 20, 1965, 12:20 a.m. (August 20, 1965, C11).

46. From the *Chicago Tribune*'s "TV Movie" guides (citations are in parentheses): early showcases on WGN airing *Casablanca* also included *Hollywood Startime,* Monday, April 17, 1961, 1:15 p.m. (April 15, 1961, B16); *Sunday's Best,* March 11, 1962 and Dec. 9, 1962, 4:00 p.m. (March 10, 1962, C4; Dec. 8, 1962, B19), and *Virginia Gale,* Wednesday, Sept. 6, 1961, 10:30 a.m. (Sept. 6, 1961, E7). Some other airing dates during the first two decades not mentioned elsewhere in the chapter include Friday, April 11, 1958, 10:00 p.m. (April 5, 1958, D12); Tuesday, May 27, 1969, 10:30 p.m. (May 24, 1969, 19); Sunday, Jan. 17, 1971, 1:30 p.m. (Jan. 17, 1971, N1); and Sunday, Feb. 13, 1972, 10:30 p.m. (Feb. 12, 1972, 19). For the shift of late afternoon program-

ming from "juveniles" to adults in Chicago's TV market, see "WNBQ's Bid for Adults; Slots Late Matinee Features," *Variety,* Jan. 25, 1961, 34. For an analysis of the industry and female audiences, see Spigel, *Make Room for TV,* 73–98.

47. From the *Chicago Tribune*'s "TV Movies" guides: WGN's later showcases aired *Casablanca* on *Those Magnificent Talkies,* Monday, Nov. 17, 1975, 10:30 p.m. (Nov. 17, 1975, C11); *When Movies Were Movies,* Sunday, Nov. 4, 1979 at 10:30 p.m. (Nov. 4, 1979, H8) and Tuesday, Feb. 27, 1990 (Feb. 27, 1990, B6); and *Here's Looking at You Kid Theater,* Saturday, Feb. 28, 1981, 11:00 p.m. (Feb. 28, 1981, 18).

48. From the *Chicago Tribune*'s "TV Movies" guides: WGN also aired *Casablanca* on *Thursday Night Movie,* Feb. 27, 1975, 7:00 p.m. (Feb. 27, 1975, B11); and *Movie Greats,* Sunday, Jan. 17, 1971, 1:30 p.m. (Jan. 17, 1971, N1).

49. "Old Features Never Die; They Just Go Onward and Upward," *Variety,* April 29, 1959, 28.

50. Arjun Appadurai and Carol A. Breckenridge, "Museums Are Good to Think: Heritage on View in India," in *Museums and Communities: The Politics of Public Culture,* ed. Ivan Karp, Christine Mullen Kreamer, and Steven Levine (Washington, DC: Smithsonian Institution Press, 1992), 36–37.

51. Michael Bhaskar, *Curation: The Power of Selection in a World of Excess* (London: Piatkus, 2016), 6–8, 85.

52. Pierre Bourdieu, *Distinction: A Social Critique of the Judgement of Taste,* trans. Richard Nice (Cambridge, MA: Harvard University Press, 1984), 1–7.

53. E. Dean Kolbas, quoted in Jonathan Lupo, "Loaded Canons: Contemporary Film Canons, Film Studies, and Film Discourse," *Journal of American Culture* 34, no. 3 (Sept. 2011): 220.

54. Lisa Dombrowski, "Canon and Canonicity," Encyclopedia.com, www.encyclopedia.com/arts/encyclopedias-almanacs-transcripts-and-maps/canon-and-canonicity.

55. Janet Staiger, "The Politics of Film Canons," *Cinema Journal* 24, no. 3 (Spring 1985): 4–23.

56. Michael Bommes and Patrick Wright, "'Charms of Residence': The Public and the Past," in *Making Histories: Studies in History Writing and Politics,* ed. Richard Johnson et al. (Birmingham, UK: Centre for Contemporary Cultural Studies, 1982), 253, 291.

57. Earl B. Abrams, "Fan Magazines," *Broadcasting, Telecasting,* Nov. 22, 1954, 43, 50, 54, 56. For more on *TV Forecast,* see "Chicago TV Forecast 1948–1953," http://epguides.com/comics/tvf.html.

58. For more on TV and video movie guides, see Daniel Herbert, *Videoland: Movie Culture at the American Video Store* (Berkeley: University of California Press, 2014), 183–85.

59. From the *Chicago Tribune*'s "TV Movie" guides: Oct. 11, 1958, C14; March 10, 1962, C4; April 13, 1968, A20. For other examples of such variations, see April 15, 1961, B16; June 30, 1962, B27; and April 29, 1967, I17.

60. From the *Chicago Tribune*'s "TV Movie" guides: May 24, 1969, 19; and Jan. 17, 1971, SCL2.

61. Chicago's Clark Theatre, for example, ran Bogart films, including *Casablanca,* during its summer film festivals in the 1960s. Other repertory houses and theaters screening Bogart festivals at this time included the Carnegie, Playboy, Rhodes, and Wilmette theaters. See the *Chicago Tribune:* August 7, 1962, A4; May 4, 1965, B21; Oct. 30, 1965, 5; June 10, 1966, C17; Nov. 25, 1966, C6; May 31, 1967, C7; July 12, 1968, B19; Nov. 18, 1970, C5; Sept. 5, 1969, B12; and Dec. 5, 1970, 14.

62. "TV Movies Reviewed by Anna Nangle," *Chicago Tribune:* July 29, 1967, F17; and Sept. 2, 1967, C21.

63. "TV Movies," *Chicago Tribune,* July 16, 1986, D6; and July 15, 1986, D8.

64. For example, Harriet Choice rates *Casablanca* in its 1:30 p.m. Sunday slot as "outstanding" (*Chicago Tribune,* Jan. 17, 1971, R17), and an anonymous writer rated it as "excellent" in its 4:00 p.m. Sunday slot ("TV Week: Movie Guide," *Chicago Tribune,* Dec. 8, 1962, B19).

65. See, for example, Andrew Sarris, "Notes on the Auteur Theory in 1962," *Film Culture* 27 (Winter-Spring 1962–63): 1–8; Andrew Sarris, *The American Cinema: Directors and Directions, 1929–1968* (New York: Dutton, 1968); Pauline Kael, "Circles and Squares," *Film Quarterly* 16, no. 3 (Spring 1963): 12–26; and Pauline Kael, *I Lost It at the Movies: Film Writings, 1954–1965* (New York: M. Boyars, 1965).

66. *Sneak Previews* (1975–96), developed by Chicago PBS affiliate WTTW, began as *Opening Soon in a Theater Near You.* Its name changed to *Sneak Previews* in 1977. Eventually airing nationwide on PBS, the show continued with other critics after Siskel and Ebert departed.

67. Peter Bosma, *Film Programming: Curating for Cinemas, Festivals, Archives* (New York: Wallflower, 2015), 68–69.

68. Ien Ang, *Desperately Seeking the Audience* (London: Routledge, 1991), 18–19.

69. See Haidee Wasson, *Museum Movies: The Museum of Modern Art and the Birth of Art Cinema* (Berkeley: University of California Press, 2005), 149–84; and Julian Stringer, "Raiding the Archive: Film Festivals and the Revival of Classic Hollywood," in *Memory and Popular Film,* ed. Paul Grainger (Manchester, UK: Manchester University Press, 2003), 81–96.

70. Purcelli, "On Channel 9," C18 (see note 17 above); and Gowran, "On TV 9," 16 (see note 23 above). For festival film broadcast dates and blurbs, see Anna Nangle, "TV Movies," *Chicago Tribune:* Sept. 10, 1966, C38 *(The Maltese Falcon);* Sept. 17, 1966, C20 *(High Sierra);* Sept. 24, 1966, C20 *(Casablanca);* Oct. 1, 1966, G20 *(The Two Mrs. Carrolls);* Oct. 8, 1966, C17 *(Key Largo);* Oct. 29, 1966, E16 *(Passage to Marseille);* Nov. 12, 1966, D17 *(The Treasure of the Sierra Madre);* Jan. 14, 1967, E17 *(The Big Sleep);* Feb. 25, 1967, F17 *(All through the Night);* April 8, 1967, H7 *(Dark Passage);* April 15, 1967, C17 *(Across the Pacific);* April 22, 1967, D17 *(They Drive by Night);* April 29, 1967, I17 *(Casablanca);* May 6, 1967, F20 *(Petrified Forest);* May 27, D17 *(Chain Lightning);* June 10, 1967, F17 *(The Maltese Falcon);* July 15, 1967, C17 *(The Two Mrs. Carrolls);* July 22, 1967, G17 *(San Quentin);* July 29, 1967, F17 *(High Sierra);* August 12, 1967, E17 *(Marked Woman);* August 19, 1967, E17 *(Angels with Dirty Faces);* August 26, 1967, E17 *(Action in the North Atlantic);* and Sept. 2, 1967, C21 *(The Treasure of the Sierra Madre).*

71. The *Here's Looking at You Kid Theater* promo, with Bob Bell narrating, is available on YouTube, www.youtube.com/watch?v=wZk6z1sHkPY. The promotional montage, a collection of some of Bogart's memorable screen moments, aired on February 7, 1981.

72. *Here's Looking at You Kid Theater,* Museum of Classic Chicago Television (www.FuzzyMemories.TV). The films and broadcast dates were *The Maltese Falcon,* Nov. 15, 1980; *The Roaring Twenties,* Nov. 22, 1980; *The Desperate Hours,* Dec. 6, 1980; *Marked Woman,* Dec. 13, 1980; *The Amazing Dr. Clitterhouse,* Dec. 27, 1980; *The Two Mrs. Carrolls,* Jan. 3, 1981; *The Petrified Forest,* Jan. 10, 1981; *The Barefoot Contessa,* Jan. 24, 1981; *Dark Passage,* Feb. 7, 1981; *High Sierra,* Feb. 21, 1981; *Casablanca,* Feb. 28, 1981; *You Can't Get Away with Murder,* March 7, 1981; *Deadline U.S.A.,* March 21, 1981; *They Drive by Night,* March 28, 1981; *Across the Pacific,* April 4, 1981; *All through the Night,* April 11, 1981; *The Battling Bellhop/Kid Galahad,* April 18, 1981; *Conflict,* April 25, 1981; *The Maltese Falcon,* May 2, 1981.

73. Kompare, *Rerun Nation,* 55; Curtin and Shattuc, *The American Television Industry,* 75.

74. In the 1970s and 1980s, for example, WGN's *Morning Movie,* broadcast Mondays through Fridays, stripped a week of Bob Hope and Bing Crosby "road" movies, such as *The Road to Singapore* (1940) and *The Road to Morocco* (1942). "Ministrips" thematized movies during part of the week, such as Rock Hudson's films with director Douglas Sirk, *All That Heaven Allows* (1955), *Written on the Wind* (1956), and *Tarnished Angels* (1957). See Chris Tufts, "WGN Morning Movie," http://epguides.com/WGNMorningMovie.

75. Tufts.

76. Tania Modleski, *Loving with a Vengeance: Mass-Produced Fantasies for Women* (New York: Methuen, 1982), 85–109.

77. According to the *Chicago Tribune*'s 1986 "TV Movie" guides (July 14, C6; July 15, D8; July 16, D6; July 17, D15; and July 18, N4), films in this vertical strip were Monday, July 14: *The Maltese Falcon,* 7:00–9:15 p.m.; *The Treasure of the Sierra Madre,* 11:30 p.m.–2:10 a.m.; *Crime School,* 3:00–4:30 a.m.; Tuesday, July 15: *Casablanca,* 7:00–9:10 p.m.; *High Sierra,* 11:30 p.m.–1:30 a.m.; *Action in the North Atlantic,* 3:00–5:20 a.m.; Wednesday, July 16: *The Big Sleep,* 7:00–9:30 p.m.; *To Have and Have Not,* 11:30 p.m.–1:35 a.m.; *The Two Mrs. Carrolls,* 3:00–5:20 a.m.; Thursday, July 17: *The African Queen,* 7:00–9:10 p.m.; *Sahara,* 11:30 p.m.–1:30 a.m.; *Passage to Marseille,* 3:00–5:20 a.m.; Friday, July 18: *Key Largo,* 7:00–9:10 p.m.; *The Harder They Fall,* 11:30 p.m.–1:45 a.m.

78. These TV festival films were reportedly aired "in their entirety—untouched by the film butchers," an impression supported by the TV movie guides above. Guides listed their ORTs (original running times) with their more expansive broadcasting times—possibly WGN's response to premium cable TV's uninterrupted film reruns. See Robert Feder, "NBC Grants Asner Chance for Weekly TV Comeback," *Chicago Sun-Times,* July 10, 1986, 68. YouTube has several promotions for this festival; See, for example, www.youtube.com/watch?v=dpjLwXCKoXo.

79. Robert Feder, "Channel 11 Wraps Year with Record Riches," *Chicago Sun-Times,* Dec. 15, 1991, 51.

80. Jérôme Bourdon, "Some Sense of Television: Remembering Television," *History and Memory* 15, no. 2 (Fall/Winter 2003): 19, 20.

81. Paddy Scannell, "Radio Times: The Temporal Arrangements of Broadcasting in the Modern World," in *Television and Its Audience,* ed. Phillip Drummond and Richard Paterson (London: BFI, 1988), 27–28.

82. Scannell, 5–7.

83. Funkdragon23, Comment, "Bogart Weeks on WGN," www.youtube.com/watch?v=uoZAQC9qd1Y.

84. Steve F. Anderson, cited in Kristyn Gorton and Joanne Garde-Hansen, *Remembering British Television: Audience, Archive, and Industry* (London: BFI, 2019), 2; Alison Landsberg, *Prosthetic Memory: The Transformation of American Remembrance in the Age of Mass Culture* (New York: Columbia University Press, 2004), 8–9.

85. Kompare discusses these powers of programming in relation to telefilm stripping (*Rerun Nation,* 55, 93–94), but they also illuminate other intensified forms of access to content.

86. Herm., "Bogart," *Variety,* April 26, 1967, 173.

87. Lisa Glebatis Perks, *Media Marathoning: Immersions in Morality* (New York: Lexington Books, 2015), 5, ix. Perks defines key aspects of the relationships that can develop between viewers and marathoned texts, offering, like Kompare, insights useful to understanding other programming-enabled modes of intensified access to TV content.

88. Ellen Jaffe, "There's No Movie like an Old Movie," *Seventeen,* Jan. 1972, 135.

89. Part of the appeal of old movies at repertory theaters and on TV was that their datedness made them a "laugh riot." See Larry Wolters's review of *Hollywood: The Fabulous Era* in "Cinema's Great Era Comes Alive on TV," *Chicago Daily Tribune,* Jan. 20, 1963, SW16.

90. Jaffe, "There's No Movie," 135.

91. Gorton and Garde-Hansen, *Remembering British Television,* 14.

92. Michael Curtin, *Redeeming the Wasteland: Television Documentary and Cold War Politics* (New Brunswick, NJ: Rutgers University Press, 1995), 2, 139–40.

93. Leonard Maltin, "Remembering *Hollywood and the Stars,*" *Movie Crazy* blog, Dec. 30, 2010, https://leonardmaltin.com/remembering-hollywood-and-the-stars.

94. Wolper's TV series were produced in association with United Artists Television. His documentaries are available online at the Internet Archive and via YouTube: *Hollywood: The Golden Years,* https://archive.org/details/hollywoodthegoldenyears; *Hollywood: The Fabulous Era,* https://archive.org/details/Hollywood_The_Fabulous_Era; *Hollywood: The Great Stars,* www.youtube.com/watch?v=mFNB16P6NOs; and "The Man Called Bogart" on *Hollywood and the Stars,* www.youtube.com/watch?v=zhOh4yWAu2M.

95. "Sponsorscope," *Sponsor,* June 10, 1963, 22.

96. Ad, "Hollywood: The Golden Years," *Variety,* Nov. 29, 1961, 25; "Hollywood: The Fabulous Era," www.davidlwolper.com/shows/details.cfm?showID=7; Bill., "Television Review: *Hollywood: The Great Stars,*" *Variety,* March 20, 1963, 43.

97. Bill., "Television Review," 43.

98. Herm., "Hollywood: The Fabulous Era," *Variety,* Jan. 30, 1963, 33; "The New Life in Old Film," *Broadcasting,* Dec. 9, 1963, 27–29; Charles Champlin, "American Films in Focus at Expo," *Los Angeles Times,* July 5, 1967, D15.

99. Bill., "Television Review," 43; "'H'wood Story' as NBC Mon. Entry," *Variety,* March 27, 1963, 27.

100. "Wolper Series on NBC Designed for Big H'wood Promo," *Variety,* May 1, 1963, 35, 42.

101. English, *The Economy of Prestige,* 75.

102. Bourdon, "Some Sense of Television," 30.

103. Champlin, "American Films in Focus," D15.

104. Anderson, *Hollywood TV,* 72, 85, 131, 289, and, on TV spectaculars, 70–132.

105. Steven Cohan, *Hollywood by Hollywood: The Backstudio Picture and the Mystique of Making Movies* (New York: Oxford University Press, 2019), 5, 10, 11 (Cohan's emphasis). Cohan contends that, as the studio system disintegrated, harsher takedowns of Hollywood, such as *Whatever Happened to Baby Jane?* (1962), eroded the industry's glamorous facade, but films that focused on the past, such as *The Way We Were* (1973), soon nostalgically depicted the loss of old Hollywood.

106. *Thank Your Lucky Stars* (1943) is a Hollywood musical comedy about a WWII charity show, with stars appearing as themselves. WGN reran it on March 29, 1976; March 28, 1977; and July 1, 1982. Bogart parodies his gangster persona, as he had done many times on radio, in a scene featuring his *Casablanca* costar S. Z. Sakall (Karl, the waiter), offering an in-joke to audiences.

107. See Anderson, *Hollywood TV,* 169, 171, 184, 191–92.

108. Alison Trope, *Stardust Monuments: The Saving and Selling of Hollywood* (Hanover, NH: Dartmouth College Press, 2011), 129. Trope's book, in featuring an image of Bogart and Bergman from *Casablanca* on its title page, suggests that the film signifies Hollywood itself. On industrial self-reflexivity, see also John Thornton Caldwell, *Production Culture: Industrial Self-Reflexivity and Critical Practice in Film and Television* (Durham, NC: Duke University Press, 2008).

109. See Jaimie Baron, *The Archive Effect: Found Footage and the Audiovisual Experience of History* (New York: Routledge, 2014), 1–15, for a synthesis of the scholarship on documentaries that studies the issues of compilation and evidence.

110. Anne Reading, quoted in Gorton and Garde-Hansen, *Remembering British Television,* 10.

111. Bogart's behavior received substantial press during his life. See, for example, Cameron Shipp, "Humphrey Bogart's Dark Side," *Saturday Evening Post,* August 2, 1952, www.saturdayeveningpost.com/2017/06/humphrey-bogarts-dark-side. This account, like others, treats his behavior as a humorously perplexing news item of interest.

112. Gene., "Television Review: *Hollywood and the Stars,*" *Variety,* Oct. 2, 1963, 36.

113. "The Man Called Bogart," YouTube, www.youtube.com/watch?v=zhOh4yWAu2M.

114. For example, Marlon Riggs' *Color Adjustment* (1992) explores the history of Black representation on TV. Vito Russo's book *The Celluloid Closet* (New York: Harper & Row, 1981) was made into a documentary of the same title in 1995; book and film both address the repression and expression of homosexuality in movies. *Without Lying Down: Frances Marion and the Powerful Women of Early Hollywood,* Cari Beauchamp's book about women in the industry (Berkeley: University of California Press, 1998), was made into a documentary of the same name in 2000.

115. Amy Holdsworth, *Television, Memory, and Nostalgia* (Basingstoke: Palgrave Macmillan, 2011), 101.

CHAPTER 4. MOVIE VALENTINES

1. In "Doing the Thinking for All of Us: *Casablanca* and the Home Front," *Journal of Popular Film and Television* 27, no. 4 (April 2000): 5–15, Jack Nachbar writes about a couple's Valentine's Day trip to see *Casablanca* in 1943. This is an imaginary story, however, not an empirical event. While the film no doubt had earlier uptakes in relation to Valentine's Day, by the 1970s, it consistently materialized in this vein on TV schedules. For example, in February 1976, Los Angeles' KHJ-TV broadcast *Casablanca* during prime time to counterprogram CBS's airing of the TV special "Be My Valentine, Charlie Brown" (1975). "Television: Wednesday," *Los Angeles Times,* Feb. 8, 1976, O20.

2. Ernest Mathijs, "Time Wasted," *Flow,* March 29, 2010, www.flowjournal.org/2010/03/time-wasted-ernest-mathijs-the-university-of-british-columbia. Mathijs depicts the iterative watching of *Casablanca* and other seasonal cult films as a "form of resistance against the compartmentalization of time [and] the usage of time as an economic form of measurement." While I do not address fan practices here, my Valentine's Day research is more akin to Matt Hills's observation in *Fan Cultures* (London: Routledge, 2002) that fandoms are "enmeshed within the rhythms and temporalities" of platforms that deliver content (178). In my work, it seems similarly clear that the holiday and the discursive practices around it operate to temporally discipline audiences into watching certain films on video on February 14.

3. As Caetlin Benson-Allott contends in *Killer Tapes and Shattered Screens: Video Spectatorship from VHS to File Sharing* (Berkeley: University of California Press, 2013), 12–14, *video* is a polyvalent and amorphous term, applying to different kinds of analog and digital video and an array of platforms, material bases, distribution models, and experiences. I embrace its status as an umbrella term, though with certain specifications. I make a distinction between physical-format video (VHS, laser disc, DVD, Blu-ray) and digital video (forms of streaming). I use the term *video* in either manifestation to connote, on the one hand, a mode of film exhibition that presents movies to viewers in homes through noncelluloid technologies and, on the other hand, a mode of experience that fosters the viewers' personalization of movies.

Personalization includes selection/curation (that consumers pursue through sites ranging from video stores to video-on-demand [VOD]), control/manipulation (through the remote control's functions and facsimiles thereof), ownership and collection, and private screenings.

4. I. Q. Hunter, *Cult Film as a Guide to Life: Fandom, Adaptation, and Identity* (London: Bloomsbury Academic, 2016), 19.

5. Barbara Herrnstein Smith, *Contingencies of Value: Alternative Perspectives for Critical Theory* (Cambridge, MA: Harvard University Press, 1991), 47.

6. As opposed to official, critically recognized genres, like the western or film noir, that transcend historical eras and involve a group of films that demonstrate shared formal conventions, a vernacular genre is a transient historical entity, often generated by the industry or within popular culture, based on popularly recognized similarities among films, like the stars who perform in them.

7. Joe Neumaier, "Valentine's Day: From *Casablanca* to *Wuthering Heights:* What to Rent to Impress Your Date," *New York Daily News,* Feb. 14, 2012, www.nydailynews.com/entertainment/tv-movies/valentine-day-casablanca-wuthering-heights-rent-impress-date-article-1.1022275. This article is written during the DVD era, which adopted strategies from the earlier videocassette era for Valentine's Day.

8. Packaging strategies that continued to promote Bogart include, for example, Warner Home Video's 2000 VHS and DVD reissue of "The Humphrey Bogart Collection," a group of nineteen Bogart films and extra features.

9. Sheila Benson, "Still in Love with Romantic Movies," *Los Angeles Times,* Jan. 29, 1989, 5.

10. Gendy Alimurung, "Casablanca on St. Valentine's Day," *Los Angeles Weekly,* Feb. 20, 2008, www.laweekly.com/casablanca-on-st-valentines-day/; Joe Holleman, "Valentine's Day Is Monday, and the Pressure is On. Be Romantic—Or Else," *St. Louis Dispatch,* Feb. 13, 2000, F3.

11. The commercializing of the Valentine's Day cult was noticeable in repertory house screenings of *Casablanca* that I attended in the 1990s and 2000s at the Brattle Theatre in Cambridge, the Music Box Theatre in Chicago, and the Buskirk-Chumley Theater in Bloomington, Indiana. Programming strategies promoted the film's cult status and provided instructions on audience participation. The Buskirk-Chumley, for instance, had a lobby area with costumes that customers could don to have their pictures taken as Rick and Ilsa, while, as we saw in the introduction, the Music Box defined its screening as a participatory experience—a "Sweetheart Sing-Along *Casablanca.*" Although the screenings had attracted large audiences, in each case, the theaters were largely silent. Hence, *Casablanca* was still an attraction that these theaters could sell as a ritual Valentine's Day event, but the spontaneous audience participation that once defined it was not a part of the experience.

12. Jeff Springer, "The Commercialization of Our 25 Favorite Holidays," *Business Pundit,* August 14, 2008, www.businesspundit.com/the-commercialization-our-25-favorite-holidays.

13. The tension among cults, cult fandoms, and commercialization is long-standing. For a discussion of these tensions that demonstrates the importance,

rather than the disparagement, of the commercial aspects of these phenomena, see Hills, *Fan Cultures,* 27–45.

14. Mark Jancovich, Antonio Lázaro Reboll, Julian Stringer, and Andy Willis, introduction to *Defining Movies: The Cultural Politics of Oppositional Taste,* ed. Mark Jancovich, Antonio Lázaro Reboll, Julian Stringer, and Andy Willis (Manchester, UK: Manchester University Press, 2003), 4; and Hunter, *Cult Film,* 17.

15. Elena Gorfinkel, "Cult Film or Cinephilia by Any Other Name," *Cineaste* 34, no. 1 (2008): 37. See also Joan Hawkins, *Cutting Edge: Art-Horror and the Horrific Avant-Garde* (Minneapolis: University of Minnesota, 2000), 33–49.

16. David Church, *Grindhouse Nostalgia: Memory, Home Video, and Exploitation Film Fandom* (Edinburgh: Edinburgh University Press, 2015), 16–17.

17. Patrick Geary, "Sacred Commodities: The Circulation of Medieval Relics," in *The Social Life of Things: Commodities in Cultural Perspective,* ed. Arjun Appadurai (Cambridge: Cambridge University Press, 1986), 169–70.

18. For scholarship on *Casablanca* as a western, see John G. Cawelti, *Adventure, Mystery, and Romance: Formula Stories as Art and Popular Culture* (Chicago: University of Chicago Press, 1976), 250–51; and Robert B. Ray, *A Certain Tendency of the Hollywood Cinema, 1930–1980* (Princeton, NJ: Princeton University Press, 1985), 89–112. For *Casablanca* as a war movie, see, among others, Clayton R. Koppes and Gregory D. Black, *Hollywood Goes to War* (New York: Free Press, 1987).

19. This definition of cult glosses J. Hoberman in Joe Bob Briggs et al., "Cult Cinema: A Critical Symposium," *Cineaste* 34, no. 1 (2008): 44.

20. Eric Hoyt, *Hollywood Vault: Film Libraries before Home Video* (Berkeley: University of California Press, 2014), 4.

21. For more on the US industry history of video, see Janet Wasko, *Hollywood in the Information Age: Beyond the Silver Screen* (Austin: University of Texas Press, 1995), 113–70; Frederick Wasser, *Veni, Vidi, Video: The Hollywood Empire and the VCR* (Austin: University of Texas Press, 2001); and Joshua M. Greenberg, *From Betamax to Blockbuster: Video Stores and the Invention of Movies on Video* (Cambridge, MA: MIT Press, 2008).

22. Wasko, *Hollywood,* 132; Wasser, *Veni, Vidi, Video,* 120.

23. Wasko, *Hollywood,* 100–101, 113, 149. For a study of video stores, see Daniel Herbert, *Videoland: Movie Culture at the American Video Store* (Berkeley: University of California Press, 2014).

24. Wasser, *Veni, Vidi, Video,* 67; Wasko, *Hollywood,* 124.

25. "Videotapes: A Crowded Field," *New York Times,* Feb. 13, 1982, 31; Wasko, *Hollywood,* 113; Greenberg, *From Betamax to Blockbuster,* 72.

26. Wasko, *Hollywood,* 130, 158.

27. Wasko, 135–36.

28. Jim McCullaugh, "Panel Sells the Idea That Sell-Thru Is on Growth Track," *Billboard,* April 11, 1992, 53, 60.

29. Chris McGowan, "The Classic Question: What Makes a Movie a True Candidate for the Classics Section?," *Billboard,* May 30, 1987, C2–3; Earl Paige, "A Retailer's Guide to Selling the Stars of Yesteryear," *Billboard,* May 30, 1987, C2,

C10–12. In video stores, vintage international films tended to be classified as "foreign cinema."

30. Wasko, *Hollywood,* 142.

31. Greenberg, *From Betamax to Blockbuster,* 93.

32. Anne Gilbert, "Push, Pull, Rerun: Television Reruns and Streaming Media," *Television & New Media* 20, no. 7 (2019): 687–88.

33. Wasser, *Veni, Vidi, Video,* 77–79. See also Kimberly K. Massey and Stanley J. Baran, "VCRs and People's Control of Their Leisure Time," in *Social and Cultural Aspects of VCR Use,* ed. Julia R. Dobrow (Hillsdale, NJ: Erlbaum, 1990), 93–106.

34. Mark Jancovich, Lucy Faire, and Sarah Stubbings, *The Place of the Audience: Cultural Geographies of Film Consumption* (London: BFI, 2003), 197.

35. As I discussed in chapters 2 and 3, in 1956 Warner Bros. sold more than seven hundred of its pre-1948 films, including *Casablanca,* to PRM Inc. and Associated Artists Productions (AAP), followed by its 1948–50 films.

36. Peter Decherney, *Hollywood's Copyright Wars: From Edison to the Internet* (New York: Columbia University Press, 2012), 169–81.

37. "Feature Films Top List of Shows Sears Offers," *Billboard,* March 25, 1972, 33; Joe Radcliffe, "Cartridge Rental Network Distribution Set," *Billboard,* August 26, 1972, 61. See also Wasko, *Hollywood,* 118–19; Wasser, *Veni, Vidi, Video,* 62–63; and Greenberg, *From Betamax to Blockbuster,* 48–49.

38. Bryan Sebok characterizes format wars as "defined by two or more competing, incompatible technologies that function in similar ways, entering the marketplace at around the same historical moment," in "Convergent Consortia: Format Battles in High Definition," *Velvet Light Trap* 64 (Fall 2009), 36.

39. "United States CED Title Database," CED Magic, www.cedmagic.com/title-database/ced-titles.html.

40. Wasko, *Hollywood,* 121–22; Wasser, *Veni, Vidi, Video,* 65–68.

41. Ad, "Own a Movie Forever at the Cost of Seeing It Once," *American Film* 10, no. 7 (May 1, 1985): 5.

42. As its changing ownership suggests, beginning in 1972, *Casablanca*'s history of distributors in domestic home video was also varied. It included UA, Magnetic Video, 20th Century Fox Video, CBS-Fox Video, MGM/UA Home Entertainment, Time-Life Video, and Warner's Home Video. On video distribution more generally, see Wasser, *Veni, Vidi, Video,* 95–98; and Wasko, *Hollywood,* 131–32, 140–44.

43. Wasko, *Hollywood,* 65.

44. Dennis Hunt, "Colorized *Casablanca* Coming Soon to Home Video," *Los Angeles Times,* Feb. 17, 1989, www.latimes.com/archives/la-xpm-1989-02-17-ca-3062-story.html. The colorization controversies are broadly covered. See, for example, Decherney, *Hollywood's Copyright Wars,* 144–50; and Paul Grainge, *Monochrome Memories: Nostalgia and Style in Retro America* (Westport, CT: Praeger, 2002), 155–79. See also my analysis of colorization from the perspective of historical circulation in "Cinema and Immortality: Hollywood Classics in an Intermediated World," in *Cultures in Conflict/Conflicting Cultures,* ed. Christina Ljungberg and Mario Klarer (Tubingen: Narr Verlag, 2013), 22–24.

45. Thomas S. Mulligan, "Turner–Time Warner Merger Approved by Shareholders," *Los Angeles Times,* Oct. 11, 1996, www.latimes.com/archives/la-xpm-1996-10-11-fi-52676-story.html. Elliott Forbes and David Pierce discuss the specific library holdings of major companies in "Who Owns the Movies?," *Film Comment* 30, no. 6 (Nov.-Dec. 1994): 43–46, 48–50.

46. Liam Cole Young, *List Cultures: Knowledge and Poetics from Mesopotamia to BuzzFeed* (Amsterdam: Amsterdam University Press, 2017), 50–57.

47. Beginning in 1980, *Billboard* compiled figures from weekly retail sales for best-selling videos in both Betamax and VHS.

48. For a selection of chart rankings for *Casablanca* in *Billboard,* see "Videotape Top 40," *Billboard,* August 15, 1981, 62; Sept. 12, 1981, 60; Sept. 19, 1981, 53; Nov. 14, 1981, 80; Dec. 19, 1981, 61; Jan. 16, 1982, 33; Feb. 6, 1982, 58; March 20, 1982, 46; Dec. 25, 1982, TIA38.

49. In a rare showing on rental charts, *Casablanca* placed in the top twenty-five (at number twenty-two) as a new entry in April 1982. "Videocassette Top 25 Rentals," *Billboard,* April 3, 1982, 46. It did not, however, have the same staying power in rentals that it did in sales.

50. Ad, "Own the Treasures of the Silver Screen," *American Film,* Sept. 1, 1986, 10, 11.

51. Jim McCullaugh, "Videobeat '86: Reading the Clear Signposts to the Sell-Through Market," *Billboard,* August 30, 1986, V68.

52. "Number One Awards: Top Videocassette Sales," *Billboard,* Dec. 27, 1986, 52, 98.

53. McCullaugh, "Videobeat '86"; "Video News: US Home Viewing Relegates Theatres with Video Films Now in 3 Formats," *Screen International,* May 3, 1986, 338, 343; "CBS/Fox Warns of Border War," *Billboard,* March 1, 1986, 1, 73; and Tony Seideman, "CBS/Fox Video Fall Promotion Is Launched," *Billboard,* Sept. 13, 1986, 65.

54. Tom Bierbaum, "Homevideo: CBS/Fox Promo May Be the Best Even If It's the Last," *Variety,* April 9, 1986, 41–42; "Number One Awards," 52, 98.

55. "Video News," 338, 343.

56. "Top Video Sales," *Billboard,* Sept. 19, 1992, 72.

57. "Top Video Sales," *Billboard,* Sept. 26, 1992, 74; Oct. 3, 1992, 59; Nov. 28, 1992, 72; Dec. 12, 1992, 56; Dec. 26, 1992, 72; Jan. 23, 1993, 67; Feb. 13, 1993, 60; Feb. 27, 1993, 53.

58. "Top Video Sales," *Billboard,* Nov. 7, 1992, 62.

59. "1992, the Year in Video: Top Video Sales," *Billboard,* Jan. 9, 1993, V4. *Citizen Kane*'s fiftieth-anniversary edition was ranked at forty-two, *It's a Wonderful Life*'s forty-fifth at sixty-eight, *King Kong*'s sixtieth at seventy-three, and *Singin' in the Rain*'s fortieth at eighty-seven. These films, though, did not approach the success of Disney reissues. *Fantasia* and *101 Dalmatians* were numbers one and two, respectively, generating unit sales in the millions and out-earning most other films.

60. Young, *List Cultures,* 64, 48.

61. On the ability of lists to shape film culture, although my study is not broad enough to address racial disparities in the video market, the industry lists that fea-

tured classical Hollywood films tended to exclude films by or with people of color in major roles. Furthermore, video vendors often stocked titles by white directors and starring white performers while, despite demand from Black patrons, failing to stock films by Black directors in sufficient numbers. See Marc Berman, "Are Retailers Selling Black Movies Short?," *Variety,* Nov. 18, 1991, 16.

62. Young, *List Cultures,* 45.

63. Scott D. Apel, "Are You Video Literate?," *Video Review* 14 (May/June 1993): 55–59.

64. Herbert, *Videoland,* 58, 183–217. For one of the many influential video guides that canonized *Casablanca,* see Roger Ebert, "My Ten Great Films, and Why," *Roger Ebert's Movie Home Companion* (New York: Andrews and McMeel, 1989), 803–7.

65. See Mattias Frey, "The Internet Suggests: Film, Recommender Systems, and Cultural Mediation," *Journal of Cinema and Media Studies* 59, no 1 (Fall 2019): 163–69, on the connection between contemporary and past recommendation systems.

66. James F. English, *The Economy of Prestige: Prizes, Awards, and the Circulation of Cultural Value* (Cambridge, MA: Harvard University Press, 2005), 76. English explains, after Daniel Bell, that the postindustrial social formation after WWII manifested itself, in part, by the rise in the production of cultural capital as a form of power and knowledge (69–106). This set the stage for a "frenzy" of prizes and awards beginning in the late 1960s, wherein an economy of prestige, "distinct from the economy of postindustrial goods and services," grew exponentially (22, 75).

67. Young, *List Cultures,* 10, 121.

68. Leigh Eric Schmidt, "The Fashioning of a Modern Holiday: St. Valentine's Day, 1840–1870," *Winterthur Portfolio* 28, no. 4 (Winter 1993): 210–13, 244. Gifting beyond cards was practiced in seventeenth-century England but became widespread during the industrial revolution.

69. Schmidt, 227–29.

70. Schmidt, 241–43, 222.

71. Schmidt, 214–15; 218, 244–45.

72. National Retail Federation, "Valentine's Day Data Center," https://nrf.com/insights/holiday-and-seasonal-trends/valentines-day/valentines-day-data-center.

73. Herbert, *Videoland,* 50.

74. Thomas Elsaesser, "Touch and Gesture: On the Borders of Intimacy," *Framework* 60, no. 1 (Spring 2019), 22.

75. Jancovich et al., *Place of the Audience,* 192.

76. Lynn Spigel's *Make Room for TV: Television and the Family Ideal in Postwar America* (Chicago: University of Chicago Press, 1992) exemplifies a discursive approach to how new media are culturally understood in the gendered and intimate sphere of the home. Ann Gray's *Video Playtime: The Gendering of a Leisure Technology* (London: Routledge, 1992) approaches the VCR through an empirical study aimed at a similar understanding.

77. Leah Wallace, "The Human Side: How the VCR Is Changing Us," *San Francisco Chronicle,* May 4, 1986, 51. See also David Denby, "Fatal Attraction: The

VCR and the Movies," *New York Magazine,* June 6, 1988, 28; and Calvin Trillin, "Gimme a Break: Vacationing in a Room with a VCR View," *Philadelphia Inquirer,* August 25, 1988, A23.

78. Lauren Berlant, "Intimacy: A Special Issue," *Critical Inquiry* 24, no. 2 (Winter 1998): 281–82.

79. Robert Ferrigno, "Credit Ratings, Sex Appeal, and VCRs Combine as America Falls in Love with the New Romance," *Orange County Register,* May 28, 1987, J01.

80. Jack Curry, "One VCR—Two Tickets to Romance," *Cosmopolitan,* Dec. 1985, 118, 120–22.

81. Curry, 118, 120–22 (Curry's emphasis).

82. Lou Aguilar, "Romance Movies: 7 Love Stories You Can Snuggle Up to for Valentine's Day," *Cincinnati Enquirer,* Feb. 7, 1988, 180.

83. Joe Saltzman, "Video Valentines," *Los Angeles Times,* Feb. 10, 1991, 82.

84. "All One Needs Is a Loaf of Bread, a Bottle of Wine and Thou . . . and a VCR," *Los Angeles Times,* Feb. 11, 1989, W9.

85. Young, *List Cultures,* 20, 45, 56.

86. Michael Patrick Allen and Anne E. Lincoln, "Critical Discourse and the Cultural Consecration of American Films," *Social Forces* 82, no. 3 (March 2004): 877.

87. Stephen Hunter, "Eighties-Style Valentines: Old Movies Can Put Romance in Your VCR," *Baltimore Sun,* Feb. 14, 1985, 1B; Jami Bernard, "A Movie Lovers' Guide: Just the Two of You, a Darkened Room . . . and a Classic Romance on the VCR," *New York Daily News,* Feb. 8, 1998, 15.

88. Maltin published these guides between 1969 and 2014. For example, see his *TV Movies and Video Guide* (New York: Signet, 1989).

89. Leonard Maltin, "Leonard Maltin's Ten Most Romantic Movies," *Ladies Home Journal,* Feb. 1993, 66. In order, the films that followed were *The Clock* (1945), *Brief Encounter* (1945), *The Ghost and Mrs. Muir* (1947), *Roman Holiday* (1953), *Love in the Afternoon* (1947), *Moonstruck* (1987), *Love Affair* (1939), *To Catch a Thief* (1955), and *Out of Africa* (1985).

90. "The Ten Most Romantic Movies of All Time," *Cosmopolitan,* Feb. 1998, 35; Joe DeChick, "Star Crossed," *Cincinnati Enquirer,* Feb. 13, 1993, C1.

91. "All One Needs," W9 (see note 84 above).

92. Rebecca Goodman, "Play Love Again with Mumm," *Cincinnati Enquirer,* Feb. 11, 2004, 35. The correct line is "Louis, I think this is the beginning of a beautiful friendship."

93. John Hartl, "Video Valentines—If You Want a Romantic Movie Tomorrow, You'll Need a VCR," *Seattle Times,* Feb. 13, 1985, G1.

94. Hunter, "Eighties-Style Valentines."

95. Amy Hufft, "The 10 Most Romantic Movies on Video," *Redbook,* March 1997, G1 (Hufft's emphasis). Her remaining nine are *Roman Holiday, Dr. Zhivago* (1965), *The Way We Were* (1973), *The Year of Living Dangerously* (1982), *An Officer and a Gentleman, The Last of the Mohicans* (1992), *When Harry Met Sally* (1989), *An Affair to Remember,* and *Four Weddings and a Funeral* (1994).

96. Neumaier, "Valentine's Day" (see note 7 above).

97. Judith Viorst, "You Must Remember Bliss . . . Judith Viorst Picks the 10 Most Romantic Movies," *Redbook,* Feb. 1991, 64.

98. Dennis Hunt, "From the Heart: 10 Romantic Movies for Valentine's Day," *Los Angeles Times,* Feb. 9, 1990, F27.

99. Cawelti, *Adventure, Mystery, and Romance,* 41–42. Although Cawelti discusses *Casablanca* as a western rather than a romance, his classifications of romance shed better light on how the film was addressed by mass media critics in the 1980s and 1990s.

100. The appeal of Rick and Ilsa's romance did not dominate, for example, early critics' comments. See "Film Review: *Casablanca,*" *Variety,* Dec. 2, 1942, 8, which extols the cast and the song while calling the film "splendid anti-Axis propaganda" and highlighting the emotionalism of the "La Marseillaise" scene for wartime America.

101. Hunter, "Eighties-Style Valentines"; Warren Epstein, "Warren's Picks for 10 Most Romantic Movies," *Colorado Springs Gazette,* Feb. 8, 2012.

102. Michael Malice, *The New Right: A Journey to the Fringes of American Politics* (New York: All Points Books, 2019).

103. Hunter, "Eighties-Style Valentines."

104. Viorst, "You Must Remember Bliss," 64.

105. Ruthe Stein, "Today, Love in the Movies Is a Sad Affair—Dysfunctional Hearts Dominate Many Modern 'Romantic' Films," *San Francisco Chronicle,* Feb. 13, 1996, E1.

106. Sheila Benson, "Still in Love with Romantic Movies; Filmmakers Are Re-Igniting Those Old Flames of Desire," *Los Angeles Times,* Jan. 29, 1989, 5.

107. Mick LaSalle, "10 Favorite Examples of Onscreen Romance," *San Francisco Chronicle,* Feb. 13, 1996, E1.

108. Viorst, "You Must Remember Bliss," 64, 66, 68, 70–71. In order, her films were *Casablanca, Brief Encounter, Waterloo Bridge* (1940), *Wuthering Heights, Random Harvest* (1942), *An Affair to Remember, The Philadelphia Story* (1940), *Roman Holiday, Gigi* (1958), and *The African Queen.*

109. On 1940s censorship in relation to this scene and other elements of *Casablanca,* see Richard Maltby, "'A Brief Romantic Interlude': Dick and Jane Go to 3½ Seconds of the Classical Hollywood Cinema," in *Post-Theory: Reconstructing Film Studies,* ed. David Bordwell and Noël Carroll (Madison: University of Wisconsin Press, 1996), 445–50. On Bergman's career and the scandal, see Ora Gelley, "Ingrid Bergman's Star Persona and the Alien Space of *Stromboli,*" *Cinema Journal* 47, no. 2 (Winter 2008): 26–51.

110. Robert Coover, "You Must Remember This," *Playboy,* Jan. 1985, 122, 200, 241–49.

111. Joe Holleman and Patricia Corrigan, "Valentine's Day Is Monday, and the Pressure Is On. Be Romantic—or Else," *St. Louis Post-Dispatch,* Feb. 13, 2000, F3.

112. Mick LaSalle and Ruthe Stein, "He Says, She Says—20 Romantic Videos," *San Francisco Chronicle,* Feb. 13, 1998, C1.

113. Hunter, "Eighties-Style Valentines"; James Verniere, "Real Men Watch Chick Flicks," *Boston Herald,* Feb. 12, 2006, O35.

114. Diane Baroni, "Boy Meets Girl," *Ladies Home Journal* (June 1991): 100, 102–103, 108.

115. Nora Burns, "*Casablanca* Farewell," *Cosmopolitan,* May 1979, 356–58.

116. On *Cosmopolitan*'s treatment of sex during the 1970s and 1980s, see Kathryn McMahon, "The *Cosmopolitan* Ideology and the Management of Desire," *Journal of Sex Research* 27, no. 3 (August 1990): 381–96.

117. Nancy Friday, Kamala Devi, Carol Tavris, Susan Sadd, "Cosmo's Sex Sampler: The Power of Sexual Tension," *Cosmopolitan* (March 1978): 208–11.

118. *People* staff, "Ann Landers Learns That Most Women Would Rather Be Hugged Than You-Know-What," *People,* Jan. 21, 1985. https://people.com/archive/ann-landers-learns-that-most-women-would-rather-be-hugged-than-you-know-what-vol-23-no-3/.

119. Associated Press, "Surprised Columnist Gets 100,000 Replies: Dear Ann: Tenderness Beats 'the Act,'" *Los Angeles Times,* Jan. 15, 1985, www.latimes.com/archives/la-xpm-1985-01-15-mn-7352-story.html.

120. Mike Royko, "Cuddle Up with This Survey, Ann," *Chicago Tribune,* Jan. 29, 1985, www.chicagotribune.com/news/ct-xpm-1985-01-29-8501060417-story.html.

121. Sharon Cohen, "Sex Experts Say Results of Ann Landers' Survey 'Dangerous,'" AP News, Jan. 15, 1985, https://apnews.com/74b9c12ab4cc08a48cd06b7c76500131.

122. Carol Tavris and Susan Sadd, *The Redbook Report on Female Sexuality: 100,000 Married Women Disclose the Good News about Sex* (New York: Delacorte Press, 1975). Also see Linda Wolfe, *The Cosmo Report* (New York: Arbor House, 1981).

123. Susan Faludi, *Backlash: The Undeclared War against American Women* (New York: Crown, 1991). Other publications examining the reaction against feminism in the 1980s include Susan Jeffords, *The Remasculinization of America: Gender and the Vietnam War* (Bloomington: Indiana University Press, 1989); and Susan Jeffords, *Hard Bodies: Hollywood Masculinity in the Reagan Era* (New Brunswick, NJ: Rutgers University Press, 1994).

124. Hunter, "Eighties-Style Valentines."

125. Robert Ferrigno, "The New Romance Isn't What It Used to Be," *Sun-Sentinel,* June 24, 1987, 1E.

126. It is also possible that critics embraced reissued classical Hollywood films, with their insistent heterosexuality and indirect expressions of sexuality, as a reactive response to AIDs in the 1980s and 1990s.

127. Church, *Grindhouse Nostalgia,* 16.

128. On prosthetic memories see Alison Landsberg, *Prosthetic Memory: The Transformation of American Remembrance in the Age of Mass Culture* (New York: Columbia University Press, 2004).

129. Grainge, *Monochrome Memories,* 4.

130. Young, *List Cultures,* 59, 120.

131. Berlant, "Intimacy," 282.

132. In February 2020, theaters across the US screened *Casablanca,* including the Brattle Theatre, Philadelphia Film Society (for a BYOB sold-out screening), Music Box in Chicago (for its "*Casablanca* and Sweetheart Sing-Along"), Athena Cinema in Athens, Ohio, Chehalis Theater in Chehalis, Washington, American Cinematheque at the Aero in Los Angeles, and New Parkway Theater in Oakland, California (offering dinner with the film), along with symphony hall live orchestra performances in Portland, Oregon, and Indianapolis, Indiana. In these venues, the film was still "an undisputed masterpiece and perhaps Hollywood's quintessential statement on love and romance that has only improved with age" ("Olympia Film Society Presents: *Casablanca,* Valentine's Day Movie!," Feb. 14, 2017, https://olympiafilmsociety.org/valentines-day-movie-ofs-silver-screenings-presents-casablanca).

133. Young, *List Cultures,* 118.

134. Holleman and Corrigan, "Valentine's Day Is Monday," F3. See also Hufft, "10 Most Romantic Movies," G1; Epstein, "Warren's Picks"; Shalayne Pulia, "25 Valentine's Day Movies to Stream Because There's No Way You're Going Out," *InStyle,* Feb. 1, 2017, www.instyle.com/shopping/valentines-day-movies-streaming-guide; Evette Dion, "15 Black Romance Movies You Can Watch This Month," *BitchMedia,* Feb. 14, 2018, https://bitchmedia.org/article/black-romance-movies-ranked/; The BUZZ staff, "9 Black Movies to Watch on Valentine's Day," The BUZZ, Feb. 14, 2019, https://thebuzzcincy.com/541251/9-black-movies-to-watch-on-valentines-day/; and Erin Crabtree, "Valentine's Day Movies to Stream," Ask-Men, Feb. 7, 2019, https://www.askmen.com/recess/fun_lists/valentine-s-day-movies-to-stream.html.

135. Neumaier, "Valentine's Day" (see note 7 above); Sandra Barrera, "22 Romantic Movies to Watch on Valentine's Day," *New York Daily News*, Feb. 12, 2016, n.p.

136. Justin Kirkland and Emma Carey, "The 30 Best Romantic Movies of All Time," *Esquire,* March 27, 2020, www.esquire.com/entertainment/movies/g26027881/best-romantic-movies-of-all-time. See also Karl Smith, "What's the Most Romantic Movie of All Time," *Patch,* Feb. 3, 2012, https://patch.com/pennsylvania/doylestown/what-s-the-most-romantic-movie-of-all-time.

137. Holleman and Corrigan, "Valentine's Day Is Monday," F3.

138. Allen and Lincoln, "Critical Discourse," 879.

139. American Film Institute, "AFI's 100 Years . . . 100 Passions," www.afi.com/afis-100-years-100-passions. *Casablanca*'s credentials as a romance have been central, as well, to its promotion and packaging for consumption in other sales' strategies. In 2013, for example, in honor of the studio's ninetieth anniversary, Warner Bros. released several DVD series under the title "The Best of Warner Bros." This included a twenty-film collection of its romances from different periods of its history. *Casablanca* is in the first set (from 1938–42), along with *Gone with the Wind, Jezebel* (1938), *The Philadelphia Story, Mrs. Miniver* (1942), and *Now, Voyager* (1942).

140. American Film Institute, "AFI's 100 Years . . . 100 Movies," www.afi.com/afis-100-years-100-movies; *Casablanca* falls to third place in the 2008 poll,

American Film Institute, "AFI's 100 Years . . . 100 Movies—Tenth Anniversary Edition," www.afi.com/afis-100-years-100-movies-10th-anniversary-edition; and American Film Institute, "AFI's 100 Years . . . 100 Stars," www.afi.com/afis-100-years-100-stars.

141. Allen and Lincoln, "Critical Discourse," 877.

142. At number thirty-seven, *Casablanca* also made another AFI list, "AFI's 100 Years . . . 100 Thrills," www.afi.com/afis-100-years-100-thrills.

143. Pierre Bourdieu, *The Rules of Art: Genesis and Structure of the Literary Field,* trans. Susan Emanuel (Stanford, CA: Stanford University Press, 1996), 254; see also Allen and Lincoln, "Critical Discourse," 876. A mismatch with contemporary standards took place in 2020, when streaming service HBO Max temporarily pulled the classic but racist *Gone with the Wind* from its lineup due to George Floyd's murder by police and the Black Lives Matter movement.

144. David Allen, "21 Best Valentine's Day Movies Ever: From Classics to Rom Coms," Feb. 13, 2019, https://patch.com/us/across-america/21-best-valentines-day-movies-ever-classics-rom-coms.

145. "The Ten Most Romantic Movies of All Time," *Cosmopolitan,* Feb. 1998, 35; "The Best Valentine's Day Movies," *Just Poppin*', Feb. 7, 2013, http://blog.justpoppin.com/tag/casablanca.

146. Brandon Gregg, "Culture Vulture: Valentine's Day Gets the Cold Shoulder," *Salt Lake Tribune,* Feb. 11, 2008, 3; Edward Guthman, "For Valentine's Day, Catch True Love on Film—Putting Myths Aside for Genuine Romance," *San Francisco Chronicle,* Feb. 10, 2002, 41.

147. As part of bringing *Casablanca* into the present, researchers in a big data project, combining Rotten Tomatoes' top one hundred romantic films and Google Trends, tracked the state-by-state popularity of films for Valentine's Day (*Casablanca* held sway in Texas). Chris Brantner, "The Romantic Movies Each State Loves," *Streaming Observer,* Feb. 6, 2019, www.streamingobserver.com/romantic-movies-by-state.

148. *Grateful* staff, "15 Most Romantic Movies to Watch on Valentine's Day," *Grateful,* Jan. 24, 2019, www.makeitgrateful.com/living/celebrate/valentines-day/15-most-romantic-movies-to-watch-on-valentines-day.

149. Barrera, "22 Romantic Movies."

150. Rotten Tomatoes, "Top 100 Romance Movies," www.rottentomatoes.com/top/bestofrt/top_100_romance_movies.

151. Barrera, "22 Romantic Movies."

152. *Grio* staff, "10 Black Love Movies to Watch and Chill Valentine's Day Weekend," *The Grio,* Feb. 13, 2019, https://thegrio.com/2019/02/13/10-black-love-movies-to-watch-and-chill-v-day-weekend. In order, others included were *Purple Rain* (1984), *With This Ring* (2015), *The Inkwell* (1994), *Poetic Justice* (1993), *Boomerang* (1992), *Mahogany* (1975), *Jason's Lyric* (1994), and *Beyond the Lights* (2014).

153. Advocate editors, "42 LGBTQ Valentine's Day Movies for Every Mood," *Advocate,* Feb. 14, 2019, www.advocate.com/film/2019/2/14/42-valentines-day-movies-every-mood#media-gallery-media-3.

154. Herrnstein Smith, *Contingencies of Value*, 49. Of course, not all such trajectories lead to total extinction, nor is extinction necessarily a permanent state of affairs.

155. Herrnstein Smith, 50–53 (Herrnstein Smith's emphasis).

156. Herrnstein Smith, 48.

CHAPTER 5. HAPPY ANNIVERSARIES

1. Brian Hannan, *Coming Back to a Theater Near You: A History of Hollywood Reissues* (Jefferson, NC: McFarland, 2016), 301; Kirk Honeycutt, "Classics Pay Their Way in Pre-Vid Theatrical Runs," *Hollywood Reporter*, June 4, 1992, 1, 8, 11; "Promo for Reissue of *Casablanca*," *Variety*, June 1, 1992, 25. Turner licensed video rights to his library, including pre-1950 Warner Bros. films, to distributor MGM/UA. See Paul Verna, "Turner Ventures into TV Films, Miniseries with ACI," *Billboard*, April 25, 1992, 51, 55, 57.

2. Jim McCullaugh, "Retailers Honor Top Vid Titles at VSDA Confab," *Billboard*, August 7, 1993, 56. For *Casablanca*'s chartings, see *Billboard*'s "Top Video Sales": Sept. 19, 1992, 72; Sept. 26, 1992, 74; Nov. 28, 1992, 72; Dec. 26, 1992, 72; Jan. 23, 1993, 67; and Feb. 27, 1993, 53.

3. Verna, "Turner Ventures," 55; Stuart Miller, "Old Vids Are New Again with Special Packages," *Variety*, Nov. 18, 1991, 16; Earl Paige, "Classics Coming Back into Style," *Billboard*, Jan. 30, 1993, 65, 70; Jim McCullaugh, "1992 The Year in Video: Top Video Sales," *Billboard*, Jan. 9, 1993, V4.

4. McCullaugh, "1992 The Year in Video."

5. While space does not allow me to examine cable TV, *Casablanca*'s anniversary was promoted on cable, particularly Turner's cable channels, TNT, TBS, and TCM. For more on classical Hollywood films on cable, see my *Beyond the Multiplex: Cinema, New Technologies, and the Home* (Berkeley: University of California Press, 2006), 91–134; Alison Trope, *Stardust Monuments: The Saving and Selling of Hollywood* (Hanover, NH: Dartmouth College Press, 2011), 127–69; and, on TCM in particular, Caetlin Benson-Allott, *The Stuff of Spectatorship: Material Cultures of Film and Television* (Oakland, CA: University of California Press, 2021), 94–132.

6. Eileen Fitzpatrick, "Slow Year for Classic-Vid Promos," *Home Video—Billboard's Video Newsweekly*, Nov. 13, 1993, 79.

7. The laser disc market at this time was small, with about 750,000 to one million players in the US. One laser edition of *Casablanca* was in the lower-resolution format CLV (constant linear velocity) and included the film and documentary. The other was in the high-end format CAV (constant angular density) and featured a boxed set with a booklet and two discs with the film, documentary, and two trailers. Jim McCullaugh, "MGM, Taster's Choice Team on 'Casablanca' Bow," *Billboard*, May 30, 1992, 51, 56.

8. Anne Sherber, "Studios Find More Videos Worthy of 'Anniversary' Rereleases," *Billboard*, Nov. 14, 1998, 75, 78; Honeycutt, "Classics Pay Their Way," 1, 8, 11.

9. John Thornton Caldwell, *Production Culture: Industrial Reflexivity and Critical Practice in Film and Television* (Durham, NC: Duke University Press, 2008), 287, 289.

10. Ross P. Garner, "'The Series That Changed Television'? *Twin Peaks,* 'Classic' Status, and Temporal Capital," *Cinema Journal* 55, no. 3 (Spring 2016), 138.

11. Daniel Herbert, *Videoland: Movie Culture at the American Video Store* (Berkeley: University of California Press, 2014), 180; Felix Richter, "Streaming Dominates US Home Entertainment Spending," *Statista,* Jan. 24, 2019, www.statista.com/chart/7654/home-entertainment-spending-in-the-us. In 2016, US video streaming subscription revenues exceeded DVD/Blu-ray sales for the first time. By 2018, subscription streaming accounted for $12.91 billion in revenue, while sell-through and rental DVDs/Blu-rays produced just over $4 billion. According to Richter, "the future of video distribution for home use is digital."

12. Caldwell, *Production Culture,* 306.

13. Robert Brookey and Robert Westerfelhaus, "Hiding Homoeroticism in Plain View: *The Fight Club* DVD as Digital Closet," *Critical Studies in Media Communication* 19, no. 1 (March 2002): 22.

14. Other new media platforms have contributed to *Casablanca*'s classic canonicity. In 2005 under the auspices of an NEH grant and a Digital Humanities initiative, Janet Murray et al., the Georgia Institute of Technology, the AFI, and Warner Bros. produced a digital critical edition of *Casablanca.* The grantees aimed to make the film available in a form that would appeal to educators and students, rendering it in pedagogical form through interactive, annotated web design that drew from DVD special edition extras for commentary. At this time, *Casablanca* joined Digital Humanities projects in literature focused on Charles Dickens, William Shakespeare, and other "great books" authors, earning, by association, a boost in its own standing. Such "great books" and "great films" approaches are inspired by the judgment that the texts involved are central to historical, cultural, and textual literacies. In *Casablanca*'s case, these literacies are largely shaped by industry discourses from DVDs.

15. "Home Video: Criterion Releasing 'Casablanca' with Trailer, Notes," *Variety,* August 30, 1989, 72; Chris McGowan, "Here's Looking at Voyager's Restored 'Casablanca' Disk," *Billboard,* Oct. 7, 1989, 61–62.

16. Keith M. Johnston, "Reclaiming the 'Vanilla' DVD: Brand Packaging and the Case of Ealing Studios," *Screen* 55, no. 1 (Spring 2014): 85, writes that "most people don't buy discs with supplemental features," opting instead for less-expensive vanilla versions. By contrast, Trope cites surveys showing that consumers are motivated to buy DVDs because of these features (*Stardust Monuments,* 152). See also Catherine Cella, "DVD: Bells & Whistles & Wonders: What Makes a Hit?," *Billboard,* May 27, 2000, 130, 138, 140.

17. See Jonathan Gray, *Show Sold Separately: Promos, Spoilers, and Other Media Paratexts* (New York: New York University, 2010), 102, on the use of artistic creation myths in *The Lord of the Rings* DVDs.

18. Janet Staiger, "The Politics of Film Canons," *Cinema Journal* 24, no. 3 (Spring 1985): 4–23.

19. As I mentioned in chapter 1, *Casablanca* has a colonialist resonance. The anniversary editions here not only project whiteness as a standard that eclipses African Americans; they also remove any attention to Morocco, North Africa, and the Middle East.

20. The special value of milestone anniversaries dates to practices in the Roman Empire around wedding anniversaries. In twentieth-century America, arbiter of social niceties Emily Post treated milestone wedding anniversaries as an established convention; see Emily Post, *Etiquette: The Blue Book of Social Usage* (1922; New York: Funk & Wagnalls, 1960), 404–5.

21. Alfred Andrea, "Some Musings on Historical Anniversaries," *The Historian* 58, no. 1 (Autumn 1995): 205.

22. William M. Johnston, *Celebrations: The Cult of Anniversaries in Europe and the United States Today* (New Brunswick, NJ: Transaction, 1991), 4–8, 63, 102, 161–62.

23. Johnston, 174.

24. Although research on film anniversaries is not bountiful, some work engages in revisionism with respect to revered film-related anniversary events. See, for example, Ginette Vincendeau, "In Focus: The French New Wave at 50: Pushing the Boundaries," *Cinema Journal* 49, no. 4 (Summer 2010): 135–66.

25. Ray Greene, "The Big Picture," *Boxoffice,* Dec. 1, 1998, 58. As Elliot Forbes and David Pierce write in "Who Owns the Movies?," *Film Comment* 30, no. 6 (Nov.-Dec. 1994), 43: "The past few years have produced the greatest realignment and consolidation of library ownership since the advent of television in the 1950s." Libraries matter because they figure into the conglomerates' financial operation and health, supporting them through rough economic patches. Wall Street considers them in valuing the conglomerate's stock, and banks accept them as collateral. A succession of new media innovations that can renovate older titles means that the catalog will appreciate over time, further enhancing its value.

26. As Time Warner subsidiaries, Turner's company and Warner Bros. have reissued anniversary editions from their library of RKO's *Citizen Kane* and *King Kong* and of MGM's *Gone with the Wind* and *The Wizard of Oz.*

27. The stand-alone studio era ended in the 1950s and 1960s, when larger companies, unaffiliated with the film business, bought studios (e.g., the former parking operation Kinney National Company's 1969 purchase of Warner Bros.). In the 1980s and 1990s, the government's deregulatory measures further energized the assimilation of film studios into larger corporations, enabling media ownership to consolidate into a few multinational corporations. With Time Warner's 2018 transition into the AT&T-owned WarnerMedia, this trend continued.

28. Caldwell, *Production Culture,* 276.

29. Simone Murray, "Brand Loyalties: Rethinking Content within Global Corporate Media," *Media, Culture, and Society* 27, no. 3 (2005): 418.

30. Murray, 418.

31. Eileen Fitzpatrick, "Shelf Talk—Southern Calif. Steps Up Street-Date Enforcement," *Billboard,* Nov. 8, 1997, 72, 73.

32. Bradley Schauer, "The Warner Archive and DVD Collecting in the New Home Video Market," *Velvet Light Trap* 70 (Fall 2012): 37.

33. Eileen Fitzpatrick, "Warner Vid Brews Anniv. Effort: Synergy Is Key Strategy for 75th Birthday Campaign," *Billboard,* Nov. 1, 1997, 6, 101.

34. Schauer, "The Warner Archive," 36–37.

35. Craig Hight, "Making-of Documentaries on DVD: *The Lord of the Rings* Trilogy and Special Editions," *Velvet Light Trap* 56 (Fall 2005): 4.

36. Schauer, "The Warner Archive," 36.

37. Robert Alan Brookey, "The Format Wars: Drawing the Battle Lines for the Next DVD," *Convergence* 13, no. 2 (2007): 201.

38. Motion Picture Association of America, "2018 Theme Report," www.motionpictures.org/wp-content/uploads/2019/03/MPAA-THEME-Report-2018.pdf, esp. 5–6, 33, 36–37; Samuel Axion, "DVD and Blu-ray Sales Nearly Halved Over Five Years, MPAA Report Says," *Ars Technica,* April 12, 2019, https://arstechnica.com/gadgets/2019/04/dvd-and-blu-ray-sales-nearly-halved-over-five-years-mpaa-report-says.

39. Brookey, "The Format Wars," 200–201.

40. Giorgio Bertellini and Jacqueline Reich, "DVD Supplements: A Commentary on Commentaries," *Cinema Journal* 49, no. 3 (Spring 2010): 103; James Kendrick, "What Is the Criterion? The Criterion Collection as an Archive of Film as Culture," *Journal of Film and Video* 53, nos. 2/3 (Summer/Fall 2001): 124–39.

41. Erika Balsom, "Original Copies: How Film and Video Became Art Objects," *Cinema Journal* 53, no. 1 (Fall 2013): 101–2, 116.

42. Gary Crowdus, "Providing a Film Archive for the Home Viewer: An Interview with Peter Becker of the Criterion Collection," *Cineaste* 25, no. 1 (1999): 49; Matt Neapolitan, "Quality Is the Trademark of Criterion Collection DVDs," *Billboard,* May 17, 2003, 46.

43. Kendrick, "What Is the Criterion?," 126.

44. Miller, "Old Vids Are New Again," 16.

45. Catherine Applefeld Olson, "Classic Titles Dominate 4th Quarter," *Billboard,* Oct. 12, 1996, 87; Paige, "Classics Coming Back," 65, 70; Miller, "Old Vids Are New Again," 16.

46. Sherber, "Studios Find More Videos," 75, 78.

47. Brookey and Westerfelhaus, "Hiding Homoeroticism," 22.

48. Caldwell, *Production Culture,* 298, 291.

49. Johnston, "Reclaiming the 'Vanilla' DVD," 86.

50. Brookey, "The Format Wars," 201.

51. Trope, *Stardust Monuments,* 129.

52. For an analysis that emphasizes positive aspects of the knowledge that extras generate for fans, see Pat Brereton, *Smart Cinema, DVD Add-Ons, and New Audience Pleasures* (New York: Palgrave Macmillan, 2012).

53. Eileen Fitzpatrick, "VSDA '98: Happy Birthday, Baby," *Billboard,* July 11, 1998, 60.

54. Media conglomerates honed synergy as a central practice, but, as a staple of capitalist media enterprise, synergy characterized Hollywood's earlier history as well. For Warner Bros.' fiftieth anniversary, in 1973, Warner Communications Inc.'s subsidiaries participated in a yearlong celebration. These offshoots included Warner Bros. Inc. Films, Warner Bros. Television, Warner/Reprise Records, Atlantic Records, Elektra Records, Warner Cable Corp., Warner Paperback Library, Warner National Periodical Publication, and more. See "Golden Anniversary for Warners," *Independent Film Journal,* Feb. 19, 1973, 25.

55. See, for example, Ray Greene, "Warner's @ 75," *Boxoffice,* May 1, 1998, 28.

56. Fitzpatrick, "Shelf Talk," 72, 73; Fitzpatrick, "VSDA '98," 60; Fitzpatrick, "Warner Vid Brews," 6; Adam Sandler, "Warner Marking 75th Anni with Video Push," *Variety,* Oct. 23, 1997, https://variety.com/1997/digital/features/warner-marking-75th-anni-with-video-push-1116674580. Independent companies participating were Act II Microwave Popcorn and Princess Cruise Lines.

57. Alex Fung, "Warner Bros. 75th Anniversary Festival of Film Classics," https://letterboxd.com/alexfung/list/warner-bros-75th-anniversary-festival-of. In another act of synergy, the festival also played at the Showcase Theater at the *Six Flags Great Adventure* theme park in Jackson, New Jersey, from April 9 to September 21, 1998; see https://sixflags.fandom.com/wiki/Warner_Bros._75th_Anniversary. Time Warner owned the park from 1991 to 1998 but remained a major stakeholder after selling it to Premier Parks.

58. Christine James, "Warner's Winner," *Boxoffice,* April 1, 1998, SW14–15; "Reel News in Review: New Warners Wing Offers Classics," *Film Journal International* 101, no. 7 (July 1, 1998): 6. Warner Bros.' creation of its classics division was not the first time these films had been sold in this way. In 1975, United Artists formed "United Artists Classics" as a specialized theatrical sales division to sell the same library of films. See "Vintage Film Release Set via UA Classics," *Boxoffice,* May 26, 1975, 10.

59. Fitzpatrick, "Warner Vid Brews," 101.

60. Tim Sheridan, "Warner Brothers 75 Years Entertaining," *AllMusic,* May 19, 1998, https://www.allmusic.com/album/warner-brothers-75-years-entertaining-mw0000036485?1648310077355.

61. After a long working relationship, Warner Bros. purchased Wolper's production company in 1976. By the 1990s, Wolper was in the Time Warner fold, making him a part of in-house, synergistic operations. See "Warner Bros. & Wolper," *Back-Stage,* Oct. 1, 1976, 22; Todd McCarthy, "Pictures: Wolper in New Warners Deal," *Variety,* August 10, 1988, 21; "News: Warner Bros. to Team Up with Wolper," *Broadcast,* Oct. 11, 1996, 6.

62. Fitzpatrick, "Warner Vid Brews," 6, 101; Fitzpatrick, "Shelf Talk," 72, 73.

63. Fitzpatrick, "Warner Vid Brews," 6, 101; Fitzpatrick, "VSDA '98," 65.

64. Fitzpatrick, "VSDA '98," 60.

65. Murray, "Brand Loyalties," 424, 422.

66. Murray, 422.

67. Greene, "Warner's @ 75," 34–36.

68. Murray, "Brand Loyalties," 424.

69. On this point, see also Benson-Allott, *The Stuff of Spectatorship,* 41–42.

70. NCM Fathom Events, Turner Classic Movies, and Warner Bros. Entertainment jointly presented *Casablanca*'s nationwide screenings in five hundred movie theaters. They programmed it as a special event on November 12 and 15 through Fathom's Digital Broadcast Network. See Aljean Harmetz, "*Casablanca* Is Back: Turner Classic Movies Presents 70th Anniversary Event," *IndieWire,* March 9, 2012, www.indiewire.com/2012/03/casablanca-is-back-turner-classic-movies-presents-70th-anniversary-event-182381.

71. Robert Kapsis, *Hitchcock: The Making of a Reputation* (Chicago: University of Chicago Press, 1992), 11, 85. For more on these relationships, specifically with museums, see Trope, *Stardust Monuments,* 11–43.

72. "The Smithsonian," www.si.edu; "American History Museum," www.si.edu/museums/american-history-museum; "Warner Bros. Theater," www.si.edu/theaters/warnerbrostheater.

73. See Haidee Wasson, *Museum Movies: The Museum of Modern Art and the Birth of Art Cinema* (Berkeley: University of California Press, 2005).

74. Alison Griffiths, *Shivers Down Your Spine: Cinema, Museums, and the Immersive View* (New York: Columbia University Press, 2008), 196.

75. Kurt and Gladys Lang, quoted in Kapsis, *Hitchcock,* 119.

76. As a sign of this priority, executives from Warner Home Video's theatrical catalog and publicity divisions ran NMAH's gala. Lou Lumenick, "*Casablanca* Restoration Premieres at Smithsonian," *New York Post,* Feb. 4, 2012, https://nypost.com/2012/02/04/casablanca-restoration-premieres-at-smithsonian.

77. Lou Lumenick; "*Casablanca:* Evening Film Screening," *Smithsonian Associates,* Feb. 3, 2012, https://smithsonianassociates.org/ticketing/tickets/223815. Beyond spearheading *Casablanca*'s limited rerelease in theaters in 2012 for its seventieth anniversary and showing it on its cable channel, TCM contributed in other ways to its circulation, including, in 2010, featuring the film in its Classic Film Festival in Los Angeles and, in 2011, embarking on its first Classic Movie Cruise, with a theme night devoted to *Casablanca.* See Nick Thomas, "Cruising with the Stars: The 2011 Turner Classic Movies Film Cruise," *Classic Images,* Feb. 2012, www.getnickt.com/newstcm.pdf.

78. On this subject, see also Daniel Mackay, "*Star Wars:* The Magic of Anti-myth," in *Performing the Force: Essays on Immersion into Science Fiction, Fantasy, and Horror Environments,* ed. Kurt Lancaster and Tom Micotowicz (Jefferson, NC: McFarland, 2001), 44–54.

79. Jason Combs, "Warner Bros. Theater to Open at Smithsonian in February," *IndieWire,* Dec. 5, 2011, www.indiewire.com/2011/12/warner-bros-theater-to-open-at-smithsonian-in-february-183868.

80. Kapsis, *Hitchcock,* 88–89.

81. Griffiths, *Shivers Down Your Spine,* 199, 202, 226.

82. Griffiths, 219.

83. Lumenick, "'*Casablanca*' Restoration."

84. For the week ending April 1, 2012, *Casablanca* ranked twenty-fourth on the DVD sales charts (with 21,132 units sold) and fifteenth in Blu-ray sales (with 19,593 units sold). "United States DVD Sales Chart" and "United States Blu-ray Sales Chart," *The Numbers*, www.the-numbers.com/home-market/dvd-sales-chart/2012/04/01 and www.the-numbers.com/home-market/bluray-sales-chart/2012/04/01; see also "Top-Selling Blu-rays in the United States," *The Numbers*, www.the-numbers.com/home-market/bluray-sales/2012.

85. In terms of saturation, not counting its VHS releases, between 1998 and 2018 *Casablanca* received US reissue in at least fourteen different DVD and ten Blu-ray editions, plus one on HD DVD, all of which demonstrate the importance of repackaging in reselling oldies. See "Casablanca: DVD," *Blu-ray.com*, www.blu-ray.com/dvd/Casablanca-DVD/80423; "*Casablanca:* Blu-ray," *Blu-ray.com*, www.blu-ray.com/movies/Casablanca-Blu-ray/746/; and appendix 2 of this book.

86. Kenneth Brown, "*Casablanca* Blu-ray Review," www.blu-ray.com/movies/Casablanca-Blu-ray/33623/#Review.

87. Miller, "Old Vids Are New Again," 16.

88. Miller, 16.

89. Miller, 16; Paige, "Classics Coming Back," 65, 70. As Paige recounts, retailers reported that purchasers gravitated to *Casablanca*'s deluxe boxed set so enthusiastically that some stores were "sold out to the last piece."

90. Johnston, "Reclaiming the 'Vanilla' DVD," 86. For more on DVD packaging for contemporary films, see Trope, *Stardust Monuments*, 160–61.

91. Jim McCullaugh, "Sell-Thru Sales Judged by Cover," *Home Video*, Oct. 24, 1992, 1.

92. Catherine Applefeld, "DVD: The Growth of a Format," *Billboard*, June 13, 1998, 85, 90, 92, 98.

93. Caldwell, *Production Culture*, 300–301.

94. The supplementary materials are mainly in standard definition.

95. Hight, "Making-of Documentaries on DVD," 7.

96. Johannes Mahlknecht, *Writing on the Edge: Paratexts in Narrative Cinema* (Heidelberg: Universitätsverlag, 2016), 19, 22.

97. Benson-Allott, *The Stuff of Spectatorship*, 50.

98. Rudy Behlmer, *Inside Warner Bros. (1935–1951): The Battles, the Brainstorms, and the Bickering* (New York: Simon & Schuster, 1985).

99. See also Trope, *Stardust Monuments*, 157.

100. Pavel Skopal, "'The Adventure Continues on DVD': Franchise Movies as Home Video," *Convergence* 13, no. 2 (2007): 193.

101. Kendrick, "What Is the Criterion?," 124–39.

102. Nathan Carroll, "Unwrapping Archives: DVD Restoration Demonstrations and the Marketing of Authenticity," *Velvet Light Trap* 56 (Fall 2005), 20.

103. Jaimie Baron, *The Archive Effect: Found Footage and the Audiovisual Experience of History* (London: Routledge, 2014), 5, 8.

104. Bridget Terry's documentary *Without Lying Down: Frances Marion and the Powerful Women of Early Hollywood* (2000) was based on a book of the same title

by Cari Beauchamp (1997). Beauchamp reported that Jack Warner was "abusive with a capital 'A.'" The documentary, shown on TCM and circulated by Criterion, demonstrates that such observations can attain industry-level exposure in nonanniversary contexts. See also, Thelma Adams, "Casting-Couch Tactics Plagued Hollywood Long before Harvey Weinstein," *Variety*, Oct. 17, 2017, https://variety.com/2017/film/features/casting-couch-hollywood-sexual-harassment-harvey-weinstein-1202589895.

105. Hight, "Making-of Documentaries on DVD," 7, 12–14.

106. Brookey and Westerfelhaus, "Hiding Homoeroticism," 21, 22; Klinger, *Beyond the Multiplex*, 115.

107. Skopal, "'The Adventure Continues on DVD,'" 186.

108. The documentaries include Bacall's "Introduction"; *You Must Remember This: The Warner Bros. Story;* "You Must Remember This: A Tribute to *Casablanca*"; "As Time Goes By: The Children Remember"; "Great Performances: Bacall on Bogart"; and "*Casablanca:* An Unlikely Classic."

109. For a detailed analysis of the differences between the play and the film script, see Noah Isenberg, *We'll Always Have "Casablanca": The Life, Legend, and Afterlife of Hollywood's Most Beloved Movie* (New York: Norton, 2017), 1–41.

110. See Danae Clark, *Negotiating Hollywood: The Cultural Politics of Actors' Labor* (Minneapolis: University of Minnesota Press, 1995). As Benson-Allott points out, labor in DVD/Blu-ray supplements is not so much completely obscured as it is transformed into "infotainment" (*The Stuff of Spectatorship*, 43).

111. Aljean Harmetz, *The Making of "Casablanca": Bogart, Bergman, and World War II* (New York: Hyperion, 2002). Harmetz did not invent the film's legend—it circulated in pieces in earlier sources—but she gave the most comprehensive account of it at the time. For a book composed almost entirely of Warner Bros. studio memos for its approach to the studio's and film's history, see Behlmer, *Inside Warner Bros.*, 194–221.

112. The bulk of the Warner Bros. paper archive is located at the Warner Bros. Archive, USC School of Cinematic Arts, Los Angeles. See also Emily Carman, "That's Not All, Folks! Excavating the Warner Bros. Archives," *Moving Image: The Journal of the Association of Moving Image Archivists* 14, no. 2 (Spring 2014): 30–48.

113. For a recent book that celebrates the origins and legacy of the film, see Isenberg, *We'll Always Have "Casablanca,"* published in 2017, the year of *Casablanca*'s seventy-fifth birthday. See also Horace Martin Woodhouse, *The Essential "Casablanca": 101 Things You Didn't Know about America's Favorite Movie* (Ithaca, NY: History Company, 2013) for a work that exhibits the influence of the film's origin story on what constitutes its essence.

114. Harmetz, *The Making of "Casablanca,"* 338–54.

115. Benson-Allott, *The Stuff of Spectatorship,* 16. Benson-Allott contends that DVD/Blu-ray box sets obscure TV series' historical origins and television history itself, thus offering a sense of the different impact that this mode of content distribution can have (22–58) on different media.

116. Jörg Arnold et al., "Forum: Anniversaries," *German History* 32, no. 1 (2014): 79, 84–85, 90, 97.

117. Arnold et al., 79, 86–89. See also Clara Calvo and Coppelia Kahn, eds., *Celebrating Shakespeare: Commemoration and Cultural Memory* (Oxford: Cambridge University Press, 2016).

118. Anne Reading, quoted in Gorton and Garde-Hansen, *Remembering British Television,* 10.

119. Trope, *Stardust Monuments,* 4.

120. See, for example, Dan Burley, "Wilson's Role in 'Casablanca' Tops for Hollywood," *New York Amsterdam Star-News,* Feb. 6, 1943, 17; Leon Hardwick, "To Honor Actors Responsible for the Rise of Negroes in Films," *Chicago Defender,* April 22, 1944, 8; and Billy Rowe, "Nation Hails Dooley Wilson in 'Casablanca': Star Leads Trend Toward Uplifting Roles for Negroes," *Pittsburgh Courier,* May 15, 1943, 21.

121. Delia Malia Konzett, "Classical Hollywood, Race, and *Casablanca,*" in *Critical Insights: Film—"Casablanca,"* ed. James Plath (Amenia, NY: Grey House Publishing, Inc., 2016), 97–113.

122. Maryann Erigha, *The Hollywood Jim Crow: The Racial Politics of the Movie Industry* (New York: New York University Press, 2019), 6, 9–10, 56.

123. Konzett, "Classical Hollywood," 110–111.

124. "The AFI List," American Film Institute, www.afi.com/afi-lists.

125. Fitzpatrick, "VSDA '98," 65.

126. The AFI was involved in promotion meant to drive video sales. Its "100 Films" list was publicized by a CBS television special dedicated to revealing the list for the first time, a ten-week TNT series that discussed the selections, a traveling exhibition of films involved, and promotions aimed at video retailers and stores. See Fitzpatrick, "VSDA '98," 60, 65.

127. Fitzpatrick: "VSDA," 60, 65; "Columbia, MGM Celebrate Sweet 75," *Billboard,* Feb. 13, 1999, 95, 97.

128. Jonathan Rosenbaum, *Movie Wars: How Hollywood and the Media Limit What Movies We Can See* (Chicago: A Cappella Books, 2000), 93–94. For more on Rosenbaum and canon building, see Christopher Long, "Revising the Film Canon: Jonathan Rosenbaum's *Movie Mutations* and *Essential Cinema,*" *New Review of Film and Television Studies* 4, no. 1 (2006): 17–35.

129. Elena Gorfinkel, "Against Lists," *Another Gaze,* Nov. 29, 2019, www.anothergaze.com/byline/elena-gorfinkel/.

130. Erigha, *The Hollywood Jim Crow,* 52–81.

131. Howard Becker writes, "The common solution to the problem of identifying what is best is to appeal to common sense and collective experience, to what 'everyone knows.'" Howard S. Becker, *Art Worlds* (Berkeley: University of California Press, 1982), 365.

132. Jonathan Lupo, "Loaded Canons: Contemporary Film Canons, Film Studies, and Film Discourse," *Journal of American Culture* 34, no. 3 (2011): 224–25.

133. Todd Boyd and Amy Heller, quoted in Kyle Buchanan and Reggie Ugwu, "The Criterion Collection's 'Blind Spots,'" *New York Times,* August 23, 2020, 6–7.

Criterion has taken steps to address this situation by streaming, for example, Black directors Justin Simien and Janicza Bravo's series *Adventures in Moviegoing,* which questions the racial bias of the film canon and discusses the work of Black filmmakers.

134. Spike Lee's *Do the Right Thing* (1989) and Julie Dash's *Daughters of the Dust* (1991) celebrated their twentieth and twenty-fifth anniversaries, respectively, with theatrical reissues and special editions.

135. Ellen C. Scott, *Cinema Civil Rights: Regulation, Repression, and Race in the Classical Hollywood Era* (New Brunswick, NJ: Rutgers University Press, 2015), 2–3, 11–67.

136. Erigha, *The Hollywood Jim Crow,* 4.

137. Donald Bogle, *Toms, Coons, Mulattoes, Mammies, and Bucks: An Interpretive History of Blacks in American Films* (New York: Continuum, 1991), 140; Konzett, "Classical Hollywood."

138. John Guillory, *Cultural Capital: The Problem of Literary Canon Formation* (Chicago: University of Chicago Press, 1993), 340.

139. Ankhi Mukherjee, "'What Is a Classic?': International Literary Criticism and the Classic Question," *PMLA* 125, no. 4 (2010): 1038.

140. Rachel Martin, "'Gone with the Wind' Returns to HBO Max with Intro by Expert in African American Film," NCPR, June 29, 2020, www.northcountrypublicradio.org/news/npr/884551356/gone-with-the-wind-returns-to-hbo-max-with-intro-by-expert-in-african-american-film; Jacqueline Stewart, "Why We Can't Turn Away from 'Gone with the Wind,'" *CNN Opinion,* June 25, 2020, www.cnn.com/2020/06/12/opinions/gone-with-the-wind-illuminates-white-supremacy-stewart/index.html. For a contrasting view on pedagogy and race, see Racquel Gates, "The Problem with 'Anti-Racist' Movie Lists," *New York Times,* July 17, 2020, www.nytimes.com/2020/07/17/opinion/sunday/black-film-movies-racism.html.

141. Martin, "'Gone with the Wind' Returns."

142. Burley, "Wilson's Role," 17; Hardwick, "To Honor Actors," 8; "Actors' Guild Fetes Dooley Wilson in N.Y.," *Chicago Defender,* July 3, 1943, 18.

143. Bill Chandler, "Hollywood Has Respect for Negro Fans' Wishes," *Chicago Defender,* Oct. 14, 1944, 7.

144. Quoted in Robin Pogrebin, "A Movie Museum in a Changing World," *New York Times,* June 7, 2021, C1, C6.

145. See, for example, Eric S. Faden, "Defining Classical Hollywood Narration in *Casablanca,*" in *Critical Insights: Film—"Casablanca,"* ed. James Plath (Amenia, NY: Grey House, 2016), 114–29.

146. Longxi Zhang, "Meaning, Reception, and the Use of Classics: Theoretical Considerations in a Chinese Context," *Intertexts* 19, nos. 1–2 (Spring–Fall 2015): 5. For a foundational work on this matter, see Hans Robert Jauss, *Toward an Aesthetic of Reception* (Minneapolis: University of Minnesota Press, 1982).

147. On TCM's deployment of the "classic" designation, see Benson-Allott, *The Stuff of Spectatorship,* 97–100.

148. Klinger, *Beyond the Multiplex,* 94.

149. James F. English, *The Economy of Prestige: Prizes, Awards, and the Circulation of Cultural Value* (Cambridge, MA: Harvard University Press, 2005), 244. See also J. M. Coetzee "What Is a Classic?" in *Stranger Shores: Literary Essays, 1986–1999* (London: Vintage, 2002).

150. Brown, "*Casablanca* Blu-ray Review" (see note 86 above).

151. Balsom, paraphrasing Isabelle Graw, "Original Copies," 100.

152. See, for example, *Life* magazine's special edition, "*Casablanca*": *The Most Beloved Movie of All Time* (New York: Time, 2018); the *CBS Morning Show*'s interview with scholar and author of *We'll Always Have "Casablanca"* Noah Isenberg; and coverage like Kenneth Turan, "*Casablanca* Returns to Theaters to Celebrate 75th Anniversary," *Los Angeles Times*, Nov. 8, 2017, www.latimes.com/entertainment/movies/la-et-mn-critics-choice-20171108-story.html.

153. In 2021, AT&T instituted a bid to "unmerge" with WarnerMedia and merge it with Discovery, forming a media-content business called Warner Bros. Discovery, which would be separate from the phone company. At the time of this writing, the federal government and the boards of AT&T and Discovery had approved of this plan. See Jennifer Maas, "Discovery Shareholders Approve $43 Billion WarnerMedia Merger," *Variety*, March 11, 2022, https://variety.com/2022/tv/news/discovery-warnermedia-merger-approvbed-investor-vote-1235201881.

154. For coverage of this event, see, for example, Amanda Kondolojy, "TCM Classic Movie Festival Celebrates *Casablanca, Cabaret,* and More on the Big Screen," *Orlando Sentinel,* Dec. 24, 2021, www.orlandosentinel.com/entertainment/movies/os-et-tcm-classic-movie-festival-2022-20211224-gccwcxze7bc77dmh62lmpmauhy-story.html.

EPILOGUE

1. See, for example, Dina Iordanova and Stuart Cunningham, eds., *Digital Disruption: Cinema Moves On-Line* (St. Andrews, UK: St. Andrews Film Studies, 2012), esp. 1–31.

2. An early book on cinema in the digital era focused on the struggles between Hollywood and Silicon Valley that made their partnership seem unlikely. See John Geirland and Eva Sonesh-Kedar, *Digital Babylon: How the Geeks, the Suits, and the Ponytails Tried to Bring Hollywood to the Internet* (New York: Arcade, 1999).

3. Felix Richter, "Streaming Dominates U.S. Home Entertainment Spending," *Statista*, Jan. 24, 2019, www.statista.com/chart/7654/home-entertainment-spending-in-the-us. In 2018, "US consumers spent $12.9 billion on subscription to services such as Netflix (up 30 percent compared to 2017)," while "all physical formats, both sell-through and rental, suffered double-digit declines."

4. Brooks Barnes, "Building and Managing a Warner Bros. Multiverse," *New York Times,* Dec. 28, 2020, B1, B3; Alex Weprin, "Netflix Adds 1.5 Million Total Subscribers, but Loses Ground in US/Canada," *Hollywood Reporter,* July 20,

2021, www.hollywoodreporter.com/business/digital/netflix-q2-2021-earnings-1234985080.

5. Lev Manovich, quoted in Derek Kompare, "Reruns 2.0: Revising Repetition for Multiplatform Television Distribution," *Journal of Popular Film and Television* 38, no. 2 (2010): 82; Anne Gilbert, "Push, Pull, Rerun: Television Reruns and Streaming Media," *Television & New Media* 20, no. 7 (2019): 687.

6. Chuck Tryon, "'Make Any Room Your TV Room': Digital Delivery and Media Mobility," *Screen* 53, no. 3 (Autumn 2012): 289–90; Kompare, "Reruns 2.0," 82.

7. Tryon, "'Make Any Room,'" 289–90; Charles Acland, "Curtains, Carts, and the Mobile Screen," *Screen* 50, no. 1 (Spring 2009): 150.

8. Kompare, "Reruns 2.0," 82.

9. Caetlin Benson-Allott, *The Stuff of Spectatorship: Material Cultures of Film and Television* (Oakland: University of California Press, 2021), 51–57.

10. Anna Menta, "HBO Max Movies: 11 Classic Films for You to Stream," *Decider,* May 27, 2020, https://decider.com/2020/05/27/classic-films-hbo-max-criterion-citizen-kane-casablanca/.

11. Barry Willis, "Broadcast.com's *Casablanca* Will Be 1st Internet Major Motion Picture," *Sound & Vision* (Dec. 20, 1998): www.soundandvision.com/content/broadcastcoms-casablanca-will-be-1st-internet-major-motion-picture.

12. Ben Fritz, "*Casablanca* to Screen on Facebook Wednesday Night," *Los Angeles Times,* May 15, 2012, www.latimes.com/entertainment/envelope/la-xpm-2012-may-15-la-et-ct-casablanca-facebook-20120515-story.html; Darren Franich, "*Casablanca* on Facebook," *Entertainment Weekly,* May 12, 2012, https://ew.com/article/2012/05/15/casablanca-facebook-free.

13. "Willem Dafoe Announces *Casablanca,*" YouTube, April 14, 2020, www.youtube.com/watch?v=Oj_ZgqFkzPk. *Casablanca* also has a social media presence with dedicated pages on Facebook, Twitter, Instagram, and Tumblr, and GIFs on numerous sites. See www.facebook.com/CasablancaTheMovie; https://twitter.com/hashtag/casablanca?lang=en; www.instagram.com/explore/tags/casablancamovie/?hl=en; www.tumblr.com/tagged/casablanca?sort=top; https://giphy.com/explore/casablanca.

14. On some of Warner Bros.' other digital endeavors, see Chuck Tryon, *On-Demand Culture: Digital Delivery and the Future of Movies* (New Brunswick, NJ: Rutgers University Press, 2013), 29, 112, 132–33.

15. Bradley Schauer, "The Warner Archive and DVD Collecting in the New Home Video Market," *Velvet Light Trap* 70 (Fall 2012): 35–48.

16. Jeffrey M. Anderson, "Now Streaming: The Best Movies to Stream This Valentine's Day," *TechHive,* Feb. 10, 2017, www.techhive.com/article/3168390/best-movies-for-valentines-day.html. *Casablanca* was rentable at that time on Vudu, Amazon Prime, Google Play, and iTunes.

17. Todd Spangler, "*Casablanca, Citizen Kane,* and More Will Finally Be Available to Stream as FilmStruck Adds Warner Bros. Classics to Library," *Variety,* Feb. 26, 2018, https://decider.com/2018/02/26/casablanca-citizen-kane-filmstruck-warner-bros; Todd Spangler, "WarnerMedia's FilmStruck Subscription-Streaming

Service to Shut Down," *Variety,* Oct. 26, 2018, https://variety.com/2018/digital/news/filmstruck-shutdown-warnermedia-turner-1202998364; Rick Marshall, "Everything Coming to HBO Max, WarnerMedia's Streaming Service," *Digital Trends,* Jan. 17, 2020, www.digitaltrends.com/movies/everything-coming-to-hbo-max-streaming-movies-tv-warnermedia; Hoai-Tran Bui, "HBO Max Will Host a Collection of Classic Movies Curated by TCM," *Film: Blogging the Reel World,* Oct. 30, 2019, www.slashfilm.com/hbo-max-classic-movies-tcm.

18. Angie Errigo, "Casablanca Review," *Empire,* Jan. 2000, www.empireonline.com/movies/reviews/casablanca-review.

19. Franich, "*Casablanca* on Facebook."

20. Barbara Herrnstein Smith, *Contingencies of Value: Alternative Perspectives for Critical Theory* (Cambridge, MA: Harvard University Press, 1988), 48.

21. Menta, "HBO Max Movies" (Menta's emphasis).

22. Wesley Morris, "For Me, Rewatching *Contagion* Was Fun until It Wasn't," *New York Times,* March 10, 2020, www.nytimes.com/2020/03/10/movies/contagion-movie-coronavirus.html.

23. A. O. Scott and Manohla Dargis, "Viewing Party! Let's All Watch *Jurassic Park,*" *New York Times,* June 25, 2020, www.nytimes.com/2020/06/25/movies/jurassic-park.html.

24. Emma Baty, "Low-Key Highbrow Oldies: 'Casablanca' Still Slaps, Guys," *Cosmopolitan,* April 10, 2020, www.cosmopolitan.com/entertainment/movies/a32097726/casablanca-rewatch-review.

25. Reggie Ugwu, "Urgent Discussions by 'Inessential' Workers," *New York Times,* Dec. 29, 2020, C3.

26. Marc Augé, *"Casablanca": Movies and Memory,* trans. Tom Conley (Minneapolis: University of Minnesota Press, 2009), 49. For more discussion of the film's global manifestations, see also Noah Isenberg, *We'll Always Have "Casablanca": The Life, Legend, and Afterlife of Hollywood's Most Beloved Movie* (New York: Norton, 2017), 158–62, 254–58.

27. Isabelle Ross, "What's *Casablanca* without Nazis? After WWII, German Audiences Found Out," NPR.org, Dec. 17, 2017, www.npr.org/2017/12/17/565777766/whats-casablanca-without-nazis-after-wwii-german-audiences-found-out. Thanks also to Jan Distelmeyer and Hans-Michael Bock for our conversation about this German print.

28. On this troupe, see Jennifer Robertson, *Takarazuka: Sexual Politics and Popular Culture* (Berkeley: University of California Press, 1998). The Japanese-language Region 2 DVD of Takarazuka's performance was released in 2009.

SELECTED BIBLIOGRAPHY

For the sake of economy, this bibliography lists only the scholarly books and articles that I have referenced for the writing of this book. It does not represent a comprehensive record of the sources that appear in my notes, including industry trade journals, archival materials, newspapers and magazines, and internet sites that have also informed my research.

Acland, Charles. "Curtains, Carts, and the Mobile Screen." *Screen* 50, no. 1 (Spring 2009): 148–66.

———. *Screen Traffic: Movies, Multiplexes, and Global Culture.* Durham, NC: Duke University Press, 2003.

Allen, Michael Patrick, and Anne E. Lincoln. "Critical Discourse and the Cultural Consecration of American Films." *Social Forces* 82, no. 3 (March 2004): 871–94.

Altman, Rick. *Sound Theory, Sound Practice.* London: Routledge, 1992.

Anderson, Christopher. *Hollywood TV: The Studio System in the Fifties.* Austin: University of Texas Press, 1994.

Andrea, Alfred. "Some Musings on Historical Anniversaries." *The Historian* 58, no. 1 (Autumn 1995): 205–6.

Andrew, Dudley. *What Cinema Is!* West Sussex, UK: Wiley-Blackwell, 2010.

Ang, Ien. *Desperately Seeking the Audience.* London: Routledge, 1991.

Appadurai, Arjun. "Introduction: Commodities and the Politics of Value." In *The Social Life of Things: Commodities in Cultural Perspective,* edited by Arjun Appadurai, 3–63. Cambridge: Cambridge University Press, 1986.

Appadurai, Arjun, and Carol A. Breckenridge. "Museums Are Good to Think: Heritage on View in India." In *Museums and Communities: The Politics of Public Culture,* edited by Ivan Karp, Christine Mullen Kreamer, and Steven Levine, 34–55. Washington, DC: Smithsonian Institution Press, 1992.

Arnheim, Rudolph. *Radio: An Art of Sound.* Translated by Margaret Ludwig and Herbert Read. New York: Da Capo, 1972.

Arnold, Jörg, Thomas A. Brady, Feargal McGarry, Tim Grady, and Dan Healey. "Forum: Anniversaries." *German History* 32, no. 1 (2014): 79–100.

Augé, Marc. *"Casablanca": Movies and Memory.* Translated by Tom Conley. Minneapolis: University of Minnesota Press, 2009.
Balio, Tino, ed. *Hollywood in the Age of Television.* Boston: Unwin Hyman, 1990.
Balsom, Erika. "Original Copies: How Film and Video Became Art Objects." *Cinema Journal* 53, no. 1 (Fall 2013): 97–118.
Baron, Jaimie. *The Archive Effect: Found Footage and the Audiovisual Experience of History.* New York: Routledge, 2014.
Bazin, André. "The Death of Humphrey Bogart." In *Cahiers du cinéma: The 1950s: Neo-realism, Hollywood, and the New Wave,* edited and translated by Jim Hillier, 98–101. Cambridge, MA: Harvard University Press, 1985.
———. *What Is Cinema?* Translated by Hugh Gray. Berkeley: University of California Press, 1967.
Becker, Christine. *It's the Pictures That Got Small: Hollywood Film Stars on 1950s Television.* Middleton, CT: Wesleyan University Press, 2008.
Becker, Howard S. *Art Worlds.* Berkeley: University of California Press, 1982.
Bennett, James, and Tom Brown. "Introduction: Past the Boundaries of 'New' and 'Old' Media." In *Film and Television after DVD,* edited by James Bennett and Tom Brown, 1–18. London: Routledge, 2008.
Benson-Allott, Caetlin. *Killer Tapes and Shattered Screens: Video Spectatorship from VHS to File Sharing.* Berkeley: University of California Press, 2013.
———. *The Stuff of Spectatorship: Material Cultures of Film and Television.* Oakland: University of California Press, 2021.
Berlant, Lauren. "Intimacy: A Special Issue." *Critical Inquiry* 24, no. 2 (Winter 1998): 281–88.
Bertellini, Giorgio, and Jacqueline Reich. "DVD Supplements: A Commentary on Commentaries." *Cinema Journal* 49, no. 3 (Spring 2010): 103–5.
Bhaskar, Michael. *Curation: The Power of Selection in a World of Excess.* London: Piatkus, 2016.
Billips, Connie, and Arthur Pierce. *Lux Presents Hollywood: A Show-by-Show History of the "Lux Radio Theatre" and the "Lux Video Theatre," 1934–1957.* Jefferson, NC: McFarland, 1995.
Bloom, Allan. *The Closing of the American Mind.* New York: Simon & Schuster, 1987.
Bloom, Harold. *The Western Canon: The Books and School of the Ages.* New York: Riverhead, 1995.
Boddy, William. *Fifties Television: The Industry and Its Critics.* Urbana: University of Illinois Press, 1990.
Bogle, Donald. *Toms, Coons, Mulattoes, Mammies, and Bucks: An Interpretive History of Blacks on American Film.* New York: Continuum, 1991.
Bolter, Jay David, and Richard Gruisin. *Remediation: Understanding New Media.* Cambridge, MA: MIT Press, 1999.
Bommes, Michael, and Patrick Wright. "'Charms of Residence': The Public and the Past." In *Making Histories: Studies in History Writing and Politics,* edited by Richard Johnson, Gregor McLennan, Bill Schwarz, and David Sutton, 253–302. Birmingham, UK: Centre for Contemporary Cultural Studies, 1982.

Bordwell, David. "Classical Hollywood Cinema: Narrational Principles and Procedures." In *Narrative, Apparatus, Ideology: A Film Theory Reader*, edited by Philip Rosen, 17–34. New York: Columbia University Press, 1986.

Bordwell, David, Janet Staiger, and Kristin Thompson. *The Classical Hollywood Cinema: Film Style & Mode of Production to 1960*. New York: Columbia University Press, 1985.

Bosma, Peter. *Film Programming: Curating for Cinemas, Festivals, Archives*. New York: Wallflower, 2015.

Bourdieu, Pierre. *Distinction: A Social Critique of the Judgement of Taste*. Translated by Richard Nice. Cambridge, MA: Harvard University Press, 1984.

———. *Homo Academicus*. Translated by Peter Collier. Stanford, CA: Stanford University Press, 1988.

———. *The Rules of Art: Genesis and Structure of the Literary Field*. Translated by Susan Emanuel. Stanford, CA: Stanford University Press, 1996.

Bourdon, Jérôme. "Some Sense of Television: Remembering Television." *History and Memory* 15, no. 2 (Fall/Winter 2003): 5–35.

Brookey, Robert Alan. "The Format Wars: Drawing the Battle Lines for the Next DVD." *Convergence* 13, no. 2 (2007): 199–211.

Brookey, Robert, and Robert Westerfelhaus. "Hiding Homoeroticism in Plain View: *The Fight Club* DVD as Digital Closet." *Critical Studies in Media Communication* 19, no. 1 (March 2002): 21–43.

Caldwell, John Thornton. *Production Culture: Industrial Self-Reflexivity and Critical Practice in Film and Television*. Durham, NC: Duke University Press, 2008.

Carman, Emily. "That's Not All, Folks!: Excavating the Warner Bros. Archives." *Moving Image: The Journal of the Association of Moving Image Archivists* 14, no. 2 (Spring 2014): 30–48.

Carroll, Nathan. "Unwrapping Archives: DVD Restoration Demonstrations and the Marketing of Authenticity." *Velvet Light Trap* 56 (Fall 2005): 18–31.

Casetti, Francesco. *The Lumière Galaxy: Seven Key Words for the Cinema to Come*. New York: Columbia University Press, 2015.

Cawelti, John G. *Adventure, Mystery, and Romance: Formula Stories as Art and Popular Culture*. Chicago: University of Chicago Press, 1976.

Chatman, Seymour. *Story and Discourse: Narrative Structure in Fiction and Film*. Ithaca, NY: Cornell University Press, 1978.

Chion, Michel. *The Voice in Cinema*. Edited and translated by Claudia Gorbman. New York: Columbia University Press, 1999.

Church, David. *Grindhouse Nostalgia: Memory, Home Video, and Exploitation Film Fandom*. Edinburgh: Edinburgh University Press, 2015.

Coetzee, J.M. "What Is a Classic?" In *Stranger Shores: Literary Essays, 1986–1999*, 1–16. London: Vintage, 1992.

Cohan, Steven. *Hollywood by Hollywood: The Backstudio Picture and the Mystique of Making Movies*. New York: Oxford University Press, 2019.

———. *Masked Men: Masculinity and the Movies in the Fifties*. Bloomington: Indiana University Press, 1997.

Condry, Ian. *The Soul of Anime: Collaborative Creativity and Japan's Media Success Story.* Durham, NC: Duke University Press, 2013.
Cripps, Thomas. *Making Movies Black: The Hollywood Message Movie from WWII to the Civil Rights Era.* New York: Oxford University Press, 1993.
Crowdus, Gary. "Providing a Film Archive for the Home Viewer: An Interview with Peter Becker of the Criterion Collection." *Cineaste* 25, no. 1 (1999): 47–50.
Curtin, Michael. *Redeeming the Wasteland: Television Documentary and Cold War Politics.* New Brunswick, NJ: Rutgers University Press, 1995.
Curtin, Michael, and Jane Shattuc. *The American Television Industry.* London: Palgrave Macmillan, 2009.
Davis, Ben. *Repertory Movie Theaters of New York City: Havens for Revivals, Indies, and the Avant-Garde, 1960–1994.* Jefferson, NC: McFarland, 2017.
Davis, Fred. *Yearning for Yesterday: A Sociology of Nostalgia.* New York: Free Press, 1979.
Day, Barry. "The Cult Movies: *Casablanca.*" *Films and Filming* 20 (August 1974): 20–24.
Decherney, Peter. *Hollywood's Copyright Wars: From Edison to the Internet.* New York: Columbia University Press, 2012.
Desjardins, Mary R. *Recycled Stars: Female Film Stardom in the Age of Television and Video.* Durham, NC: Duke University Press, 2015.
De Valck, Marijke. "Fostering Art, Adding Value, Cultivating Taste." In De Valck, Kredell, and Loist, *Film Festivals,* 100–116.
———. Introduction. In De Valck, Kredell, and Loist, *Film Festivals,* 1–11.
De Valck, Marijke, Brendan Kredell, and Skadi Loist, eds. *Film Festivals: History, Theory, Method, Practice.* New York: Routledge, 2016.
Dinerstein, Joel. *The Origins of Cool in Postwar America.* Chicago: University of Chicago Press, 2017.
Dombrowski, Lisa. "Canon and Canonicity." Encyclopedia.com. www.encyclopedia.com/arts/encyclopedias-almanacs-transcripts-and-maps/canon-and-canonicity.
Dyer, Richard. *Heavenly Bodies: Film Stars and Society.* New York: Routledge, 1986.
Eco, Umberto. "*Casablanca:* Cult Movies and Intertextual Collage." In *Travels in Hyperreality.* Translated by William Weaver, 197–211. New York: Harcourt Brace, 1983.
Eliot, T. S. "What Is a Classic?" In *On Poetry and Poets,* 52–74. New York: Farrar, Straus and Cudahy, 1957.
Elsaesser, Thomas. *Metropolis.* London: BFI, 2000.
———. "Touch and Gesture: On the Borders of Intimacy." *Framework* 60, no. 1 (Spring 2019): 9–25.
Elsaesser, Thomas, and Malte Hagener. *Film Theory: An Introduction through the Senses.* London: Routledge, 2010.
English, James F. *The Economy of Prestige: Prizes, Awards, and the Circulation of Cultural Value.* Cambridge, MA: Harvard University Press, 2005.
Erb, Cynthia. *Tracking King Kong: A Hollywood Icon in World Culture.* 2nd ed. Detroit: Wayne State University Press, 2009.

Erigha, Maryann. *The Hollywood Jim Crow: The Racial Politics of the Movie Industry.* New York: New York University Press, 2019.
Faden, Eric S. "Defining Classical Hollywood Narration in *Casablanca.*" In *Critical Insights: Film—"Casablanca,"* edited by James Plath, 114–29. Amenia, NY: Grey House, 2016.
Faludi, Susan. *Backlash: The Undeclared War against American Women.* New York: Crown, 1991.
Flinn, Caryl. *Strains of Utopia: Gender, Nostalgia, and Hollywood Film Music.* Princeton, NJ: Princeton University Press, 1992.
Frey, Mattias. "The Internet Suggests: Film, Recommender Systems, and Cultural Mediation." *Journal of Cinema and Media Studies* 59, no 1 (Fall 2019): 163–69.
Gadamer, Hans-Georg. *Truth and Method.* Translated by Joel Weinsheimer and Donald G. Marshall. New York: Crossroad, 1991.
Garner, Ross P. "'The Series That Changed Television'? *Twin Peaks,* 'Classic' Status, and Temporal Capital." *Cinema Journal* 55, no. 3 (Spring 2016): 137–42.
Gaudreault, André, and Philippe Marion. *The End of Cinema? A Medium in Crisis in the Digital Age.* Translated by Timothy Barnard. New York: Columbia University Press, 2015.
Gauntlett, David, and Annette Hill. *TV Living: Television, Culture, and Everyday Life.* London: Routledge, 1999.
Geary, Patrick. "Sacred Commodities: The Circulation of Medieval Relics." In *The Social Life of Things: Commodities in Cultural Perspective,* edited by Arjun Appadurai, 169–91. Cambridge: Cambridge University Press, 1986.
Gelley, Ora. "Ingrid Bergman's Star Persona and the Alien Space of *Stromboli.*" *Cinema Journal* 47, no. 2 (Winter 2008): 26–51.
Gilbert, Anne. "Push, Pull, Rerun: Television Reruns and Streaming Media." *Television & New Media* 20, no. 7 (2109): 686–701.
Gillespie, Tarleton. "The Politics of Platforms." *New Media and Society* 12, no. 3 (2010): 1–19.
Gitelman, Lisa. *Always Already New: Media, History, and the Data of Culture.* Cambridge, MA: MIT Press, 2008.
Gomery, Douglas. *Shared Pleasures: A History of Movie Presentation in the United States.* Madison: University of Wisconsin Press, 1992.
Gorbman, Claudia. "The Master's Voice." *Film Quarterly* 68, no. 2 (Winter 2014): 8–21.
———. *Unheard Melodies: Narrative Film Music.* Bloomington: Indiana University Press, 1987.
Gorfinkel, Elena. "Against Lists." *Another Gaze,* Nov. 29, 2019. www.anothergaze.com/byline/elena-gorfinkel.
———. "Cult Film or Cinephilia by Any Other Name." *Cineaste* 34, no. 1 (2008): 33–38.
Gorton, Kristyn, and Joanne Garde-Hansen. *Remembering British Television: Audience, Archive, and Industry.* London: BFI, 2019.
Grainge, Paul. *Monochrome Memories: Nostalgia and Style in Retro America.* Westport, CT: Praeger, 2002.

Gray, Ann. *Video Playtime: The Gendering of a Leisure Technology.* London: Routledge, 1992.
Gray, Jonathan. *Show Sold Separately: Promos, Spoilers, and Other Media Paratexts.* New York: New York University Press, 2010.
Greenberg, Joshua M. *From Betamax to Blockbuster: Video Stores and the Invention of Movies on Video.* Cambridge, MA: MIT Press, 2008.
Griffiths, Alison. *Shivers Down Your Spine: Cinema, Museums, and the Immersive View.* New York: Columbia University Press, 2008.
Guillory, John. *Cultural Capital: The Problem of Literary Canon Formation.* Chicago: University of Chicago Press, 1993.
Hannan, Brian. *Coming Back to a Theater Near You: A History of Hollywood Reissues, 1914–2014.* Jefferson, NC: McFarland, 2016.
Harbord, Janet. "Contingency, Time, and Event." In De Valck, Kredell, and Loist, *Film Festivals,* 69–82.
Harmetz, Aljean. *The Making of "Casablanca": Bogart, Bergman, and World War II.* New York: Hyperion, 1992/2002.
Hebdige, Dick. *Subculture: The Meaning of Style.* London: Methuen, 1979.
Herbert, Daniel. *Videoland: Movie Culture at the American Video Store.* Berkeley: University of California Press, 2014.
Herrnstein Smith, Barbara. *Contingencies of Value: Alternative Perspectives for Critical Theory.* Cambridge, MA: Harvard University Press, 1988.
Hight, Craig. "Making-of Documentaries on DVD: *The Lord of the Rings* Trilogy and Special Editions." *Velvet Light Trap* 56 (Fall 2005): 4–17.
Hills, Matt. "Cult Movies with and without Cult Stars: Differentiating Discourses of Stardom." In *Cult Film Stardom: Offbeat Attractions and Processes of Cultification,* edited by Kate Egan and Sarah Thomas, 21–36. Basingstoke, UK: Palgrave Macmillan, 2013.
———. *Fan Cultures.* London: Routledge, 2002.
Hilmes, Michele. *Hollywood and Broadcasting: From Radio to Cable.* Chicago: University of Illinois Press, 1990.
———. *Radio Voices: American Broadcasting, 1922–1952.* Minneapolis: University of Minnesota Press, 1997.
Hoberman, J., Joe Bob Briggs, Damien Love, Tim Lucas, Danny Peary, Jeffrey Sconce, and Peter Stanfield. "Cult Cinema: A Critical Symposium." *Cineaste* 34, no. 1 (2008): 43–50.
Hoberman, J. and Jonathan Rosenbaum. *Midnight Movies.* New York: Da Capo, 1983.
Holdsworth, Amy. *Television, Memory, and Nostalgia.* Basingstoke: Palgrave Macmillan, 2011.
Hoyt, Eric. *Hollywood Vault: Film Libraries before Home Video.* Berkeley: University of California Press, 2014.
Hunter, I. Q. *Cult Film as a Guide to Life: Fandom, Adaptation, and Identity.* London: Bloomsbury, 2016.
Hutcheon, Linda. *A Theory of Adaptation.* New York: Routledge, 2006.

Iordanova, Dina, and Stuart Cunningham, eds. *Digital Disruption: Cinema Moves On-Line.* St. Andrews, UK: St. Andrews Film Studies, 2012.

Isenberg, Noah. *We'll Always Have "Casablanca": The Life, Legend, and Afterlife of Hollywood's Most Beloved Movie.* New York: Norton, 2017.

Jancovich, Mark. "Cult Fictions: Cult Movies, Subcultural Capital and the Production of Cultural Distinctions." *Cultural Studies* 16, no. 2 (2002): 306–22.

Jancovich, Mark, and Shane Brown. "'The Screen's Number One and Number Two Bogeymen': The Critical Reception of Boris Karloff and Bela Lugosi in the 1930s and 1940s." In *Cult Film Stardom: Offbeat Attractions and Processes of Cultification,* edited by Kate Egan and Sarah Thomas, 243–58. Basingstoke, UK: Palgrave Macmillan, 2013.

Jancovich, Mark, Lucy Faire, and Sarah Stubbings. *The Place of the Audience: Cultural Geographies of Film Consumption.* London: BFI, 2003.

Jancovich, Mark, Antonio Lázaro Reboll, Julian Stringer, and Andy Willis, eds. *Defining Movies: The Cultural Politics of Oppositional Taste.* Manchester, UK: Manchester University Press, 2003.

Jauss, Hans Robert. *Toward an Aesthetic of Reception.* Translated by Timothy Bahti. Minneapolis: University of Minnesota Press, 1982.

Jeffords, Susan. *Hard Bodies: Hollywood Masculinity in the Reagan Era.* New Brunswick, NJ: Rutgers University Press, 1994.

———. *The Remasculinization of America: Gender and the Vietnam War.* Bloomington: Indiana University Press, 1989.

Jennings, Wade. "The Star as Cult Icon: Judy Garland." In Telotte, *The Cult Film Experience,* 90–101.

Jerslev, Anne. "Semiotics by Instinct: 'Cult Film' as a Signifying Practice between Film and Audience." In *Media Cultures: Reappraising Transnational Media,* edited by Michael Skovmand and Kim Schroder, 181–98. London: Routledge, 1992.

Johnson, Kathy Merlock. "Playing It Again and Again: *Casablanca*'s Impact on American Mass Culture." *Journal of Popular Film and Television* 27, no. 4 (2000): 33–41.

Johnston, Keith M. "Reclaiming the 'Vanilla' DVD: Brand Packaging and the Case of Ealing Studios." *Screen* 55, no. 1 (Spring 2014): 85–101.

Johnston, William M. *Celebrations: The Cult of Anniversaries in Europe and the United States Today.* New Brunswick, NJ: Transaction, 1991.

Kapsis, Robert. *Hitchcock: The Making of a Reputation.* Chicago: University of Chicago Press, 1992.

Karabel, Jerome. *The Chosen: The Hidden History of Admission and Exclusion at Harvard, Yale, and Princeton.* New York: Houghton Mifflin, 2005.

Kendrick, James. "What Is the Criterion? The Criterion Collection as an Archive of Film as Culture." *Journal of Film and Video* 53, nos. 2/3 (Summer/Fall 2001): 124–39.

Kindem, Gorham. "The Postwar Motion Picture Industry: SAG, HUAC, and Postwar Hollywood." In *Boom and Bust: American Cinema in the 1940s,* edited by Thomas Schatz, 313–19. Berkeley: University of California Press, 1999.

Klinger, Barbara. *Beyond the Multiplex: Cinema, New Technologies, and the Home.* Berkeley: University of California Press, 2006.

———. "Cinema and Immortality: Hollywood Classics in an Intermediated World." In Ljungberg and Klarer, "Cultures in Conflict/Conflicting Cultures," 17–29.

———. *Melodrama and Meaning: History, Culture, and the Films of Douglas Sirk.* Bloomington: Indiana University Press, 1994.

———. "Pre-Cult: *Casablanca,* Radio Adaptation, and Transmedia in the 1940s." *New Review of Film and Television Studies* 13, no. 1 (2015): 45–62.

Kompare, Derek. *Rerun Nation: How Repeats Invented American Television.* New York: Routledge, 2005.

———. "Reruns 2.0: Revising Repetition for Multiplatform Television Distribution." *Journal of Popular Film and Television* 38, no. 2 (2010): 79–83.

Konzett, Delia Malia. "Classical Hollywood, Race, and *Casablanca.*" In *Critical Insights: Film—"Casablanca,"* edited by James Plath, 97–113. Amenia, NY: Grey House, 2016.

Koppes, Clayton R., and Gregory D. Black. *Hollywood Goes to War: How Politics, Profits, and Propaganda Shaped World War II.* Berkeley: University of California Press, 1990.

Kopytoff, Igor. "The Cultural Biography of Things: Commoditization as Process." In *The Social Life of Things: Commodities in Cultural Perspective,* edited by Arjun Appadurai, 64–91. Cambridge: Cambridge University Press, 1986.

Kozloff, Sarah. *Overhearing Film Dialogue.* Berkeley: University of California Press, 2000.

Kunze, Peter. "Beautiful Friendship: Masculinity and Nationalism in *Casablanca.*" *Studies in Popular Culture* 37, no. 1 (Fall 2014): 19–37.

Lampel, Joseph, and Shivasharan S. Nadavulakere. "Classics Foretold? Contemporaneous and Retrospective Consecration in the UK Film Industry." *Cultural Trends* 18, no. 3 (Sept. 2009): 239–48.

Landsberg, Alison. *Prosthetic Memory: The Transformation of American Remembrance in the Age of Mass Culture.* New York: Columbia University Press, 2004.

Lane, Jim. "Critical and Cultural Reception of the European Art Film in 1950s America: A Case Study of the Brattle Theatre (Cambridge, Massachusetts)." *Film History* 24, nos. 3–4 (1994): 51–64.

Langkjær, Birger. "*Casablanca* and Popular Music as Film Music." *P.O.V.* 14 (Dec. 2002): http://pov.imv.au.dk/Issue_14/section_1/artc7A.html.

Lawrence, Amy. "The Voice as Mask." In *Dietrich Icon,* ed. Gerd Gemünden and Mary R. Desjardins, 79–99. Durham, NC: Duke University Press, 2007.

Littau, Karin. "Media, Mythology, and Morphogenesis: *Aliens.*" *Convergence: The International Journal of Research into New Media Technologies* 17, no. 1 (2011): 1–16.

Ljungberg, Christina, and Mario Klarer, eds. "Cinema and Immortality: Hollywood Classics in an Intermediated World." Special issue, *SPELL: Swiss Papers in English Language and Literature* 29 (Fall 2013).

Long, Christopher. "Revising the Film Canon: Jonathan Rosenbaum's *Movie Mutations* and *Essential Cinema*." *New Review of Film and Television Studies* 4, no. 1 (2006): 17–35.
Lupo, Jonathan. "Loaded Canons: Contemporary Film Canons, Film Studies, and Film Discourse." *Journal of American Culture* 34, no. 3 (Sept. 2011): 219–33.
Malice, Michael. *The New Right: A Journey to the Fringes of American Politics.* New York: All Points, 2019.
Maltby, Richard. "'A Brief Romantic Interlude': Dick and Jane Go to 3 ½ Seconds of the Classical Hollywood Cinema." In *Post-Theory: Reconstructing Film Studies,* edited by David Bordwell and Noel Carroll, 434–59. Madison: University of Wisconsin Press, 1996.
———. "New Cinema Histories." In Maltby, Biltereyst, and Meers, *Explorations in New Cinema History,* 3–40.
Maltby, Richard, Daniel Biltereyst, and Philippe Meers, eds. *Explorations in New Cinema History: Approaches and Case Studies.* West Sussex, UK: Blackwell, 2011.
Manovich, Lev. *The Language of New Media.* Cambridge, MA: MIT Press, 2001.
Mathijs, Ernest. "Time Wasted." *Flow* (March 29, 2010): www.flowjournal.org/2010/03/time-wasted-ernest-mathijs-the-university-of-british-columbia.
Mathijs, Ernest, and Jamie Sexton. *Cult Cinema.* West Sussex, UK: Wiley-Blackwell, 2011.
Mayne, Laura. "Assessing Cultural Impact: Film4, Canon Formation, and Forgotten Films." *Journal of British Cinema and Television* 11, no. 4 (2014): 459–80.
McArthur, Colin. *The "Casablanca" File.* London: Half Brick Images, 1992.
Modleski, Tania. *Loving with a Vengeance: Mass-Produced Fantasies for Women.* New York: Methuen, 1982.
Montfort, Nick, and Ian Bogost. *Racing the Beam: The Atari Video Computer System.* Cambridge, MA: MIT Press, 2009.
Morley, David. *Television, Audiences, and Cultural Studies.* London: Routledge, 1992.
Mukherjee, Ankhi. "'What Is a Classic?': International Literary Criticism and the Classic Question." *PMLA* 125, no. 4 (2010): 1026–42.
Murray, Simone. *The Adaptation Industry: The Cultural Economy of Contemporary Literary Adaptation.* London: Routledge, 2012.
———. "Brand Loyalties: Rethinking Content within Global Corporate Media." *Media, Culture, and Society* 27, no. 3 (2005): 415–35.
Murray, Susan. *Hitch Your Antenna to the Stars: Early Television and Broadcast Stardom.* New York: Routledge, 2005.
———. "I Know What You Did Last Summer: Sarah Michelle Gellar and Crossover Teen Stardom." In *Undead TV: Essays on "Buffy the Vampire Slayer,"* edited by Elana Levine and Lisa Parks, 42–55. Durham, NC: Duke University Press, 2007.
Nachbar, Jack. "Doing the Thinking for All of Us: *Casablanca* and the Home Front." *Journal of Popular Film and Television* 27, no. 4 (April 2000): 5–15.
———. "'Nobody Ever Loved Me That Much': A *Casablanca* Bibliography." *Journal of Popular Film and Television* 27, no. 4 (2000): 42–45.

Naremore, James. Introduction to *Film Adaptation,* edited by James Naremore, 1–18. New Brunswick, NJ: Rutgers University Press, 2000.

———. *More Than Night: Film Noir in Its Contexts.* Berkeley: University of California Press, 1998/2008.

Newman, Michael Z., and Elana Levine. *Legitimating Television.* New York: Routledge, 2012.

Patterson, Eleanor. "Capturing the Flow: The Growth of the Old-Time-Radio Collecting Culture in the United States during the 1970s." *Journal of Cinema and Media Studies* 59, no. 3 (Spring 2020): 46–68.

Peary, Danny. *Cult Movies: Over 100 Films from the Silent Era to the Present.* New York: Gramercy, 1981.

Peltzman, Shira, and Casey Scott. "This Is DCP: Digital Projection in Repertory Theatres." Tisch Preservation Program (Spring 2012). www.miap.hosting.nyu.edu/program/student_work/2012spring/12s_3049_Peltzman_Scott_a2.docx (download only).

Perks, Lisa Glebatis. *Media Marathoning: Immersions in Morality.* New York: Lexington Books, 2015.

Polan, Dana. *Scenes of Instruction: The Beginnings of the U.S. Study of Film.* Berkeley: University of California Press, 2007.

Porst, Jennifer. *Broadcasting Hollywood: The Struggle over Feature Films on Early TV.* New Brunswick, NJ: Rutgers University Press, 2021.

Raskin, Richard. "*Casablanca* and United States Foreign Policy." *Film History* 4, no. 2 (1990): 153–64.

Ray, Robert B. *A Certain Tendency in Hollywood Cinema, 1930–1980.* Princeton, NJ: Princeton University Press, 1985.

Rodowick, D.N. *The Virtual Life of Film.* Cambridge, MA: Harvard University Press, 2007.

Rosenbaum, Jonathan. *Movie Wars: How Hollywood and the Media Limit What Movies We Can See.* Chicago: A Cappella, 2000.

Ross, T.J. "*Beat the Devil* or Goodbye, *Casablanca.*" In Telotte, *The Cult Film Experience,* 79–89.

Scannell, Paddy. "Radio Times: The Temporal Arrangements of Broadcasting in the Modern World." In *Television and Its Audience,* edited by Phillip Drummond and Richard Paterson, 27–47. London: BFI, 1988.

Schauer, Bradley. "The Warner Archive and DVD Collecting in the New Home Video Market." *Velvet Light Trap* 70 (Fall 2012): 35–48.

Schlotterbeck, Jesse. "Radio Noir in the USA." In *A Companion to Film Noir,* edited by Helen Hanson and André Spicer, 423–39. New York: Wiley-Blackwell, 2013.

Schmidt, Leigh Eric. "The Fashioning of a Modern Holiday: St. Valentine's Day, 1840–1870." *Winterthur Portfolio* 28, no. 4 (Winter 1993): 209–45.

Scott, Derek B. "Orientalism and Musical Style." *Musical Quarterly* 82, no. 2 (Summer 1998): 309–35.

Scott, Ellen C. *Cinema Civil Rights: Regulation, Repression, and Race in the Classical Hollywood Era.* New Brunswick, NJ: Rutgers University Press, 2015.

Sebok, Bryan. "Convergent Consortia: Format Battles in High Definition." *Velvet Light Trap* 64 (Fall 2009): 34–49.
Segrave, Kerry. *Movies at Home: How Hollywood Came to Television.* Jefferson, NC: McFarland, 1999/2009.
Sexton, Jamie. "From Bad to Good and Back to Bad Again: Cult Cinema and Its Unstable Trajectory." In *B Is for Bad Cinema: Aesthetics, Politics, and Cultural Value,* edited by Claire Perkins and Constantine Verevis, 129–45. Albany: State University of New York Press, 2014.
Shohat, Ella, and Robert Stam. *Unthinking Eurocentrism: Multiculturalism and the Media.* London: Routledge, 1994.
Silverstone, Roger. *Television and Everyday Life.* London: Routledge, 1994.
Sklar, Robert. *City Boys: Cagney, Bogart, Garfield.* Princeton, NJ: Princeton University Press, 1992.
Skopal, Pavel. "'The Adventure Continues on DVD': Franchise Movies as Home Video." *Convergence* 13, no. 2 (2007): 185–98.
Smit, David. *Ingrid Bergman: The Life, Career, and Public Image.* Jefferson, NC: McFarland, 2012.
Smith, Jacob. *Spoken Word: Postwar American Phonograph Cultures.* Berkeley: University of California Press, 2011.
———. *Vocal Tracks: Performance and Sound Media.* Berkeley: University of California Press, 2008.
Solomon, Ben. *"Ben-Hur": The Original Blockbuster.* Edinburgh: Edinburgh University Press, 2016.
Solomon, Matthew. "Adapting 'Radio's Perfect Script': 'Sorry Wrong Number' and *Sorry, Wrong Number.*" *Quarterly Review of Film and Video* 16, no. 1 (1997): 23–40.
Spigel, Lynn. *Make Room for TV: Television and the Family Ideal in Postwar America.* Chicago: University of Chicago Press, 1992.
Staiger, Janet. *Interpreting Films: Studies in the Historical Reception of American Cinema.* Princeton, NJ: Princeton University Press, 1992.
———. "The Politics of Film Canons." *Cinema Journal* 24, no. 3 (Spring 1985): 4–23.
Stearns, Peter N. *American Cool: Constructing a Twentieth-Century Emotional Style.* New York: New York University Press, 1994.
Steinberg, Marc. *The Platform Economy: How Japan Transformed the Consumer Internet.* Minneapolis: University of Minnesota Press, 2019.
Street, Seán. *The Memory of Sound: Preserving the Sonic Past.* London: Routledge, 2015.
Stringer, Julian. "Raiding the Archive: Film Festivals and the Revival of Classic Hollywood." In *Memory and Popular Film,* edited by Paul Grainge, 81–96. Manchester, UK: Manchester University Press, 2003.
Studlar, Gaylyn. *This Mad Masquerade: Stardom and Masculinity in the Jazz Age.* New York: Columbia University Press, 1996.
Taylor, Greg. *Artists in the Audience: Cults, Camp, and American Film Criticism.* Princeton, NJ: Princeton University Press, 1999.

Telotte, J. P. "Beyond All Reason: The Nature of the Cult." In Telotte, *The Cult Film Experience*, 5–17.
———. "*Casablanca* and the Larcenous Cult Film." In Telotte, *The Cult Film Experience*, 43–54.
———. "The Classical Cult Film." In Telotte, *The Cult Film Experience*, 39–41.
———, ed. *The Cult Film Experience: Beyond All Reason*. Austin: University of Texas Press, 1991.
Thomas, Sarah. *Peter Lorre: Face Maker: Constructing Stardom and Performance in Hollywood and Europe*. New York: Berghahn, 2012.
Thornton, Sarah. *Club Cultures: Music, Media, and Subcultural Capital*. Middletown, CT: Wesleyan University Press, 1996.
Trope, Alison. *Stardust Monuments: The Saving and Selling of Hollywood*. Hanover, NH: Dartmouth College Press, 2011.
Tryon, Chuck. "'Make Any Room Your TV Room': Digital Delivery and Media Mobility." *Screen* 53, no. 3 (Autumn 2012): 287–300.
———. *On-Demand Culture: Digital Delivery and the Future of Movies*. New Brunswick, NJ: Rutgers University Press, 2013.
Usai, Paolo Cherchi. *The Death of Cinema: History, Cultural Memory, and the Digital Dark Age*. London: BFI, 2001.
Verma, Neil. *Theater of the Mind*. Chicago: University of Chicago Press, 2012.
Vincendeau, Ginette, ed. "In Focus: The French New Wave at 50: Pushing the Boundaries." *Cinema Journal* 49, no. 4 (Summer 2010): 135–66.
———. *Pépé le Moko*. London: BFI Classics, 1998.
Wasko, Janet. *Hollywood in the Information Age: Beyond the Silver Screen*. Austin: University of Texas Press, 1995.
Wasser, Frederick. *Veni, Vidi, Video: The Hollywood Empire and the VCR*. Austin: University of Texas Press, 2001.
Wasson, Haidee. *Museum Movies: The Museum of Modern Art and the Birth of Art Cinema*. Berkeley: University of California Press, 2005.
Wong, Cindy Hing-Yuk. "Publics and Counterpublics: Rethinking Film Festivals as Public Spheres." In De Valck, Kredell, and Loist, *Film Festivals*, 83–99.
Wyatt, Justin. *High Concept: Movies and Marketing in Hollywood*. Austin: University of Texas Press, 1994.
Young, Liam Cole. *List Cultures: Knowledge and Poetics from Mesopotamia to BuzzFeed*. Amsterdam: Amsterdam University Press, 2017.
Zhang, Longxi. "Meaning, Reception, and the Use of Classics: Theoretical Considerations in a Chinese Context." *Intertexts* 19, nos. 1–2 (Spring–Fall 2015): 5–21.

INDEX

Note: Page numbers in italics refer to figures.